Library Services from Birth to Five

Delivering the best start

Edited by

Carolynn Rankin and Avril Brock

facet publishing

© This compilation: Carolynn Rankin and Avril Brock 2015
The chapters: the contributors 2015

Published by Facet Publishing,
7 Ridgmount Street, London WC1E 7AE
www.facetpublishing.co.uk

Facet Publishing is wholly owned by CILIP: the Chartered Institute of Library
and Information Professionals.

British Library Cataloguing in Publication Data
A catalogue record for this book is available from the British Library.

ISBN 978-1-78330-008-2

First published 2015

Text printed on FSC accredited material.

Typeset from editors' files by Facet Publishing Production
in 10/13 pt University Old Style and Chantilly
Printed and made in Great Britain by CPI Group (UK) Ltd,
Croydon, CR0 4YY.

Every purchase of a Facet book helps to fund CILIP's
advocacy, awareness and accreditation programmes
for information professionals.

Contents

    Carolynn Rankin and Avril Brock

    Carolynn Rankin and Avril Brock

    Avril Brock and Carolynn Rankin

    Paula Kelly

    Caroline Barratt-Pugh and Nola Allen

    Carolynn Rankin and Avril Brock

    Carolynn Rankin and Avril Brock

    Francesca de Freitas and Tess Prendergast

    Rachel Payne

Figures and tables

Figures

Tables

Contributors

Nola Allen

Over the past 30 years, Nola Allen has worked in the library and education sectors specializing in services for children and families. From 2004 to 2013, Nola was the Program Co-ordinator of the Better Beginnings Family Literacy Program, the State Library of Western Australia's state-wide literacy initiative promoting reading and book sharing with children from birth. With a special interest in the fields of children's literature, literacy and reading promotion, Nola has co-authored two children's books, regularly contributes to professional journals and publications and is a past awards judge and long-standing member of the Children's Book Council of Australia.

Caroline Barratt-Pugh

Caroline Barratt-Pugh is Professor and Director of the Centre for Research in Early Childhood Education at Edith Cowan University (ECU), in Western Australia (WA). She worked in the UK as an early years teacher and teacher educator before joining ECU. Caroline is internationally and nationally renowned for her work in early childhood, focusing on early language and literacy in diverse communities. She teaches on postgraduate courses, has directed a number of national and local research projects and authored several books, journal articles and reports. During the past decade she has been involved in the evaluation of early literacy family programmes and has directed the evaluation of Better Beginnings, working closely with librarians and the State Library of WA. This has led to the development of a number of changes in policy and practice in relation to creating a better future for children and families.

Avril Brock

Avril Brock has written several books in partnership with Carolynn Rankin on language, literacy and library services. She has recently published *The Early Years Reflective Practice Handbook* for early childhood educators. Avril has also written books and journal articles on play, professionalism, bilingualism and early language development. She has worked in higher education since 1989 at Bradford College and Leeds Metropolitan University, having been a deputy head, primary and early years teacher in West Yorkshire, often working with linguistically diverse children. Avril's PhD longitudinal research elicited early years educators' thinking about their professionalism and this resulted in a typology of professionalism which has been developed across the early years interdisciplinary team. She has been involved in interdisciplinary partnerships with colleagues in West Yorkshire, Europe and the USA.

Shelley Bullas

Shelley Bullas co-ordinates the Children and Young People's Library Service for Calderdale Metropolitan Borough Council in West Yorkshire. She represents Yorkshire and The Humber on the National YLG (Youth Libraries Group) committee and is also secretary for the Kirklees and Calderdale Children's Book Group. Shelley has delivered training on family learning, story-telling and using songs and rhymes to practitioners across Calderdale as well as training specifically for Children's Library professionals. Shelley studied music at the University of Hull and specialized in 20th-century music and performance. She completed an MSc in Librarianship from Leeds Metropolitan University and wrote a dissertation on Bookstart schemes in the North West. Her previous roles have included working as the Literacy Development Officer in Blackburn with Darwen, which involved setting up early years libraries within children's centres across the borough.

An accomplished signer, Shelley has volunteered with Music and the Deaf, which allowed her to get involved in a 'Sing Up' project. In her spare time Shelley studies bassoon with Laurence Perkins, Principal Bassoonist of Manchester Camerata, and enjoys participating in wind chamber courses. She currently plays with the Orchestra of Square Chapel and Todmorden Symphony Orchestra.

Francesca de Freitas

Francesca de Freitas is a Children's Librarian with the Vancouver Public Library. She works with young children and their families and caregivers, leading programmes and education sessions to help families support their children's developing early literacy skills. She has presented at professional conferences and training programmes on the subject of effectively using technology as a tool for early literacy development. With a BA and MA from University College Galway, an MLIS from the University of British Columbia and 11 years' experience as an IT project manager, Francesca now delights in sharing the wondrous world of stories available to children – in all its forms, including electronic ones.

Anne Harding

Anne Harding is an independent trainer specializing in children's and young people's reading and children's and school libraries. She is a former children's librarian and manager of Young People's Library Services. She has eight years' experience as a school governor, including three as literacy governor.

Anne's UK clients include CILIP, the Youth Libraries Group, the School Library Association, the Welsh Government and the National Centre for Language and Literacy as well as many local authorities and schools. Internationally, Anne has delivered training for the British Council and Ministry of Education in the Czech Republic, UCL Qatar, the British Virgin Islands Department of Education, the University of Missouri, Library Council Ireland and for international school staff. Anne frequently gives training on library provision for under-fives and is an assessor for accredited learning on early years literacy and language development and on rhyme times for Agored Cymru. There is more information on her website: www.anneharding.net.

Paula Kelly

Appointed in 2013 as the City of Melbourne's Library Service Manager, Paula Kelly leads and manages the City Library, East and North Melbourne Libraries, the Southbank Library at Boyd and the Library at the Dock. Paula's previous role as Reader Development and Offsite Learning Manager at the State Library of Victoria focused on young people in schools, family and community settings. Leadership of the Centre for Youth Literature was a significant component of this work, alongside the management of the Victorian Government's Young Readers Program. A passionate advocate for reading and the positive outcomes it produces in people's lives, Paula works with public libraries, schools, community and philanthropic organizations and commercial partners.

Alongside a broad background in education, community development and public libraries, Paula also has a passion for architecture and the development of public building facilities. She helped establish Australia's first Children's Laureate program, and was awarded a Churchill Fellowship which supported an international study tour of reading promotion organizations in 2010. Paula helped scope Australia's first National Year of Reading, delivered in 2012. She is currently undertaking a PhD with the University of Melbourne examining early literacy and disadvantaged families - a nested study within the E4kids project.

Ben Lawrence

Ben Lawrence has worked in libraries all his working life and is Calderdale's

Early Years Librarian and Bookstart Coordinator, a job he finds incredibly rewarding. He loves sharing his passions for music and literature with the families in and around Halifax, West Yorkshire. He is also Chair of both Yorkshire and Humber Youth Libraries Group and the Kirklees and Calderdale Children's Bookgroup. Ben regularly delivers training on using songs and rhymes for Children's Centre and Early Years staff as well as Children's Library professionals.

Ben studied music at the University of Huddersfield, studying viola with Helen Brackley Jones, and graduated in 2008. He continues to study the viola with Louise Lansdown, Head of Strings at Birmingham Conservatoire, and Sarah-Jane Bradley. Ben can be seen playing with the Fields String Quartet and Bolton Symphony Orchestra. He is a member of the British Kodály Academy and endeavours to apply Kodály's principles of music education in all his sessions. In 2013, Ben was awarded the Cecilia Vajda Memorial Scholarship to further his studies at the British Kodály Academy Summer School.

Rachel Payne

Rachel Payne is the co-ordinator of early childhood services at Brooklyn Public Library; previously she ran the Early Childhood Resource and Information Center of the New York Public Library. A graduate of Hampshire College, Rachel received her MS Ed from Bank Street College of Education and her MLS from the Palmer School of Long Island University. She is a co-author of *Reading with Babies, Toddlers, and Twos: a guide to laughing, learning and growing together through books* (Sourcebooks, 2013). She has written about play and early literacy for *School Library Journal* and reviewed children's books for *Kirkus*. She served on the 2009 Caldecott Award Selection Committee and she is chairing the 2016 Committee. Rachel has presented on early literacy at the American Library Association Conference, Bank Street Infancy Institute, Young Child Expo, Public Library Association Conference and at other professional gatherings. She serves on the advisory boards of Reach and Read of Greater New York and the New York City Infant Toddler Technical Assistance Resource Center. Rachel lives in Brooklyn with her husband and son.

Tess Prendergast

Tess Prendergast has worked as a children's librarian for almost two decades and her doctorate in early literacy is well under way at the University of British Columbia. Her dissertation project explores early literacy in the lives of children with disabilities and she has interviewed both parents and children's librarians on this important topic. She is also currently surveying and critiquing some of the ways that children with disabilities are depicted in contemporary picture books. Tess has written about how digital technology can be leveraged to help extend early literacy-learning opportunities for *all* children. She and her colleagues at www.littleelit.com believe that children's librarians can and should play a key role in supporting parents and other caregivers as they make critical and informed media decisions in support of children's early learning. Diversity themes permeate Tess's scholarly and professional work as she endeavours to contribute to the advancement of universal access and inclusion for all in the public library world and beyond. She lives with her husband and their teenaged son and daughter, as well as two cats, in Vancouver, British Columbia. Tess blogs at www. InclusiveEarlyLiteracy.wordpress.com and can be found on Twitter @tess1144.

Carolynn Rankin

Carolynn Rankin is currently a Visiting Fellow in the Faculty of Arts, Environment, and Technology at Leeds Beckett University. Carolynn worked as an information management specialist for 20 years before moving into professional education in 2000. Carolynn has interdisciplinary research interests, exploring the connections between civil society, social justice and access to literacy and learning via libraries and her PhD thesis focused on the role of the public library in supporting young children and their families. Her current research projects include a longitudinal evaluation of the development of the Sister Libraries programme for the International Federation of Library Associations (IFLA). Carolynn's professional activities include the role of External Examiner for the Chartered Institute of Library and Information Professionals (CILIP) Professional Registration Board, and Assessor for CILIP Accreditation for Learning Providers. She is a member of the IFLA Standing Committee Library Theory and Research Section.

By chance, Carolynn met Dr Avril Brock during a coffee break about nine years ago, and as research partners they have now co-authored and edited four books, including *Library Services for Children and Young People: challenges and opportunities in the digital age*, published by Facet, *Professionalism in the Interdisciplinary Early Years Team*, published by Continuum, and *Communication, Language, and Literacy from Birth to Five*, published by Sage.

Rachel Van Riel

Rachel Van Riel founded and shaped the reader development movement which changed the way public libraries in the UK engage with their customers. Opening the Book's reader-centred approach released new energy into library work, re-motivating many library staff and delivering wider cultural change in organizations.

Libraries moved from largely passive provision of books and computers to actively engaging the audience. Opening the Book's online training courses have been taken by 12,000 library staff in three continents.

Rachel has designed and installed 100 libraries in the UK as well as giving consultancy advice on library design in Norway, Sweden, Ireland, the Netherlands and North America. With Helen Thomas, Rachel developed the BookSpace concept and range to encourage reading for pleasure in primary schools. Rachel is a passionate advocate for public and school libraries in the wider cultural and educational sector.

International perspectives: country case study contributors
Jessica Bates

Jessica Bates PhD, MA, BSocSc joined the staff of the University of Ulster as Course Director for the Library and Information Management programmes in the School of Education in 2009, having previously held a lecturing post in the School of Information and Library Studies at University College Dublin. Jessica has research publications across a range of library and information areas. She is a member of the Institute for Research in the Social Sciences and Research Coordinator for the School of Education at the University of Ulster, as well as being a Fellow of the Higher Education Authority.

Carolyn Bourke

Carolyn's work as Outreach and Marketing Co-ordinator at Fairfield City Library Service in New South Wales allows her to be involved in researching, planning, marketing, implementing and evaluating the outreach services and programmes, including those for babies, children, youth and adults from a huge range of cultural and socio-economic backgrounds. As well as library qualifications, she holds a Master of Education degree, specializing in literacy, and is interested in expanding the current thinking on emergent literacy and numeracy in order to encourage parents to help prepare their children for lifelong learning. Working in a highly multicultural environment, Carolyn is passionate about demonstrating that public libraries provide opportunities to build social capital in their communities through the processes of connecting and engaging with local government, community groups, schools, businesses, families and individuals.

Dajana Brunac

Dajana Brunac is Children and Youth Services Librarian at Zadar Public Library,

Zadar, Croatia, where she is in charge of programes and services for all age groups of children, including for babies and toddlers, and early reading promotion. She was president of the Children and Youth Services Section - a professional body of the Croatian Library Association - from 2010 to 2012. Since 2009 Dajana has been an adjunct teacher at the Zadar University Department of Library and Information Science, and she has lectured at the Croatian Center for Permanent Professional Education of Librarians since 2010. Dajana is currently a member of the IFLA Libraries for Children and Young Adults Section - Standing Committee.

Andrew Carlin

Andrew Carlin PhD, ACIEA is a school librarian. He also teaches part time on the Library and Information Management programmes in the School of Education at the University of Ulster. Andrew was a postdoctoral fellow and lecturer in the School of Information and Library Studies at University College Dublin. Andrew has published in sociology and in library and information science, and has particular interests in research methods, library space, information theory and the foundations of information science.

Tatiana Kalashnikova

Tatiana Kalashnikova is the Director of the A. P. Gaidar Central City Children's Library, Moscow and a Board member of the Russian Children's Fund. A graduate of the Moscow State University of Culture as a librarian-bibliographer, she has over 30 years' experience as a librarian. Tatiana is an active participant in the cultural life of the city. During her professional career she has been involved in the preparation and implementation of citywide programmes, including 'Culture of Moscow', 'Programme of development public libraries in Moscow as intelligence information centers' and 'Reading Moscow'. Today her children's library, 'Gaidarovka', is a place of communication, exciting trips and holidays, creative competitions, clubs, workshops and art exhibitions. The library robots Chuk and Gek greet library visitors and conduct tours and there is active social networking, book crossing and a Wi-Fi zone.

Ingrid Källström

Ingrid Källström is a children's librarian currently working at the Swedish Agency for Accessible Media. A qualified teacher who graduated as a librarian in 1984, she has worked as a preschool teacher and has many years' experience as a school librarian and children's librarian, including work at the House of Cultur, Stockholm and the Book Bus for Children, Stockholm Public Library. Ingrid's professional activities include Chairman of the jury for Children's Books Awards of the Swedish Library Association, 2003-2013, and she is currently Vice President of IBBY (International Board on Books for Young People) Sweden, having been a Board member since 2011. Ingrid has served on the selection committee for Barnbokskatalogen, the annual Children's Books Catalogue of the Swedish Arts Council, and has been a Standing Committee member of the International Federation of Library Association section Libraries for Children and Young Adults since 2009.

Giovanna Malgaroli

Giovanna Malgaroli is a qualified librarian, specializing in children's librarianship and publishing. She has worked in municipal libraries in the province of Milan (1984-2004) and for the social services of a small municipality (2004-9). She has been engaged in the Italian Library Association's activities since 1989. Giovanna has been a member of the Coordinating Council of the national programme 'Nati per Leggere' (Born to Read) since 2000 and is the regional co-ordinator for 'Nati per Leggere Lombardia' (Born to Read, Lombardia region). Since 2009 she has worked for the national secretariat of the programme, supporting the activities of the regional co-ordinators. She is interested in children's literature and the promotion of reading aloud - as a planner, co-ordinator and trainer.

Maria Sjøblom

Maria Sjøblom has worked at Aalborg Public Libraries since 1999. Currently she is Head of Library Activities, with a staff of 35 innovative and creative people. Maria works in library development as well as strategic leadership and communication and is represented in a wide range of national boards and work groups, e.g. the Danish Library Association. Her main focus is related not only to development in the physical and digital aspects of libraries but also to the changing of the staff mindset and adapting to the challenges of modern library service. Maria works with both children and adult library services and has run substantial award-winning projects targeting children.

Marie-Elaine Tierney

Marie-Elaine Tierney MSc, HNC joined the Western Education and Library Board (WELB) in 1983, based in Derry Central Library. She worked in the Lending Library before being promoted to Senior Library Assistant in 1996, and worked within the Reference/Local Studies Department. She then left the WELB and moved to Scotland, where she worked for Bank of Scotland before returning to Northern Ireland and taking up a position again with the WELB. Marie-Elaine presently works for Libraries NI (previously libraries across Northern Ireland were part of the five education boards). Her areas of interest are local heritage and early years development.

Acknowledgements

Our grateful thanks are due to the contributing authors and to all the librarians, children and families who willingly shared their viewpoints and experiences of both libraries and reading; the ever-helpful staff in the reading room at the British Library in Boston Spa; and our families - once again we thank you for your patience.

Thanks are also due to our colleagues at Facet Publishing who again have provided excellent support and guidance in enabling us to bring this revised publication to fruition.

Many thanks to those who have provided or appeared in the photographs used in this book. In particular we would like to thank the State Library of Western Australia for permission to use the photographs in Chapter 4; Crystel Bijasson-Elliott for Figure 5.2; Philip Greenberg for Figures 8.1 and 8.2 and Opening the Box for Figures 13.1 and 13.2.

Carolynn Rankin and Avril Brock

Thanks for the patience of my husband, Jonathan, and to my family, particularly my grandchildren who are my delight and source of inspiration.

Avril Brock

Introduction

Carolynn Rankin and Avril Brock

Introduction

Literacy, language and communication skills are vital in society today and an early introduction to literacy through a breadth of experiences of rhymes, stories, pictures and books supports these skills. The first edition of *Delivering the Best Start: a guide to early years libraries*, published in 2009, was one of our first collaborations as researchers and co-authors. The Preface to this notes 'We want to help early years librarians find a voice in promoting and sharing their own professional experiences and expertise – that is, how they develop and provide services that support young children and their families. This may often be achieved by working in partnership with others.'

This new title, *Library Services from Birth to Five: delivering the best start*, moves information, knowledge and ideas further forward and adds important new voices to the message. Experienced practitioners share their knowledge about strategies to maximize access to services and the book considers how young children and their families will be provided with relevant and accessible services, resources and programmes. This is an edited book, with invited contributions from nationally and internationally known practitioners and Library and Information Service (LIS) academics. The hand-picked team of contributors has meant that we have been able to capitalize on the knowledge, expertise and wide experience of the authors, who are innovators, researchers and respected practitioners in their own right.

Because we are based in the UK and have a greater awareness of developments and political drivers within the UK, the chapters we have contributed as editors tend to focus on examples and case studies from these shores. For our overseas readers we hope that this is balanced by the quantity and quality of international contributions in the other chapters and country case studies. As with the first book, this revised and expanded edition would not have been possible without practitioners, parents and families also sharing their knowledge and providing rich examples. We have capitalized on their experiences – taking advantage of shared episodes from professional and family lives. The case studies, scenarios and vignettes, drawn from UK and international sources, show that the key issues have an international dimension. The use of vignettes is intended to help focus and give particular insight into a setting, an event or an experience. Innovative initiatives are used to present diverse views of early years library services. Examples from best practice – what others have tried and what works well – permeate the book and we reflect upon good practice from both the UK and a range of international examples. Experienced practitioners share their knowledge about strategies to maximize access to services, and the book considers how young children and their families will be provided with relevant and accessible services, resources and programmes.

This book is an innovative and valuable text for anyone working in the fields of early years library services and early years education. It establishes a sound background in various aspects of library provision for 0- to five-year-olds. It provides professional insight, backed up by an evidence base, for those who have to strategically plan or deliver early years library services and programmes at a local community level or in nursery schools. The book's underpinning philosophy is that theory and practice are closely interrelated. The developmental needs of children between the ages of 0 and 5 years vary greatly and designing programmes that are age appropriate and engaging for children can prove particularly challenging for library staff who are not early childhood specialists. Our aim is that this book should be an accessible, informative and inspiring text that offers practitioners the knowledge, ideas and confidence to work in partnership with other key professionals in delivering services and programmes.

A note about terminology

This book discusses the work of librarians who specialize in providing services and resources to support the needs of young children from birth to five years, often just referred to as the 'under-fives'. These library practitioners will usually be employed in the public library service and may have a variety of different career titles, depending on which part of the world they are from. The examples we came across include: children's librarian, early years librarian, community librarian, co-ordinator of early childhood services, Bookstart Co-ordinator, literacy development officer. We have not attempted to 'standardize' the name of the role, so please be aware that in the chapters of this book you will encounter a range of different job titles for the practitioners who are active intermediaries in providing library services for the under-fives. The little people who are the focus of this book are also called different things, and we have been happy to use a variety of words to describe the babies, toddlers, preschoolers, infants, young children and the under-fives who feature in each chapter and country case study. Similarly, we have not standardized names of things such as the all-important 'gear and accoutrements' known as buggies, prams, pushchairs and strollers, depending on where in the world you live - so please be prepared to code-switch.

Structure of the book

The book is organized into 14 chapters. The opening chapter, written by the editors, Carolynn Rankin and Avril Brock, sets the scene by discussing how encouraging young children and their families to access a library with all its resources can provide a great foundation for developing early literacy. Children's services are receiving a high profile today, as policy makers are concerned about effective education and the level of reading skills in contemporary society. We make the case that professional intervention provided by the librarian in supporting the development of communication, language and literacy is much more than just the 'telling of stories', as access is provided to resources that encourage emergent literacy and parents and carers are encouraged to play an active part in the learning process. Library practitioners are at the forefront of promoting children's rights, helping to give young users the best start in life and disseminating key messages about the importance of early literacy. We discuss how the librarian provides one of the universal services which potentially offers the 'pathway of opportunity' for young children. The role of the librarian is therefore very important in drawing families into the world of literacy and all that it can offer, but we note that there are issues to consider around professional and political recognition and the perceived value of this intervention.

The evidence suggests that we should also be paying attention to the very structure and nature of the places we are creating. Although it is a contested concept, we argue that the library has a role in helping to stimulate social capital at the individual or micro level, providing support for families and parenting. It has been proposed that libraries can help to build social capital by providing a safe place to meet, socialize and relax. Governments have been recognizing the crucial importance of understanding these inter- and intragenerational relationships and transmission processes. This has implications for the role of the librarian in supporting family learning and providing a place for intergenerational encounters. The chapter introduces the role of the public library in offering an environment where young children and their families can gain a sense of belonging to the community through using a shared resource and where they are made welcome in a community space that celebrates diversity.

The first chapter concludes by looking at the politics of the situation. Libraries can change children's lives, but, despite compelling evidence about the value and impact of library services, many are currently under threat, due to funding cuts in public services; public libraries are in the spotlight as local authorities make decisions about what can and cannot be provided through the public purse. We argue that the job of the early years librarian and the children's librarian is undervalued where the role is not understood. In this chapter we hope we have shown that this is not a simplistic perception, but that what is done in the early years library does indeed make a difference to social capital, educational achievement and future life chances, as well as to an enjoyment of reading and of being literate in today's fast-moving world.

In **Chapter 2** Avril Brock and Carolynn Rankin discuss 'What you need to know about promoting early reading with young children.' There is much more to reading than just decoding symbols and stringing words together to make sense. Children need to become critical readers and thinkers, and it is important for librarians to gain an understanding of the reading process and the skills of reading in the 21st century. We highlight some of the underpinning knowledge about early literacy, early language acquisition and the stages of language development. In order to become competent and active readers and writers, children need a multitude of experiences of oral language, of talking, listening, storying, rhyming, reading and singing. These are the building blocks of literacy and make a difference as to how quickly and easily they acquire reading and writing. Until recently, literacy was seen primarily as reading and writing, and children were not thought to be ready to learn to read or write before the ages of 6 or 7. However, the principles behind the concept of 'emergent literacy' are that literacy begins at birth and is a social process. This new knowledge about child development and emergent literacy has highlighted the needs of babies and toddlers and this can be incorporated into providing appropriate services for young children and their families. In discussing what practitioners need to know about young children, practical guidance is provided for the librarian to develop strategies for promoting early reading skills.

Chapter 3 provides a glimpse of the three-year intervention programme planned by the City of Melbourne and due to commence in 2015. Librarian Paula Kelly writes about 'City of Literature ... it all starts with ABCD! The City of Melbourne and the Abecedarian Approach'. This chapter discusses the development of the City of Melbourne's Early Literacy Strategy, which intentionally looks at developing the parenting practices of parents as their child's first teachers. It aims to improve parent–child interactions and subsequent early language development and is framed by the Abecedarian Approach, which focuses on an interventionist approach that promotes learning and positive educational and social outcomes for children who begin life 'at risk'. The investment in the proposed programme is significant as a cross-council commitment to the City's focus on early literacy and early intervention. Evaluation is planned, and the programme delivery and its impact will be measured.

We stay in Australia and with the theme of research evidence for **Chapter 4**, where Caroline Barratt-Pugh and Nola Allen provide an overview of the Better Beginnings Family Literacy Program, an initiative of the State Library of Western Australia based on the UK's Bookstart. The authors describe how, since its launch in 2005 to the present time, Better Beginnings, has grown to be one of the most extensive and successful family literacy programmes in Australia. Delivered through public libraries and community health centres throughout Western Australia, this universal programme is designed to provide positive early literacy experiences for all families with young children aged from birth to three.

A significant aspect of this is that Edith Cowan University has conducted an independent, longitudinal evaluation of the programme since its inception, which has been invaluable to the programme's sustainability and has contributed to the evidence base that demonstrates the key role that libraries can and do play in literacy development. Barratt-Pugh and Allen make the case that the Better Beginnings programme, founded on international research, has transformed theory into practice.

In **Chapter 5** the editors, Carolynn Rankin and Avril Brock, focus on 'People and partnerships, skills and knowledge', addressing the role of professionals in the interdisciplinary work involved in meeting the varied needs of the local community. The chapter is particularly concerned with the roles of librarians and other early years specialists as they seek to develop effective partnerships across the disciplines as well as to foster partnerships with parents and carers. Partnership working is seen as an important strategy for tackling complex issues such as social inclusion and supporting the lifelong learning agenda. The chapter includes a discussion on community profiles, which form the basis on which to identify community needs for library services and facilities. The authors consider understanding the information needs of parents, and opportunities for involving fathers and grandparents.

Chapter 6, 'Resources for early years libraries: books, toys and other delights', by Carolynn Rankin and Avril Brock, starts by considering the underlying principles and requirements of collection development. Library authorities can take a number of different approaches to the procurement and supply of books and other resources and we look in detail at collection development in the early years library using picture books as the core of the collection. The chapter illustrates why early years librarians need to have knowledge of diverse resources such as treasure baskets, toy libraries, storysacks and Bookstart packs. We discuss how to select books that are appropriate for babies and young children, girls and boys, additional-language learners and children with special educational needs, not forgetting the needs of their parents. The chapter points readers in the direction of sources of information on a range of materials for early years stock selection.

Francesca de Freitas and Tess Prendergast, from Vancouver Public Library in Canada, are innovators. In **Chapter 7**, 'Using digital media in early years library services', they focus specifically on the role of early years library work in the digital age and open up a topic of professional debate. The wide availability of digital technology means that more and more children across a range of socio-economic and cultural groups now have access to digital tools in their daily lives with their families. The authors pose the questions how and why does this concern early years library staff?

In particular, tablet computers such as iPads and the applications (apps) that are designed to run on them represent an area of particular promise for early years libraries. Many of these apps are 'book-based' and represent a natural place for early years library collections to jump into the digital realm. This chapter focuses on approaches to learning about tablets and apps and how they might be incorporated into your existing early years work in libraries. The authors are both librarians and they set the scene in the light of underpinning research and the importance of modelling early literacy activities using digital media. They present a case study at Vancouver Public Library, including practical advice on using apps in family story time sessions.

Chapter 8 turns the focus to the importance of play in the library. Rachel Payne describes how Brooklyn Public Library has been exploring play activities that get parents talking with their little ones. Read, Play, Grow! is an early literacy curriculum of simple play activities using everyday household objects and materials. In this chapter, Payne gives an outline of the curriculum and includes suggested play activities and practical tips for setting up 'play stations' in traditional story time programmes or in full-scale play events. She discusses the ages and stages of play for little ones and explains what play looks like for babies and toddlers. For the past three years, the annual Big Brooklyn Playdate has been hosted by the Central Library, and each time, over 100 babies and toddlers (and their parents or caregivers) have come out to play. Three 'zones' at the playdate direct the children to appropriate areas based on their development. Rachel makes the point that, since libraries are often the first cultural and educational institutions where the very young can fully participate, we are uniquely positioned to support parents in these first interactions.

She proposes redirecting children's energy to more appropriate play in the library where small-scale, temporary play experiences can be created in multipurpose programme rooms and even in the children's library. A key message is that we need to see playtime as a core component of our programmes, not an afterthought. (Additional note from the editors: if you want to know the secrets of how to run a 'No-Mess Finger Painting' session, we can recommend this chapter!)

In Chapter 9 Tess Prendergast lays a firm foundation for helping early years librarians consider their role in the provision of inclusive early literacy resources for children with disabilities. The terms 'inclusive' and 'inclusion' in early childhood settings are thoroughly explored, with a definition and illustrative examples which help towards an understanding of what is meant by the term 'inclusive early literacy'. Prendergast argues that in order to best meet the needs of *all* children, including those with developmental disabilities, the public library's early literacy resource provisions should include a range of intentionally designed inclusive approaches. She challenges us as readers to expand our conception of what constitutes early childhood literacy.

Prendergast identifies that there is currently a distinct lack of library studies that deal with the needs of children with disabilities and how to adapt early literacy resources to effectively meet their needs. This chapter aims to partially fill that gap, while acknowledging the critical need for further research about libraries, early literacy and children with disabilities. Inclusive early literacy involves *anticipating, planning and preparing for the participation of children with diverse development* and ensuring that they are provided with opportunities to experience and learn alongside their age peers. The chapter describes some critical features of inclusive story times and, alongside challenges to conventional wisdom, offers some recommendations for adapting programmes to meet the needs of diverse young children, including those with developmental disabilities.

Chapter 10 is written by two children's librarians who are also very talented musicians in their own right. Shelley Bullas and Ben Lawrence celebrate the fact that singing and rhyme time sessions are perfectly placed in the local library; singing helps to develop speech, language and communication skills as well as fine and gross motor skills. It also enriches the family unit by boosting emotional and social well-being. Their chapter on 'Music and rhyme time sessions for the under-fives' focuses on the practical aspects of running singing sessions in public libraries for young children and their parents and carers. The authors recognize that their readers may include library assistants, librarians, chief librarians, managers, early years professionals and students, and because of the wide-ranging audience they combine a case study with a step-by-step how-to guide. They want to empower readers to feel confident about delivering high-quality sessions and they also hope to inspire complete beginners.

The way Bullas and Lawrence plan and deliver their rhyme time sessions is directly informed by the writings and philosophical approach to music education of the Hungarian composer Zoltán Kodály. It is a methodical and sequential approach to music education, and in the early years has a huge emphasis on musical play. They provide detailed practical guidance on 'planning and preparing your session', and include reassuring sections on 'encouraging participation' and how to deal with 'what if it goes horribly wrong?' Choosing appropriate material is essential for these sessions and an extensive list of recommended songs and rhyme books and other resources (including parachutes, Lycra and puppets!) is provided at the end of the chapter.

Chapter 11 is arranged in two parts. In Part 1, 'Reaching your audience', authors Carolynn Rankin and Avril Brock look at how practitioners can provide opportunities for young children and their families to enjoy literacy and language development activities together. Many early years librarians tell stories at sessions, providing entertainment and enlightenment for their local community. Acknowledging the skills required to effectively connect and engage with a family audience, the authors offer practical guidance for the librarian as performer, including strategies for sharing stories with children and voice projection and performance skills. The chapter also includes a discussion on using treasure baskets with babies, using picture books to help to build vocabulary and telling stories in other languages to support the bilingual learner. Continuing the theme of partnerships, three examples of outreach work are provided, looking at Traveller families, teenage fathers and culturally diverse communities. Partnerships are a key aspect of campaigns and promotional schemes, and some UK-based initiatives are discussed.

Early years library provision is also delivered by partnerships in other parts of the world. There are a wealth of initiatives in operation, both in the UK and overseas, and Part 2 of the chapter presents case studies of excellent practice from Australia, Croatia, Denmark, Italy, Northern Ireland, Russia and Sweden.

Early years activities in libraries and, of course, library books can play a huge role in supporting babies' and young children's learning and development. **Chapter 12** considers that role and identifies successful library activities and book promotion for under-fives.

Anne Harding, the author, is an experienced independent trainer specializing in children's and young people's reading and children's and school libraries. Well-planned sessions and well-chosen books deliver enormous benefits to children and families and Anne discusses the key ingredients of successful early years provision. She challenges practitioners to consider how early years-friendly the library feels to the first-time visitor. Planning and practicalities are discussed, with a message that early years activities should feel informal, but meticulous planning is vital in order to achieve this. The chapter includes guidance on the types of books that work well for reading to groups of babies and young children.

Chapter 13 considers what makes for a good design in providing library spaces for babies and young children and their families. Choosing, sharing and expressing views on books all start long before children can read, and the challenges and opportunities relating to library-space design for the birth-to-five age range are discussed by Carolynn Rankin and Rachel Van Riel, the latter an experienced library designer. The premise in this chapter is that librarians should be concerned about architecture and design and take an active interest in the place and space in which services are delivered to the user community. The role of the library building as a community space is considered, but there is recognition that the personal development needs of different age groups can cause conflicts in terms of location and design. The authors suggest issues to consider in planning the use of space, designing to create boundaries, dealing with noise and book displays for different age groups. Practical guidance is provided on choosing colour schemes, furniture and equipment, carpets and soft furnishings.

The theme in **Chapter 14**, the final chapter, is planning, and Carolynn Rankin discusses some of the issues associated with planning in organizations and multidisciplinary teams. Financial planning is discussed as an important means of allocating resources to enable development. Practical aspects of project planning are also covered, as librarians may have opportunities to set up schemes and initiatives, often in partnership work. Impact and evaluation are also discussed, as these are important stages in the planning cycle for any project or activity. The final sections look at planning at the individual level, and Carolynn discusses aspects of continuous professional development and developing skills for the reflective practitioner.

Final comments

We hope that this book will provide a deeper understanding of the connections and interdependencies between the government policy agendas that shape the delivery of early years library services, and the ways in which we connect and engage with our communities, the ways in which we design baby-friendly library space fit for purpose and the ways that we seek to maintain high, professional standards. We hope you will enjoy reading this book and draw inspiration, enthusiasm and challenge from the ideas presented here and be encouraged to put them into practice in your own early years library service. Your professional intervention will provide the 'pathway of opportunity' for young children and their families.

CHAPTER 1

Take them to the library: the pathway of opportunity

Carolynn Rankin and Avril Brock

PART 1 TAKE THEM TO THE LIBRARY: THE PATHWAY OF OPPORTUNITY

Introduction

Literacy and communication skills are vital in society today and an early introduction to literacy through a breadth of experiences of rhymes, stories, pictures and books supports these skills. Encouraging young children and their families to access a library, with all its resources, can provide a great foundation for developing early literacy. There are many routes into reading and practitioners - early years librarians, carers and educators - should capitalize on all of them. This introductory chapter will discuss literacy as a human right and the importance of early childhood as a time for becoming competent learners and readers.

Librarians know that reading to babies and young children is one of the most effective ways of enhancing language development in a child (Brock and Rankin, 2008; Greene, 1991; Walter, 2009). In terms of cognitive skills development, librarians have a contribution to make to the early years by providing activities that support the development of language, communication and literacy skills. Encouraging young children and their families to access a library and its resources can provide a great foundation for developing early reading skills (Anderson, 2006; Rankin, 2011; Rankin and Brock, 2008). This chapter will discuss the role of the public library and the role of the librarian in providing books and other resources and a place to access them.

Intervention and opportunity

The professional intervention provided by the librarian in supporting the development of communication, language and literacy is much more than just the 'telling of stories', as access is provided to resources that encourage emergent literacy and parents and carers are encouraged to play an active part in the learning process. The librarian provides positive interventions through an offer of universal services and by engaging in partnerships.

We suggest that this intervention, or direct involvement, provides a pathway of opportunity for young children and their families if they take advantage of the library's services and resources. The term 'intervention' is used here to mean becoming directly involved in something in order to have an influence on what happens. In early years library sessions where children (and their families) are encouraged to participate the learning is interactive, experiential and social. Early intervention works on the basis that the care a child receives in the first three years can largely determine future outcomes. This means that it is important to intervene to tackle any problems emerging for children such as diagnosed disabilities or developmental delays, as soon as possible, so that they receive resources to maximize development. This can be through providing targeted services and support universally to all children and families or through targeted support for those more likely to suffer poor outcomes (Brock, 2015, 95).

Bronfenbrenner, a co-founder of the USA's Head Start programme (1979; 1989), was well known for his cross-cultural studies on families. He defined the importance of context to a child's well-being and suggested that behaviour and development are influenced by the interactions with the social system around them. Bronfenbrenner's model of the universal child places her at the centre of concentric circles of influence: the family, the immediate context and the wider cultural context, and so indicates the influences that affect young children's life experiences. Bronfenbrenner's main concern has been to examine how the groups or settings surrounding the child work, and how the child is influenced by these systems. The model 'A child's world – a social ecological perspective of professional intervention' (Brock, 2011, 11) is an adaptation of Bronfenbrenner's model and indicates how universal and targeted services have an impact and are developed around the child (Figure 1.1). In this model the librarian is shown as providing one of the universal services which potentially opens the 'pathway of opportunity', but there are issues to consider around professional and political recognition and the perceived value of this intervention.

The phrase 'pathway of opportunity' reflects how the public library and librarians offer opportunities across the spectrum of age groups, from the youngest baby all the way along the life course to grandparents and family elders. By offering interactive sessions and building library collections to mirror local community profiles, librarians can work to ensure that children's diverse literacies are accepted and built upon in library settings, and Tayler (2007, vii) notes 'the natural learning strategies and the agency that very young children demonstrate

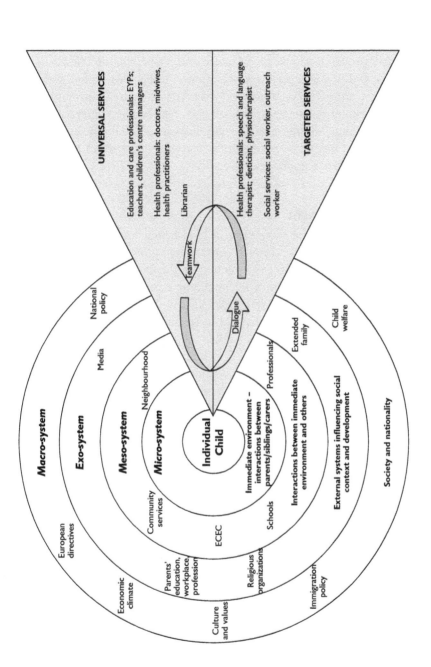

Figure 1.1 *A child's world – a social ecological perspective of professional intervention (Brock, 2011, 11)*

The figure contains the following labels:

UNIVERSAL SERVICES

Education and care professionals: EYPs; teachers, children's centre managers

Health professionals: doctors, midwives, health practitioners

Librarian

TARGETED SERVICES

Health professionals: speech and language therapist; dietician, physiotherapist

Social services: social worker, outreach worker

Teamwork

Dialogue

Macro-system

Exo-system

Meso-system

Micro-system

Individual Child

Immediate environment – interactions between parents/siblings/carers

Interactions between immediate environment and others

External systems influencing social context and development

Society and nationality

National policy

Media

Neighbourhood

Professionals

Extended family

Child welfare

Community services

ECEC

Schools

Parents' education, workplace, profession

Religious organizations

Immigration policy

European directives

Economic climate

Culture and values

in their everyday lives are sound bases upon which to build education'.

Children's services are receiving a high profile today, as policy makers are concerned about effective education and the level of reading skills for the Information Age. Political policies influence and shape what is offered to our communities, and it is important for practitioners to be effective in developing and delivering a range of services to meet local needs. Proactive library authorities develop and customize services specifically for their local communities, using community profiling. Funding, sustainability and accountability are at the centre of most initiatives, but many practitioners may not be aware of the political landscape in which services are delivered.

Literacy is a human right

Basic education, within which literacy is the key learning tool, was recognized as a human right in 1948 in the Universal Declaration of Human Rights. In 1989 the United Nations endorsed the Convention on the Rights of the Child, which afforded children the same range of civil, political, economic, social and cultural rights as adults. It is the most complete statement of children's rights ever produced and it came into force in the UK in 1992. It requires that services for children should develop policies that are responsive to the wide range of children's needs, encompassing all spheres of their lives (Lewis and Lindsay, 2000).

The Convention on the Rights of the Child is the first legal instrument to focus solely on the child, regardless of where the child was born and to whom, and regardless of sex, religion and social origin. It sets out in detail what every child needs to have for a safe, happy and fulfilled childhood. The rights focus on three key aspects - the three 'Ps' of protection, provision and participation. All of the rights in the Convention apply to all children and young people without discrimination. These include the rights to:

- receive special protection measures and assistance
- have access to services such as education and health care
- develop their personalities, abilities and talents to the fullest potential
- grow up in an environment of happiness, love and understanding
- be informed about and participate in achieving their rights in an accessible and active manner.

Key rights include the right to education, the right to literacy and the right to play. Literacy is acknowledged as a major global issue.

The Arts Council England states that access to knowledge, experiences and treasures within libraries is every child's birthright (Arts Council England, 2011).

Libraries and librarians are a vital aid to literacy development, providing resources to help parents make sure their child has the best start in life. The generic message is that reading with young children is important, irrespective of first language, heritage or cultural background. The pleasure of stories and story-telling is universal, and this will be explored further in later chapters.

A working group from the Chartered Institute of Library and Information Professionals (CILIP) provided an overview of library services to children and young people in the *Start with the Child* report published in 2002. This report is at the centre of advocacy activity and argues that libraries can change children's lives. Libraries are a hugely important part of children's and young people's lives because they bring books and children together; they provide reading opportunities free of charge, and so they encourage experimentation and learning (CILIP, 2002, 9). Books can inspire imagination, help emotional growth and develop understanding of the world and our place in the local and global community, past and present.

> Literacy takes many forms: on paper, on the computer screen, on TV, on posters and signs. Those who use literacy take it for granted – but those who cannot use it are excluded from much communication in today's world.
>
> (UNESCO, 2003)

The babies and young children of today represent the first generation to grow up spending their entire lives surrounded by and using computers, mobile phones and all the other gadgets, toys and tools of the digital age. Prensky (2001, 1) has designated this generation as the Digital Natives - all 'native speakers' of the digital language of computers, video games and the internet. In the library profession, there is a recognition that service providers need to embrace the world of these digital natives - the born-digitals who have experienced sound and visual surroundings of ever-increasing complexity since birth.

Advocating for children's rights in the contemporary global society

Library practitioners are at the forefront of promoting children's rights and helping to give young users the best start in life. They can play a key role in disseminating information about the importance of early literacy to parents, childcare providers, early childhood teachers, children's advocates and political decision makers. Librarians are advocates for literacy, and their practices are the tools of such advocacy. In her paper on 'Children's Rights and Library Best Practices', Koren draws attention to this opportunity:

> For all who are concerned with children and young people, the United Nations Convention on the Rights of the Child offers support in library policy and practice.
>
> (Koren, 2003,1)

In considering the issue of child rights in terms of access to books,

> The idea of the child having rights is a crucial one. We are used to thinking of children as unformed extensions of their parents, and it is easy to overlook that they have rights, which may differ from their parents, particularly when considering the early years and the right to access books and information.
>
> (Halpin et al., 2012, 231)

Using the public library is an important first step in local citizenship, and Halpin et al. (2013) propose that 'The public library, in the UK and also around the world, can be seen as a fundamental human right, a basic expectation of society, community, and individuals.'

The development of new knowledge, thinking, policy and practice occurs constantly and practitioners operate within the context of where and with whom they work, accepting or adapting to change. New developments might feel positive or negative to the individual practitioner, but whatever the immediate and personal/professional feelings she or he might have, it is necessary to engage in critical reflection on any change. It is a key professional attribute to be able to reflect on the impact of change on the children and families with whom you work and the effects on working practice (Brock, 2015, 22).

Reflect on the different approaches in the following scenario.

SCENARIO: Having a voice as an advocate for early years policy

'Hello, what do you do?'

'I work as an early years librarian in a children's centre.'

'Gosh, it must be great fun to spend all day just reading stories and running play times, though I'm not sure I could cope with all those little children crawling about ...'

Reply option 1

'Yes, I do spend part of my day reading to young children and their parents and carers and helping them to choose books. It is great fun.'

Reply option 2

'Yes, I do spend part of my day helping young children and their parents and carers with story times and reading activities. I and my colleagues also address some of the key issues in 21st-century society – we tackle social inclusion, support lifelong learning. We encourage community cohesion and build social capital and foster cultural activity.'

Social capital and the public library

Policy makers have been interested in the importance of social capital, deprivation and community cohesion. The concept of 'social capital' is a focus of interest and debate in the research and policy communities. This interest is driven by a growing body of evidence that social capital has enormous effects on economic growth, health, crime and even the effectiveness and functioning of governments. However, the concept is contested and used for varying purposes, largely by social theorists (Sullivan, 2010). There has been considerable discussion – and disagreement – about what should be counted as social capital. It has been described as the complex web of relationships between organizations, communities and groups which make up civil society. This is used to describe the social relationships, networks and community strength, including the reciprocity, good neighbourliness and trust. According to Halpern (2004), social capital refers to the social networks, informal structures and norms that facilitate individual and collective action. He argues that the essence of the concept is simple enough, as people are connected with one another through immediate social structures – webs of association and shared understandings of how to behave (Halpern, 2004, 3). This social fabric greatly affects with whom and how we interact and co-operate. Field (2008) suggests that the term 'social capital' is a way of defining the intangible resources of community, shared values and trust upon which we draw in daily life.

Social capital is considered important in the building of an individual's human capital. Dex and Joshi (2005) are undertaking the longitudinal UK Millennium Cohort Study of babies born in the year 2000. Children will have levels of capital stock from their parents' financial circumstances and wealth, from their parents' human capital in the forms of education and knowledge, from their parents' and wider family's social and relationship capital and from the neighbourhood's social capital and infrastructure of services. Governments have recognized the crucial importance of understanding these inter- and intragenerational relationships and transmission processes. This has implications for the role of the librarian in supporting family learning and providing a place for intergenerational encounters, and Pateman and Vincent (2010) provide a well-argued justification for extending the social justice role of the public library and the provision of needs-based services.

The evidence suggests that we should also be paying attention to the very structure and nature of the places we are creating. It has been proposed that libraries can help to build social capital by providing a safe place to meet, socialize and relax. Bourke (2005) argues that public libraries can build social capital through networking, and this potential for the community has been noted by other researchers (Aabø, 2005; Aabø and Audunson 2012; Johnson, 2010; Neuman, 2009; Rankin et al 2007; Svendsen, 2013; Vårheim, 2009).

Research by Johnson (2012) in three neighbourhood branch libraries in a large American Midwestern city suggests that public libraries may contribute to social capital through the relationships and interactions that occur between staff and patrons. Some of the ways in which these relationships and interactions may contribute to social capital include connecting people to both community and library resources, providing social support for patrons/users, reducing social isolation and providing a positive place for local residents to gather. Ferguson (2012) examines the idea, commonly expressed in the library and information services literature, that public libraries have a growing role as developers of social capital, and brings to bear some of the growing body of research into public libraries and social capital. He outlines the main strategies taken by public librarians who attempt to contribute to social capital, such as community outreach, provision of meeting places and the provision of universal services to the public.

It can be argued that the library therefore has a role in helping to stimulate social capital at the individual or micro level; the library can provide greater support for families and parenting. Halpern advocates that the relationships between parents and their children is important for the development of both bonding and bridging social capital (Halpern, 2004, 295). In the early years of a child's development, attentive and responsive adults draw the child into the social world, reinforcing and echoing the child's own interactions (Halpern, 2004, 144). Parents' social networks, parent–parent connections, and parent–school interactions have significant impacts on children's educational attainment, delinquency and later-life chances. This approach underpins interventions such as the US Head Start and the UK Sure Start programmes, both of which are intended to help parents support their children (see later in this chapter for information about these programmes).

Literacy as a social tool

Literacy can be considered as a social tool in which we communicate and function on an everyday basis. This includes talking, listening, reviewing and drawing as well as critiquing. There are many different types of literacy available to us, and we consume and interpret texts in many different ways across a variety of social, cultural and linguistic situations (Jones Diaz, 2007). Marsh provides a strong reminder that

Communication, language and literature permeate all aspects of daily living. Consequently these skills are essential for life. If children are not proficient communicators they are vulnerable to the many varied and significant disruptions to their learning and development in all areas.

(Marsh, 2011, 137)

The literacy practices that are important to the everyday lives of children do not take place in isolation from other social practices and interactions. In everyday life children gain expertise in literacy practices that are directly relevant to their social and cultural experiences. The concept of 'seemingly inconsequential actions' plays a key role in supporting the development and socialization of babies and young children. Because literacy is embedded in almost everything we do, its connections to social situations and practices are significant (Jones Diaz, 2007, 33).

Reading can be a very social activity, encouraging community involvement. Young children can certainly be socialized as they participate in reading as a social activity. This is very popular, judging by the number of rhyme time and story sessions offered in public libraries and other early years settings across the British Isles. Reading has social benefits and the power to build relationships, and can help to form and nurture relationships from the earliest act of parents sharing books with babies. (See Chapters 3, 4, 10 and 12.)

Parents' involvement with their children's early literacy experiences

Parents' involvement with their children's early literacy experiences has a positive impact on their children's reading performance and is the key to young children's future literacy achievement and educational success (Desforges and Abouchaar, 2003). Hannon and Nutbrown's work in Sheffield (Hannon and Nutbrown, 2001) provided parents with ways of thinking about their own literacy and their roles with their children and how this reflected a socio-cultural change in family literacy for the families. These children made more literacy progress than did comparable children not participating in the study. Research has repeatedly shown that one of the most accurate predictors of a child's achievement is not only parental income or social status, but the extent to which parents are able to create a home environment that encourages learning and communicates high, yet reasonable, expectations for achievement (NLT, 2011). This UK research report, *Literacy: a route to addressing child poverty*, stresses the importance of parents' involvement in their own literacy skills and their understanding of the hugely important role they play in developing their children's educational outcomes.

PART 2 EARLY CHILDHOOD: THE MOST IMPORTANT TIME

Children's early experiences have significant effects on early cognitive development, and affect literacy outcomes. It is important for professionals who work with young children to have a theoretical underpinning and build their knowledge on a critical understanding of how children perceive the world; of how they think, learn and develop. Early childhood is high on the political agenda globally, and the shaping of children's and their families' daily and future lives through policy development (Brock and Rankin, 2011). This has evolved through growing awareness of the significance of the first five years of life for intellectual, social and emotional development and growing interest and research in the early years within the disciplines of psychology, education, social policy, social care and neuropsychology.

This interest in policy has been stimulated by recent studies highlighting that the nurturing, care and education received from parents and carers are vital for optimal brain development, emotional intelligence, learning and educational achievement (Brock and Rankin, 2011). There is growing evidence 'from neuroscience, from longitudinal development studies and from population studies that the period of early childhood is crucial in establishing a child's self-identity, learning and achievement' (Gammage, 2006, 236). A child's life chances are most heavily predicated on their development in the first five years of life and 'the period from birth to age 5 is one of opportunity and vulnerability for healthy physical, emotional, social, and cognitive development' (Karoly et al., 2005, xv). Family background, parental education, good parenting and the opportunities for learning and development in the early years have more impact on children's emotional and social development than money, and so determine potential and attainment (Field, 2010).

The international conference 'Prepare for Life! Raising Awareness for Early Literacy Education' held in Leipzig in March 2013 involved 130 participants from over 35 different countries. The assembled experts developed 'The Leipzig Recommendations on Early Literacy Education', a set of recommendations based on the assumption that early literacy education is a prerequisite for any kind of skill acquisition, and it is important to recognize that early literacy is much more than learning the alphabet (Stiftung Lesen, 2013).

A 'good start' in the early years

A 'good start' in the early years can be a way of compensating for any negative effects of children's developmental context (Sylva et al., 2004). The quality of the home environment as a strong contributor to young children's literacy and social competence and to their subsequent educational success has been strongly established by longitudinal research by The Abecedarian Approach (Ramey et al., 2012) and Head Start in the USA, and in the UK by the Effective Provision of Pre-School Education (EPPE) project. Research by Foster et al. (2005, 13) with children in three Head Start programmes finds that 'family social risk and home learning experiences mediate the association between socio economic status and Head Start children's school readiness in the areas of emergent literacy competence and social functioning'.

The Effective Pre-School, Primary and Secondary Education research project (EPPSE) is a notable large-scale, UK longitudinal study that focuses specifically on the effectiveness of early years education. The EPPSE project has tracked the progress and development of children from preschool to post-compulsory education, considering the aspects of preschool provision that have a positive impact on children's attainment, progress and development (Siraj-Blatchford et al., 2011). The project's aims were to identify the impact and effectiveness of preschool on children's intellectual and social/behavioural development. The EPPSE researchers followed the children to the end of Key Stage 1 (age seven), and their development was monitored until they entered school around the age of five. The findings demonstrated the importance of parents in children's early educational achievements. This comprehensive study undertaken by Siraj-Blatchford et al. (2011, 33) explores why some 'at risk' children 'succeed against the odds', while others fall further behind. Disadvantaged children significantly benefit from good-quality preschool experiences and Siraj-Blatchford et al.'s (2011) research finds that this is the case internationally. The EPPSE study finds that the evidence from France indicates that preschool appears to reduce socio-economic inequalities, and in Switzerland the expansion of early childhood care and education has improved intergenerational educational mobility (Brock, 2015, 90).

The early years: an important foundation for future literacy

Most other European countries do not promote formal literacy experiences with young children until they are at least six or even seven years old! They then normally find that their children acquire both reading and writing skills with little difficulty. In the UK there is a strong emphasis on young children acquiring formal literacy skills from a very early age. 'Focusing on educational achievement may lead to less emphasis on individual young children's personal, social and emotional needs and ... children may not gain the emotional well-being that is so important for holistic learning and development' (Brock, 2015, 61).

Low socio-economic status does not mean low aspirations, but it is more likely that there will be barriers to achieving them (Hirsch, 2007). The gap in attainment is evidenced in Feinstein's (2003) research, which found that children from high socio-economic status groups at 22 months overtook the children from low socio-economic status groups as their age increased to forty months, five years and ten years of age. This was further substantiated by the Sutton Trust-funded report which showed that children in the poorest fifth of families were already nearly a year behind children from middle-income families in vocabulary tests (Brock, 2015, 90). This research by Waldfogel and Washbrook (2010) indicates that children's educational achievements are strongly linked to parents' income, which can therefore be a key barrier to social mobility. Maisey et al. (2013) find that children's attendance at high-quality settings has a positive impact on language ability and on the parent–child relationship. Good-quality, teacher-led early years education helps children to develop the social skills and vocabulary they need for learning.

The Bercow Report (2008) and research by Roulstone et al. (2011) both demonstrate that a 'child's communication environment influences language development' and that this is a 'more dominant predictor of early language than social background' and can strongly influence 'performance at school entry'. The number of books available to the child, frequency of visits to the library, parents teaching a range of activities, the number of toys available and attendance at preschool are all-important predictors of children's vocabulary at the age of two (Siraj-Blatchford, 2010). Research by Dickinson et al. (2012) in the USA evaluates how countries internationally have initiated programmes that distribute books to parents through libraries and medical clinics. They find that there has been a rapid spread of intervention programmes to promote the power of book reading and literacy. The EU High Level Group of Experts on Literacy reported that family literacy programmes that focus on both parents and children, and their interaction, are highly cost-effective in increasing the literate environment at home. These are powerful, low-cost interventions (European Commission, 2012).

McElwee (2004) writes that Bookstart has been the catalyst for the development of new public library services aimed at this user group – such as rhyme times, interactive sessions using songs and action rhymes which encourage interaction between parent and baby – and to develop communication, bonding and enjoyment. It is interesting to note that Bookstart was different from many other projects in that it was offered to *all* families in the chosen areas rather than being targeted at families considered as being deprived (Cooling, 2011, 6). As a pioneering initiative in children's-book gifting, the programme has been of interest to researchers investigating its impact on language and literacy development in babies and toddlers, and the Bookstart idea has been copied internationally (Allen, 2010; Barratt-Pugh and Allen, 2011). (See Chapter 4 by Barratt-Pugh and Allen, which discusses the evaluation of Better Babies.) Libraries can therefore play a really important role in supporting parents in their children's communication, language and literacy development.

PART 3 THE ROLE OF THE PUBLIC LIBRARY IN SUPPORTING YOUNG CHILDREN

The International Federation of Library Associations (IFLA) has produced guidelines for children's library services to help public libraries implement high-quality children's services. Published by the Libraries for Children and Young Adults Section in 2003, the guidelines state that

> Library services have never been as important for children and their families all over the world as they are today. Access to the knowledge and the multicultural riches of the world, as well as lifelong learning and literacy skills have become the priority of our society. A quality children's library equips children with lifelong learning and literacy skills, enabling them to participate and contribute to the community.
>
> (IFLA, 2003, 3)

IFLA also says that by providing a wide range of materials and activities, public libraries provide an opportunity for children to experience the enjoyment of reading and the excitement of discovering knowledge and works of the imagination. Children and their parents should be taught how to make the best use of a library and how to develop skills in the use of printed and electronic media (IFLA, 2003).

Since the late 19th century public libraries in the UK have been at the heart of their local communities, providing services for children and young people, reflecting the diversity of the population they serve. In the past public library services mainly focused on children who already knew how to read. Public libraries in many parts of the world are now actively encouraging the parents and carers of babies and very young children to join in language and literacy activities:

> The family support workers would tell everyone about the library and they'd bring them down to the library for a visit. They see it as their own, it's not just a library for Sure Start but for all the partners working with it.
>
> Senior librarian

Public libraries have always been community spaces designed to support learning, reading and wider community objectives. The public library service in the UK has many unique selling points and benefits. There is a strongly held view that libraries offer a welcoming, neutral space providing opportunities for personal, cultural and community development. Goulding (2006) writes about how public libraries are playing a role in multi-agency working and in enabling community involvement, cohesion and capacity building (Goulding, 2006, 237). Public libraries also give children and their families access to a vast amount of reading at all levels and for all interests. Ross et al. (2006) sum this up when they highlight that the public library offers

> The opportunity to try out a book with no risks and the importance of no-cost use, the assistance of knowledgeable staff, wide choice, and the ability to browse freely, choosing reading material independently, support readers of all ages.
>
> (Ross et al. 2006, 99)

Creating the right environment

Children, and their families, can gain a sense of belonging to the community through using a shared resource, and they are made welcome in a community space that celebrates diversity. Libraries should be safe and secure, as well as a welcoming environment for children. Long gone are the days of our expecting children to creep into a library, choose a book and creep out again. It is important to make information available to parents that will encourage them to bring their child to the library. The library should be a community hub - welcoming all. It is important to think about how the traditional barriers to access and use can be broken down and removed.

SCENARIO Oscar's first visits to the library
Visit 1

Oscar, at four years and two months old, was not at all interested in going to the library and protested all the way there. However, he did wait patiently in a queue, with his Grandma Avril and ten-year-old sister Melissa, to be registered and get a library card. The three then trooped down to the children's library area, where there were hundreds of books on shelves and in boxes, with seating areas around the window and some tables. Oscar immediately started to rearrange the small, red plastic stacking chairs and the large beanbags and he worked hard, though rather noisily, at this self-allotted task. He didn't look at a single book, so whilst Melissa selected several Jacqueline Wilson books, Grandma chose Oscar's books – two Julia Donaldson stories, a book about dog detectives in London, a pirate book and one entitled *The Big Yellow Digger*. Melissa and Grandma both decided this needed to be a quick visit and they all went to the self-issuing machine. Oscar tried to get behind the machine, where all the wires were. Grandma started to get a bit flustered, so they all made a hasty retreat!

Oscar has several shelves full of story books in his bedroom and he enjoys his bedtime stories every night. He loved his new library books and Mum and Dad read and reread these books every night for the next two weeks. Oscar kept repeating that he did not want to go to the library again, crying 'I don't want to swap the library books, I'm going to keep them!'

Visit 2

'I don't want to go to the library, I want to go home. I don't want to swap my library books, I like *my* books, I'm going to keep them. I don't want new books!' Grandma Avril enticed Oscar out of the car to put money in the parking meter, whilst Melissa carried the heavy bag of books into the library. Oscar returned his library books one by one into the self-issuing machine. A book entitled *Why Reindeers Have Antlers* was next to the machine and Oscar appropriated this for himself. He then went down the stairs by himself to the children's area and once more commenced his task of rearranging the furniture. He didn't look at any books and Grandma chose him five and Melissa chose him two. Melissa had got seven books this week, again mainly Jacqueline Wilson plus one about Space for her school project. Oscar was a bit less noisy than on his last visit and knew how to put his books on the machine one by one to check them out. Yet again, it was a fairly rapid visit, but Oscar enjoyed it more this time and he helped Melissa carry all the books to the car.

That evening's bedtime, Grandma read him the reindeer story, *The Midnight Library* and a nature discovery book about being an insect detective. They planned to go on a bug hunt when the weather improved and Oscar would take his magnifying glass, rucksack and bug-hunting kit. Oscar saved Julia Donaldson's *Super Worm* for Mummy to read and he told both his parents that the library has thousands of books that you can borrow and read.

Visit 3

By visit three, Oscar was now quite familiar with the library routines, although he did muddle the returning of his library books by trying to experiment if they could all go through the self-issuing machine at once. On this visit he did not rearrange the furniture but spent some time watching a nine-month-old girl in a tiger suit who was visiting the library with her dad and her six-year-old brother. This time he did select his own books and was quite insistent on what he wanted and that he needed 12 books this week. Oscar chose information books about going to the hospital and on insect spotting as well as storybooks. He also insisted on getting a comic book of *The Hobbit*, which was too old for him and not very suitable (according to his parents)! Oscar also insisted on again putting his books through the self-issuing machine and we had to ask the librarian to help us, as he was too quick and again there was a muddle. As soon as we got home from the library, Oscar wanted to 'read' his library books.

Oscar is still a regular borrower from the library and the library staff are always patient and helpful with whatever chaos he creates!

The scenario 'Oscar's first visits to the library' exemplifies how young children accessing the library environment provide experiences that are both challenging and rewarding. Calmness, patience and interest in young children are all key elements required by the professional librarian working at the forefront of vital practice. What a child experiences in these early visits will make a difference to their continuing to access the public library resources at different stages in their life.

In Chapter 13 we look at some of the ways in which space and design can be used effectively to create a welcoming environment. Young children will make the most of all their experiences in the library. They will enjoy the range of interesting materials to play with and the opportunity to socialize in a relaxed atmosphere. They will like the colourful environment and revel in the variety of sights, sounds and activities. If their parents and carers are relaxed and made to feel welcome, this will enhance the experience for all and should lead to repeat visits. Word of mouth is an important means of promoting library services for the early years.

Take them to the library: early reading experiences and the 'pathway of opportunity'

There is considerable evidence in the literature to support the value of library provision for young children and their families and in encouraging early reading experiences (Elkin and Kinnell, 2000; Lonsdale, 2000; Fasick, 2011; Roulstone et al., 2011). Maynard suggests that the role played by librarians in providing access to reading material cannot be over-emphasized, and this applies to all kinds of material, not just books (Maynard, 2011). The *Start with the Child* report (CILIP, 2002) recognized the contribution libraries can make in delivering government policies on lifelong learning, combating social exclusion and improving the quality of life of children and young people in the United Kingdom.

In Canada, Stooke and McKenzie undertook an observational study of library and community programmes for babies and toddlers with their caregivers and suggested that important work related to early child development and getting 'ready to learn' at school was embedded in seemingly inconsequential leisure activities (Stooke and McKenzie, 2009, 672). They contend that their findings, because they are based on empirical data and because they are somewhat counter-intuitive, have practical implications for library and information professionals and researchers. McKechnie's observations of library settings (2006, 198) 'story-times for babies and toddlers are complex and usually noisy events, with many activities of different types going on at the same time', emphasizes the professional interventions by the librarian and the 'seemingly inconsequential' actions that support the foundations of early literacy.

Rowsell (2006) suggests that community programme organizers can learn from public librarians who provide engagement and multimodality. In library-based programmes, children were invited to experience the pleasures of playful language, the beauty of books as physical objects and social symbolic play through interactions with puppets. For young children, and especially for parents and caregivers learning English, the multimodal nature of such library activities scaffolds language acquisition.

The role of the children's librarian in providing access to the universal service: promoting communication, language and literacy

It is said that two conditions essential to creating a reader are early experiences of a print-filled environment (and adults reading these materials) and a caring adult to introduce the child to literary pleasure. It would seem that the public library can meet both these requirements (Greene, 1991; Wilkie, 2002), and the institution has a key role to play in supporting the development of communication, language and literacy through the professional intervention provided by librarians. Dugdale and Clark (2008) note that public libraries, with their welcoming presence in communities, are well placed to help address the literacy challenge. Context is important to well-being and development, and babies and young children are influenced by their interactions with the social system around them. Other factors such as family background and ethnic identities, national and cultural heritages, parents' health and educational levels will have an influence. For example, Dex and Joshi (2005) describe the babies in the Millennium Cohort Study as growing up within a series of concentric circles - within their immediate family, within the wider family, within the local area, within the country, its institutions and policies and so on. At the heart of this set of concentric circles are a set of intergenerational relationships.

This resonates with Bronfenbrenner's model of the universal child (1979; 1989) discussed earlier in this chapter, and Brock's model showing the librarian as one of the key professions in providing access to the universal service (see Figure 1.1). The skills of the children's librarian go far beyond story-telling and, in fact, provide professional intervention at the micro level that reflects Bronfenbrenner's model of concentric circles of influence for the child and the family (Rankin, 2011). Kropp (2013) strongly advocates that early literacy programmes need to be regarded as 'essential' - especially if we want the job of children's librarian to be considered a necessary community service. She makes the case succinctly:

When we provide these services, we become more than children's librarians: We're early learning experts. We introduce nursery rhymes to new generations of learners and share the power of rhyme with caregivers. We show parents how to build the early literacy foundation that kids need to enter school ready to learn. We take that first step in creating lifelong library users.

(Kropp, 2013, 18)

Community-based early years libraries are uniquely placed to support families and young children, as they offer accessible learning opportunities for intergenerational groups. Librarians are more than just good story-tellers, and evidence from around the world is showing this vital role in supporting early literacy and family learning (Bohrer, 2005; Feinberg et al., 2007; Prendergast, 2011).

Librarians supporting the early years need to provide positive conditions for all children and their families so that they can access the vast range of books and literacy resources available within libraries. According to IFLA, effective and professionally run children's libraries require trained and committed staff. Desired skills include:

- enthusiasm
- strong communication, interpersonal, team-working and problem-solving skills
- the ability to network and co-operate
- the ability to initiate, be flexible and be open to change
- the ability to analyse user needs, plan, manage and evaluate services and programmes
- eagerness to learn new skills and develop professionally.

The public library should be attractive to the early years community, as it provides access to library staff who know about children's books and care about children's reading. However, it not only needs to be a welcoming place, it also should be able to stimulate and inspire. Creative spaces should enable creative experiences, and public libraries should provide a mix of cultural and creative resources and experiences. Many public librarians have fostered strong links with writers, illustrators and story-tellers, and library practitioners get involved in holding events which draw in the local community. So, whether working in a large central library with extensive 'creative space' for running such events or in a more modest local setting, practitioners can use the power of a story-telling, story-sharing experience to encourage and foster early literacy. The role of the librarian is therefore very important in drawing families into the world of literacy and all that it can offer. Story time for preschool children involves social learning, being part of the group, learning how to listen and following the activities modelled by the librarian. Story and rhyme sessions for children are designed to help language development and reading skills, and we look at aspects of planning for these in Chapters 10 and 11. These activities normally form part of the forward planning of library managers.

Reading and story-telling activities in the early years library

Reading aloud to children is a well-developed aspect of library provision. Neuman and Wright (2007) provide a key message for parents when they emphasize the importance of reading aloud to young children. By providing quality children's books and holding activities and events, librarians can show, by modelling, how to read aloud to young children. Chapter 2 provides knowledge about and activities of the reading process and how/why/what to promote and model for families and young children.

Knowledge is key. Librarians need to have knowledge not only about stories, books and collection development (as illustrated in Figure 1.2), but also about key initiatives and how to work in partnership with other organizations. For example, the NLT is an independent charity that changes lives through literacy and promotes reading to young families. The NLT links home, school and the

Figure 1.2 *An early years librarian preparing for a story-telling session*

wider community to inspire learners and create opportunities for everyone. The 'Talk to Your Baby' initiative encourages parents and carers to talk to and enjoy communicating with their baby. There is a wealth of information about the initiatives of the NLT and many varied, valuable resources on its website. See the end of this chapter for details of this and other useful organizations both in the UK and overseas.

PART 4 POLICY

The politics of the situation

In this chapter we have argued that public libraries support well-being, encourage reading, spread knowledge, contribute to learning and skills and help to foster identity, community and a sense of place for people of all ages, backgrounds and cultures. The political, economic, social, cultural and technological environment influences how professionals work and how they develop their personal professional values and ethics. To support professional practice, practitioners should be aware of the political environment influencing the public library service and its partner organizations. Public library activities that promote reading are playing a key role in supporting learning.

There has been a significant increase in activity around early years provision in recent years and there are now many cross-sector initiatives, recognizing the key role of language in children's development. Multi-agency working and integrated service delivery are key aspects of government strategy to improve standards in the early years, and complex structural models (with associated challenges) have been devised where a range of professionals endeavour to work together to provide services to children and their families (Rankin and Butler, 2011). Agency partnerships are helping parents to support their children's early language and literacy, as well as communicating important messages about emotional and social development and health issues. The challenge for librarians is to implement policies in libraries and work effectively with partners to achieve the effective delivery of services while not losing the unique selling point of the library. This will be discussed further in Chapter 5. Karoly et al. (2005, xxiv) report that economic analyses of several early childhood interventions demonstrate that effective programmes can repay the initial investment with savings to government and benefits to society down the road.

Recession and sustainability

As mentioned earlier in this chapter, Field's (2010) *Independent Review on Poverty and Life Chances* acknowledged that the first five years of young children's lives are those which predicate their future life chances. In recent years policy regarding young children and their families has been concerned with reducing poverty, getting parents into employment, increasing training, aspiration and educational achievement, but the recession has created even more difficulties. Recession affects the sustainability of libraries – yet surely there has never been such an important need for libraries as the gap between rich and poor, the 'haves and the have-nots' is increasing. In this age of the 'digital natives', privileged children will have ready access to a range of information technology and digital literacy. However, the cost of getting on to the internet and purchasing devices to enable this access must lead to ever more division in rights to literacy. Libraries are so important for children living in poverty or restricted-income families. Neuman (2009, 133) describes a community-based initiative in Pennsylvania where a key issue was 'Recognising the critical if little-understood role that libraries may play in hard-pressed communities'.

Sustainability is dependent on links with other mainstream activities and funding opportunities and libraries too are involved in this particular focus on those at risk of social exclusion. Some individuals, groups or communities may feel deliberately excluded from access to mainstream services and may face barriers to using those services. This may be because of their own literacy skills, because they have never used libraries in their schooling years or because they have not found schools or other institutions to provide positive experiences. It is therefore important that early years services – children's centres, nurseries and libraries – welcome families and aim to meet all their clients' needs.

Evidence has shown that librarians are good at reaching hard-to-reach groups and can successfully build partnerships based on reading. For young children and their families there is the chance to develop and achieve in a community setting through accessing the local library. The Carnegie Trust UK found that the services provided by public libraries appear to have the potential to contribute directly to individual and community well-being. It states that if this is the case, they should continue to be provided to all, with the core service being provided free of charge (Macdonald, 2012). This report identified that 'there is a strong link between library services and education, digital participation, access to information, the promotion of literacy and social inclusion which support the argument for this service remaining a universal public service' (Macdonald, 2012, 42). Findings from phases one and two of the *Envisioning the Library of the Future* project (Arts Council England, 2012) indicate that over the next ten years, the core *purpose* of libraries looks set to remain the same as it has been for many years: enabling people to access, explore and enjoy books, reading and other forms of knowledge, the provision of quality-assured information, support for learning and literacy. Making parents and others in communities aware that librarians are a resource for early literacy information and guidance will help to position libraries as community partners in the common public goal of helping children to become successful readers and learners. Libraries can change children's lives.

However, despite compelling evidence about the value and impact of library services, many are currently under threat in the UK, due to funding cuts in public services. This is a challenging time for publicly funded services in the UK, and public libraries are in the spotlight as local authorities make decisions about what can and cannot be provided through the public purse. The public funding of a core library service is a topic of political debate in the UK, particularly as it is a statutory requirement under the terms of the Public Libraries and Museums Act 1964 (Great Britain, 1964). In this environment, many libraries are cutting both professional and paraprofessional staff and making increased use of volunteers (Locality, 2013a, 2013b). As Markless and Streatfield (2012) observe:

> Public services are widely viewed by politicians as requiring constant rationing and reduction, although they usually prefer to talk about 'cutting out waste' rather than admitting that they want to reduce or remove highly regarded services such as libraries.
>
> (2012, 9)

In commenting on library budgets and libraries under threat, Cooling notes that 'we lose these services at our peril, for their disappearance would change the educational chances of many of our children' (Cooling, 2011, 10). In referring to the Leipzig Recommendations on Early Literacy Education (Stiftung Lesen, 2013), Flewitt (2013) also registers concern that 'the current lack of funding for public library facilities does not augur well for the emancipatory vision of literacy promoted internationally'.

We can argue that where the role is not understood, the job of the early years librarian and the children's librarian is undervalued. However, librarians themselves need to be more 'politically' astute about the value of their role. A challenging question still to be addressed is how to ensure that the decision makers responsible for educational and literary initiatives fully understand the potential of the public library and the many pathways of opportunity on offer.

Positive outcomes from the Sunshine Library
Jane is a mum who, despite having literacy problems, is determined that her children will have better chances than she has had. She was encouraged to come to the library after receiving her Bookstart Plus Bag and listening to the Bookstart Plus worker on how to share books together.

A mum who has a daughter with Down's syndrome recorded the comment:
'I love to come to the Sunshine because nobody minds if you stay all afternoon.'

A mum who has mental health problems comes to the library for time out –
she knows that our staff will make her feel welcome, make her a drink and
read with her children – giving her some precious time for herself. (See
Chapter 9 on inclusive early literacy.)

Conclusion: helping to create positive experiences and memories in your library: the pathway of opportunity

As we stated at the beginning of this chapter – encouraging young children and
their families to access a library, with all its resources, provides a great foundation
for developing early literacy. This introductory chapter has discussed literacy as
a human right and the importance of early childhood for developing this.

Reflective moment

How well prepared are you to ensure that you can provide positive and enjoyable
learning experiences for young children and their parents and carers? Katherine
Ross suggests that one good way to think about the role of the reader is to think
about your own experiences and reflect on your own reading history (Ross et al.,
2006, 56):

- Were you read to as a child?
- Does your memory include a physical experience such as being bounced
  up and down to nursery rhymes?
- What can you remember about the first stages of reading on your own?

Your professional practice, your partnership with parents and the activities and
service offered in your library setting will shape the recollections and experiences
of the next generation. We rather like that thought, and it sits comfortably with
all the stuff about government policies, missions and targets. The library practitioner
provides positive interventions for the 'digital native' – the young child and her
family – thus leading to the journey along the 'pathways of opportunity'.

This chapter has made links to the other chapters throughout the book,
signposting where you can read more about key issues raised here. The contributors
demonstrate how these issues are international, contemporary and important.
They demonstrate how librarians can have, and should have, a powerful role in
making a difference to the literacy skills of young children and their families. In

this chapter we hope we have shown that this is not a simplistic perception, but that what is done in the early years library does indeed make a difference to social capital, educational achievement and future life chances, as well as an enjoyment of reading and of being literate in today's fast-moving world.

Useful organizations

Booktrust, www.booktrust.org.uk/home

Bookstart, www.bookstart.co.uk

Chartered Institute of Library and Information Professionals (CILIP), www.cilip.org.uk

Effective Pre-School, Primary and Secondary Education (EPPSE) project, www.ioe.ac.uk/research/153.html

International Federation of Library Associations, www.ifla.org

National Literacy Trust, www.literacytrust.org.uk

Sure Start, www.surestart.gov.uk

The Reading Agency, www.readingagency.org.uk

UNESCO, www.unesco.org

References

Aabø, S. (2005) The Role and Value of Public Libraries in the Age of Digital Technologies, *Journal of Librarianship and Information Science*, **37** (4), 205–11.

Aabø, S. and Audunson, R. (2012) Use of Library Space and the Library as Place, *Library and Information Science Research*, **34** (2), 138–40.

Allen, N. (2010) Making a Difference: the Western Australia Better Beginnings family literacy program, *Australasian Public Libraries and Information Services*, **23** (1), 33–7.

Anderson, S. (2006) Books for Very Young Children. In Rosenkoetter, S. E. and Knapp-Philo, J. (eds), *Learning to Read the World: language and literacy in the first three years*, Zero To Three Press.

Arts Council England (2011) *Culture, Knowledge and Understanding: great museums and libraries for everyone*, Arts Council England.

Arts Council England (2012) *Envisioning the Library of the Future Project*, Arts Council England.

Barratt-Pugh, C. and Allen, N. (2011) Making a Difference: findings from Better Beginnings a family literacy intervention programme, *The Australian Library Journal*, **60** (3), 195–204.

Bercow, J. (2008) *The Bercow Report: a review of services for children and young people (0–19) with speech, language and communication needs*, Ref 00632-2008-DOC-EN, DCSF Publications.

Bohrer, C. N. (2005) Libraries as Early Literacy Centers, *Public Libraries*, May/Jun, **44** (3), 127–32.

Bourke, C. (2005) *Public Libraries: building social capital through networking*. Australasian Public Libraries and Information Services (APLIS) **18** (1), 71–5.

Brock, A. (2011) The Child in Context: policy and provision. In Brock, A. and Rankin, C. (eds), *Professionalism in the Interdisciplinary Early Years Team: supporting young children and their families*, Continuum.

Brock, A. (ed.) (2015) *The Early Years Reflective Practice Handbook*, Routledge.

Brock, A. and Rankin, C. (2008) *Communication, Language and Literacy from Birth to Five*, Sage Publications.

Brock, A. and Rankin, C. (2011) (eds) *Professionalism in the Early Years Interdisciplinary Team: supporting young children and their families*, Continuum.

Bronfenbrenner, U. (1979) *The Ecology of Human Development, Experiments by Nature and Design*, Harvard University Press.

Bronfenbrenner, U. (1989) Ecological Systems Theory, *Annals of Child Development*, **6**, 187–249.

CILIP (Chartered Institute of Library and Information Professionals) (2002) *Start with the Child. Report on the CILIP Working Group on Library Provision for Children and Young People*, CILIP.

Cooling, W. (2011) It's Never Too Soon to Start. In Court J. (ed.), *Read to Succeed: strategies to engage children and young people in reading for pleasure*, Facet Publishing.

Desforges, C. and Abouchaar, A. (2003) *The Impact of Parental Involvement, Parental Support and Family Education on Pupil Achievement and Adjustment: a literature review*, DfES Research Report 433, DfES.

Dex, S. and Joshi, H. (2005) (eds), *Children of the 21st Century: from birth to nine months*, The Policy Press.

Dickinson, D. K., Griffith, J. A., Golinkoff, R. M. and Hirsh-Pasek, K. (2012) How Reading Books Fosters Language Development around the World, Hindawi Publishing Corporation, *Child Development Research*, 2012, Article ID 602807.

Dugdale, G. and Clark, C. (2008) *Literacy Changes Lives: an advocacy resource*, National Literacy Trust.

Elkin, J. and Kinnell, M. (2000) *A Place for Children: public libraries as a major force in children's reading*, British Library Research and Innovation Report 117, Library Association.

European Commission (2012) *EU High Level Group of Experts on Literacy*, Final Report, September 2012. Publications Office of the European Union.

Fasick, A. (2011) *From Boardbook to Facebook: children's services in an interactive age*, Libraries Unlimited.

Feinberg, S., Deerr, K., Jordan, B., Byrne, M. and Kropp, L. (2007) *The Family-centered Library Handbook*, Neal-Schuman Publishers.

Feinstein, L. (2003) Inequality in the Early Cognitive Development of British Children in the 1970 Cohort, *Economica*, **70**, 73–98.

Ferguson, S. (2012) Are Public Libraries Developers of Social Capital? A review of their contribution and attempts to demonstrate it, *The Australian Library Journal*, **61** (1), 22–33.

Field, F. (2010) *The Foundation Years: preventing poor children becoming poor adults. The report of the Independent Review on Poverty and Life Chances*, Cabinet Office, http://webarchive.nationalarchives.gov.uk/20110120090128/http://povertyreview. independent.gov.uk/media/20254/poverty-report.pdf.

Field, J. (2008) *Social Capital*, 2nd edn, Routledge.

Flewitt, R. (2013) *Early Literacy: a broader vision*, TACTCY Occasional Paper 3, Association for the Professional Development of Early Years Educators, http://eprints.ncrm.ac.uk/3132/1/flewitt_occasional-paper3.pdf.

Foster, M. A., Lambert, R., Abbott-Shim, M., McCarty, F. and Franze, S. (2005) A Model of Home Learning Environment and Social Risk Factors in Relation to Children's Emergent Literacy and Social Outcomes, *Early Childhood Research Quarterly*, **20** (1), 13–36.

Gammage, P. (2006) Early Childhood Education and Care: politics, policies and possibilities, *Early Years: An International Journal of Research and Development*, **26** (3), 235–48.

Goulding, A. (2006) *Public Libraries in the 21st Century: defining services and debating the future*, Ashgate.

Great Britain (1964) *Public Libraries and Museums Act* (ch. 75), The Stationery Office.

Greene, E. (1991) *Books, Babies and Libraries: serving infants, toddlers, their parents and caregivers*, American Library Association.

Halpern, D. (2004) *Social Capital*, Polity Press.

Halpin, E., Rankin, C., Chapman, E. L. and Walker, C. (2013) Measuring the Value of Public Libraries in the Digital Age: what the power people need to know, *Journal of Librarianship and Information Science*, published online ahead of print 3 September 2013, doi: 10.1177/0961000613497746.

Halpin, E., Trevorrow, P., Topping, L. and Rankin, C. (2012) The Rights of the Child and Youth Advocacy – Issues for Professional Practice. In Rankin, C. and Brock, A. (eds), *Library Services for Children and Young People: challenges and opportunities in the digital age*, Facet Publishing.

Hannon, P. and Nutbrown, C. (2001) Outcomes for Children and Parents of an Early Literacy Education Parental Involvement Programme, paper presented at the *Annual Conference of the British Educational Research Association*, Leeds.

Hirsch, D. (2007) *Chicken and Egg: child poverty and educational inequalities*, Child Poverty Action Group.

IFLA (2003) *Guidelines for Children's Library Services*, IFLA Children and Young Adults Section.

Johnson, C. A. (2010) Do Public Libraries Contribute to Social Capital? A preliminary investigation into the relationship, *Library and Information Science Research*, **32** (2), 147–55.

Johnson, C. A. (2012) How Do Public Libraries Create Social Capital? An analysis of interactions between library staff and patrons, *Library and Information Science Research*, **34** (1), 52–62.

Jones Diaz, C. (2007) Literacy as a Social Practice. In Makin, L., Jones Dias, C. J. and McLachlan, C. (eds), *Literacies in Childhood, Changing Views, Challenging Practice*, 2nd edn, Elsevier Australia.

Karoly, L. A., Kilburn, M. R. and Cannon, J. S. (2005) *Early Childhood Interventions: proven results, future promise*, RAND Corporation.

Koren, M. (2003) Children's Rights and Library Best Practices. In *World Library and Information Congress, 69th IFLA General Conference and Council: proceedings from an international conference held on 1–9 August 2003, Berlin*, IFLA.

Kropp, L. G. (2013) Chew that Book: why babies belong in libraries. *School Library Journal*, **59** (11), 18.

Lewis, A. and Lindsay, G. (2000) *Researching Children's Perspectives*, Open University Press.

Locality (2013a) *Community Libraries – 10 Case Studies*, Arts Council England, www.artscouncil.org.uk/media/uploads/pdf/Community_libaries_research_2013_case_studies.pdf.

Locality (2013b) *Community Libraries – Learning From Experience: guiding principles for local authorities*, Arts Council England, www.artscouncil.org.uk/media/uploads/pdf/Community_libraries_research_2013_guiding_principles.pdf.

Lonsdale, R. (2000) The Role of the Children's Library in Supporting Literacy. In Elkin, J. and Kinnell, M. (2000) *A Place for Children: public libraries as a major force in children's reading*, British Library Research and Innovation Report 117, Library Association Publishing.

Macdonald, L. (2012) *A New Chapter, Public Library Services in the 21st Century*, Carnegie UK Trust.

McElwee, G. (2004) It's Never Too Early, *Library and Information Update*, **3** (11), 23–5.

McKechnie, L. (2006) Observations of Babies and Toddlers in Library Settings, *Library Trends*, **55** (1), 190–201.

Maisey, R., Speight, S., Marsh, V. and Philo, D. (2013) *The Early Education Pilot for Two-Year-Old Children: age five follow-up research report, March 2013*, Ref: DFE- RR225, NatCen Social Research, Department for Education.

Markless, S. and Streatfield, D. (2012) *Evaluating the Impact of Your Library*, 2nd edn, Facet Publishing.

Marsh, T. (2011) The Speech and Language Therapist: laying the foundations of communication. In Brock, A. and Rankin, C. (eds), *Professionalism in the Interdisciplinary Early Years Team: supporting young children and their families*,

Continuum.

Maynard, S. (2011) Children's Reading Habits and Attitudes. In Baker, D. and Evans, W. (eds), *Libraries and Society: role, responsibility and future in an age of change*, Chandos.

Neuman, S. B. (2009) *Changing the Odds for Children at Risk: seven essential principles of educational programs that break the cycle of poverty*, Praeger.

Neuman, S. B. and Wright, T. S. (2007) *A Parent's Guide to Reading with Your Young Child*, Scholastic Inc.

NLT (National Literacy Trust) (2002) *Getting a Head Start. A good ideas guide for promoting reading to young families*, National Literacy Trust.

NLT (National Literacy Trust) (2011) *Literacy: a route to addressing child poverty*, National Literacy Trust.

Pateman, J. and Vincent, J. (2010) *Public Libraries and Social Justice*, Ashgate.

Prendergast, T. (2011) Beyond Storytime: children's librarians collaborating in communities, *Children & Libraries, The Journal of the Association for Library Service to Children*, **9** (1), 20–40.

Prensky, M. (2001) *Digital Natives, Digital Immigrants*, www.marcprensky.com/writing/Prensky%20-%20Digital%20Natives,%20Digital%20Immigrants%20-%20Part1.pdf.

Ramey, C. T., Sparling, J. J. and Ramey, S. L. (2012) *Abecedarian: the ideas, the approach, and the findings*, Sociometrics Corporation.

Rankin, C. (2011) The Librarian – a Key Partner in Promoting Early Language and Literacy. In Brock, A. and Rankin, C. (eds), *Professionalism in the Interdisciplinary Early Years Team: supporting young children and their families*, Continuum.

Rankin, C. and Brock, A. (2008) *Delivering the Best Start: a guide to early years libraries*, Facet Publishing.

Rankin, C. and Butler, F. (2011) Issues and Challenges for the Interdisciplinary Team in Supporting the 21st Century Family. In Brock, A. and Rankin, C. (eds), *Professionalism in the Early Years Interdisciplinary Team: supporting young children and their families*, Continuum.

Rankin, C., Brock, A., Halpin, E. and Wootton, C. (2007) *The Role of the Early Years Librarian in Developing an Information Community: a case study of effective partnerships and early years literacy within a Sure Start project in Wakefield*, paper presented in the conference proceedings of the Canadian Association of Information Sciences, Montreal, 2007.

Ross, C. S., McKechnie, L. E. F. and Rothbauer, P. M. (2006) *Reading Matters: what research reveals about reading, libraries and community*, Libraries Unlimited.

Roulstone, S., Law, J., Rush, R., Clegg, J. and Peters, T. (2011) The Role of Language in Children's Early Educational Outcomes, Research Brief, DFE-RB 134, Department for Education.

Rowsell, J. (2006). *Family literacy experiences: creating reading and writing opportunities that support classroom learning*, Pembroke.

Siraj-Blatchford, I. (2010) Learning in the Home and in School: how working class children succeed against the odds, *British Educational Research Journal*, **36** (3), 463–82.

Siraj-Blatchford, I., Mayo, A., Melhuish, E., Taggart, B., Sammons, P. and Sylva, K. (2011) *Performing against the Odds: developmental trajectories of children in the EPPSE 3–16 study*. Research Report DFE-RR128. Department for Education/Institute of Education, University of London.

Stiftung Lesen (2013) *Prepare for Life!: raising awareness for early literacy education*, Leipzig Recommendations on Early Literacy Education, www.readingworldwide. com/fileadmin/dokumente/Leipzig_Recommendations_2013.pdf.

Stooke, R. and McKenzie, P. J. (2009) Leisure and Work in Library and Community Programs for Very Young Children, *Library Trends*, **57** (4), 657–75.

Sullivan, A. (2010) Ethnicity, Community and Social Capital. In Hansen, K., Joshi, H. and Dex, S. (eds), *Children of the 21st Century: the first five years*, The Policy Press.

Svendsen, G. L. H. (2013) Public Libraries as Breeding Grounds for Bonding, Bridging and Institutional Social Capital: the case of branch libraries in rural Denmark, *Sociologia Ruralis*, **53** (1), 52–73.

Sylva, K., Melhuish, E. C., Sammons, P., Siraj-Blatchford, I. and Taggert, B. (2004) *The Effective Provision of Pre-school Education [EPPE] Project: final report*, Department for Education and Skills/Institute of Education, University of London.

Tayler, C. (2007) Foreword in Makin, L. , Diaz, C. J., and McLachlan, C., *Literacies in Childhood: changing views , challenging practice*, 2nd edn, Elsevier Australia.

UNESCO (2003) United Nations Literacy Decade 2003-2012, http://portal.unesco.org/education/en/ev.php-URL_ID=22420&URL_DO=DO_TOPIC&URL_SECTION=201.html.

Vårheim, A. (2009) Public Libraries: places creating social capital?, *Library Hi Tech*, **27** (3), 372–81.

Waldfogel, J. and Washbrook, E. (2010) *Low Income and Early Cognitive Development in the U.K.*, The Sutton Trust, www.suttontrust.com/our-work/research/download/35/.

Walter, V. (2009) *Twenty-First-Century Kids, Twenty-First-Century Librarians*, American Library Association.

Wilkie, S. (ed.) (2002) *Take Them to the Library*, Youth Libraries Group.

CHAPTER 2

What you need to know about promoting early reading with young children from birth to five

Avril Brock and Carolynn Rankin

Introduction

Competence in literacy is essential for life in contemporary society, and it dramatically contributes to people's emotional well-being, mental health and economic success. A range of particular skills, a breadth of reading materials, a depth of knowledge and understanding and positive attitudes are important for enabling young children to become capable, competent and active readers. The achievement of these skills lies not only with the children themselves but also with parents, carers, early years teachers, librarians and politicians. Books and other literacy materials, public libraries, early years settings, schools and school libraries all have roles to play in the successful development of children who will read for pleasure; for information and knowledge acquisition; and for educational attainment. How they engage in the reading process, the materials they access and their developing attitudes to reading are all key elements in achieving competence in literacy. There is much more to reading than just decoding symbols and stringing words together to make sense. Children need to become critical readers and thinkers, and the early years librarian can play a key role in ensuring that children do become so. It is therefore, important for librarians to gain an understanding of the reading process and the skills of reading in the 21st century.

Opening up the world of knowledge and understanding and finding there is lifelong satisfaction in communicating both with and without words, and in reading and writing, also equips children for survival in a fast-developing global world economy where the future is both known and unknown (Bruce and Spratt, 2011, 13).

In the USA MacLean (2008) observes how librarians are, to an extent, teachers – teaching children how to love to read, making literacy fun and setting the early literacy foundations needed for reading success. Therefore public libraries have a crucial role to play in helping young children to develop early reading skills. Knowledge of these skills and how to promote them with children, how to plan and deliver preschool story times, how to promote these in partnership with parents will enable librarians to make a difference to children's literacy and educational success. Not all children grow up in a literacy-rich environment, having parents who read to them, as some parents may not understand that reading to young children is so important; they may have different cultural traditions, lack literacy skills themselves or not have the financial resources to purchase books (Bohrer, 2005; MacLean, 2008). Librarians can help parents to overcome these difficulties through working in partnership. Public libraries are valuable in that they can nurture and prepare young children for the more structured learning situations they will experience in schools (Diamant-Cohen, 2007).

CASE STUDY A family visit to the library

Nathan (aged 6) and Callum (aged 5) visit the library with their mum. Nathan always asks the library staff for help or information even though his mum is sitting there next to him. 'No mummy you don't know what to do. Let the lady do it.' Tricia (Nathan and Callum's mum) observes: 'The librarians have a fantastic attitude to the children – very approachable, really friendly and always willing to help them. They promote a chatty, friendly and relaxed atmosphere. It's a great place. There are comfortable places to sit and read, bright displays and it's light and airy.

'I bring them here, but I'm not sure what they are getting out of it – that is, to what level. I think that bringing them into this environment is very important. If they get used to it and when they go to secondary school, working in a library and handling books, accessing information from textbooks and doing homework won't be a problem for them. They will be comfortable in a library setting. My mum never ever took me to a library. You can go into Smiths and look at some books and buy the boys books, but look at the range of books that are here; you couldn't possibly buy them all. The whole concept is fantastic. Callum is fascinated by the non-fiction. I couldn't provide him with all this. These are the building blocks to set them up now for later life – using reference books and reading stories. This environment is great for Callum – he doesn't run around or shout – he has really calmed down here.' Nathan, who is 'working' at the computer, but listening in on the discussion shouts: 'Callum hasn't calmed down!'

What practitioners need to know about young children

Some of you reading this book may already have a background in theories of early child development and preschool literacy. However, many managers or co-workers may not have this knowledge base. In common with parents and carers, they will also have questions that you may need to answer. The following sections highlight some of the underpinning knowledge and useful things to know about early literacy. This will help you to develop your role as an effective advocate for early years library services.

There are now many studies on the development of the brain that suggest that a young child's early years are important, as the learning that takes place during this time contributes to brain development and functioning. Humans learn as they interact with the world and the resulting stimulation of neurons in body and brain passes messages through the nervous system. This networking of the neurons effectively produces thought - the source of language. From thought comes meaning, and it is meaning that helps us to understand and interpret the world - the ultimate goal of any learning experience. Each new experience adds to the previous, to create a rich tapestry of learning and communication. The early interactions that occur between children and their parents and carers are crucially important for young children's personal, social, cultural, emotional and linguistic development. These interactions not only promote close relationships and early language development, but also contribute to children's intellectual development. It is important for young children to have natural experiences and types of active learning that will encourage thinking, learning and communication. Practitioners should be providing young children with the following opportunities to:

- have interaction with adults as listeners
- practise movements, sounds and rhythms
- practise language patterns repeatedly
- play imaginatively
- discover and investigate creative means of expressing themselves
- be able to move around on their tummies to explore their personal space and the physical environment around them.

Children's centres, nurseries and libraries often provide rhyme, song, music and movement activities for young children. They will have interesting names such as 'Jo Jingles', 'Moving Minnies', 'Sing-a-long with Sheree'. Baby yoga and baby massage are also on offer in many settings. These experiences are an important part of early literacy development, as well as being social activities with other children and their parents. Librarians have always been interested in a 'reading child', but now, due to new understandings about child development and emergent literacy, we also need to be aware of the needs of babies and toddlers and provide opportunities to support their learning.

Early language acquisition and the stages of language development

Quality early language development is the key to early literacy! In order to become competent and active readers and writers, children need a multitude of experiences of oral language, of talking, listening, storying, rhyming, reading and singing. These are the building blocks of literacy and make the difference as to how quickly and easily they acquire reading and writing. Young children acquire language through interaction with others in their immediate environment, through responding to sounds, sentences and experiences expressed by their parents, family and other carers. They begin by absorbing, listening and then imitating and practising. Gradually they learn to reproduce sounds and words, and establish an understanding of how language works, the structure and grammatical sense of putting these sounds and words together.

Human language is a most powerful communication system. Humans use rules in conjunction with words, which enables infinite generativity - the ability to produce and understand an infinite number of utterances from a finite number of words. Words are made up of sounds. Phonemes are the smallest units of sounds and morphemes are the phonemes combined into the smallest units of meaning to form a vocabulary of words. Syntax is the grammatical rules of language by which words can be combined, and this is important, as the same words in a different order can have different meanings. Human communication also involves the use of pragmatics, such as how language is used in context and the taking of turns in conversation. We also employ paralinguistics in communicating with others - through gestures, signs and facial expressions.

Children acquire language through imitation with reinforcement - they associate an object with the word and the reinforcement provided by the adult when the child points to an object. The roots of language lie in the early attempts of young children and their carers' interactions and communications with each other. The beginnings of language are in early conversation or 'proto-conversation' in everyday routines and play. Babies are born with the propensity to be sociable, particularly with their carers, and they respond first with face and body movements, later with gesture, intonation and ultimately with words. When communicating and talking to their babies and young children, parents will accommodate their language use to promote attentive listening, understanding and then reproduction of sounds, words and ultimately sentences. Bruner (1983) viewed language development as overall cultural transmission from parent (or carer) to child, with the parents as the facilitators of language, scaffolding children's learning through participation, so that children become familiar with routines of communication and can gradually take more initiative. Children know a lot of language before they use words, and when the child comes to use her first words they fit readily into an established pattern of communication. Vygotsky (1978) proposes that language enables us to negotiate or renegotiate our understanding and that language and thinking processes must interact in order for intellectual development to occur. Children develop emotional attachments and social relationships, learning language and communication strategies through interacting with significant others. They learn through social situations embedded in their immediate environment, shaped by cultural expectations of the family and the community. How adults and children interact is crucial in the co-construction of language and learning.

A child's ability to develop language depends on being immersed in a rich environment of words, sounds, rhythm and verbal and non-verbal expression from birth. A useful guide is that children are usually able to communicate as follows:

- birth: language learning starts here through listening to sounds in the environment
- 0–3 months: they turn to you when you speak, and smile when a familiar voice is heard
- 4–6 months: they are interested in sounds and are responsive to changes in tone of voice
- 7–12 months: they love peek-a-boo and recognize labels such as mummy; dog; milk; more
- 12 months: they point to pictures in books; follow commands; understand questions; utter single words
- 18 months: children have a vocabulary of approximately 5–20 words made up chiefly of nouns.

Language and vocabulary development now begins to explode, and by the age of 6 years children can produce 6000 words and comprehend 14,000 words. You should read and reflect on the stages of speech and language development produced by ICAN in Figure 2.1. It is organized through the ages of 0–5 in four sections of: listening and talk; understanding; speech and sounds and talk; social skills. ICAN (www.ican.org.uk/) is the children's communication charity, which is expert in helping children to develop the speech, language and communication skills they need to thrive in a 21st-century world and has a plethora of valuable resources that you can access.

Reading to babies and young children and getting them involved in the whole literacy process is one of the most effective ways of enhancing language development in a child. Librarians have a number of great selling points – there is access to free books at the local library and children's centres, and it is never too early for parents and carers to bring their babies and toddlers to the library.

Stages of Speech and Language Development

For more information visit www.talkingpoint.org.uk

	Listening and attention	Understanding	Speech sounds and talk	Social skills
Up to 3 months	• Turns towards a familiar sound • Startled by loud noises	• Recognises parent's voice • Often calmed by familiar friendly voice, e.g. parent's	• Frequently cries especially when unhappy or uncomfortable • Makes vocal sounds, e.g. cooing, gurgling	• Gazes at faces and copies facial movements, e.g. sticking out tongue! • Makes eye contact for fairly long periods
3–6 months	• Watches a face when someone talks	• Shows excitement at sound of approaching voices	• Makes vocal noises to get attention • Makes sounds back when talked to • Laughs during play • Babbles to self	• Senses different emotions in parent's voice and may respond differently, for example, smile, quieten, laugh • Cries in different ways to express different needs
6–12 months	• Locates source of voice with accuracy • Focuses on different sounds, e.g. telephone, doorbell, clock	• Understands frequently used words such as 'all gone', 'no' and 'bye-bye' • Stops and looks when hears own name • Understands simple instructions when supported by gestures and context	• Uses speech sounds (babbling) to communicate with adults; says sounds like 'ba-ba, no-no, go-go' • Stops babbling when hears familiar adult voice • Uses gestures such as waving and pointing to help communicate • Around 12 months begins to use single words e.g. 'mummum', 'dada', 'tete' (teddy)	• Enjoys action rhymes and songs • Tries to copy adult speech and lip movements • Takes 'turns' in conversations (using babble)
12–15 months	• Attends to music and singing • Enjoys sound-making toys/objects	• Understands single words in context, e.g. cup, milk, daddy, when the object is there • Understands more words than they can say • Understands simple instructions, e.g. 'kiss mummy', 'give to daddy', 'stop'	• Says around 10 single words, although these may not be clear • Reaches or points to something they want whilst making speech sounds	• Likes being with familiar adults • Likes watching adults for short periods of time

Figure 2.1 Stages of Speech and Language Development (ICAN) – getting babies and young children involved in literacy (Continues on facing page)

	Listening and attention	Understanding	Speech sounds and talk	Social skills
15–18 months	• Listens and responds to simple information/instructions, e.g. 'Ben, put on shoes', 'Mohammed, give to daddy'	• Understands a wide range of single words and some two-word phrases, e.g. 'give me', 'shoe on' • Recognises and points to objects and pictures in books if asked • Gives named familiar objects to adult, e.g. coat, car, apple, book	• Still babbles but uses at least 20 single words correctly, although may not be clear • Copies gestures and words from adult • Constant babbling and single words used during play • Uses intonation, pitch and changing volume when 'talking'	• Simple pretend play • Plays alone, although likes to be near familiar adult • Although increasingly independent, happiest when near familiar adult
18 months to 2 years	• Focuses on activity of their own choice but finds it difficult to be directed by an adult • Use of child's name beginning to help them to attend to what an adult says, e.g. 'Sarah, eat sandwiches', 'Ali, put coat on'	• Understanding of single words develops rapidly during the stage: anything between 200 and 500 words are known • Understands more simple instructions, e.g. 'Get mummy's shoes', 'Get your bricks', 'Tell dad tea's ready'	• Uses up to 50 words • Begins to put two or three words together • Frequently asks questions, e.g. the names of people and objects (towards two years of age) • Uses speech sounds, p, b, m, w	• 'Pretend' play developing with toys, such as feeding a doll or driving a car • Becomes frustrated when unable to make self understood – this may result in tantrums • Follows adult body language including pointing, gesture and facial expressions
2–3 years	• Beginning to listen to talk with interest, but easily distracted • Listens to talk addressed to him/herself, but finds it difficult if prompts are not provided, e.g. use of name, 'stop and listen'	• Developing understanding of simple concepts including in/on/under, big/little • Understands phrases like 'put teddy in the box', 'get your book, coat and bag', 'draw a big brown dog' • Understands simple 'who' and 'what' and 'where' questions but not why • Understands a simple story when supported with pictures	• Uses 300 words, including descriptive language, time, space, function • Links four to five words together • May stutter or stammer when thinking what to say • Able to use pronouns (me, him, she), plurals and prepositions (in, on, under) • Has problems saying speech sounds: l/n/w/y, f/th, s/sh/ch/dz	• Holds conversation but jumps from topic to topic • Interested in other's play and will join in • Expresses emotions towards adults and peers using words, not just actions

Figure 2.1 (Continues overleaf)

	Listening and attention	Understanding	Speech sounds and talk	Social skills
3–4 years	• Enjoys listening to stories • Still finds it difficult to attend to more than one thing at a time, so can't easily listen to a speaker whilst still carrying on an activity; has to switch attention between speaker and task	• Understands questions or instructions with two parts: **'get your jumper'** and **'stand by the door'** • Understands **'why'** questions • Aware of time in relation to past, present and future, e.g. **'Today is sunny, yesterday was rainy. I wonder what the weather will be like tomorrow?'** (towards four years)	• Uses sentences of four to six words, e.g. **'I want to play with cars'**, **'What's that thingy called?'** • Uses future and past tense, e.g. **'I am going shopping, I walked home'** • May continue to have problems with irregular words, **'runned'** for **'ran'**, **'swimmed'** for **'swam'** • Able to remember and enjoys telling long stories or singing songs • Has problems saying r, j, th, ch, and sh	• Understands turn-taking as well as sharing with adults and peers • Initiates conversations • Enjoys playing with peers • Able to argue with adults or peers if they disagree – uses words, not just actions
4–5 years	• Attention is now more flexible – the child can understand spoken instructions related to a task without stopping the activity to look at the speaker	• Able to follow simple story without pictures • Understands instructions containing sequencing words: **'first... after... last'** • Understands adjectives: **'soft, hard, smooth'**, etc. • Aware of more complex humour, laughs at jokes that are told	• Uses well formed sentences, e.g. **'I played with Ben at lunch time'** but there may still be some grammatical errors • Easily understood by adults and peers, with only a few immaturities in speech sounds, for example, **'th'**, **'r'**, and three consonant combinations, **'scribble'** • Frequently asks the meaning of unfamiliar words and may use them randomly	• Chooses own friends • Generally co-operative with playmates • Able to plan construction and make believe play activities, e.g. building models from Lego • Takes turns in longer conversations • Uses language to gain information, negotiate, discuss feelings/ideas and give opinions

Figure 2.1 *(Continued)*

Encouraging the development of early language skills in children also means providing support and guidance for parents and carers. Babies can learn to handle books from a very young age. They will acquire vocabulary as parents and carers provide the words that match the pictures, imitating sounds with enthusiasm. The following case study illustrates the importance of involving babies in choosing books to read.

CASE STUDY Amy, aged 8 months, and her books

Reading a book together now forms part of our daily routine. There is a large box full of books and before bed every night we choose a book to read together with the baby. Sticking a hand in the box and rummaging around makes an interesting noise and Amy responds excitedly. We do not specifically choose books for babies or young children, rather we read lots of stories together and she appreciates the rhythm and sounds made. Amy also likes turning the pages and will sometimes want to turn back to the first page. She is also excited by pages with particular colours on them.

(Brock and Rankin, 2008, 27)

Amy's mum tells us something about how they share the reading experience. Practitioners advise parents that it is important to get into a routine with their baby. Each night before bed, it is good to choose a book together; it can be a very simple book with just a few words on a page. In holding a conversation with the baby, the adult provides an opportunity to model turn taking by waiting for the baby's response before continuing. The baby is also learning book-handling skills, even at this young age. This illustrates the importance of reading to babies and involving them in the process of choosing books to read. Although the baby may not yet be able to understand the words or articulate formulated responses, clearly she is enjoying the experience. She is looking at the pictures and learning how to turn the pages. Many books are quite tactile, with different materials to touch and feel, flaps to lift up or buttons to press. It is good to point out that reading before bed can settle the baby and ensure that there are fewer interruptions during the night (Brock and Rankin, 2008, 27). As you can see, young children don't wait to begin their early literacy experiences of reading and writing until they start school!

Bookstart is the first national baby book-giving programme in the world and is run by Booktrust, a national charity in the UK. Bookstart offers the gift of free books to all children at key ages before they start school, to inspire a love of reading that will give children a flying start in life, encouraging all parents and carers to enjoy books with children from as early an age as possible. Parents can get their child's free Bookstart pack in the baby's first year from a health visitor at the eight months' health check, or they can get information at their local library. The pack contains baby books, advice booklets for parents on sharing stories and an invitation to join the local library. Wade and Moore (1998) introduced the idea of Bookstart in 1992 in Birmingham with 300 babies and by 2001 there had been over one million Bookstart babies! They found that Bookstart babies were six times more likely to be library members and their parents were more confident about reading to their children. There are packs for children with additional needs - Bookshine for children who may be hearing impaired or Booktouch for children with visual impairments. 'Some parents may have limited literacy skills, but they can be encouraged to look at the pictures with their child and talk about the illustrations' (Brock and Rankin, 2008, 29). Collins and Svensson (2008) explored the reading behaviours of ten competent nursery and reception children involved in the national Bookstart evaluation study - Bookstart: Planting a Seed for Life. This research examined the children's attitudes to reading, their responses to selected texts and their understanding of early phonological and letter knowledge. The researchers also interviewed the parents in order to discover the home literacy events that shaped these young children's reading competences. They found that this group of young readers, from different socio-economic groups, were reading in advance of their peers.

Emergent literacy

Until recently, literacy was seen primarily as reading and writing, and children were not thought to be ready to learn to read or write before the ages of 6 or 7. However, the principles behind the concept of 'emergent literacy', a term first used by Marie Clay in 1966, are that literacy begins at birth and is a social process (Riley, 2006; Makin, 2007). Studies on the development of the brain suggest that the early years are very important as the learning that takes place at this time contributes to brain development and functioning (Clay, 1991). Children will acquire language and literacy skills from their earliest years, and throughout their preschool years babies and young children develop knowledge of language and the sounds that form words. The onset of literacy acquisition is at birth rather than at the start of formal reading instruction at school. Emergent literacy (Clay, 1991) is about young children's early explorations into reading and writing. As they are singing rhymes, listening to stories, looking at pictures, handling books, scribbling and drawing with varied writing implements, they are acquiring early literacy skills.

Knowledge about child development and emergent literacy has highlighted the needs of babies and toddlers, and this knowledge can be incorporated into providing appropriate services for young children and their families. Butler (1986,

1992, 1995) and Huebner (2000) have described how the early interactions that occur between young children and their parents and carers are important for personal, social, cultural, emotional and linguistic development. Research by Makin (2006) demonstrates how the interactions during shared book reading between babies aged 8-12 months and their mothers enhance language and literacy acquisition. From an 'emergent' perspective, literacy is now recognized as beginning from birth, and shared book reading in families is strongly linked with successful school literacy and thus with identity, belonging and participation in literate societies. Trivette et al. (2010) found that early expressive language development was helped by joint reading strategies that engaged, supported and promoted children's active participation in book-reading opportunities. Picture books help infants and toddlers to begin to understand symbols and babies begin to understand the representative meaning of pictures as they touch, look at and share feelings about the pictures with an adult (Bus and de Jong, 2006, 125).

Young children soon begin to incorporate patterns and incidents from stories into their everyday conversation. Stories can have a tremendous impact on many aspects of children's lives, as children incorporate stories into their everyday activities and these then permeate their language experiences, enabling them to use advanced linguistic structures (Fox, 1993). Most children cannot escape literacy, as it permeates their environment and real-life settings - in their home, in nursery, on the television, in the supermarket and in the high street. They are surrounded by signs and notices in our highly literate environment, and all young children will have everyday experiences with literacy. They will have received birthday cards, visited a favourite restaurant, observed electronic signs and digital screens, looked through catalogues, scribbled on pictures and handled (and possibly chewed) packaging in the supermarket.

Librarians can foster emergent literacy by modelling reading and showing an interest in and enjoyment of books. They can:

- provide opportunities for listening and following directions
- introduce sentences, words, letters and numbers
- introduce new vocabulary
- help children with story-lines
- create social learning through group activities
- support discussion in story time.

The librarian can help parents and carers to understand that they are the best teachers to help their children to enjoy books and to get ready for learning to read. Learning occurs through interaction with what is available in the immediate environment, and the caregiver's task is to provide the child with an enriched environment. Reading together and sharing books encourages talking, which helps to develop speaking and listening skills. Fluent readers do well in school and reading and literacy skills will stand them in good stead for life in the 21st century.

The role of the librarian in supporting the early years

As children and teachers in classrooms around the world struggle to maintain control over literacy learning and teaching within narrow governmental agendas and mandates, the knowledge, research and robust theory regarding early literacy development is critical to explaining how young children come to be literate members of society.

(Whitmore et al., 2004, 291)

The role of practitioners – whether in early years settings, libraries or schools – is obviously crucial to promoting young children's communication, language and literacy. Effective early years librarians ensure that the development of these skills receives a high profile in their practice. It is important that they expand their own knowledge and understanding to plan for optimum language opportunities for young children. The librarian should:

- provide high-quality books and other reading resources
- promote diverse story experiences to promote children's imagination and knowledge
- tell stories as well as read stories
- have books available in community languages
- promote access to books, tapes, videos, computers
- provide story and rhyme times
- emphasize key vocabulary from stories
- model the language used in story and match it to practical activities
- get children actively involved in talking and doing
- contextualize language through play and active experiences
- encourage socio-dramatic play opportunities inspired by story
- interact verbally with children
- praise, encourage and ask open questions
- create an atmosphere of fun where children want to participate
- use practical resources, visual support and other children
- use magnet boards, laminated figures, finger puppets
- provide storysacks with small-world resources of a story
- create role-play areas with a story as theme for children to enact stories.
  (Adapted from Brock and Power, 2006; Brock and Rankin, 2008; Brock, 2015)

Librarians need to develop positive relationships with parents and carers and promote anti-discriminatory practice to meet children's needs in terms of ethnicity, culture, home language, family background, special educational needs, disability, gender and ability (Power and Brock, 2006). Knowledge of parental expectations, culture, literacy experiences, development of bilingualism and support for first language and English as an additional language are key to success in early literacy. Gillanders and Jiménez (2004) examined the home environments of a sample of immigrant Mexican kindergarteners of low socio-economic status in the USA and found that the parental role in promoting positive bilingualism and literacy learning, along with the 'school's use of Spanish facilitated the dynamic of the families' belief in active support of their children's literacy learning and subsequent literacy practices'. In the UK, Brooker (2002) compared the early literacy experiences of two children, one from an English background and the other from a Bangladeshi background, analysing the differences in their experiences and outcomes. She found that the English child was able to 'make up' for home disadvantages in ways which were not readily available to the Bangladeshi child. She suggests that partnership and communication is key to successful adaptation to literacy learning. Through providing readily available information in the early years, librarians can encourage parents to:

- make reading a high priority
- promote a love of story and books
- read with and talk to their children about the books they are sharing
- be role models through reading for themselves, enjoying reading and writing
- make it an enjoyable and sharing time and provide quality time for reading
- involve all members of the family in reading with babies and young children – including siblings and grandparents
- show that it's important for everyone to read, including for different purposes and in different places
- promote a wide variety of story, picture, rhyming and information books
- help their children to choose books for themselves
- be aware of what books and stories their children are likely to be interested in
- ask the early years practitioner for advice
- read with expression and intonation
- read familiar stories again and again
- give children time to look at pictures
- get children to participate in the story-telling
- encourage anticipation and prediction

- make connections to familiar experiences
- read different materials - poems, books, stories, messages, newspapers, instructions, advertisements
- write for a range of purposes - notes, letters, lists, invitations, diary entries, filling in forms.

Environmental print, the signs, labels, logos of everyday life that appear in homes, on the street and shops, surrounds young children's lives. An environment replete with books, environmental print and new technology where children have opportunities to browse through books, engage in shared reading, listen to stories, use computers and other technological devices are crucial for young children to develop their understandings and purposes of literacy (Brown et al., 2012). Effective library services advertise a warm welcome to parents of young children and invite them into the local authority's libraries. They invite babies and young children, are happy to receive even newborn babies and do not mind if babies cry or children make a noise, or even if a book gets damaged occasionally! Libraries should promote a variety of activities, including story times/rhyme times, special events, holiday activities and the 'Bookstart Book Crawl'. Leeds City Libraries advertises that it can help parents in lots of ways to help children gain a head start to developing early reading skills. Parents can join a family readers group to share stories, develop basic skills and learn about books that children will enjoy. The library staff are skilful and helpful in providing valuable information and all Leeds' libraries have dedicated areas for children. Parents can borrow from a huge range of books, including board and picture books, story tapes, CDs and DVDs, and there is free internet access.

Families reading stories to young children

Reading stories to children is thought to be the most important activity for their successful future reading capabilities on entry to school. If children can get used to using the library and its resources at an early age, then they will feel confident about handling books, reading stories and finding information from reference books to support later learning. Becoming a reader involves developing many skills, but of key importance is how young children view themselves as readers (Levy, 2011). Children become readers not just through learning the skills of reading, but most powerfully through listening and enjoying stories and through looking at books:

- Listening to stories is very, very enjoyable and reading and telling stories to children are very worthwhile activities.

- Everyone in a family can be involved in story-telling.
- A breadth of stories and books is important.
- Early story experiences can make a huge difference to language development.
- Stories and books are the routes into literacy.

Practitioners know that reading stories to children is obviously worthwhile, but there is a wealth of value gained – much more than just hearing a story. Experience of stories promotes language development, develops understanding of the world and the people in it, and enriches imagination. It is never too soon to begin to share books and read to children. Even very young babies develop their love of books and stories before they are able to understand the words or see the illustrations clearly. Avril's grandsons, Oscar and James (Figure 2.2), have been listening to stories since they were two months old and soon learnt to handle books and turn pages. By the age of 14 months they could sit for 20 minutes at a time with an adult, listening to stories and pointing at the pictures. Intonation is important, as the more an adult uses it in reading, the more actively the child . listens. Oscar and James's favourite stories at age three and a half included:

Figure 2.2
Oscar and James reading their favourite books

- *We're Going on a Bear Hunt* (Rosen, 1992)
- *Once upon a Time* (Prater, 1995)
- *Room on the Broom* (Donaldson and Scheffler, 2001)
- *Charlie Cook's Favourite Book* (Donaldson and Scheffler, 2005)
- *Where the Wild Things Are* (Sendak, 2000)
- *Not Now Bernard* (McKee, 1980)
- *The Owl Babies* (Waddell, 1992)
- *Peace at Last* (Murphy, 2007)
- *The Little Mouse, Big Hungry Bear and the Red Ripe Strawberry* (Wood and Wood, 2004).

(Brock, 2015, 241)

In Carolynn's family every new baby is presented with a copy of the Ahlbergs' *The Baby's Catalogue* (Ahlberg and Ahlberg, 1982), as the pictures reflect what they do in family life. Illustrations provide images of the characters in a story, what they look like, what they are doing, what they are feeling and the setting of the story and their place in it (Brock and Rankin, 2008, 67). Children develop their 'imaginative looking' (Meek, 1991) when they examine and talk about illustrations, becoming creative in gaining cues and discovering the meanings being transmitted. Large picture and storybooks enable children to get physically involved in pointing out what is happening and labelling the characters and objects (Brock and Rankin, 2008). As children listen, participate, retell and respond they are creating stories in the mind and this 'storying' is one of the most fundamental means of making meaning (Wells, 2009). Children have a natural impulse to tell stories as a means of making connections between what they are learning and what they already know (Wells, 2009). One of James's favourite stories at three years old was 'Little Rabbit Foo Foo' and one afternoon he told his own version to his granddad. It is easy to see how he has acquired a story-telling repertoire, cueing his audience into the story, using key vocabulary and repeating the phrases from the original story:

> James: This is a book about a bunny rabbit Little Rabbit Foo Foo. I'm trying to read this granddad. Don't laugh granddad. So this is about Little Rabbit Foo Foo. Do you want to listen about Little Rabbit Foo Foo?
> Granddad: Riding through the forest
> James: Scooping up all the mouses
> Granddad: Scooping up all the mice
> James: Together and bopping them on the heads
> Granddad: I'll turn you into a ...
> James: Granddad. It says I'll turn you into a Goonie. It says Little Rabbit Foo Foo. It's got a fairy on it. Little Rabbit Foo Foo riding through the forest and bopping them on the heads. Down came the good fairy and said Little Rabbit Foo Foo stop frightening the mouses. I don't like your attitude.
>
> (Brock, 2015, 241)

There is rich evidence from research of the importance of promoting books and high-quality story experiences with very young children. Shared book reading in families is strongly linked with successful school literacy and the development of an identity of belonging and participation in a literate society (Makin, 2006). The rich detail of Dylan's unique responses to sharing picture books with his parents and grandparents is captured in Whitehead's (2002) research through month-by-month observations of his first three years. Wells's (1986) research in the Bristol literacy projects involved audio-taping the language use of 128 young children from the age of 15 months to 39 months in their family lives. The tape recorders were placed in the children's homes and captured the conversations that the children naturally engaged in throughout the two and a half years. The results showed that the quality of young children's early language experiences could vary greatly. The team tracked the children in their sample as they entered formal schooling and found that the impact of these early 'story' experiences made a difference to the children's capability and their literacy achievements (Brock and Rankin, 2008, 30).

The importance of story

Children love to listen to, and to read, stories they like over and over again, enjoying that familiar themes are unchanging and that the same ending always occurs. They will naturally begin to use the words in a story and experience the repetition, prediction, sequencing and text/illustration correlation promoted in a story. Stories are so important for early language and literacy development because they promote:

- varied linguistic structures
- vocabulary and rich description
- organization of thought processes
- complex narrative sequences
- pace, mood, atmosphere, suspense, anticipation
- intonation, gestures, paralinguistics
- plots, characters, events, places, problems
- emotions, morals, moods and the words to express these
- semantics, syntax and grapho-phonemics for early reading skills
- enjoying language for its own sake
- enjoying the story itself!

(Adapted from Brock and Rankin, 2008)

Children's metacognition in action - the thinking through and making meaning - can be seen through their story repertoires. Observing children's story-play can provide a window into their thinking. Jed, aged 4 and Holly, aged 2, have listened to Hairy McClary and Going on a Bear Hunt stories and are now in role protecting the two wooden dogs from Tasha cat, aged 20. 'We're going on a bear hunt. We've got to save the dogs. I'll take the big dogs and we'll take them to the safe room.' Young children are active meaning makers and it is exciting to watch them demonstrate their capabilities as they play. Two-year-old Jeremy wore a pyjama collar round his neck for weeks because 'if you don't wear a collar, you get taken to the pound'. This originated from his first video of Walt Disney's *Lady and the Tramp* and it engendered lots of family story-telling. This two-year-old was able to use and understood 'pound' in the connotation of 'dog prison' (Brock and Rankin, 2008, 31). Carmen was a wicked stepmother chanting 'Mirror mirror on the wall', allocating her parents a role in her Sleeping Beauty; Katie, when wearing a shawl, would say 'I'm the poor, poor peasant woman' or 'I'm Red Riding Hood' and the 'Tiger came to tea' often at Karolina's house – these three-year-old girls were often in roles from their favourite picture books (Brock and Rankin, 2008, 68).

A range of stories from different cultures and backgrounds should be made available. Storysacks (Griffiths, 2011) are a valuable resource available in many libraries to lend to parents so that they can become involved in story-telling. They contain the storybook, models of characters and practical objects from the story and parents can read and then role play using the language of story with their children whilst handling the characters and props. Sargent's (2008) *Little Book of Story Bags* contains a wealth of ideas for how to create and use storybags to enhance story-telling for both practitioners and parents.

Early years librarians should be story readers and story-tellers

Reading aloud to children is a well-developed aspect of library provision. By providing quality children's books and holding activities and events, early years librarians can show by modelling how to read aloud to young children. Librarians may read straight through a book, whereas nursery teachers often interact with children by asking questions and encouraging questions. Using the technique of dialogic reading helps children to stay actively involved with a story and develop reading comprehension. Instead of reading the story straight through, ask open-ended questions about the story – 'Why do you think Goldilocks ate Baby Bear's porridge?' 'What do you think will happen next?':

> Stories are a means of learning about life, emotion, culture and morals. History, culture and family experiences have been handed down the generations through traditions of storytelling. New ideas and knowledge, history, real life issues and different characters can be explored and experienced through story. Hearing and reading stories from different genres is important, so consider the potential in traditional fairy and folk tales, myths and legends, fantasy and adventure, fiction and non-fiction, family and animal stories. In this way a rich diet of life patterns – real and imaginative – helps develop knowledge, thinking and empathy.
>
> (Brock and Rankin, 2008, 65)

Telling stories also shows children how they too can be story-tellers and learn to create imaginative and factual happenings. This can empower children to make things happen in story-telling, and in this way confidence is developed. Children are beginning to journey down the road of creativity in all its forms. As a story-teller you can:

- make use of voice, rhythm, tenor and songs to create pace, surprise, suspense and anticipation
- contextualise through use of props and story resources
- characterise through intonation, emphasis, accent, dialect
- use gestures and movement to create effects of size, space, weather
- create effects of mood, atmosphere and anticipation
- create fluency and flow that suits the story
- observe and assess children's listening abilities and engagement in the story
- tell and retell favourite parts or aspects that need reiterating for effect or comprehension
- include the children in telling and acting out the story
- include children's names so they feel they are part of the story (this can also be a means of re-engaging a child's attention and involvement)
- include personal and shared information to further develop a story.

(Brock and Rankin, 2008, 69)

Reading stories to children can fire their imaginations for story reading and story-telling. By providing prompts, scaffolding and asking key questions, you can assist in developing children's vocabulary and concepts. By posing problems and challenges you can encourage children to use their imagination and enhance their story-telling skills (Brock and Rankin, 2008, 69). Points to remember are:

- ensure your stories reflect a child's home and cultural knowledge, enabling them to build on what they clearly know
- don't limit children's story and imaginative experiences
- provide children with words and chunks of language to use in stories
- model new structures or chunks of language repetitively through story
- puppets are valuable to tell stories to children and for children to use to tell stories
- audio stories on CDs, tapes and DVDs enable children to listen again and again, internalising phrases and chunks of language.

(Brock and Rankin, 2008, 76)

Reflect on the following challenges to your knowledge base and skill or expertise:

- Are you confident enough to tell stories as well as read them? This takes more confidence and may require some practice; however, the benefits can be enormous. You will probably feel empowered if you tell a story to an audience of enthralled young listeners. Start with something familiar such as 'The Gingerbread Man' or 'The Enormous Turnip'.

- Are you aware of the behavioural characteristics of your clientele and the implications of these for library services? For example, babies and toddlers may dribble on and chew books, so materials and quality of resources are important. Babies and toddlers require space to move and crawl around and many settings now have cushions, bolsters, small comfy chairs and carpeted areas for them to explore in between handling the books.
- Do you provide activities for children to dress up and engage in role play? Many library settings now provide for play and the developing of emergent literacy through role play. In addition to the books do you offer interesting materials, such as dressing-up clothes, and musical instruments?
- Are you aware of the importance of active activities and of enabling children to scribble and begin to write? Are there opportunities for children to draw, paint and be actively engaged in craft sessions around story themes? Do you have crayons, paint, paper, card, envelopes, glue, clay, playdough, etc.? How do you cope with these resources in surroundings that cater for 'expensive' books?

Stories can provide adults with a focus for their talk with young children and develop imaginative conversations. They can promote a two-way process of co-construction in narratives, shared sustained thinking and problem-solving contexts with young children. This is important for both practitioners and parents, facilitating everyone's involvement in children's language development and early literacy skills, as everyone understands story!

Promoting early reading skills

Competence in literacy results from success in speaking, listening, reading and writing. Adults - parents, teachers and librarians - should encourage children's reading through a range of experiences - listening to stories, singing songs, creating rhymes, relating anecdotes and playing word games. Children need to access a range of literary/literacy materials - fiction and non-fiction books, electronic programs, internet communications, notices, comics and magazines, to name a few. In this way, children's reading repertoires are developed and can be broadened by enabling them to relate these varied activities to their previous and diverse experiences. Therefore, adults have important roles in supporting and scaffolding children's reading through introducing a range of reading activities, facilitating children's selection and use of a range of reading materials, giving children time to think, look and choose for themselves and encouraging them to use a variety of clues in the reading process.

When we *can* read, we probably take being able to read for granted. One definition of reading is 'the cognitive process of understanding a written linguistic message'. Reading is a complicated process and learning to make sense of those funny squiggles on the page (Figure 2.3) involves a wide range of skills.

> Imagine that no-one had encouraged you to understand the funny little squiggles on the page called words that can make you gasp or can make you cry. You'd be a smaller person living in a smaller world. We believe that everyone deserves the right to those amazing moments that reading can bring us. And that we should all have more of them.
>
> The Reading Agency, http://readingagency.co.uk

Early years librarians therefore require knowledge and understanding about children's capabilities through the 0-5 age range and phases of learning; children's literacy skill acquisition; promoting opportunities for appropriate communication, language and literacy resources and activities. Motivating young children to want to learn to read and write is the route to achievement, but early literacy experiences

Figure 2.3
Sharing a story in the garden

need to be fun and easily acquired. You should access 'Development Matters' and the 'Characteristics of Effective Learning' in the Early Years Foundation Stage (DfE, 2012) to find out more about the phases of children's language and literacy development. Figure 2.4 provides you with a sample of what is in these documents.

Rhyme, rhythm, sound, song – and phonics!

Rhyme, rhythm, sound and song are very important elements of learning a language and they are also routes into developing children's knowledge of letter sounds, i.e. phonics or phonemic awareness, required for developing their early reading strategies. Rhymes are also important, as they support children's sentence structure and vocabulary development. The importance of young children listening, singing and saying rhymes has been well researched and well substantiated (Bradley and Bryant, 1985; Goswami and Bryant, 1989; 1990). These early experiences ease children into early phonemic development and can make a real difference to beginning and developing reading skills. In this way children will learn to sound out, blend and decode words. Maclean, Bryant and Bradley (1987)

Literacy: Reading			
	A Unique Child: observing what a child is learning	**Positive Relationships:** what adults could do	**Enabling Environments:** what adults could provide
Birth–11 months	• Enjoys looking at books and other printed material with familiar people.	• Use finger play, rhymes and familiar songs from home to support young babies' enjoyment.	• Collect a range of board books, cloth books and stories to share with young babies.
8–20 months	• Handles books and printed material with interest.	• Notice and support babies' developing responses as they learn to anticipate and join in with finger and word play.	• Let children handle books and draw their attention to pictures. • Tell, as well as read, stories, looking at and interacting with young babies. • Make family books using small photo albums with photos of family members, significant people in the child's life, familiar everyday objects.
16–26 months	• Interested in books and rhymes and may have favourites.	• Encourage and support children's responses to picture books and stories you read with them. • Use different voices to tell stories and encourage young children to join in wherever possible.	• Provide CDs of rhymes, stories, sounds and spoken words. • Provide picture books, books with flaps or hidden words, books with accompanying CDs and story sacks. • Provide story sacks for parents to take them home to encourage use of books and talk about stories.

Figure 2.4 *Literacy: reading as an area of learning and development (DfE, 2012, 28–9)*
(Continues on facing page)

	A Unique Child: observing what a child is learning	**Positive Relationships:** what adults could do	**Enabling Environments:** what adults could provide
22–36 months	• Has some favourite stories, rhymes, songs, poems or jingles. • Repeats words or phrases from familiar stories. • Fills in the missing word or phrase in a known rhyme, story or game, e.g. 'Humpty Dumpty sat on a ...'.	• Encourage children to use the stories they hear in their play. • Read stories that children already know, pausing at intervals to encourage them to 'read' the next word.	• Create an attractive book area where children and adults can enjoy books together. • Find opportunities to tell and read stories to children, using puppets, soft toys, or real objects as props. • Provide stories, pictures and puppets which allow children to experience and talk about how characters feel.
30–50 months	• Enjoys rhyming and rhythmic activities. • Shows awareness of rhyme and alliteration. • Recognises rhythm in spoken words. • Listens to and joins in with stories and poems, one-to-one and also in small groups. • Joins in with repeated refrains and anticipates key events and phrases in rhymes and stories. • Beginning to be aware of the way stories are structured. • Suggests how the story might end. • Listens to stories with increasing attention and recall. • Describes main story settings, events and principal characters. • Shows interest in illustrations and print in books and print in the environment. • Recognises familiar words and signs such as own name and advertising logos. • Looks at books independently. • Handles books carefully. • Knows information can be relayed in the form of print. • Holds books the correct way up and turns pages. • Knows that print carries meaning and, in English, is read from left to right and top to bottom.	• Focus on meaningful print such as a child's name, words on a cereal packet or a book title, in order to discuss similarities and differences between symbols. • Help children to understand what a word is by using names and labels and by pointing out words in the environment and in books. • Provide dual language books and read them with all children, to raise awareness of different scripts. Try to match dual language books to languages spoken by families in the setting. • Remember not all languages have written forms and not all families are literate either in English, or in a different home language. • Discuss with children the characters in books being read. • Encourage them to predict outcomes, to think of alternative endings and to compare plots and the feelings of characters with their own experiences. • Plan to include home language and bilingual story sessions by involving qualified bilingual adults, as well as enlisting the help of parents.	• Provide some simple poetry, song, fiction and non-fiction books. • Provide fact and fiction books in all areas, e.g. construction area as well as the book area. • Provide books containing photographs of the children that can be read by adults and that children can begin to 'read' by themselves. • Add child-made books and adult-scribed stories to the book area and use these for sharing stories with others. • Create an environment rich in print where children can learn about words, e.g. using names, signs, posters. • When children can see the text, e.g. using big books, model the language of print, such as letter, word, page, beginning, end, first, last, middle. • Introduce children to books and other materials that provide information or instructions. Carry out activities using instructions, such as reading a recipe to make a cake. • Ensure access to stories for all children by using a range of visual cues and story props.

Figure 2.4 *(Continues overleaf)*

	A Unique Child: observing what a child is learning	Positive Relationships: what adults could do	Enabling Environments: what adults could provide
40–60+ months	• Continues a rhyming string. • Hears and says the initial sound in words. • Can segment the sounds in simple words and blend them together, and knows which letters represent some of them. • Links sounds to letters, naming and sounding the letters of the alphabet. • Begins to read words and simple sentences. • Uses vocabulary and forms of speech that are increasingly influenced by their experiences of books. • Enjoys an increasing range of books. • Knows that information can be retrieved from books and computers. **Early Learning Goal** Children read and understand simple sentences. They use phonic knowledge to decode regular words and read them aloud accurately. They also read some common irregular words. They demonstrate understanding when talking with others about what they have read.	• Discuss and model ways of finding out information from non-fiction texts. • Provide story sacks and boxes and make them with children for use in the setting and at home. • Encourage children to recall words they see frequently, such as their own and friends' names. • Model oral blending of sounds to make words in everyday contexts, e.g. *'Can you get your h-a-t hat?'* • Play games like word letter bingo to develop children's phoneme–grapheme correspondence. • Model to children how simple words can be segmented into sounds and blended together to make words. • Support and scaffold individual children's reading as opportunities arise.	• Encourage children to add to their first-hand experience of the world through the use of books, other texts and information, and information and communication technology (ICT). • Help children to identify the main events in a story and to enact stories, as the basis for further imaginative play. • Provide story boards and props which support children to talk about a story's characters and sequence of events. • When children are ready (usually, but not always, by the age of five) provide regular systematic synthetic phonics sessions. These should be multisensory in order to capture children's interests, sustain motivation and reinforce learning. • Demonstrate using phonics as the prime approach to decode words while children can see the text, e.g. using big books. • Provide varied texts and encourage children to use all their skills including their phonic knowledge to decode words. • Provide some simple texts which children can decode to give them confidence and to practise their developing skills.

Figure 2.4 (*Continued*)

found that the number of nursery rhymes known by preschool children predicted later reading success. Rhyme and song should be a natural event in young children's lives, and practitioners should transmit this to parents. Most parents will naturally sing, rhyme and story with their children, but practitioners can ensure that parents understand the importance through creating resources and providing information (Brock, 2014). Many libraries offer rhyme time sessions, such as this one visited by two-year-old Alana and her mother:

> We tried the singing and sign classes last week and so we are trying to teach her. I don't think we have got very far yet, but it is quite interesting going into the class and

seeing those that are at the end of it. They are so excited – singing the songs and doing the movements – seeing them actually doing it is quite amazing. They are doing 'The elephant went through the jungle' and we are learning to mime the actions.

(Brock and Rankin, 2008, 84)

Muter et al.'s (2004) longitudinal study of 90 British children's early reading skills at school entry finds that the children's word-recognition skills were consistently predicted by their early knowledge of letters and phonemes, whilst, contrastingly, reading comprehension was predicted by prior word-recognition skills, vocabulary knowledge and grammatical skills. Usha Goswami (2012), of the Centre for Neuroscience in Education, University of Cambridge, is now researching how the brain encodes speech, and her work on brain imaging and phonology is fascinating. Her research explores how the brain forms word representations through hearing the acoustic signals and creates both a semantic (meaning) and phonological (sound) representation. The implications for young children learning are that:

- children need to hear as much language as possible
- rich language can be enhanced in story reading interactions
- parents and practitioners can train children's hearing and listening skills through activities that emphasise rhythms and metrical structure of speech such as:
  - learning nursery, number, finger/hand rhymes and poems
  - listening to music, making music and sounds, singing songs
  - engaging in rhythmic experiences such as dancing, marching, playing instruments.

(Goswami, 2011)

The Early Years Foundation Stage (DfE, 2012, 15) advises that practitioners and children should have opportunities to:

- share and enjoy a wide range of rhymes, music, songs
- link language with physical movement in action songs and rhymes
- develop children's phonological awareness through small-group and individual teaching
- link sounds to letters, naming and sounding the letters of the alphabet
- use phonic knowledge to write simple regular words and make phonetically plausible attempts at more complex words
- explore and experiment with sounds, words and texts.

Most cultures have their own long-established rhymes and these can be an important part of heritage and life experience. Young children can learn very complicated words through acquiring them in rhymes and songs. They will learn about sequences, events, motives, causes and effects and this will contribute to their pleasure in language for its own sake.

Phonics

> There are many different factors involved in teaching children how to read, and it could be argued that no single method is applicable to all children on all occasions. However, it is equally important to consider all the methods and understand their possibilities and limitations. Phonics is important in learning to read, and though it is not the only important element, it needs to be given due care and consideration in order for it to meet the needs of every individual child.
>
> (Brock and Thornton, 2015, 183)

Phonics is a way of teaching children to read quickly and skilfully through learning to:

- recognize the sounds that each individual letter makes
- identify the sounds that different combinations of letters make – such as '*sh*' or '*oo*'
- blend these sounds together from left to right to make a word.

Children can then use this knowledge to 'decode' new words that they hear or see. This is the first important step in learning to read (DfE, 2013). The Rose Review (Rose, 2006) recommended the 'Simple View of Reading' as the most effective approach for teaching young children to read. This approach separates the process of reading into two elements, decoding and comprehension, which children need to develop in order to become fluent, confident readers. Within this context, the Rose Review recommended systematic synthetic phonics as the most efficient approach to teaching the skills children need so as to decode (Keen, 2014, 281). Both decoding and comprehension are necessary, but neither is enough on its own: children need to be able to recognize and decode words as well as develop language comprehension and so understand and interpret both written and spoken language. (If you would like to find out more about phonics, visit the phonics section of the Department for Education website; access the Simple View of Reading or the Rose Report; explore Jolly Phonics or other published materials.)

Comprehension is important

It may seem obvious to state that understanding or comprehension is key to children's becoming fluent readers. They need to make sense of a text, first through developing a literal interpretation and then moving on to explore complex meanings that are embedded in texts through using the processes of inference and deduction. They can begin to learn these strategies from the earliest stages of learning to read. Children need to purposefully engage with texts so as to gain understanding, and effective comprehension of the meaning of texts is best acquired when combined with direct instruction or guidance from an adult/teacher. Good reading needs to be modelled for children to achieve independence and autonomy. Children need to acquire a range of reading comprehension strategies and be encouraged to reflect on their own understanding and learning. In 2005 the English Primary National Strategy produced a useful booklet entitled *Understanding Reading Comprehension* that drew on research that sees the child, as an active participant, develop strategies through engaging in authentic reading, influenced by experience and sociocultural context rather than by acquiring a specific set of skills. Children develop comprehension and understanding of texts through:

- active engagement with the text to create meaning
- critically evaluating the text
- monitoring their own understanding
- making connections with existing knowledge
- making decisions about which strategies will help
- reflecting upon responses
- applying cognitive, interpretive and problem-solving strategies
- drawing on their interests and personal experiences.

(Adapted from DfES, 2005, 2)

The most effective way to develop comprehension and improve reading is therefore through encouraging extensive reading, and obviously the early years librarian has a key role in this. Reading varied books and literacy texts should not only promote an increased acquisition and understanding of new vocabulary, but should also develop knowledge and generate questions. Most readers construct mental images during reading, and, as they are able to understand and reflect on these, this enables readers to develop their metacognitive awareness. Metacognition has an important role in the reading process – an ability to reflect on one's understanding and learning will produce a 'self-awareness' of being an active reader.

Developing the skills for reading

Reading with children brings a shared closeness and can be an important part of creating close relationships for parents and practitioners. Adults should read with, and talk to, developing readers about stories, books and reading, as well as ensuring that they value the knowledge and the culture that children bring to the process. Modelling the reading of books can apprentice children into reading and so guide them to understanding and success. If you listen to emergent readers reading and making sense of text, you can observe the strategies they bring to the reading process. Ensure that you read with and talk to children about the text and encourage children to:

- handle books and orient left to right, turning pages in different directions
- discover how texts and stories work
- make sense of the whole text
- make connections to familiar experiences
- talk about and understand what they are reading
- ask questions about the reading process
- see patterns in words and letters
- gain visual images of words
- use illustrations to help meaning
- scan backwards and forwards for cues
- examine punctuation and how it is used.
              (Adapted from Brock and Rankin, 2008; Rankin and Brock, 2008)

Widen children's repertoire by relating everything to their previous experiences and helping them to make connections, scaffolding their knowledge. Children need to be interested, to be motivated and learn to achieve through building on early success. When reading with children:

- give them time to think, look and reread for themselves
- support by introducing the book – title, characters, content
- encourage them to use a variety of clues – if one doesn't work try another
- encourage them to think 'Does that look right?' 'Does that sound right?' 'Does that make sense?'

(Rankin and Brock, 2008, 27)

As well as building on their knowledge of oral language, stories, books and phonics, Brock and Rankin (2008, 102-3) advise that children will make sense of the reading process through using the following four cueing systems:

Grapho-phonic (letters and sounds)
- trying to find patterns in the print
- sounding out words or parts of words using phonics
- discovering that sounds are important for making sense of the text

Semantic (meaning)
- looking at pictures - interpreting them in different ways
- guessing words from context and revising the guess as more of the meaning is revealed
- filling in words to 'make meaning' of the sentence
- returning to a previous part of the text
- using knowledge of traditional stories

Syntactic (grammar)
- using knowledge of word order in sentences
- using knowledge of word endings and their grammatical functions
- using knowledge of 'function words' and their grammatical purposes

Social
- seeking confirmation from others
- repeating each other's utterances
- discussing what it might mean
- discussing the picture and testing out hypotheses.

(Brock and Rankin, 2008, 102-3)

To summarize all the aforementioned strategies, the following checklist provides an encompassing view of reading for practitioners. These ten points promote an understanding of all that is involved in learning to read, promoting a holistic view of the range of skills that is required for developing successful reading:

1   previous experience: personal knowledge, cultural experiences and early language development, through opportunities for speaking, listening, story, rhyme and singing experiences
2   practice: repetition and practice of words, phrases and structures, throughout the reading experience
3   knowledge of how language works: all that children have intuitively acquired, through hearing and using language
4   grapho-phonemic cues: letter/sound correspondence, through sounding out words or parts of words using phonics
5   semantics: gaining the meanings of words from the context and revising

guesses, as more of the meaning is revealed, as a text develops
6 syntax and grammatical knowledge: using knowledge of word order in sentences, in order to determine the grammatical function of words
7 social learning: seeking confirmation from others and discussing what the text means
8 comprehension and inference: making sense of a text, understanding obvious and hidden meanings, creating opinions and drawing conclusions
9 positive attitudes: gender, ethnicity, a family's socio-economic status and role models all influence reading success
10 reading materials: a diversity of genres in texts and a range of reading materials, including books, computers and magazines.

(Rankin and Brock, 2012, 77).

Conclusion: reading is a social activity

This chapter should have given you a good appreciation of all that is involved in children's learning to read. Children need active and varied experiences to help them master the complex skills involved in reading. They need to achieve through experience and success, as failure can lead to frustration and cause barriers to learning. Children try to make sense of their world and the learning process by using all strategies available, and this is the same for reading, as for everything else they learn.

Useful organizations

Booktrust, www.booktrust.org.uk/home
Bookstart, www.bookstart.co.uk
Chartered Institute of Library and Information Professionals (CILIP), www.cilip.org.uk
IFLA, www.ifla.org
National Literacy Trust, www.literacytrust.org.uk
The Reading Agency, www.readingagency.org.uk
UNESCO, www.unesco.org

References

Ahlberg, J. and Ahlberg, A. (1982) *The Baby's Catalogue*, Viking Kestrell Picture Books.
Bohrer, C. N. (2005) Libraries as Early Literacy Centers, *Public Libraries*, **44** (3), 127–32.
Bradley, L. and Bryant, P. E. (1985) *Rhyme and Reason in Reading and Spelling*, University of Michigan Press.

Brock, A. (2014) Let's Get Talking: promoting communication, language and literacy for young children in multicultural England. In Swiniarski, L. B. (ed.), *Moving Forward in a Global Age,* Springer.

Brock, A. (2015) *The Early Years Reflective Practice Handbook*, Routledge.

Brock, A. and Power, M. (2006) Promoting Learning in the Early Years. In Conteh, J. (ed.), (2006) *Promoting Learning for Bilingual Pupils 3–11: opening doors to success*, PCP/Sage Publications.

Brock, A. and Rankin, C. (2008) *Communication, Language and Literacy from Birth to Five*, Sage Publications.

Brock, A. and Thornton, T. (2015) Capable, Confident Children: a reception class teacher's pedagogical reflections. In Brock, A. (ed.), *The Early Years Reflective Practice Handbook*, Routledge.

Brooker, L. (2002) *Starting School: young children learning cultures*, Open University Press.

Brown, M. P., Byrnes, L. J., Raban, B. and Watson, L. (2012) Young Learners: the home literacy environments of Australian four-year-olds, *Journal of Research in Childhood Education*, **26**, 450–60.

Bruce, T. and Spratt, J. (2011) *Essentials of Literacy: a whole child approach to communication, language and literacy*, Sage Publications.

Bruner, J. S. (1983) *Child's Talk: learning to use language,* Oxford University Press.

Bus, A. and de Jong, M. (2006) Book Sharing: a developmentally appropriate way to foster pre-academic growth. In Rosenkoetter, S. E. and Knapp-Philo, J. (eds), *Learning to Read the World: language and literacy in the first three years*, Zero To Three Press.

Butler, D. (1986) *Five to Eight: vital years for reading*, Bodley Head.

Butler, D. (1992) *Telling Tales: the 1992 Margaret Mahy Award lecture*, New Zealand Children's Book Foundation, www.storylines.org.nz/site/storylines/files/downloads/Awards/Storylines_Dorothy_Butler_lecture_Telling_Tales.pdf.

Butler, D. (1995) *Babies Need Books: sharing the joy of books with children from birth to six*, 3rd edn, Penguin Books.

Clay, M. M. (1991) *Becoming Literate: the construction of inner control*, Heinemann.

Collins, F. M. and Svensson, C. (2008) If I Had a Magic Wand I'd Magic Her out of the Book: the rich literacy practices of competent early readers. *Early Years, An International Journal of Research and Development*, **28** (1), 81–91.

Department for Education (DfE) (2012) *Development Matters. The early years foundation stage*, Department for Education.

Department for Education (DfE) (2013) *Learning to Read through Phonics. Information for parents*, Department for Education.

Department for Education and Skills (DfES) (2005) *Understanding Reading Comprehension: 1. What is reading comprehension?* Primary National Strategy. DfES Publications 1310-2005, https://bso.bradford.gov.uk/userfiles/file/Primary%20Literacy/Guided%20 Reading/reading%20comprehension%201.pdf.

Diamant-Cohen, B. (2007) First Day of Class: the public library's role in 'school readiness', *Education Research Journal*, **30** (5), 691–712.

Donaldson, J. and Scheffler, A. (2001) *Room on the Broom*, Macmillan.

Donaldson, J. and Scheffler, A. (2005) *Charlie Cook's Favourite Book*, Macmillan.

Fox, C. (1993) *At the Very Edge of the Forest. The influence of literature on story-telling by children*, Cassell.

Gillanders, C. and Jimenez, R. T. (2004) Reaching for Success: a close-up of Mexican immigrant parents in the USA who foster literacy success for their kindergarten children, *Journal of Early Childhood Literacy*, **4** (3), 243–69.

Goswami, U. (2011) *Language Development and the Brain: a phonological perspective*, keynote presentation at the TACTYC Conference 'Ready' for School? Research, Reflection and Debate. A research into practice conference, 11 and 12 November 2011, York.

Goswami, U. (2012) Entraining the Brain: applications to language research and links to musical entrainment, *Musicology Review*, **7** (1–2), 57–63.

Goswami, U. and Bryant, P. E. (1989) The Interpretation of Studies Using the Reading Level Design, *Journal of Reading Behavior*, **21** (4), 413–24.

Goswami, U. and Bryant, P. (1990) *Phonological Skills and Learning to Read*, Lawrence Erlbaum Associates.

Griffiths, N. (2011) *Storysacks*, www.storysack.com.

Huebner, C. E. (2000) Promoting Toddlers' Language Development through Community-based Intervention, *Journal of Applied Development Psychology*, **21** (5), 513–35.

Keen, B. (2014) Reflecting on the Process of Learning how to Teach Reading Using Systematic Synthetic Phonics. In Brock, A. *The Early Years Reflective Practice Handbook*, Routledge.

Levy, R. (2011) *Young Children Reading at Home and at School*, Sage.

MacLean, J. (2008) *Library Preschool Storytimes: developing early literacy skills in children*, https://www.ed.psu.edu/.../Judy%20MacLean%20Library%20Preschool.

Maclean, M., Bryant, P. and Bradley, L. (1987) Rhymes, Nursery Rhymes, and Reading in Early Childhood, *Merrill-Palmer Quarterly*, **33**, 255–81.

Makin, L. (2006) Literacy 8–12 Months: what are babies learning? *Early Years*, **26** (3), 267–77.

Makin, L. (2007) Surveying the Landscape. In Makin, L., Jones Diaz, C. J., and McLachlan, C. (eds), *Literacies in Childhood: changing views, challenging practice*, 2nd edn, Elsevier Australia.

McKee, D. (1980) *Not Now Bernard*, Anderson.

Meek, M. (1991) *How Texts Teach What Readers Learn*, Thimble Press.

Murphy, J. (2007) *Peace at Last*, Macmillan Children's Books.

Muter, V., Hulme, C., Snowling, M. J. and Stevenson, J. (2004) Phonemes, Rimes, Vocabulary, and Grammatical Skills as Foundations of Early Reading Development: evidence from a longitudinal study, *Developmental Psychology*, **40** (5), 665-81.

Power, M. and Brock, A. (2006) Promoting Positive Links between Home and School. In Conteh, J. (ed) *Promoting Learning for Bilingual Pupils 3-11: opening doors to success*, PCP/Sage Publications.

Prater, J. (1996) *Once upon a time*, Candlewick.

Rankin, C. and Brock, A. (2008) *Delivering the Best Start: a guide to early years libraries*, Facet Publishing.

Rankin, C. and Brock, A. (eds) (2012) *Library Services for Children and Young People: challenges and opportunities in the digital age*, Facet Publishing.

Riley, J. (2006) *Language and Literacy 3-7*, Paul Chapman Publishing.

Rose, J. (2006) *The Independent Review of the Teaching of Reading*, Department for Children, Schools and Families, http://webarchive.nationalarchives.gov.uk/ 20130401151715/https://www.education.gov.uk/publications/ eOrderingDownload/0201-2006pdf-EN-01.pdf.

Rosen, M. (1992) *We're Going on a Bear Hunt*, Walker Books.

Sargent, M. (2008) *Little Book of Story Bags*, Featherstone Education, Black Publishers Ltd.

Sendak, M. (2000) *Where the Wild Things Are*, Red Fox.

Trivette, C. M., Dunst, C. J. and Hamby, D. W. (2010) Influences of Family-systems Intervention Practices on Parent–Child Interactions and Child Development, *Topics in Early Childhood Special Education*, **30** (1), 3-19.

Vygotsky, L. (1978) *Mind in Society*, Harvard University Press.

Waddell, M. (1992) *The Owl Babies*, Walker Books.

Wade, B. and Moore, M. (1998) *A Gift for Life: Bookstart, the first five years – a description and evaluation of an exploratory British project to encourage sharing books with babies*, Booktrust, 1998 98/11791.

Wells, G. (1986) *The Meaning Makers: children learning language and using language*, Heinemann.

Wells, G. (2009) *The Meaning Makers*. Channel View Publications Ltd.

Whitehead, M. (2002) Dylan's Routes to Literacy: the first three years with picture books, *Journal of Early Childhood Literacy*, **2** (3), 269-89.

Whitmore, K. F., Martens, P., Goodman, Y. M. and Owock, G. (2004) Critical lessons from the transactional perspective on early literacy research, *Journal of Early Childhood Literacy* **4** (3), 291-325.

Wood, D. and Wood, A. (1984) *The Little Mouse, Big Hungry Bear and the Red Ripe Strawberry*, Child's Play International.

CHAPTER 3

City of Literature ... it all starts with ABCD! The City of Melbourne and the Abecedarian Approach

Paula Kelly

Introduction

Melbourne was designated as a UNESCO City of Literature in 2008, in recognition of its focus on literature as an art form, the high prevalence of bookshops and well-resourced libraries, and its investment in public programming promoting reading and engagement with literature. The National Year of Reading campaign has grown into a proactive movement across Australia in public libraries, schools and workplaces to promote the inherent 'goodness' of reading as well as the power of literacy to change lives. The Australian Bureau of Statistics' Yearbook 2012, in its feature article on the National Year of Reading (Kelly and McKerracher, 2012) refers to the Adult Life Skills Survey conducted in 2006 which prompted libraries to act. The nation's statistician highlighted that literacy is 'a basic prerequisite for full participation in Australian society' (Pink, 2012, 1). This chapter will discuss the City of Melbourne's parenting education programme, which aims to make a difference by breaking cycles of disadvantage and thus contribute to Melbourne's status as a City of Literature (and literacy) for all.

Australian literacy levels

Alarmingly, Australia's literacy levels are dropping. In 2012, 46% of Australians did not meet Level 3 literacy standards. This includes functional literacy tasks like the ability to read newspapers and a novel for pleasure, decipher medicine-bottle information and read a recipe. There are significant issues associated with almost half the population of our country not meeting the literacy levels required for everyday functioning in today's society. As a state, Victoria is the second-lowest after Tasmania in its literacy levels, as identified by the Australian Bureau of Statistics in the same survey. Australia's literacy rates have dropped amongst OECD countries in recent years.

In Australia the federal and state governments have made commitments to the significance of learning to read and 'keeping on' reading. Initiatives include the Get Reading Campaign, the Centre for Youth Literature, South Australia's Little Big Books Club's *It's Rhyme Time* booklet and DVD, the Victorian Government's Young Readers Program, Western Australia's Better Beginnings Family Literacy Program, as well as federal government support for the National Year of Reading and National Literacy and Numeracy Week. However, no national universal early years-targeted literacy interventions are currently funded across Australia. Australia does not have a national reading or literacy strategy.

City of Melbourne: growth and challenges

The City of Melbourne is proud of its cultural status and traditions, and particularly so of its literary heritage and contemporary focus on the importance of books in people's lives. Reading matters to the City of Melbourne but there are significant challenges: some 48% of Melbourne's residents were born overseas and a high proportion live with identified multiple disadvantage factors. These range from low socio-economic backgrounds, homelessness and transitional life circumstances to a high incidence of mental illness and high unemployment or underemployment in many of the city's neighbourhoods. Melbourne is a growth area and is undergoing significant urbanization, with an expected doubling of its residential population in the coming decade across its 38sq km footprint. Its growing population of under-fives is a particular focus for its efforts to become a recognized UNICEF-designated Child-Friendly City - one that values families and the development and well-being of children.

City of Melbourne's early literacy strategy

Nobel prize-winning economist James Heckman and other researchers agree that the greatest economic return on investment in human capital is in the area of early intervention (Heckman, 2008; Schweinhart et al., 2005; Grunewald and Rolnick, 2010). The University of Melbourne's E4Kids programme is focused on this area, where the development of positive life trajectories and the avoidance of subsequent more costly remediation can occur (Tayler, 2009). Other research demonstrates that programmes like the Abecedarian Approach will impact positively on the lives of disadvantaged mothers as well as their children, directly leading to greater educational and academic success (Campbell et al., 2002; Masse and Barnett, 2002; Ramey, Dorvall and Baker-Ward, 1983).

Using a cross-council approach, the City of Melbourne is developing a parenting education programme that aims to make a difference by breaking cycles of disadvantage in order to achieve better early literacy outcomes for the City's young children. This work will see the development of the City of Melbourne's Early Literacy Strategy and will incorporate many of the learning outcomes being realized by the E4Kids project in Australia. E4Kids follows a large cohort of three- to four-year-old children in Victorian and Queensland early education programmes, as well as examining outcomes for children who do not attend childcare, kindergarten and preschool. The programme goes to the heart of the home and intentionally looks at developing the parenting practices of parents as their child's first teachers. It aims to improve parent–child interactions and subsequent early language development and is framed by the Abecedarian Approach, as proposed by Professor Joseph Sparling (Sparling, 2011a).

The Abecedarian project

The Abecedarian project was a carefully controlled scientific study of the potential benefits of early childhood education for poor children, developed for and validated in the Abecedarian studies conducted in the University of Chapel Hill, North Carolina. These studies were a series of scientific investigations to test the power of a high-quality early childhood educational programme to improve the later school achievement of children from at-risk and under-resourced families. The intervention involved intensive learning and social–emotional support, starting in infancy and continuing until at least kindergarten entry, for children and their families. The long-term positive results of the first three of these randomized controlled trials are now known throughout the world and form a major part of the evidence that supports our current advocacy to ensure all young children receive high-quality learning opportunities in their homes and their early childhood programmes (Ramey, Sparling and Ramey, 2012).

The Abecedarian Approach

The Abecedarian Approach is a combination of teaching and learning enrichment strategies, demonstrating positive outcomes for disadvantaged families throughout 40 years of international research. There are additional and practical reasons for using the Abecedarian Approach:

- Many professionals and parents recognise that, even before training, they have been doing 'their version' of some of these strategies.
- Adults with substantially different educational backgrounds can successfully use the simple attractive printed materials, especially if they receive scaffolding and good training.

- It is fun, and makes the caregiving process enjoyable for both the adult and the child.

(Ramey, Sparling and Ramey, 2012)

The Abecedarian Approach focuses on an interventionist approach that promotes learning and positive educational and social outcomes for children who begin life 'at risk'. The intervention is simple but deep and is built on a tripod approach of three core components that all encourage caregiver-child interaction and language priority. This approach focuses on joint-attention activity between the enabling adult (parent or carer) and child. It is intentional, individual and focused in the way learning is facilitated. Inherently it aims to best position the child for later literacy development and a successful start to formal education.

Melbourne's road to reading ... parents and carers at the heart

The City aims to implement support for parents to achieve best outcomes for their very young children. The proposal substantiates the development of early literacy competencies on the positive outcomes for children in their education, life choices and success. The programme focuses attention on early years education and disadvantaged parents as areas of potential for significant return on investment. It is supported by best practice in mediated learning and in methods of support and parenting education.

The implementation framework being developed is underpinned by the Abecedarian Approach, and its three core elements:

- Learning Games
- Conversational Reading
- Enriched Caregiving.

This is complemented by other early literacy programme strategies delivered in community settings. These include Baby Bounce and Rhyme Time sessions, as well as community publishing projects supported by the City's Library Service in childcare, supported parent programmes, and maternal and child health environments.

The window of opportunity: early experiences

It is now recognized that 50% of language is learned by three years of age (Hamer, 2011). The young brain is most receptive to early experiences between three months and three years, peaking at about nine months of age for language development (Nelson, 2000; Mendellson, 2009). It is logical then, that the intent and focus of this programme should focus on this critical period of time in a child's developmental journey. The focus on early literacy development has considerable importance for policy makers, as division and disadvantage in our society are mirrored in school readiness, school achievement and reading ability throughout a child's schooling. It is in such windows of opportunity that the focus of this programme is nestled. Human brain development is dependent on early experiences, and whilst the plasticity of the brain is accepted and there is ongoing growth in terms of the brain's capacity for learning, there is clear evidence of the importance of acting in windows of opportunity (Ting-Fang, 2007).

A focus on oral language, nursery rhymes and reading behaviours

Book reading is well established as a universally useful activity to improve language development and literacy (Wells, 1986).The 'how to do it' focus included in the Abecedarian Approach of Conversational Reading is respectful and acknowledging of the use of home language in the 'conversation', as well as of the need for an understanding of book knowledge to be developed as part of the journey to literacy. The 'SEE, SHOW, SAY' technique adopted in the Abecedarian Approach opens up a 'back and forth' approach to book reading. The effect of this method of shared book reading facilitates early expressive language and fosters children's active participation in book-reading opportunities from a young age. Studies demonstrate that the more adults encourage sustained active participation by the child by interacting in an open-ended way, or expanding on the child's utterances, the more the child's language development is enhanced during book reading (Trivette, Dunst and Gorman, 2010).

Other reading experts emphasize all of the practices that include 'reading with enthusiasm, responsiveness to children's attempts to engage in looking at and playing with books, reading stories that include rhythms and rhymes, following children's interests, reading children's favorite stories and rhymes over and over, and engaging children in reading episodes just long enough to maintain engagement' (Dunst, Simkus and Hamby, 2012, 5). Further to these outcomes in terms of reading modelling and behaviours, shared reading supports the social and emotional connection between parent and child (Peifer and Perez, 2011).

The role of technology as motivator/facilitator/access point

There are conflicting views about the use of technology in learning, with many educators claiming problems with shortened attention spans and distracted attention (Richtel, 2012). Despite this, in this case the disruption that technology provides is actually being posed as a positive intervention – with the provision of SMS updates and 'nudges' to the parents in the programme as an intentional strategy. These 'nudges' will link parents to resources available via the mobile website now under construction. In this way short bursts of highly accessible information will be provided to support their learning. This in turn will provide a mediated learning environment that could not otherwise be supported from a resource point of view with direct, regular library staff/parent contact, due to the sheer logistics of such provision. It is actually by design that this element is included in the programme as part of the method.

Building capacity for parents

It is the social interaction and communication provided by adults, as identified by Vygotsky (1962), that points to the way forward in this programme implementation. Vygotsky's work emphasizes the importance of social learning and the role the parent takes as tutor, intentionally 'nudging' their child along in their development and playfully developing their language prowess and engagement. It is this very focus that places the development of the parent at the heart of this programme in terms of building capacity.

Interventions designed to improve language and reading engagement will be more likely to have a lasting impact if they 'include parents' own literacy habits and beliefs about their role in fostering literacy and language development' (Weigel, Martin and Bennett, 2006, 375). For this reason the proposed intervention focuses on parents as individuals, but also in small groups where parents may already be accessing support structures and learning opportunities offered in community/educational settings; namely the City of Melbourne's Family Services supported playgroups, with existing parent programmes, delivered in the City's Community Hubs, which have libraries as their anchor points.

Snow et al. (1991) also support the notion that it matters where programmes are delivered. They attest that public libraries provide the kind of community settings that have 'open' membership, are not bound by specific entry requirements and are non-secular. These are ideal places that support the strengthening of communities and the connection of people (Snow et al., 1991). They are also places accessed by a broad spectrum of individuals and groups. Libraries are places that actively work to close the literacy divide, alongside the technological one (Neuman and Celano, 2004).

Language priority

The Abecedarian Approach features language priority, emphasizing interactions that:

- are playful
- are responsive (the adult builds on the child's behaviours)
- are rich in language
- ask questions on multiple levels (using the 3S strategy: SEE, SHOW, SAY)
- carry informational content
- encourage joint attention and task orientation
- narrate the child's actions (using the 3N strategy: NOTICE, NUDGE, NARRATE) and provide a template for his later private speech
- as learning games, even though playful, are scaffolded.

(Sparling, 2011b, 8)

In the 2011 training presentation to Family Day Care workers, presented by the Melbourne Graduate School of Education, Professor Sparling refined the areas of potential to the three elements of activity focus in this programme: Learning Games, Conversational Reading and Enriched Caregiving (Sparling, 2011a). Giving priority to language means responding warmly, engaging in longer conversations and generally focusing on making every event in the child's life an opportunity for rich language stimulation.

The Learning Games

The Learning Games are a set of 200 individualized, game-like activities designed to be shared in mediated learning experiences. They are bite-sized, developmentally appropriate activities that utilize the teachings of Piaget and Vygotsky in their approach to cognitive development. Some of them are designed to be used in routine care giving, some for joining in with already 'in-progress' play and some in which the adult initiates an invitation to join. These simple but deep experiences will be applied particularly in the context of Enriched Caregiving in this programme.

Conversational Reading

Conversational Reading models a conversation with the 'prop' of a book. It engages an individual or a group of 2-3 children, together with an adult. It employs the 'SEE, SHOW, SAY' method that builds on the child's capacity for receptive and expressive language. 'SEE, SHOW, SAY' questions are scaffolded and have the ability to be made easier or more complex depending on the child's capacity to interact through looking at, pointing to and naming various elements, objects, happenings or emotions in the pages of the book being shared in the experience.

Enriched Caregiving

The Abecedarian Approach promotes the notion that care and education go hand in hand. Contingent responding, sensitivity, close physical connection (including eye contact) and respectful interactions are the basis of this area. Respectful interactions include the *narrating* of activities of care with the child as well as inviting the child to name the care-giving activities and environment. The caregiver in this case will explain and ask questions about what is happening next, and will *nudge* and support the child with active engagement in caregiving routines (e.g. nappy-changing areas and mealtime areas), incorporating educational opportunities (e.g. counting, colours, letter recognition), and doing this repeatedly and as part of everyday care (Sparling, 2011b). The Abecedarian Approach supports Vygotsky's notion that 'cooperatively achieved success lies at the foundations of learning and development' (Wood, 1998, 27).

An intentional tripod approach

Three intervention activities provide context for the programme (see Figure 13.1 – A tripod approach). The tripod approach suggested for this programme moves from the parent and child at the centre of the implementation to the 'homogenous' group experience of community publishing within the context of groups of parents, to the community context where parents will be linked into the resources and programmes of their local library, and to the Baby Bounce and Rhyme Time programmes offered by the City's Library Service.

Community publishing

The sociocultural basis for language development calls for attention to be given to meeting the parent 'where they are at', in giving credibility to their own stories and interests around parenting their child and developing meaningful contexts for language development. Being involved in a community publishing programme allows for the rich language of a shared group experience of creating a book around a centrally identified theme, e.g. healthy eating, places to visit or favourite things. Individuals at first create highly engaging and meaningful texts that are immediately accessible for parents and children as they are infused with personal

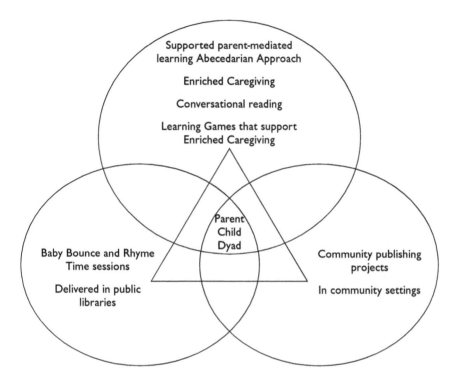

Figure 3.1 *A tripod approach*

meaning. As a collective the group then creates a cohesive, community-published book that documents a shared experience which can be enjoyed and celebrated. The artefact is a highly meaningful language and reading-skill development prop. The approach begins with what the parent knows and values, and gives hope that this will be meaningful and of inherent value. This speaks to the importance of hope as a catalyst for learning and aspirational development - a powerful ally in human development (Avrill, Catlin and Chon, 1990).

Mediated learning

The actions of 'NOTICE, NUDGE and NARRATE' as defined by the Abecedarian Approach will form the basis of the mantra for mediated learning that will support the Enriched Caregiving experience provided by parents to their children through a supported learning experience. Rhyme, rhythm and repetition form the basis of developing intentional oral language that points to the complex structures of literate behaviour. Phonetic awareness and connections, word patterns and comprehension are all communicated in a joyful and highly engaging way through the sharing of nursery rhymes and finger plays. Enriched Caregiving can be enhanced by the inclusion of nursery rhymes in everyday care alongside the turn-taking talk that accompanies the child's daily activities and nuanced interests. Musical play encourages the exploration of the environment of sound. From the first days, infants can discriminate sounds and initiate preferences. As infants do not understand words, sound is the basis of communication - consisting of intensity, pitch, rhythm and timbre. For the newborn and infant 'language is music', and experiences that foster this development of language through the medium of music and its rhyme, rhythm and repetition are important (Hart, Burts and Charlesworth, 1997). Nursery rhymes and interactive language games develop the underpinning skills required for reading, including vocabulary development, letter identification and phonological awareness (Whitehurst and Lonigan, 1998).

Alongside this, the use of 'parentese' or babytalk will be encouraged in Enriched Caregiving situations, as this is the language through which babies learn best (Berstien Ratner, 2012). Culturally, this is relevant for most Westernized societies where it is accepted practice to directly interact with babies and small children. However, in some cultural contexts children are cared for, and spoken to, by other older siblings, or parents do not directly interact with them as a means of language socialization. Encouragement of this direct interaction between parent and baby is a design feature of the programme.

Quality Implementation Framework

Based on the work of Fixsen et al. (2005), a Quality Implementation Framework will be utilized in the selection of the host settings, creating the 'team/s' involved in the programme (including the City of Melbourne's Maternal and Child Health nurses, Supported Parent Group leaders, Child Care workers, the Melbourne Library Service's Children's Librarians and the City's Neighbourhood Development Officers), establishing structure to keep the momentum of the programme going and also communicating the evaluation strategies to all involved.

Phase 1 - Initial considerations: host setting
1. Needs and resources assessment (target group identification and delivery setting)
2. Fitness assessment - current policy and practices in the setting
3. Capacity and readiness for change in the host setting
4. Possibility for adaptation of the primary proposed implementation
5. Obtaining explicit commitment from the critical stakeholders and fostering a supportive climate

6. Building general/organizational capacity
7. Staff recruitment to promote and advocate for the project
8. Effective induction and pre-implementation: City of Melbourne staff training utilizing the resources and expertise developed by the Children's Librarians from the Melbourne Library Service.

Phase 2 - Creating structure for the implementation
9. Creating a team - active within the host setting
10. Developing a plan of how to measure fidelity and dosage.

Phase 3 - Ongoing structure once implementation begins
11. Technical assistance
12. Process evaluation
13. Supportive feedback mechanisms.

Phase 4 - Evaluation
14. Evaluation.

It is proposed that this Quality Implementation Framework (Fixsen et al., 2005) underpins the approach to the programme, and that a qualitative assessment paradigm as outlined be applied to the evaluation of the implementation.

Implementation overview

The programme outlined is currently in development, and proposed as a three-year programme. It is due for commencement in 2015 in the City of Melbourne.

Figure 3.2 provides a summary of the theoretical background framing and underpinning research, as well as the proposed implementation. The programme delivery and its impact will be measured and outcomes communicated in a report on the programme at its culmination in 2017.

Measuring impact

Given the nature of the programme, which is based on the implementation of a three-pronged approach to helping parents develop their skills to enhance their children's language development, the importance of fidelity measures cannot be underestimated in measuring the impact of such a programme (Durlak, 2010; Knoche et al., 2010). Scrutinizing the implementation as well as the outcomes is critical here to show clear indications of the efficacy of the proposed intervention, its time-frames, the effects of the actual, rather than just reported, adherence to

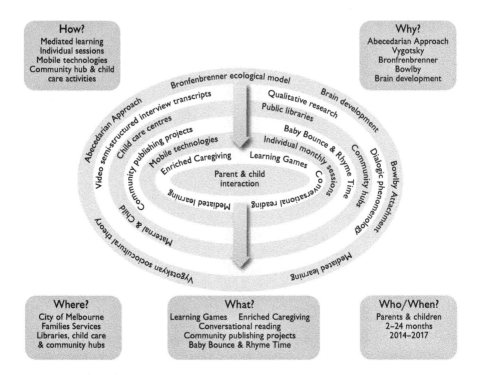

Figure 3.2 *Implementation overview*

the intervention activities, and the response to the unique offer of the intervention.

A non-implementation (or control) group is not being specifically 'measured' here; however the results of the implementation will be measured against collected data from other sources identifying 'typical' overall language indicators of children. Additionally, the baseline will be established at the beginning of the programme to ascertain the 'development' that occurs throughout the implementation of the parental behaviour observed in the programme. This will be recorded as case studies and, through the analysis of dialogic interplay noted in the transcripts of semi-structured interviews with sample parents, the current behaviours of parents compared to (over time) their recorded behaviours interacting with their children will be noted. It has already been established that children in the families that will be targeted for participation are at a disadvantage generally in terms of the effects of their own life affordances or lack thereof. Durlak (2010) asserts that it is inappropriate in the context of educational research to indicate that control groups should be used to measure the effect of implementation studies.

Whilst the strength of the data set from the Abecedarian studies is in its Randomized Control Trials design, it is proposed that the evaluation of this programme focuses on the change in attitudinal behaviours and understandings of parents over time regarding their role in their child's development (which was not measured in the Abecedarian studies). For this reason it is proposed that the evaluation activities will draw from video-recorded sessions (from a sample of the parents involved in the implementation), written observations, and information provided by the parents in online interactions as a form of parental log entry, as well as interviews with the parents at defined intervals during the implementation period. Changes in population data will also be examined, such as the differences evidenced in the Australian Early Development Index (AEDI, 2009) with specific reference to local community and language competence data.

Conclusion

The City of Melbourne's parenting education programme, utilizing the Abecedarian Approach, aims to make a difference by breaking cycles of disadvantage and help contribute to a focus on literacy for all.

The investment in the proposed programme is significant as a cross-council commitment to the City's focus on early literacy, and early intervention and its role in building strong communities. This programme is viewed as an intentional strategy to support the city's designated status as a UNESCO City of Literature, growing young readers and supporting parents, using Abecedarian* principles to lead the development of a reading and literary culture for all.

Abecedarian: rudimentary; elementary; primary (Dictionary.com, 2014)

References

Australian Early Development Index (2009) Melbourne, Victoria: Department of Education and Early Childhood Development, last updated 23 September 2013, www.education.vic.gov.au/about/research/pages/aedi.aspx.

Avrill, J. R., Catlin, G. and Chon, K. K. (1990) *Rules of Hope*, Springer-Verlag.

Berstein Ratner, N. (Producer) (2012) Babytalk 101: how parents help children learn language, *Miegunyah public lecture*, www.youtube.com/watch?v=MPgqb5H8bfA.

Campbell, F. A., Ramey, C. T., Pungello, E., Sparling, J. and Miller-Johnson, S. (2002) Early Childhood Education: young adult outcomes from the Abecedarian project, *Applied Developmental Science*, 6 (1), 42–57.

Dictionary.com (2014) http://dictionary.reference.com/browse/abecedarian.

Dunst, C. J., Simkus, A. and Hamby, D. W. (2012) Relationship between Age of Onset and Frequency of Reading and Infants' and Toddlers' Early Language and Literacy Development, *CELL Reviews*, 5 (3), 1–10.

Durlak, J. (2010) The Importance of Doing Well in Whatever You Do: a commentary on the special section, 'Implementation research in early childhood education', *Early Childhood Research Quarterly*, **25**, 348–57.

Fixsen, D. L., Naoom, S. F., Blase, K. A., Friedman, R. M. and Wallace, F. (2005) *Implementation Research: a synthesis of the literature*, University of South Florida, Louis de la Parte Florida Mental Health Institute.

Grunewald, R. and Rolnick, A. J. (2010) An Early Childhood Investment with a High Public Return, *The Regional Economist, A Quarterly Review of Business and Economic Conditions*, The Federal Reserve Bank of St. Louis, www.stlouisfed.org/publications/re/articles/?id=1987

Hamer, C. (2011) Guidance for Developing a Strategic Approach to Speech, Language and Communication in the Early Years, *Talk to Your Baby*, National Literacy Trust.

Hart, C. H. E., Burts, D. C. and Charlesworth, R. (1997) *Integrated Curriculum and Developmentally Appropriate Practice: birth to age eight*, State University of New York Press.

Heckman, J. J. (2008) *Return on Investment: cost vs. benefits*, University of Chicago, USA.

Kelly, P. and McKerracher, S. (2012) National Year of Reading, *Year Book Australia, 2012*, Australian Bureau of Statistics.

Knoche, L. L., Sheridan, S. M., Edwards, C. P. and Osborn, A. Q. (2010) Implementation of a Relationship-based School Readiness Intervention: a multidimensional approach to fidelity measurement for early childhood, *Early Childhood Research Quarterly*, **25** (3), 299–313.

Masse, L. M. and Barnett, W. S. (2002) *A Benefit-cost Analysis of the Abecedarian Early Childhood Intervention*, National Institute of Early Education Research.

Mendellson, P. F. (2009) Our Plastic Brains, *Redmond Barry Lecture* [podcast], Melbourne, VIC: State Library of Victoria, www.florey.edu.au/news-events/news/2009-07-18/our-plastic-brains.

Nelson, C. (ed.) (2000) *Neurons to Neighbourhoods: the science of early childhood development*, Office of Educational Research and Improvement.

Neuman, S. B. and Celano, D. (2004) Save the Libraries, *Educational Leadership*, **61** (6), 82–5.

Peifer, K. and Perez, L. (2011) Effectiveness of a Coordinated Community Effort to Promote Early Literacy Behaviors, *Maternal & Child Health Journal*, **15** (6), 765–71.

Pink, B. (2012) Launch Speech for the Australian Bureau of Statistics Year Book 2012 Media Release, unpublished media release, Australian Bureau of Statistics.

Ramey, C. T., Dorvall, B. and Baker-Ward, L. (1983) Group Day Care and Socially Disadvantaged Families: effects on the child and the family, *Advances in Early Education and Day Care*, **3**, 69–106.

Ramey, C. T., Sparling, J. J. and Ramey, S. L. (2012) *Abecedarian: the ideas, the approach, and the findings*, Sociometrics Corporation.

Richtel, M. (2012) For Better and for Worse, Technology Use Alters Learning Styles, Teachers Say, *New York Times*, 1 November, www.nytimes.com/2012/11/01/education/technology-is-changing-how-students-learn-teachers-say.html.

Schweinhart, L. J., Montie, J., Xiang, Z., Barnett, W. S., Belfield, C. R. and Nores, M. (2005) *Lifetime Effects: the High/Scope Perry Preschool Study through age 40*, High/Scope Press.

Snow, C. E., Barnes, S., Chandler, J., Goodman, I. and Hempell, L. (1991) *Unfulfilled Expectations: home and school influences on literacy*, Harvard University Press.

Sparling, J. (2011a) *3A: Abecedarian Approach Australia Professional Development Facilitator's Guide*, Melbourne Graduate School of Education.

Sparling, J. (2011b) A Working Document on the Abecedarian Program and Its Probable Relationships to Child Outcome Behaviours. Working Paper 2011-042. Economic Research Centre, University of Chicago.

Tayler, C. (2009) Research Interview – Q&A with Collette Tayler, www.eduweb.vic.gov.au/edulibrary/public/publ/research/publ/researchinterview_collette_tayler.pdf.

Ting-Fang, W. (2007) Executive Summary. In *Understanding the Brain: the birth of a learning science*, OECD.

Trivette, C. M., Dunst, C. J. and Gorman, E. (2010) Effects of Parent-mediated Joint Book Reading on the Early Language Development of Toddlers and Preschoolers, *Centre for Early Literacy Learning (CELL) Reviews*, **3** (2), 1–15, www.earlyliteracylearning.org/cellreviews/cellreviews_v3_n2.pdf

Vygotsky, L. S. (1962) *Thought and Language*, MIT Press.

Weigel, D. J., Martin, S. S. and Bennett, K. K. (2006) Contributions of the Home Literacy Environment to Preschool-aged Children's Emerging Literacy and Language Skills, *Early Childhood Development and Care,* **176** (3–4), 357–78.

Wells, G. (1986) *The Meaning Makers: children learning language and using language to learn*, Heinemann.

Whitehurst, G. J. and Lonigan, C. J. (1998) Child Development and Emergent Literacy. *Child Development*, **69** (3), 848–72.

Wood, D. (1998) *How Children Think and Learn*, 2nd edn, Blackwell Publishers Inc.

CHAPTER 4

Transforming practice through research: evaluating the Better Beginnings family literacy programme

Caroline Barratt-Pugh and Nola Allen

Libraries: linking families with literacy

> You need to learn to read. It helps you with every other subject and if you don't read, you struggle with everything else in life.
>
> (mother, quoted in Barratt-Pugh, Kilgallon and Statkus, 2009)

Libraries play a vital and unique role in supporting and improving the literacy levels of the communities they serve. Libraries are regarded as trusted community places that are freely available, supporting lifelong learning across the ages and contributing to the social benefit of the broader community (Krolak, 2005; Hillenbrand, 2005; Scott, 2011). In a 2013 US study, parents perceived libraries as being important and safe places for their children, cultivating within them a love of books and reading and providing information and resources not always available at home (Miller et al., 2013).

International research demonstrates the impact of low literacy on an individual's life chances, with strong links between poor literacy skills, lower educational attainment, lower earnings, poorer health and poorer social outcomes (Hartley and Hoyne, 2006). What is also widely recognized is that the most effective and efficient way to address these issues is from the very beginning of life (Heckman and Masterov, 2005).

From its launch in 2005 to the present, Better Beginnings, an initiative of the State Library of Western Australia, has grown to be one of the most extensive and successful family literacy programmes in Australia. Delivered through public libraries and community health centres throughout Western Australia, this universal programme is designed to provide positive early literacy experiences for all Western Australian families with young children aged from birth to three.

Dynamic and ever-evolving, Better Beginnings makes connections - between parents and children, families and libraries, state government and local councils, health and education services, and between research and practice. Edith Cowan University has conducted an independent, longitudinal evaluation of the programme since its inception, which has proved crucial not only to demonstrating its effectiveness but also, equally importantly, in identifying new directions and areas of need.

Better Beginnings: the why, what and how

Extensive international research shows that children's development is influenced by nature and nurture, that is, genes and the environment. Research also shows that the first five years of life are the most significant time for brain development, while the most rapid growth happens in the first three years. The experiences and relationships that young children have actually shape the architecture of their brains (Mustard, 2006).

Based on international studies on early brain development (Klass, Needlman and Zuckerman, 2003), the importance of the early years and the efficacy of family literacy programmes (Moore and Wade, 2003), Better Beginnings is founded on a strengths-based approach, recognizing that parents want the best for their children and are their child's first and most important teacher. The programme aims to:

- support and involve parents in their children's early literacy learning
- introduce young children to developmentally appropriate books and literacy activities
- raise awareness in the wider community of the value of reading to children from birth
- link families with libraries and community services that support literacy development.

Strategies and resources

To realize these aims, Better Beginnings utilizes a range of strategies and resources:

1   A reading pack (Figure 4.1) for parents of young babies that contains a high-quality children's board book, a library bag, a nursery rhyme frieze, nursery booklet and DVD, a fold-out poster and brochures with reading and book-sharing tips and book recommendations. Libraries include membership forms and invitations to join Rhyme Time and parent-information sessions.

Figure 4.1 *A Better Beginnings reading pack*

2   Baby Rhyme Time, Story Time and parenting information sessions. New
    parents are invited to attend free regular Rhyme Time sessions, which
    focus on developing early literacy skills through emphasis on nursery
    rhymes, songs and simple stories. Some libraries offer parenting sessions,
    including workshops covering speech and language development, child
    development and nutrition.

3   Story Time boxes contain a variety of literacy resources, including picture
    books, big books for group sharing, hand and finger puppets, felt board
    and magnetic board sets, musical instruments, novelty and pop-up books
    and the Story-and-Rhyme Time handbook. Libraries are provided with
    Story Time boxes to support in-house and outreach sessions at playgroups
    and childcare centres.

4   Family reading centres. Some libraries have established physical family-
    friendly spaces designed to encourage shared reading and interactive
    literacy activities, along with the provision of parenting information. Each
    centre can vary, depending upon the library's space and needs, with some
    including parenting collections of books, DVDs and magazines, children's
    picture books, book and puppet sets, child-friendly computers with
    literacy games, comfortable couches for family book sharing and children's
    furniture.

5   The Better Beginnings website (www.better-beginnings.com.au). The
    website provides high-quality literacy e-resources and e-books for children,
    practical advice and reading guidance for parents.
6   A training programme, handbook and online practitioners' portal that
    allows librarians, community child-health nurses and educators to access
    programme-delivery information, handbooks, video tutorials and
    demonstrations and to share best practice relating to programme delivery.

Co-operation for delivery

Starting from a pilot programme in six communities, Better Beginnings is now
available to all families with new babies throughout Western Australia. More than
220,000 babies and toddlers and their families have participated in the programme,
from receiving free books and reading packs, to attending family Rhyme Times
and parent-information sessions, to using material in the local library's family
reading centre.

With a population of approximately 2.5 million (Australian Bureau of Statistics,
2013) spread across an area ten times that of the United Kingdom (Geoscience
Australia; The World Bank, 2014) Western Australia presents geographical,
economic and social challenges for the provision of universal and equitable access
to resources and services. To address these challenges, the Better Beginnings
programme is built on partnerships and strong co-operation across state and
local government, public library, community health and corporate sectors. The
programme is provided free to all families and is funded under a tripartite alliance
between the Western Australian State Government, all of the 139 local governments
in Western Australia (WALGA, 2014) and founding corporate partner Rio Tinto.

Public libraries play a vital role in the programme's delivery, implementation
and sustainability. Western Australia has a network of over 230 public libraries
delivering services through a partnership between state and local governments.
These libraries are accessible and inclusive and are the only government-funded
agencies that provide year-round access to resources and services supporting
reading and literacy from birth through to adulthood. Each library is the local
contact point for Better Beginnings within its community, adapting and delivering
the programme with the community's needs in mind and liaising with diverse
agencies to increase awareness and access.

Work with community health services

To extend the reach of the programme beyond library users, public libraries work
closely with community health services. While library membership in Western

Australia sits at around 41% (National and State Libraries Australasia, 2011-12), community child-health nurses see approximately 90% of families with babies within the first few months of life (Western Australian Auditor General's Report Universal Child Health Checks, 2010). Community child-health nurses working in the 310 community health centres in metropolitan and country areas assess children's health and development as well as provide information about many aspects of parenting, maternal and family health and healthy lifestyles.

Many community child-health nurses are strong and proactive advocates for the programme, citing that it reinforces their holistic approach to child health and the links between health and literacy. This was echoed by a community child-health nurse who took part in the pilot evaluation in 2005: 'It's wonderful to have support across the community emphasizing the importance of reading and language development. It's not just a health issue, it's a community issue.' At the 6-8 weeks meeting every parent receives a personal health record 'All About Me' for their newborn, which includes topics for discussion with their community child-health nurse, including 'book sharing with your baby' and 'talking with and listening to your baby'.

Library staff liaise with the community child-health nurse to deliver free books and reading packs to parents with newborns at one of the first health visits. Libraries offer a secondary delivery point for families that may not access their community health services. Some regional libraries also deliver reading packs to local maternity hospitals. During the health-check visit, community child-health nurses discuss the contents of the reading pack and the importance of reading to children and promote library membership and use. In some instances, community child-health nurses bring 'new parents' groups' to the library, where the librarian introduces the library's services and resources, makes book recommendations and delivers Better Beginnings reading packs.

Rhyme Time sessions

Rhyme Time sessions in libraries are held regularly, on a twice-weekly, weekly, fortnightly or monthly basis, depending on staffing and resources. Trained volunteers also conduct sessions in some smaller country libraries to cater for demand. During the sessions, librarians lead parents and children in singing nursery rhymes and participating in action rhymes together. Some libraries provide multiple copies of board books (e.g. *Baby Ways,* one of the Better Beginnings gift board books) to participants so that they can read along with the librarian reading a big book version. Many libraries report increasing attendance and demand for additional Rhyme Time sessions from families with babies and toddlers, with many public libraries creating dedicated family reading spaces with Better

Beginnings resources (Barratt-Pugh, Maloney and McLean, 2012).

The sessions have provided informal opportunities for librarians to engage with less-confident parents or those with limited literacy. Recognizing that some families did not feel comfortable in the library, librarians have conducted outreach sessions using the Better Beginnings resources at childcare centres and playgroups in the local community. One librarian explains that she is careful not to alienate less-confident parents or those with limited literacy by encouraging them to talk about the pictures in books, and telling the story rather than reading the text. 'I want them to know that anything they can do is good enough, [this] is the kind of message that I try to get across.'

Figure 4.2 *Introducing books from the beginning – a librarian shows literacy resources to parents and babies*

Is it working? Evaluation and reflection

Evaluation and reflective practice have been integral to the implementation and expansion of Better Beginnings from its inception. Evaluation has been identified as central to the development of programmes (Farmer and Stricevic, 2011) and 'can and should enhance the quality of interventions (policies and programs)' (Owen, 2006, 1). Hannon and Fox (2005, 9) also claim that 'evaluation should be integral to practice, especially in a situation where the practice has to be innovative'. In the context of Better Beginnings, the programme evaluation has been designed to:

- measure the programme's effectiveness and build an evidence base
- inform programme development
- identify challenges and issues
- identify gaps in programme coverage
- encourage reflective practice.

The programme is evaluated in two ways - through an internal library-based process and an external independent study. Annually, public libraries submit statistical and anecdotal data about the programme which is collated and analysed by the State Library. Statistics collected include Rhyme Time attendance figures, the number of outreach sessions given to childcare centres and playgroups, library memberships for the target audiences and circulation of picture books and parenting resources. Librarians are also encouraged to observe and report on the programme's impact or influence on the use of the library service by families. One large metropolitan library attributed a 25% increase in the number of loans of picture books over a 12-month period to its involvement in Better Beginnings (Better Beginnings, State Library of Western Australia). Another library recorded feedback from a newly arrived, socially isolated mother with a culturally and linguistically diverse background who stated that, as a result of attending Better Beginnings parenting sessions, she had accessed playgroups and other community services which provided much needed support (Better Beginnings, State Library of Western Australia).

Individually, this information is used by libraries to build a picture of what Better Beginnings looks like in their own community and for their own progress reporting to library managers and local government. Collectively, the internal evaluation complements the independent, longitudinal evaluation conducted by Edith Cowan University on the role of public libraries in producing positive outcomes through family literacy initiatives.

Evaluation by Edith Cowan University

The Centre for Research in Early Childhood at Edith Cowan University in Western Australia has been independently evaluating Better Beginnings over a four-year period, from 2007 to 2010.[1] Three hundred parents who received a Better Beginnings reading pack in 2007 took part in the ongoing evaluation. Researchers undertook the evaluation to explore the following key questions:

1   How effective is the Better Beginnings programme from the participants' perspectives?
2   What factors helped or hindered the implementation of the Better Beginnings programme?

In order to capture the breadth and depth of the programme, researchers utilized both qualitative and quantitative methods documenting programme delivery, implementation and impact. The State Library's Better Beginnings co-ordinator, local librarians and community child-health nurses were interviewed and parents of new babies from four diverse socio-economic communities were surveyed annually over a period of four years. Table 4.1 documents the number of participants over four years.

Table 4.1 *Number of participants interviewed over four years*				
Mothers Community	**Year 1**	**Year 2**	**Year 3**	**Year 4**
Rural	74	30	22	22
Metropolitan i	87	69	36	26
Metropolitan ii	77	42	18	11
Remote	62	36	26	25
Total	**300**	**177**	**102**	**84**
Librarians	10	9	4	4
Community child-health nurses	13	8	6	6

The first survey form was presented to the parent/carer at their baby's 6–8 week health check-up at their local health clinic. All parents/carers who completed the survey identified as the baby's mother. Where appropriate, a translator was available at the clinic. Mothers were asked to complete the first survey before they received the Better Beginnings Reading Pack. In this survey mothers were asked about demographics, early literacy practices with their baby, attitudes to and confidence in sharing songs, books and nursery rhymes with their baby and library membership and use.

The following three surveys, in years two, three and four of the evaluation, were completed by telephone, after receipt of the Better Beginnings Reading Pack. In the second survey, mothers were asked about the delivery and content of the programme, the impact of the programme on literacy beliefs, attitudes and practices in relation to sharing books, nursery rhymes and songs with their baby and library membership and activities. In the third and fourth surveys, mothers were asked to provide feedback on the continuing influence and sustainability of Better Beginnings.

Researchers interviewed the State Library programme co-ordinator, librarians and community child-health nurses about their perspectives on the programme and its implementation, effectiveness and sustainability. The programme's practitioners were also surveyed about the training provided and the development of inter-agency collaboration.

Making a difference: the programme's impact on families

The Better Beginnings programme has had a positive impact on mothers' confidence, practices and beliefs about sharing books. Many mothers talked about how they would not have thought about sharing a book with their baby before becoming involved in Better Beginnings. Only 14% reported that they shared books with their baby before Better Beginnings, while one year later, 85% reported sharing books with their baby. One mother reflected that the programme introduced 'us to rhymes and stories that we can do daily at either bath time or bedtime, maybe we would have a silent house without it' (mother, 2008).

The mothers reported that Better Beginnings had increased or reinforced their confidence in sharing books. One year after receiving the Reading Pack almost two-thirds (62%) reported an increase in their confidence and by the end of the evaluation, 81% of mothers reported feeling more confident about sharing books with their child. Interestingly, a number of mothers had asked for information about what and how to read to older children, asking for a Reading Pack for 4- to 5-year-olds. One year after receiving the Reading Pack the majority of mothers (93%) reported that they had read the Better Beginnings book to their child between 1 and 99 times, the average being 26 times.

> I thought [the book] was fantastic. First of all you had every colour in there and you had every size of baby ... doing something that was naturally a baby and they all looked at you ... It's got cardboard pages and the clear pictures ... for [the baby] to focus on ... we were reading that every day, several times a day.
>
> (mother, quoted in Barratt-Pugh, Statkus and Kilgallon, 2010)

Evidence from the mothers' responses to the surveys across the four years of the evaluation suggests that the Reading Pack had influenced their language and literacy practices. Ninety-three per cent of mothers were overwhelmingly positive about the Reading Pack resources. The majority of mothers reported sharing books with their baby as well as using the information from the pamphlets. Almost all the mothers reported that they and their child liked the gift book and almost a third (29%) claimed that they had read some of the books that were recommended in the Better Beginnings pamphlet. Around two-thirds of the mothers reported that the parent-information pamphlet with tips on book sharing with babies was useful. Mothers were also asked what they liked the most about receiving the Reading Pack. The following responses illustrate two different perspectives, 'All the different ideas, basic books easy to follow. Knowledge to read to young babies [and] information for parents to follow' (mother, 2008) and 'It has encouraged me to persevere and continue bringing books into Robin's life. It is hard with his disability but I believe the books have helped with his speech development' (mother, 2010).

Three-quarters of mothers reported an increase in the frequency of reading to their child, of the child asking for a book to be read and of other people reading to their child. In addition, almost all described how their communication with their child had increased, and how the frequency of reading to other children in the family had increased. Although these changes of language and literacy practices could be attributed to the growing maturity of the child, 90% of mothers in the fourth survey indicated that these had been influenced by Better Beginnings. This is illustrated in the following comment: 'Made me more confident in reading to my children. I have taken books off the top shelf where I kept them safe and put them down where he can reach them. Now he picks up books so we can read them together or he flicks through by himself' (mother, 2010).

Figure 4.3 *Sharing* Baby Ways *together*

Library membership and use

Over the four years of the evaluation there had been a steady increase in mothers' beliefs about the importance of sharing books with their child. By the end of the fourth year, all mothers reported that they felt sharing books was either very or fairly important. Almost all of the mothers attributed this view to Better Beginnings. As well as impacting on book-sharing practices, beliefs and confidence it was evident that the programme also influenced library membership and use. By the end of the evaluation 85% of mothers reported that they were library members and 65% reported that their child had library membership. Many mothers reported that they visited the library with their child and borrowed children's books on a regular basis, as illustrated in the following comments, 'Even though I knew that babies could join the library, it encouraged and reminded me to join the library and go to it more often' (mother, quoted in Barratt-Pugh, Kilgallon and Statkus, 2009), 'Lots of activities for toddlers. Great kids section for kids to rummage through' (mother, quoted in Barratt-Pugh, Kilgallon and Statkus, 2009) and 'Encouraged me in the beginning to go to the library and attend Story Time and from there I learned different ways of reading to my child to hold his interest' (mother, quoted in Barratt-Pugh, Kilgallon and Statkus, 2009).

Impact on children's literacy

The influence of *Better Beginnings* appeared to have a ripple effect, impacting not only on the mothers but also on their children's literacy. Mothers reported an increase in their child's engagement in books, vocabulary, time spent sharing books, reading-like behaviours and the sheer joy in choosing and sharing books with siblings and other family members. Many mothers reflected that sharing books had helped them bond with their child as a baby, and supported early reading development as their child matured. The children's interaction with books, reported by mothers, such as pointing to the words, asking questions about the story and speculating about the sequence of events in the story were closely related to those outlined in the Better Beginnings brochure. They were also identified as behaviours mothers reported modelling for their children. The following comments illustrate some of these changes:

> I felt a dill reading to the baby but as he has grown and responded I realized it really was worthwhile. Now he has a great vocabulary and people comment on how well he speaks and I put that down to him being read to. Better Beginnings has made me make reading a part of the everyday routine.
> (mother, quoted in Barratt-Pugh, Statkus and Kilgallon, 2010)

> I realized how much she loved books and being read to and how much it helped her. She is always talking and makes up her own stories while looking through books.
> (mother, quoted in Barratt-Pugh, Kilgallon and Statkus, 2009)

Dynamic and evolving: informing programme development and strengthening partnerships

Over the time of their involvement in Better Beginnings, librarians have developed a strong sense of ownership of the programme's success. During interviews librarians spoke about their evolving understanding of the programme's aims, the inclusion of Better Beginnings activities into job descriptions and embedding the programme into core library business. Better Beginnings activities have become a recurrent budget item for local government libraries and facilitated increased involvement by libraries in early years and community networks. Librarians describe the programme as providing an incentive for families to engage in library activities and access resources that promote literacy and lifelong learning, as illustrated in the following comment, 'For a young parent or anyone who hasn't previously used the library or doesn't have a book-oriented household, that could be their very first introduction to making it a regular part of their child's upbringing' (Librarian, 2008).

Through the evaluation, librarians identified a need for more extensive, in-depth training to build on the initial programme-delivery workshops on offer. Continuing professional development opportunities offered by the State Library have increased as a result, with training extending beyond print handbooks to include integrated face-to-face, hands-on and web-based modules aimed at sharing best practice. Areas of professional development of high interest to library staff include baby Rhyme Time training, early childhood development, using and promoting online literacy resources and cultural-awareness workshops on services to Aboriginal families and families from culturally and linguistically diverse backgrounds (Barratt-Pugh and Rohl, 2010, year 4).

With their growing familiarity with the programme, community child-health nurses have further developed their understanding and commitment to Better Beginnings. By the fourth year of the evaluation, community child-health nurses regarded Better Beginnings as supporting their role and providing resources to demonstrate the importance of early literacy, as illustrated in the following comment, 'I think it is a fantastic lead into early literacy ... To have the babies look at [the book] is quite good for the mums and dads to see. I think it is a very important part of early learning development' (Community Child-Health Nurse, 2009).

While both groups of practitioners recognize the programme's value, limited staffing and heavy workloads have presented challenges to developing and maintaining effective working relationships. In a formal acknowledgement of this vital collaboration, the State Library and State Government's Department of Health have developed a memorandum of understanding regarding the joint delivery of Better Beginnings state-wide.

Librarians and community child-health nurses were very positive about the Better Beginnings resources, which they felt supported not only literacy practices but also understanding of the importance of literacy. Early feedback from mothers, community child-health nurses and librarians about the contents of the Reading Pack and book selection led to modifications of the material included (e.g. a growth chart was replaced with a nursery rhyme frieze). Of particular note was the development and production of a board book that featured the cultural diversity of children and families in the Western Australian community. Practitioners have also identified the need to increase the number of books for multiple-birth families and offer a variety of books including titles by Aboriginal authors and illustrators and Indigenous publishers for families living in remote Indigenous communities. Another review of the reading pack and its contents is currently under way, following participant and practitioner feedback.

The evaluation has identified central co-ordination and management of Better Beginnings by the State Library as critical to the programme's evolution and expansion. The State Library manages the programme, thereby ensuring continuity, sustainability, wide distribution and an overview of its ongoing development. Establishing and building key partnerships with founding corporate partner Rio Tinto and various government and not-for-profit organizations, the State Library strives to strengthen and build the programme's sustainability. A state-wide perspective has enabled the State Library to identify and address gaps in service provision and programme coverage. Through this central co-ordination, the State Library has initiated targeted marketing campaigns to raise awareness of the programme and its key messages on the importance of early literacy within and across metropolitan and regional communities.

Challenges and changes: identifying and addressing gaps in programme coverage

The universal approach of Better Beginnings – that is, the programme is intended for every child born in Western Australia – has meant that literacy is seen as a community-wide issue. While this is recognized as a strength of the programme, there has also been an expressed need for targeted strategies and resources to engage marginalized families. A recurrent theme throughout the evaluation reports, reiterated by both library and health practitioners, has been the concern that families who were socially and/or geographically isolated or those most in need were missing out on the benefits associated with Better Beginnings (Barratt-Pugh and Rohl, 2010).

While the collaboration between libraries and community health has resulted in increased access to and awareness of the programme it has not ensured the programme's availability to Aboriginal families living in remote communities in isolated rural areas or families from culturally and linguistically diverse backgrounds. In particular, the delivery of Better Beginnings to all Aboriginal families presents unique challenges, with just over 40% of Western Australian Aboriginal children aged five and under living in remote communities where there is no library (Commissioner for Children and Young People WA, 2011, 18).To redress this gap in service provision, a pilot programme, Read To Me I Love It! was successfully trialled in 2010 with the key aims of supporting and involving parents in their children's early literacy learning and engaging families in remote Aboriginal communities with targeted and culturally appropriate resources and strategies.

Local Aboriginal communities are assisted to facilitate the delivery of the Read to Me I Love It! programme through a network of distributors who work in Aboriginal corporations, schools, health services and other community or not-for-profit services. In this way, communities share the responsibility for the programme's delivery and develop a sense of ownership of the programme, a central tenet of Better Beginnings. It is underpinned by a belief that the communities themselves are best placed to identify how the programme is delivered and sustained, and recognizes that this varies from community to community. A series of reading packs are delivered to children and families at regular intervals over a two-year period, whereby families will receive 16 high-quality children's books and a 'virtual library' of 80 stories on DVD over the course of the programme. The books and accompanying resources are specifically chosen and designed to reflect Aboriginal history, culture and everyday life and include stories and rhymes, alphabet and number posters, DVDs, T-shirts for children and an adult Aboriginal newspaper and pamphlet about the importance of reading to children. Currently 110 remote Aboriginal communities are participating in the programme. A teacher working in one community observed:

> The kids love it when we get [the packs] ... they cheer and cheer. One mother reads
> with her 4-year-old every afternoon after school now ... She said without these
> books, they would not have any to read. I didn't realise the program was having this
> kind of an impact on families.
>
> (Teacher, remote community school, 2009)

The ongoing evaluation has continued to be instrumental in identifying new directions for the programme. Once again, as a result of participant and practitioner feedback, the State Library has developed new ways to extend and consolidate the reach of Better Beginnings into the wider community. Pilot programmes including a reading-incentive initiative for older children, a programme to engage adults with limited literacy skills and a community publishing venture with culturally diverse families have also been trialled and independently evaluated.

In response to a need articulated by parents for support of their children's reading when they commenced formal education, a programme with age-appropriate books and targeted resources is now being made available through public libraries and schools.[2] An evaluation of the pilot conducted in 2010 noted that the programme was having a positive impact on improving links between families, libraries and schools in literacy provision. In 2013 alone, 59,000 children aged four and five years received books and reading packs and the programme registered a participation rate of 86% of Western Australian primary schools.

Conclusion

The main findings of the evaluation have clearly shown that Better Beginnings has significantly influenced literacy practices, attitudes and confidence within and across families, making a positive contribution to early literacy learning in Western Australia (Barratt-Pugh and Rohl, 2010). In addition, five elements of the programme that appeared to be of central importance to its success were identified:

1   Listening to the voices of recipients and professionals involved in delivering and maintaining the programme. This enabled the programme to be informed and shaped by the participants. It helped to identify gaps in coverage, acknowledged programme strengths and highlighted challenges.

2   Central co-ordination of the programme through the State Library and local library involvement. This enabled coherent and comprehensive planning, delivery and sustainment of the programme across Western Australia.

3   Inter-agency collaboration. This strengthened the programme as professionals supported each other

Figure 4.4
Babies love books and rhymes at the library

and the programme's message and practices were reinforced through different service providers.
4   Professional development. This enabled the professionals to deliver the programme in increasingly effective ways, with developing confidence.
5   Flexibility of design. This enabled the programme to be adapted and developed to respond to diversity in different communities.

Founded on international research, the Better Beginnings programme has transformed theory into practice. From the outset, the longitudinal, independent evaluation of the programme has been invaluable to its sustainability and has contributed to the evidence base that demonstrates the key role that libraries can and do play in literacy development.

> We have to do everything we can to give all our children opportunities to get off to a strong start, and community institutions play a critical role. For parents and families, libraries and museums are a go-to resource that supports them as their child's first teacher.
>
> (Howard and Camp, 2013, 16)

Notes

1   www.better-beginnings.com.au/research/research-about-better-beginnings/better-beginnings-making-difference.
2   For more information visit www.better-beginnings.com.au/programs/four-five.

References

Australian Bureau of Statistics (2013) www.abs.gov.au/ausstats/abs@.nsf/mf/3101.0.

Barratt-Pugh, C. and Rohl, M. (2010) *Making a Difference: the report of the evaluation of the Better Beginnings (0–3 years) family literacy program, 2007–2010*, Edith Cowan University.

Barratt-Pugh, C., Kilgallon, P. and Statkus, S. (2009) *Making a Difference: the evaluation of the Better Beginnings birth to three family literacy program, 2007–2009*, Year 2, Edith Cowan University.

Barratt-Pugh, C., Maloney, C. and McLean, C. (2012) *Making a Difference: the evaluation of the Better Beginnings birth to three family literacy program*, Year 5, Edith Cowan University.

Barratt-Pugh, C., Rohl, M. and Statkus, M. (2010) *Making a Difference: evaluation of the Better Beginnings family literacy program 2007–2010*, Year 4, Edith Cowan University.

Barratt-Pugh, C., Statkus, S. and Kilgallon, P. (2010) Making a Difference: evaluation of the Better Beginnings family literacy program, 2007–2010, Year 3, Edith Cowan University.

Commissioner for Children and Young People WA (2011) *Profile of Children and Young People in Western Australia: wellbeing monitoring framework,* www.ccyp.wa.gov.au/maps/PDF/CCYP_ProfileHealthandWellbeingofChildren.pdf.

Farmer, L. and Stricevic, I. (2011) *Using Research to Promote Literacy and Reading in Libraries: guidelines for librarians,* International Federation of Library Associations and Institutions IFLA Professional Reports, No. 125, www.ifla.org/publications/ifla-professional-reports-125.

Hannon, P. and Fox, L. (2005) Why We Should Learn from Sure Start. In Weinberger, J., Pickstone, C. and Hannon, P. (eds), *Learning from Sure Start: working with young children and their families,* Open University Press.

Hartley, R. and Hoyne, J. (2006) *Social and Economic Benefits of Improved Adult Literacy: towards a better understanding,* National Centre for Vocational Educational Research, Adelaide.

Heckman, J. J. and Masterov, V. D. (2005) *The Productivity Argument for Investing in Young Children,* University of Chicago.

Hillenbrand, C. (2005) Public Libraries as Developers of Social Capital, *Aplis,* **18** (1), 4–12.

Howard, M. L. and Camp, A. (2013) *Growing Young Minds: how museums and libraries create lifelong learners,* IMLS, Washington, DC.

Klass, P., Needlman, R. and Zuckerman, B. (2003) The Developing Brain and Early Learning, *Archives of Disease in Childhood,* **88**, 651–4.

Krolak, L. (2005) The Role of Libraries in the Creation of Literate Environments, paper commissioned for the *EFA Global Monitoring Report 2006, Literacy for Life,* www.ifla.org/files/assets/literacy-and-reading/publications/role-of-libraries-in-creation-of-literate-environments.pdf.

Miller, C., Zickuhr, K., Rainie, L. and Purcell, K. (2013) *Parents, Children, Libraries and Reading,* Pew Research Center, www.libraries.pewinternet.org/2013/05/01/parents-children-libraries-and-reading.

Moore, M. and Wade, B. (2003) Bookstart: a qualitative evaluation, *Educational Review,* **55** (1), 3–13.

Mustard, J. F. (2006) Experience-based Brain Development: scientific underpinnings of the importance of early child development in a global world, *Paediatrics & Child Health,* **11** (9), 571–2.

National and State Libraries Australasia, www.nsla.org.au/publication/australian-public-library-statistics-2011-12.

Owen, J. M. (2006) *Program Evaluation Forms and Approaches,* 3rd edn, Allen & Unwin.

Scott, R. (2011) The Role of Public Libraries in Community Building, *Public Library Quarterly,* **30** (3), 191–227.

WALGA (Western Australian Local Government Association) (2014)
www.walga.asn.au/AboutWALGA.aspx.

Western Australian Auditor General, Western Australian Auditor General's Report
Universal Child Health Checks (2010) Report, 11 Nov 2010, 18,
http://audit.wa.gov.au/wpcontent/uploads/2013/05/report2010_11.pdf.

The World Bank (2014) http://data.worldbank.org/indicator/AG.LND.TOTL.K2.

Websites

Better Beginnings, State Library of Western Australia, www.better-beginnings.com.au.

Geoscience Australia, Australian Government, www.ga.gov.au/education/geoscience-
basics/dimensions/area-of-australia-states-and-territories.html.

Practitioners' Portal and Internal Online Evaluation (not for public access),
Commissioner for Children and Young People, Western Australia.

CHAPTER 5

People and partnerships, skills and knowledge

Carolynn Rankin and Avril Brock

Introduction

This chapter addresses the role of professionals in the interdisciplinary work involved in meeting the varied needs of the local community. It is particularly concerned with the roles of librarians and other early years specialists as they seek to develop effective partnerships across the disciplines as well as to foster partnerships with parents and carers. It considers how these professionals can provide quality, focused services and help to break down the barriers to those services that may be apparent in the community. Drawing on practice, the chapter also discusses the issues of developing effective communication and providing greater accountability to the stakeholders across the disciplines.

We have updated only some aspects of this chapter since it was prepared for the first edition of *Delivering the Best Start* in 2008, written after the authors had undertaken research with early years practitioners - librarians and educators - in a variety of early years settings, and mostly particularly in the Sure Start Children's Centres (SSCCs). The New Labour government promised an SSCC in every locality and commenced with developing them in areas of deprivation.

The origins of Sure Start came from the 1998 Comprehensive Spending Review led by Norman Glass, an economist, who had no experience of early years. Lees (2015, 101) demonstrates how Glass was asked 'to quantify expenditure on young children and the effectiveness on outcomes for children'. According to Lees (2015, 101), the review was 'extremely comprehensive, involving 11 different government departments (Glass, 1999; Eisenstadt, 2011; Lewis, 2011), and examined evidence from America, including Head Start and the Perry preschool programme, as well as UK research in child health'. The findings of the review concluded that a child's development in the early years is crucial and that children are more vulnerable to external adverse environmental conditions than had been realized.

Richardson's doctoral research in SSCCs (Richardson, 2013) found that Sure Start children's centres had enormous potential for supporting individual progress and possibilities for generating social change. She discovered that the reciprocity described in the staff–parent relationships and the value of the services offered emerged strongly through the detailed personal perspectives of the staff and parents. This provided insight into the challenging circumstances and complexities of individual lives and a framework for how social capital develops. Richardson's research demonstrates how inter-agency working to meet the needs of children under four years of age and their families provided good early years practice and the integration of family support services.

Rankin and Butler (2011, 41) observe, 'young children and their families do not see their needs for early education, health care, literacy support, job or housing advice as separate silos and neither should the professionals working with them'. As demonstrated in the model adapted from Bronfenbrenner in Chapter 1 (see Figure 1.1), librarians are one of the key professions that can make a difference to young children and their families' lives. Achieving literacy in the early years is key to both educational attainment and occupational success in later years. This chapter celebrates some of those successes and demonstrates some of the excellent practice that has occurred in early years settings and libraries. Unfortunately, in 2014 in the UK we have seen the removal of early years librarians and library provision from the SSCCs, following on the closure of libraries in villages and small towns since the recession started in 2010. Furthermore, due to financial difficulties and the squeeze on funding, many local authorities are closing SSCCs, and we are sad to announce that some of these authorities are the ones (namely Wakefield and Sheffield) we applauded in our 2009 book. You have already read about the importance of enhancing social capital in Chapter 1, and in this chapter you will see how good practice has evolved as librarians work in partnerships with professionals and with families. We therefore make no apology for continuing to include this practice that is no longer occurring in SSCCs, as we are sure that many early years librarians are still striving to achieve this, despite whatever cutbacks or problems arise, as they know they can make a difference to young children.

Working with diverse communities

Communities give purpose to libraries and it is important that libraries seek to reach out to the local community beyond the library walls. Reading is an invaluable tool that can be used as the basis for connecting with various groups in society - babies and their families, looked-after children, young people at risk, the housebound, as well as adults trying to improve their literacy skills. Librarians and information workers share a critical value in that it is important to understand the needs of user communities in order to perform this task/function effectively and efficiently. Success in helping people to meet their information needs lies in understanding their difficulties and problems and is dependent on forming good working relationships. Young children and their families are at the heart of the community. To increase their value, libraries can use community profiling to examine the needs of the target audience and determine how those needs can best be met. This may involve redefining the traditional role of the library as well as that of the librarian. The traditional children's department may need to be 'stretched' by expanding the age and scope of the target audience. For parents and carers, access to information and services during their children's early years is critical, particularly information about how everyday activities are linked to developing literacy and communication skills.

The development of the Children's Centre networks presented the opportunity for children's library services to become an integral part of the multi-agency services provided. It also offered new avenues for reaching the young children of disadvantaged families in order to help make a difference to their reading, listening and language skills.

Libraries that invest in services for young children and their families increase the effectiveness of the provision. This should also have the secondary effect of helping to increase membership rates and loan records. Outreach work with diverse communities will encourage new cultural groups to use the service and promote the library's role as a centre for the community. This represents an excellent opportunity to position the library as a partner in the development and education of young children. In addition, libraries that expand the role of children's services to include families may also be able to attract additional backing for their services and gain political support. As Feinberg and Feldman (1996, 2) write:

> In ranking or prioritizing services, public libraries would be loath to cut services to children even in an austerity budget. Service to children is essential, popular and an emotionally charged issue. Family centred services have the same cost benefit as children's services. They are essential, popular and emotionally or politically important services for all public or government institutions. Selecting family services as a role or strengthening children's services to include service to parents and agencies that serve parents, increases the political worth of the public library.

However this is exactly what is happening in the UK.

How to develop a family-friendly service: breaking down barriers to library use

It is vital to encourage families to use the library's services. Remember, libraries are competing with the many other places that offer facilities and activities to families, so think carefully about how your library can offer something different. First consider the physical environment and the activities on offer. As a starting point, you could ask the staff to try to visualize the library from the customer's point of view. Familiarity can cause complacency. When working in the same place day in, day out, we tend not to notice the little imperfections and begin to take the environment for granted. Perhaps it is a long time since we reflected on the layout of the furniture, or we may have failed to notice the out-of-date posters. Although the lighting is poor, and inadequate for either daytime or evening use, we have gradually become accustomed to it. Even the grumpy staff may have become accepted as part of the fittings and fixtures! It is important to challenge any complacency. Good negotiating skills may also prove to be essential, as you may need to convince management that staff time and resources used in evaluating a service or identifying a gap are time and effort well spent. Practitioners need to be aware of the library's customers and the needs of those customers.

The library environment should be designed to create appropriate physical spaces and have appropriate furniture for the age group you are supporting. Thoughtful design using soft furnishings and child-friendly furniture will help to provide a welcoming location (Figure 5.1) and we discuss space and design in more detail in Chapter 13.

Figure 5.1 *A welcoming space*

CASE STUDY

Family Place Libraries is a network of children's librarians in the USA who believe that literacy begins at birth and that libraries can help build healthy communities by nourishing healthy families. This is a joint initiative of Middle Country Public Library and Libraries for the Future, and at the time of writing the network included more than 220 sites in 23 states. Feinberg and Rogoff (1998) explain that 'The Family Place project takes a holistic and developmentally informed approach to the promotion of emergent literacy and healthy child development by addressing the needs of children at the earliest stages, and supporting the role of parent as a child's first and most important teacher' (p. 50). Family Place Libraries redesign the library environment to be welcoming and appropriate for children, beginning at birth. The services offered at the library and other family service agencies reach out to non-traditional library users. This creates the network that families need in order to nurture their children's development during the critical first years of life and helps to ensure that all children enter school ready and able to learn. It is interesting to note that, according to Kropp (2004), the core components of a Family Place Library are:

- Collections of books, toys, music and multimedia materials for babies, toddlers, parents and service providers
- A specially designed, welcoming space within the children's area for families with young children
- The parent/child workshop which is a five week program that involves toddlers and their parents and caregivers; features local professionals who serve as resources for parents; emphasizes the role of parents as the first teachers of their children; facilitates early intervention; and teaches strategies for healthy child development and early literacy
- Coalition-building with community agencies that serve families and young children to connect parents to community resources and develop programs and services tailored to meet local needs
- Outreach to new and non-traditional library users, especially parents and very young children (beginning at birth)
- Developmentally appropriate programming for very young children and their parents
- Library staff trained in family support, child development, parent education and best practices.

(Kropp, 2004)

It is also interesting that the Family Place Library network provides specific training packages for the library staff involved in the scheme. Further information is available at www.familyplacelibraries.org/whatMakes.html.

Libraries can be good meeting places, providing a neutral, non-threatening environment – a place to share information with the community. We want to present a building that is encouraging and welcoming. However, thinking beyond the bricks and mortar, the human contact is also very important. Consider the library from your family users' point of view and how the staff interact with them. Think about first impressions and how body language and non-verbal messages can either convey encouragement or show lack of interest and distain. Customer service is undoubtedly one of the most important areas for training and development in today's workplace. You might consider using recommended words or phrases to greet visitors. Review the signs and notices displayed around the library setting to ensure that your message is inclusive both culturally and from a gender perspective.

This is an opportunity for staff development. Leeds Library and Information Service is one of many authorities encouraging staff to undertake Frontline training and development. Frontline is an online course in reader-centred skills for library staff. Further details are available at www.openingthebook.co.uk/frontline. The training course is provided by Opening the Book, a company which specializes in reader development and library design and display. A customer-facing service will incorporate training into the daily work of the library service. Seek customer feedback on all aspects of your services. Consider how you can use analysis, self-assessment and observation to improve what is on offer.

Know your community: meeting needs
Community profiles

Library collections and services are shaped by the needs of the user community. Users are stakeholders, and identifying frequent users shows who the major stakeholders in the community are and which users form your current support base. Community profiles form the basis on which to identify the community needs for library services and facilities.

A community profile provides a range of information about a group of people, usually based on their geographic location. The profile can include information on:

- population
- age
- ethnic groups
- religion
- health and care
- economic status
- households

- car ownership
- travel to work
- deprivation indicators
- demographic data
- library statistics.

Developing such profiles at authority and local ward level should help in the development of services. The intelligence you gather will inform planning, target setting and performance measurement, including impact measures. The measures should also be applicable at a local level, demonstrating how libraries are responding to local needs and priorities based on the results of community profiling. The process should also help to identify those clients with special needs as a basis for designing and implementing services. This information will contribute to decisions on collection development policy. Where there is an ethnically diverse community you will have information to support decision making on the resources and services to meet the needs of that community. When undertaken periodically, community profiling can reflect the changing nature of the local community that the library serves.

Assessing local needs

You will want to reach out so as to encourage potential users to access your services. Library users are created by involving parents. You can use profiles of customers and potential customers to develop good services. General developmental information can be gathered about children, recognizing the development needs of young children - developmental stages include language levels, mobility, emotional maturity, communication skills and social development. Think about and be aware of how customers use their time in your early years library setting. Are there any ethnic or cultural time factors that you can use to encourage visits, for example celebrating particular holidays and festivals? Actually getting to your library may also be an issue if families are dependent on local public transport or if there is nowhere to park the car. Events and holidays within the school calendar will be important in terms of family visits. Think about the family constraints.

CASE STUDY Significant outcomes of the early years library provision in Wakefield in 2009

We have numerous examples of the significant impact that our Early Years Librarians have made in the lives of many young children and their parents in areas where literacy levels are particularly low.

- Approximately 95% of families using our Early Years Library have never used libraries before and perceptions of books, reading and learning are being positively changed.
- As disadvantaged young children develop a love of books and stories, literacy skills are being established.
- Children and parents from families without access to computers in the home have developed IT skills in a non-threatening environment, either to access information or to assist with writing CVs and job applications.
- Professional help has enabled parents to enrol on IT/Basic Skills training courses or to take a leading role in the community through fund raising, chairing meetings, volunteering within the Sure Start community and successfully gaining employment.
- Children with little or no confidence and poor communication skills have started to interact at story sessions and developed new social skills in the friendly environment.
- Families who feel isolated, including Asian families, asylum seekers and Travellers have discovered a safe, non-threatening environment in which to access help with literacy and information.
- Parents and children have had significant involvement in the development of the service.
- Where families have needed additional support from other agencies, librarians have been able to assist with the referral process.

Cath Threapleton, Principal Cultural Officer:
Children and Social Cohesion, Wakefield

Developing effective partnerships: with other professionals and partner organizations

Library and information practitioners have a tradition of networking with other professional groups and developing communities of practice. Working in early years provision, you are most likely to be involved in a multi-professional team made up of representatives from different professional groups or involving members from different organizations. Sullivan and Skelcher (2002) highlighted the rise in collaborative working between public, business and voluntary and community sectors. Collaboration is now central to the way in which public policy is made, managed and delivered in the UK. Funding, and the authority for the development and delivery of public policy, are increasingly located in collaborative ventures involving a range of governmental, business, voluntary and community agencies. This is the bigger picture discussed in Chapter 1, and for you as a player in a multidisciplinary team your story-time sessions fit into the increasingly complex landscape of early years provision in the UK. This is why the role of the librarian is so important. Partnership working is seen as an important strategy for tackling complex issues such as social inclusion and supporting the lifelong learning agenda. Many workplace settings now require the delivery of services or projects by a series of teams, each one a multidisciplinary team made up of a range of different professionals. This presents particular challenges for the team leaders in a complex work environment. Staff in the same teams may be employed under different contractual arrangements and line-managed by different managers working in different agencies, each with its own operating procedures and practices.

The following experience of a Sure Start librarian highlights this:

> Partnership work is fantastic most of the time. When I initially started with Sure Start they tried to give me three line managers so I said 'Can I just have one please!' We have Sure Start targets to reach and library targets to reach. Instead of me having two performance appraisals, one with the library manager and one with the Sure Start programme manager, we eventually arranged for me to have one appraisal with both managers present. That makes much more sense but it took a year to achieve this.
>
> Sure Start librarian

Partnership working can present challenges and barriers, particularly in cross-sector partnerships, where participants can often have different strategic priorities and work to different time-frames. Rankin et al. (2007) found that the early years librarians in their Wakefield case-study area were achieving very successful results in the services they offered and the varied outreach activities provided, but the funding for their posts was from non-core sources and a potential complication for sustainability was that they were not directly line-managed by the public library service. Some of the challenges associated with this type of multidisciplinary team work are discussed further in Chapter 14, where we look at projects and planning. A key message here is that librarians working in inter-organizational teams can play an important role as connectors. Networking with other organizations can provide the early years library practitioner with information about other services that are available to families, and this will enhance your role as an information provider and referral agent. In effective partnerships, there is also evidence of other professionals acting as advocates for early years library provision. For example, Sawyer, Pickstone and Hall (2007) evaluated the promotion of speech and language in 15 Sure Start local programmes. One of their key findings mentions collaboration with early years librarians, using books to promote language skills and develop an interest in books. A recommendation of theirs is that the contribution of early years librarians should be examined and developed further.

CASE STUDY Partnership work in action: successful referral

Adam, aged 3, came regularly to the story-time sessions in The Rainbow Library. His mum was worried about his speech and language development and his behaviour. She eventually felt confident enough to speak to the early years librarian about her concerns. Through the local partnership's record keeping and information sharing, the librarian made a referral to the family support team and the family now has the needed speech therapy support. The early years library staff are also working with Adam in the group activity sessions to improve his speech and his attitude to others.

Rainbow Librarian, Airedale Library and Family Centre, Castleford

Good management and leadership skills are important, and early years librarians need not only to work in a team with the other librarians but also to promote ongoing discussion and negotiation with members of staff in other services. It is important to have an understanding of your parent organization's strategy and business plan and to be able to implement decisions. The effective practitioner will develop good political and advocacy skills. Remember, an advocate is a person who publicly supports or recommends a particular cause or policy. A key part of your work will be to develop co-operative programmes with other agencies. This may also involve developing policies and procedures applying to children's services on the basis of current legislation.

CASE STUDY Partnership work: co-operating with other agencies

A young mum who regularly attended Once Upon a Rhyme with her toddler and baby stopped coming. I was concerned because I knew there was a history of post-natal depression. I contacted her and she came in to the library and asked to speak to me. After she explained what she had been experiencing, I suggested that we should make a referral to the Family Support team. A care package was put together which included some respite care for the children. She is now recovering. Allowing her time to catch up with sleep and professional help through her GP was all she needed to regain her strength and feeling of self-worth.

Rainbow Librarian, Airedale Library and Family Centre, Castleford

The librarian will need skills beyond a love of books and children, as a key part of your role is serving the whole family, as opposed to only the child. Effective teamwork has many advantages in supporting children and their families. There are challenges for organizations, agencies and managers in providing structures and systems that enable practitioners to effectively carry out their roles and responsibilities. There may be consequences for effective joint working when preconceived ideas and stereotypes influence team attitudes and practices.

Children's librarians work hard at breaking through the stereotype by engaging in challenging community outreach work and creative partnerships (Rankin and Butler, 2011).

Partnerships: encouraging parents and carers to get involved

Children's centres are key to encouraging parents to get actively involved in their children's early learning, which we know can impact positively on children's attainment when they reach school. A key part of your role is to promote active partnerships with parents and to communicate effectively with families. Babies and young children cannot visit your library setting on their own – they need to be brought there by a parent or carer. You need to encourage that adult to visit and to engage with the resources and services you have on offer. Many may be easily put off by their own early experience of using a library; maybe they have never used one. Even the name 'library' in a children's centre may be off-putting to some adults. As an effective practitioner, treat parents as partners. White reminds us that 'Librarians have the great advantage of having a relationship with a parent or care-giver that is voluntary and based on mutual trust and respect; a partnership where both are dedicated to achieving the best for the child' (White, 2002, 3). You may not be able to have a one-to-one impact on babies or young children, but you should maximize the opportunity to influence their primary carers.

CASE STUDY Local community involvement in the local library

Parents and children were actively involved throughout the planning and development of the Sunshine Library and were consulted during the drafting of the plans. They helped select stock and loan materials, furniture and equipment. They were involved in choosing the farmyard theme for the library interior and the 'Sunshine' name for the library. 'Over the five years that the services have been operating [professional library] staff have developed services to meet local needs – it is impossible to have a 'one-size-fits all service.'

Sunshine Librarian, Wakefield

Parents have the best understanding of their own children, and you can use this knowledge to help provide resources and services to meet the children's needs. When parents support their children's literacy they make much better progress. These early experiences make a great difference to children's later achievements. Encourage parents to read and write with their children at home and advocate their supporting and being part of their children's literacy development. However, do advise them against over-pressuring their child. The child's enjoyment and motivation are of utmost importance. You could organize literacy workshops for parents, or invite them in to support and be part of children's learning through play. Parents and carers are in the best position to help young children get ready to read because:

1   young children have short attention spans; they can do activities for short bits of time throughout the day.
2   parents know their children best and can help them learn in ways and at times that are easiest for them.
3   parents are tremendous role models - if children see that their parents value and enjoy reading, they will follow their lead.
4   children learn best by doing things - and they love doing things with their parents. So parents should read with their children every day.

Interactions that occur between young children and their carers are important, as they not only promote close relationships and early language development but also contribute to children's intellectual development. Practitioners in close contact with parents, such as health visitors and childcare workers, are in a good position to support and encourage parents. This includes you, the early years library practitioner, as you can all work together to suggest ways in which parents and their young children can begin the early literacy journey together.

Understanding the information needs of parents

Although we have been focusing on the needs of young children, their parents and carers are also adult learners with their own individual needs. People do not always know what information needs they have and some parents may not feel confident about asking questions. They may not know that they have an information gap, or may be unwilling to recognize it. Despite being in the very best position to introduce their children to literacy, many parents lack the confidence and knowledge to fulfil the role of their baby's first educator. According to Nicholas (2000), there are many factors involved in the meeting of information needs, including occupation, cultural background, the personality of the individual and their level of awareness and training. Time, access to available resources, costs and information overload will also play a part. The librarian should have a good knowledge of the client group - children and their families. To effectively support this community you should have an understanding of the theory of children's learning and its implications for the provision of library services. By providing support for parents through a parenting collection and referral services you are encouraging a family-friendly library environment. To enable effective communication with parents and carers it is helpful to keep the following guidelines in mind (adapted from Feinberg, Deerr et al., 2007, 87–8):

- *Anticipate that parents will ask questions.* Be ready to deal with enquiries of a sensitive nature and know how to provide referral information to partner professionals in the family support team. It is important for support staff in the library setting to be aware of partner organizations.
- *Give advice based on qualifications and experience.* It is important to remember that a librarian is not a personal friend, counsellor or social worker. There is a fine line between providing information and offering advice. Your role is to offer professional support to the family, as opposed to assuming the role of being a personal friend. Know when to refer to others who are qualified to help.
- *Be approachable but draw boundaries.* You cannot solve all problems, but use listening skills to determine what the parent actually wants. Ask pertinent questions so that you can refer parents to the appropriate agency for help or make the contact on their behalf. Personal boundaries are also important. Become familiar with local resources and family support services, as parents in need may need information quickly.

A study commissioned by the National Evaluation of Sure Start (NESS) describes how involving parents can be very empowering. The investigation used six Sure Start case-study areas to take a closer look at parents' experiences of empowerment and the types of mutual support and community action that had been developed. The researchers 'found substantial evidence for experiences of individual parent empowerment' (Williams and Churchill, 2006, 5). Parents in the study expressed the value of Sure Start in terms of increased confidence, skills and self-esteem as parents. One factor that influenced the opportunities for empowerment involved transforming professional relationships with parents. Williams and Churchill (2006) note that many parents commented that Sure Start staff treated them differently from other professionals in the health, education and welfare services; this involved being welcoming, friendly, supportive and non-judgemental. The study also found that when Sure Start local programmes provided responsive, accessible, available and inclusive services this also enhanced parents' access to resources. This involved dedicated outreach work, flexible times and locations for activities and regular information in the community, targeted at those with and without English language skills (Williams and Churchill, 2006, 7). Empowering local communities was also an element, and this meant that teams needed to have community development skills as well as family support and health-related expertise. Although the NESS study did not specifically involve library services, these findings echo the evidence gathered by the early years librarians in the Wakefield early years libraries.

More positive outcomes from the Sunshine Library

I really don't know what I would have done without the Sunshine, I really don't know how I would have coped. Nobody knew how depressed I was – it was the only place I could face coming to.

Mum who has a child with Down's syndrome

Libraries like the Sunshine should be accessible to all communities. The long-term problems resulting from low literacy levels could be vastly reduced if the first experiences of books and reading materials were like those available to the lucky children living in the Wakefield West Sure Start area.

Local parent

Librarians working with the early years can create opportunities for communication and develop relationships with parents. This can be done in an informal way by involving parents in interactive story sessions or inviting them to help with puppet shows. Some early years settings have very successfully involved parents in designing and making storysacks based on themes of interest to the local community. You are creating library users by involving parents. Librarians will be well positioned to talk to local people about what services they might like and to gather views on what is already available. Consider the potential barriers involved in local community use and be brave about considering changes. You may need to challenge the 'usual way' of doing something.

In some locations there is also the challenge of how to communicate with parents who are working long hours or are simply very busy. They may not know about your services or not be able to access the library because of restricted opening times. Consider how they can be encouraged to visit your library setting and get involved in activities with their young children. Families are all different and children may live with one or both parents, with carers or with other relatives in an extended family. Ask parents for their views on your services. One way of encouraging contact is to display lists of greeting words in English and other languages. You can then invite parents and families to contribute and add to the display. As an effective practitioner you should value each child's culture and you can help them to make connections between experiences at home, at the library and in the whole community.

Involving fathers

So far we have discussed parents and families supporting early literacy and making library visits. More often than not it is the mums who are involved. It is equally important that fathers have access to similar opportunities to interact with their babies and form close relationships through playing, chatting, singing songs and telling stories with them. They also have a part to play in promoting early language skills. The topic of fathers' involvement has been receiving recognition by groups of experts involved in securing the well-being of children and families (Pattnaik, 2013). The positive role that fathers can play in promoting early literacy has been established, and the stereotypical image of father reading the newspaper conveys an attitude about literacy and presents a powerful message about the importance of reading as an activity (Palm, 2013, 14). Male socialization around the importance of reading and what is important to read influences both attitudes and behaviours that fathers bring to their interactions with young children. The 'Story time with Dad' case study by Carolyn Bourke from Fairfield City Library in Australia is a great example of a partnership targeting preschool-aged children and their fathers or other male relatives (see page 239).

To support fathers' involvement you can select books which promote good father figures as well as good mother figures, and plan to hold events at times when fathers are most likely to be able to attend. Staff in early years settings (centres and libraries) tend to be predominantly female. This makes it doubly important that fathers get involved whenever possible, to act as positive role models. Research findings by the Pre-school Learning Alliance on fathers' involvement in early years settings highlighted the growing awareness of the important role fathers play in their children's learning and development. It is a key component of the inclusion agenda advocated by government and other organizations and agencies (Kahn, 2005). Reaching and engaging fathers is one of the core aims of children's centres and the challenge is to get fathers involved even before their baby is born. The National Literacy Trust (NLT) has produced a publication aimed at professionals who work with parents, *Getting the Blokes on Board: involving fathers and male carers with their children*, which contains ideas for getting dads and male carers reading with their children (NLT, 2007).

Some top tips for engaging dads

Children are often the biggest motivator – give dads the opportunity to do something with or for their children.

Use the mums – many mums act as 'gatekeepers' for their children's education, so involve them in encouraging dads to get on board.

Timing – as dads may be more likely to be at work during the day, think about other times when they might be available, such as early mornings, evenings or weekends.

Know your background – be persistent, creative, patient and sensitive in the
recruitment of fathers. They like to do something, not talk about it – use
hands-on, activity-based sessions.

Plan for long-term commitment – don't worry about numbers, as word of
mouth will help if you are successful. Speak to them directly – events
labelled 'for parents' tend to attract mothers. Address letters to fathers
and try other communication routes like text messages and e-mails.

Consult – ask fathers for their advice on publicity, recruitment, timings, activity
themes.

Remember that not all dads are the same.

Look at the whole organization's attitude – you have only one chance to make
a first impression and that needs to be a positive experience.

Allow time for staff training and discussion of the issues around encouraging
dads to bring their babies and young children into the early years library.

(Adapted from 'Top Tips for Engaging Dads', NLT, 2007, 6)

Fathers have an important role to play in their children's literacy development, yet a survey for the National Year of Reading (Dugdale and Clark, 2008) showed that fathers are less likely to read to their children than are mothers, and when they do it is more likely to be with young children. In a study for the NLT, Clark, Osborne and Dugdale (2009) showed that fathers are the second most important person to inspire children's reading, so it can be seen that it is really important that practitioners encourage fathers to be involved in the development of their children's literacy skills. An increased desire to read with their children was expressed by some fathers in Clark's (2009) research, evidencing the proven relationship between the father's involvement in early literacy and better child outcomes. This is further demonstrated by the comments from one father in research by Potter et al. (2013) on engaging fathers from disadvantaged areas in their children's early learning transitions. This father's confidence in his own literacy skills had led to changes in the ways in which he interacted with his daughter:

It is enjoying these times with the bairn ... when I was a young one I found it difficult to read out loud, but because of these groups, I am wanting to get more involved – these groups are making me want to – I am reading to her and she loves it – I read her a bed-time story.

(Potter et al., 2013, 8)

A valuable way of encouraging fathers is through appreciating both their and their young children's technology experiences. Marsh's (2007) research in a working-class community in the north of England identified the 'emergent techno-literacy' practices of a group of children aged between two and a half and four years and documented the importance of recognizing these family practices in early childhood education and care settings. As Levy (2011) argues, reading is no longer about just reading books, and young children are accessing a wide variety of books, comics and digital screen texts.

Involving grandparents

In today's busy society, where the vast majority of mums are out at work during the day, many grandparents have an important role in childcare and have regular contact with their grandchildren. Grandparents can make a huge contribution to the lives of their grandchildren and to their learning and development. This is potentially a large group of the population, who form an important part of

children's support networks. There is an emotional bond between children and their grandparents. Grandparents have the experience to exercise particular patience in listening to young children. They can be encouraged to tell their stories and share their experiences in library story-telling sessions (as illustrated in Figure 5.2). The 'Communicate with your Grandchild' pack has been developed by 'Talk To Your Baby', the early language campaign of the NLT which encourages parents and carers to talk more to children from birth to three. Produced in partnership with the Grandparents Association, it recognizes the important role that grandparents play in the development of their grandchildren's communication and language skills, and the pack contains ideas for grandparents on talking to children in everyday situations, sharing books together and enjoying nursery rhymes and music.

Figure 5.2
Grandfather and grandson sharing a story

The home learning environment

As affirmed in the earlier chapters of this book, what parents and carers do makes a real difference to young children's development. A child's life chances are most heavily predicated on their development in the first five years of life. Family background, parental education, good parenting and the opportunities for learning and development in the early years have more impact on children's emotional and social development than does money, and so determine potential and attainment (Field, 2010). Melhuish et al.'s (2001; 2008) research finds that the home learning environment has a greater influence on a child's intellectual and social development than parental occupation, education or income. What parents do with their children is more important in terms of the children's outcomes than who they are in terms of social class and income. Children's understanding and use of language at two predicts how well they perform on school entry assessments, including reading, maths and writing.

The Effective Provision of Pre-School Education project (Sylva et al., 2004) developed an index to measure the quality of the home learning environment. This measures a range of activities that parents undertake with preschool children that are related to improvements in children's learning and have a positive effect on their development. For example, reading to children, teaching songs and nursery rhymes, painting and drawing, playing with letters and numbers, visiting the library, teaching the alphabet, teaching numbers, taking children on visits and creating regular opportunities for them to play with their friends at home were all associated with higher intellectual and social/behavioural scores.

The My Home Library website has printable bookplates that can be downloaded and stuck into favourite books (www.myhomelibrary.org/home.html). Parents can be encouraged to stick them in the baby's first picture books. You can suggest that families write a thank-you note or a birthday card together. Another idea is to set up a home library with some favourite books on a special shelf.

More times for book sharing

Encourage parents to set aside a special time each day, such as nap time, bedtime or after meals. It is better to share books when parent and child are both in a relaxed mood. Reading together at bedtime is not only important for creating settled routines and listening to stories. It is also key in forming close, warm and sharing relationships. Parents can also take advantage of 'waiting' times to share books – on trips, at the health centre, waiting at the bus stop or queuing at the supermarket checkout. Reading just 5 or 10 minutes a day to young children helps them to get ready to read on their own.

CASE STUDY 'Picture This' in Blackburn with Darwen

The 'Picture This' project was designed to encourage adults with basic literacy skills to share books with their children. It can be embarrassing for people to admit to poor reading skills, but this can be avoided by using picture books and encouraging parents and carers to share them with their children. Reading proficiency isn't necessary when using picture books, as the illustrations usually tell the stories. This type of scheme works only with help from parents. One of the achievements in this particular area was to encourage local families to attend a series of themed sessions.

Conclusion

This chapter has looked at how librarians can be involved in partnerships with other professionals and with parents and local communities. A key aim is to develop family-friendly services and a welcoming atmosphere. We have considered how librarians can provide quality, focused services and help to break down the barriers to those services that may be apparent in the community.

Useful organizations

Chartered Institute of Library and Information Professionals (CILIP), www.cilip.org.uk
Grandparents' Association, www.grandparents-association.org.uk
National Literacy Trust, www.literacytrust.org.uk
Opening the Book, www.openingthebook.com
Pre-school Learning Alliance, www.pre-school.org.uk
Talk to Your Baby, www.literarytrust.org.uk/talktoyourbaby

References

Clark, C. (2009) *Why Fathers Matter to Their Children's Literacy*, National Literacy Trust, www.literacytrust.org.uk/assets/0000/0770/Father_review_2009.pdf.

Clark, C., Osborne, S. and Dugdale, G. (2009) *Reaching Out with Role Models*, National Literacy Trust.

Dugdale, G. and Clark, C. (2008) *Literacy Changes Lives: an advocacy resource*, National Literacy Trust.

Eisenstadt, N. (2011) *Providing a Sure Start*, The Policy Press.

Feinberg, S. and Feldman, S. (1996) *Serving Families and Children through Partnerships: a how-to-do-it manual for librarians*, Neal-Schuman Publishers.

Feinberg, S. and Rogoff, C. (1998) Diversity Takes Children to a Family Friendly Place, *American Libraries*, August, 50–2.

Feinberg, S., Deerr, K., Jordan, B., Byrne, M. and Kropp, L. (2007) *The Family-centered Library Handbook: rethinking library spaces and services*, Neal-Schuman Publishers.

Field, F. (2010) *The Foundation Years: preventing poor children becoming poor adults. The report of the Independent Review on Poverty and Life Chances*, Cabinet Office, http://webarchive.nationalarchives.gov.uk/20110120090128/http://povertyreview. independent.gov.uk/media/20254/poverty-report.pdf.

Glass, N. (1999) Sure Start: the development of an early intervention programme for young children in the United Kingdom, *Children and Society*, **13**, 257-64.

Kahn, T. (2005) *Fathers' Involvement in Early Years Settings: findings from research*, Report prepared for the Department for Education and Skills, Pre-Schooling Learning Alliance.

Kropp, L. G. (2004) Family Place Libraries: building strong families, strong libraries, *Journal of the Library Administration and Management Section of the New York Library Association*, **1** (1), 39-47.

Lees, J. (2015) A Children's Centre Manager's Perspective. In Brock, A. (ed.), *The Early Years Reflective Practice Handbook*, Routledge.

Levy, R. (2011) *Young Children Reading at Home and at School*, Sage.

Lewis, J. (2011) From Sure Start to Children's Centres: an analysis of policy change in English early years programmes, *Journal of Social Policy*, **40** (1), 71-88.

Marsh, J. (2007) New Literacies and Old Pedagogies: recontextualizing rules and practices, *International Journal of Inclusive Education*, **11** (3) 267-81.

Melhuish, E. C., Sylva, K., Sammons, P., Siraj-Blatchford, I., Taggart, B. and Phan, M. (2008) Effects of the Home Learning Environment and Preschool Center Experience upon Literacy and Numeracy Development in Early Primary School, *Journal of Social Issues*, **64** (1) 95-114.

Melhuish, E., Sylva, K., Sammons, P., Siraj-Blatchford, I. and Taggart, B. (2001) *Social, Behavioural and Cognitive Development at 3-4 years in Relation to Family Background. The effective provision of pre-school education*, EPPE project, Department for Education and Employment/The Institute of Education, University of London

Nicholas, D. (2000) *Assessing Information Needs: tools, techniques and concepts for the internet age*, Aslib.

NLT (2007) 'Top Tips for Engaging Dads', *Getting the Blokes on Board*, National Literacy Trust, www.literacytrust.org.uk/assets/0000/2298/Blokes.pdf.

Palm, G. (2013) Fathers in Early Literacy. In Pattnaik, J. (ed.), *Father Involvement in Young Children's Lives: a global analysis*. Educating the Young Child 6, Advances in Theory and Research, Implications for Practice, Springer.

Pattnaik, J. (ed.) (2013) *Father Involvement in Young Children's Lives: a global analysis*, Educating the Young Child 6, Advances in Theory and Research, Implications for Practice, Springer.

Potter, C., Walker, G. and Keen, B. (2013) 'I Am Reading to Her and She Loves It': benefits of engaging fathers from disadvantaged areas in their children's early learning transitions, *Early Years: An International Journal of Research and Development*, **33** (1), 74-89.

Rankin, C. and Butler, F. (2011) Issues and Challenges for the Interdisciplinary Team in

Supporting the 21st Century Family. In Brock, A. and Rankin, C. (eds), *Professionalism in the Interdisciplinary Early Years Team: supporting young children and their families*, Continuum.

Rankin, C., Brock, A., Halpin, E. and Wootton, C. (2007) *The Role of the Early Years Librarian in Developing an Information Community: a case study of effective partnerships and early years literacy within a Sure Start project in Wakefield*, paper presented in the conference proceedings of the Canadian Association of Information Sciences, Montreal, 2007.

Richardson, A. (2013) *Sure Start Children's Centres: a study of complex social change*. Paper presented at 23rd European Early Childhood Education Research conference, 'Values, Culture and Contexts', Tallin, Estonia, 28–31 August 2013.

Sawyer, V., Pickstone, C. and Hall, D. (2007) *Promoting Speech and Language: a themed study in fifteen Sure Start local programmes*, www.surestart.gov.uk/_doc/p0002441.pdf.

Sullivan, H. and Skelcher, C. (2002) *Working Across Boundaries: collaboration in public services*, Palgrave Macmillan.

Sylva, K., Melhuish, E. C., Sammons, P., Siraj-Blatchford, I. and Taggert, B. (2004) *The Effective Provision of Pre-school Education [EPPE] Project: final report*, Department for Education and Skills/Institute of Education, University of London.

White, D. R. (2002) Working Together to Build a Better World: the importance of youth services in the development and education of children and their parents, *OLA Quarterly*, **8** (3), Fall, 15–19.

Williams, F. and Churchill, H. (2006) *Empowering Parents in Sure Start Local Programmes*, National Evaluation of Sure Start (NESS) Institute for the Study of Children, Families and Social Issues, Birkbeck, University of London. Research Report NESS/2006/FR/018.

CHAPTER 6

Resources for early years libraries: books, toys and other delights

Carolynn Rankin and Avril Brock

Introduction

This chapter is about the most important resources in the early years library - those are, of course, the books with their exciting stories, tantalizing tales and wonderful pictures and illustrations. However, this chapter is not just about collections of books but also about how to select and collect a range of resources to meet community needs, in particular the target audience of young children and their families. A range of exciting resources should be available in the bright, welcoming environment of the early years library (as illustrated in Figure 6.1). It is important to have knowledge about children and their families' culture, heritage, language and interests, so as to ensure that a breadth of valuable resources is provided. The chapter also illustrates why early years librarians need to have knowledge of diverse resources such as treasure baskets, toy libraries, storysacks and Bookstart packs. We will discuss how to select books that are appropriate for babies and young children, girls and boys, additional-language learners and children with special educational needs, not forgetting their parents. Sources of information to facilitate selection, and reviews of resources, have been included to make this job easier.

Collection development and management

Before we take a more detailed look at the resources in an early years collection, consider the underlying principles and requirements of collection development (see Sullivan, 2013). An understanding of this is important if you are to be an effective advocate for your library and user community. To be able to manage your resources effectively it is good practice to develop an understanding of how your organization operates and knowledge of the local policies. The starting point

Figure 6.1 *A bright and welcoming environment*

in collection development is to decide what stock (resources and materials) you are going to include in the library. How is this decided? Information and guidance should be available in the documents produced by library authorities. Many libraries will create collection development policies and stock selection guides to better plan their collections and to justify the allocation of resources. This documentation should reflect statutory requirements and legislation and the requirement to provide resources within a best-value framework. Libraries are under scrutiny to get better value for money from the suppliers who provide books and other resources. Although library authorities will have different approaches to how this is managed, the underlying principles are the same. Collection development is defined as:

> the process of planning a library's stock acquisitions first to cater for immediate needs, and more importantly to acquire a collection capable of meeting future requirements. The term implies a desire for a depth and quality of stock, but it cannot be separated from the need to exploit the collection effectively.
>
> (Feather and Sturgess, 1997, 61)

As a management principle, stock should be selected on the basis of written guidelines and criteria to ensure that there will be a unified approach and that the selection methodology will be cost-effective. Some key questions to be considered are:

- how stock is selected and made accessible
- how stock is maintained and promoted
- why some stock is kept and other material is removed.

The stock policy or collection management plan will provide an overall statement relating to the acquisition, selection and withdrawal of stock for the organization. It should be kept under regular review and seen as an evolving document, to reflect the needs of the community it serves. Communities change over time and data can be gathered to aid decision making through community profiling (as discussed in Chapter 5).

Outsourced procurement

Library authorities can take a number of different approaches to the procurement and supply of books and other resources. One option is to outsource key traditional functions like book selection, cataloguing and acquisitions (Edmonds, 2012). Libraries deciding to outsource will go 'out to tender' to select the best value supplier for the procurement process. This 'supplier selection' means that all general library materials are selected by the supplier, usually based on a set of requirements provided by the customer library. It is recognized that very specific requirements, for example Asian-language materials, may need to be purchased from specialist suppliers and publishers outside of the contract. An argument in favour of using the supplier-selection approach is that time saved as a result can be used to deliver front-line services. Leeds Library and Information Services uses supplier selection to acquire stock for the 55 libraries and network of mobile libraries across the metropolitan area. A detailed specification is provided to the book supplier, which includes a stock-spending plan for the early years category. This is regularly updated and staff can add titles to the lists. High priority is given to services for children and young people, in the context of Leeds City Council's aim to be a child-friendly city:

We buy a full range of materials for children and young people regardless of age, ability and culture, to enable them to develop imagination, creativity and social skills, aid educational progress, and instil a love of books and reading. Our specification to the supplier will request the following Board books for sharing with very young children.

- Picture books for a wide range of ages including dual-language books (parallel texts in English and another language, e.g. Urdu, Chinese, French).
- Material suitable for children who are beginning to read alone.
- Stories, both contemporary and classic.
- Storytapes, CDs and eBooks and eAudio for a wide range of ages.

(Leeds Library and Information Services, 2013, 7)

A number of library authorities also gain benefits through consortium membership, where bulk-purchasing arrangements aim to reduce costs while improving efficiencies in terms of supply times and availability of materials.

Direct procurement

In contrast to the supplier-selection model, many library services still work independently by procuring stock directly from suppliers on an individual basis. Some public library authorities have established buying teams to select children's stock. Staff will use various methods to select resources, by looking at books themselves in selection meetings or in suppliers' showrooms and by using publishers' lists, catalogues and trade publications. Many staff may be involved in the selection, and some authorities will ask for feedback from readers. There are pros and cons to the different approaches to procurement, based on financial and other criteria. Effective practitioners will be familiar with the procedures in their organization.

The plan may also include:

- guidelines for collection maintenance, as worn-out stock will need to be withdrawn - this activity is often referred to as weeding the collection
- guidelines for in-service training of current and future staff.

The situation with regard to supply of library stock may not be so clear in some children's centres, as it will depend on the funding and partnership arrangements.

The early years collection

Having considered the general principles of how library authorities acquire stock, let us look in more detail at collection development in the early years library. Books will form the core, but remember also that the collection in an early years library 'is a physical entity which includes materials in print and in visual, auditory, tactile and electronic formats with appropriate forms of delivery' (Van Orden and Bishop, 2001, 12). The resources will be expanded to include babies, infants and toddlers and should provide materials in a variety of formats to encourage play, creativity and development - the emphasis is on having fun.

What is the role of the librarian in collection development? The librarian's professional skills include the selection and use of materials, and this involves decision-making skills. If we look to a professional library source, the IFLA *Guidelines for Children's Library Services* state that:

> Children's libraries should include a variety of developmentally appropriate materials in all formats, including printed materials (books, periodicals, comics, brochures), media (CDs, DVDs, cassettes), toys, learning games, computers, software and [internet] connectivity.
>
> (IFLA, 2003, 9)

The process of creating the policy for the early years is important, as it will involve a knowledge and understanding of the particular user community. As with any service provider, you need to know the needs of your market before you can begin to provide the resources. The allocation of limited budgets requires careful and well-informed decision making; this is an important aspect of business planning. The planning will identify the community or market to be serviced and will describe the product - the materials that are available and how to acquire them. It is important to involve those with a vested interest; for example, you can include parents in developing ideas for the parenting collection, which will be discussed later in this chapter. Sharing information about the collection development plan or stock plan can also be a public relations tool. For the library this can be another means of communicating with the stakeholders. Many libraries publish their collection development and stock plans on the local authority website.

The purpose of the collection development plan in an early years library setting is to establish guidelines for current and future staff on acquiring stock and developing the collection. The plan will create a collection development policy which explains why certain materials are in the collection. It could include the selection criteria and the procedures used, as selection is a complex decision-making process.

Selecting materials within a framework of given criteria can be regarded as good practice. It may not be enough to say 'I've done this for years - I just know what is needed in the early years library', or 'I like this particular author', or 'Chris, who runs the library in the community centre, makes the decisions'. Some librarians make selections based on guidelines passed on by word of mouth. The feeling may be: why bother documenting what you do in practice, as these decisions are based on experience? While not wishing to decry experience or knowledge, in our opinion this informal approach is not very professional from a management perspective. You will leave yourself open to being challenged on the type and quantity of materials you are providing, and in the current financial climate it is more than likely that you will have to defend the budget allocations. A policy designed and produced by those who have best knowledge of the library service and its users should make planning easier for the future.

Staff are an important source of information about the collection and how it is used. Librarians have a vested interest in developing language and reading skills. The selection and acquisition policies should ensure the availability of appropriate materials for both children and their parents and carers. The materials should be acquired in a planned, systematic way and should reflect language and cultural backgrounds. Involving parents in selection is a valuable way of building good partnerships with the user community.

How do you do it? Guidelines for book selection

The IFLA *Guidelines for Children's Library Services* (IFLA, 2003, 9) provide the following information on selection criteria. In building collections and services, librarians should choose materials which are

- high quality
- age appropriate
- current and accurate
- a reflection of a variety of values and opinions
- a reflection of local community culture
- an introduction to the global community.

What information should be included in a collection development document? How do librarians decide what book stock is important to acquire? We can look at examples from Kirklees Cultural Services and the Bookstart programme to get some idea of criteria for selecting the all-important children's books.

Example 1: Children's book selection – Kirklees Cultural Services
Board books
- Sturdy form. Clear photos or pictures, minimum, clear text, bright colours. Can be tactile or have flaps etc. to stimulate the senses.
- Content – everyday, familiar objects/situations. Rhythm, rhyme and repetition. Questions and sound effects. Age: suitable for babies and toddlers from birth to two years.

Picture books
- Larger format, longer stories. Language can be more challenging.
- Content as before but also can be more imaginative, abstract, dealing with the wider world and developing emotions. Pictures carry story as well as text. Age: approximately 2–5yrs.

'Learners' for beginner readers
- Generally one short story. Simple sentences. Smaller format (around 50 pages). Well illustrated – speech bubbles are clear and not too complex. Age: 5–7yrs.

Parents' collection
- Books to support parenting skills and the development of early childhood skills, e.g. reading, writing, maths and play. Age range: for parents of children aged 5 years and under.
- Hand in hand. Picture books and some information books for children that deal with special situations and are better suited for use in conjunction with an adult, e.g.
  - dealing with change: moving house, new baby, death
  - new experiences: visiting the dentist, flying in an aeroplane.

Branching Out (n.d.)

Example 2: Book selection for Bookstart

Bookstart is the national agency promoting books and reading to people of every age and culture in the UK. The Bookstart packs are very successful and well known. Wendy Cooling, Bookstart's founder, explains that the books for the packs are selected by an independent panel which includes health visitors, speech and language therapists, early years educationalists and librarians. The varied cultural and social backgrounds of the children must be taken into account so choosing them is not as easy as it might sound.

> People forget that I'm buying books to go into every household in the country. I can't send everyone a very white, middle-class book with mummy, daddy, boy and girl. They'd probably bin it. I wouldn't buy a book totally centred on a pig, because of Muslim families. I worked with one-parent teenage mothers, and the last thing they wanted was a nice 'daddy' book. I'm looking for books that can literally go into any home and not cause offence.

(Cooling, 2007)

As a charity, Bookstart cannot afford to pay standard wholesale prices, so the team negotiates with publishers to buy the books very cheaply. Not all publishers can meet Bookstart's budget, so some titles cannot be included in the scheme. Bookstart provides details of its 'Policy on the selection process and criteria for books for Bookstart' on its website. The following criteria are used for choosing Bookstart-pack books and recommending books in Bookstart book lists:

1)   Quality of materials
Books must be well produced and printed. Board books must be safe and sturdy enough for the purpose. All books must meet the stringent health and safety standards of the UK and Europe and have the CE quality mark.

2)   Content and suitability
We use two books that have a good combination of all these qualities in our packs:

- books that are well illustrated and well photographed, that have appropriate text
- feely-touchy, interactive books that are exciting for babies and toddlers
- books suitable for the age range
- books that reflect baby's/child's experiences
- rhyme, rhythm and repetition, which are fun for babies and children and help them to learn.

We are committed to Equal Opportunities and address race and gender issues.

3)   Cost and availability
We generally purchase books at cost price or below from a range of children's publishers who have offered their help and have said they are 'Proud to Support Bookstart'.

Library collections will be shaped by the needs of the user community. The needs of the community cannot be effectively assessed by relying on data about materials already in demand and being circulated. This is one way of showing the needs and wants of the community but will relate only to the current user base and the materials already in the library stock. You will want to reach out so as to encourage potential users to access your services. Data collected via community profiling can be used to inform decision making about the resources you should provide at local level.

   Consider your policies and procedures relating to collection development and the loan and circulation of material to this client group. It is important to encourage parents to borrow the library materials to use in their home environment. This means that you need to consider having multiple copies of popular books and 'easy' joining and borrowing policies and procedures. Many parents can be put off by misconceptions about complicated joining regulations and heavy fines for overdue materials.

Selecting the book stock for an early years collection should be a very enjoyable experience, and Whitehead (2007), an early years specialist, says that choosing books for young children is a great responsibility, as we are directly influencing the views they will develop about literature, books and reading.

Selecting books for the early years collection
Selecting picture books

Picture books are the core of an early years library collection and are important because they enable us to explore the world around us. They will include books with multicultural content and can help to reflect the families in your catchment area as well as a view of the wider world. When championing the 'The Big Picture', a Booktrust national campaign promoting picture books, Children's Laureate Michael Rosen said 'Picture books are the fuse that lights our awareness that reading is full of intense pleasures' (Rosen, 2007).

Picture books and illustrations encourage children's vocabulary development, as the adult supplies the word or words for the pictures. Young children soon become accomplished at matching the words with the pictures. In early stages of language acquisition they will make appropriate sounds, which gradually turn into words over time. Parents soon begin to know whether the sound being uttered is the correct 'word' for each picture, as they will have developed knowledge about their child. Animal pictures are normally a very successful way into early sound and word formation, with cows mooing, lions roaring and dogs barking. Children can communicate meanings through sounds before they can articulate words. They also gain familiarity with objects and concepts, which develops both their vocabulary and their knowledge and understanding of the world. Large picture and storybooks enable children to get physically involved in pointing out what is happening and in labelling the characters and objects. Rankin and Brock give an example of a favourite picture book being shared across the generations: 'every new baby in our family is presented with a copy of the Ahlbergs' *The Baby's Catalogue*. The pictures reflect what we do in our family life' (Rankin and Brock, 2008, 67).

Books that are good for babies and toddlers will have:

- thick, sturdy cover and pages
- small size, for little hands

- bright, colourful pictures
- simple geometric shapes
- clear pictures
- pictures of human faces
- few words
- nursery rhymes.

Selecting board books

Board books with easy-to-see pictures and high contrast between the object and the background are excellent for a baby. Board books are easy for tiny fingers to handle and the pages won't tear. Babies respond best to books that have sharp contrast between the picture and the background. Wordless picture books provide an opportunity to make up stories to go with the pictures and lift-the-flap books add an element of delicious anticipation. For toddlers, the story can be more involved and pictures can have more detail. It is good to choose things they can relate to, such as pets or animals, dressing and meal times, and what they see and do as part of everyday life. Stories with rhyme and rhythm are also good, as are stories with repeated phrases or repeated happenings. To be inclusive, try to select books which have good father figures as well as mums.

Selecting dual-language books for the bilingual child

As stated in previous chapters, librarians should have knowledge about their client group, about the diversity of the communities and families. This should include knowledge of and respect for their different cultures, heritage and languages:

> In government documentation, the term most commonly used for children who speak other language beside English is EAL (English as an additional language) learners ... we use the term 'bilingual' because we believe it is broader and more inclusive, and represents more accurately the important idea, that for bilingual children, all their languages contribute to their whole language experience and their knowledge of the world.
>
> (Conteh and Brock, 2006, 2)

Through books, stories and illustrations, bilingual children can be introduced to new and complex language, contextualized in meaningful and interesting experiences. Story is thus an effective vehicle for shaping language in powerful and exciting ways (Conteh and Brock, 2007). Language and culture are central to identity, personal, social and emotional development, and it is therefore very important to reflect children's linguistic diversity and cultural heritage in the books they look at and have read to them. Parents also need to feel that they are involved in the learning processes and so need to have access to books that reflect their own cultural heritage, with stories and information that can help them to expand their children's experiences and knowledge. Parents in Bradford's Earlystart Project (Power and Brock, 2006) valued the books that had dual-language texts in their own first language and in English. They also appreciated that their children's first language and their burgeoning bilingualism was valued and respected by practitioners:

> 'I particularly like borrowing dual language books because my husband can't speak English but can read to our child in Bengali, which makes him feel involved.'
>
> (Power and Brock, 2006, 23)

There are now quite a number of books that have been translated into dual-language texts - including the 'Where's Spot?' (Hill, 1980) series, *Dear Zoo* (Campbell, 2010) and *Elmer's Weather*, (McKee, 1998) to mention only a few, which are in languages as diverse as Vietnamese, Gujarati, Chinese and Urdu. There are valuable organizations and websites noted at the end of this chapter to guide you to lists of books and stories that are ideal to use when working with bilingual children. The International Children's Digital Library provides free internet access to children's books in their original languages and this resource is discussed in more detail later in this chapter.

Selecting books for young boys

It is important to dispel the myth that boys do not like books. On the contrary, find a topic that engages a boy's interest, and he can easily be engrossed in a book. Favourites are topics such as pirates, castles, vehicles, dinosaurs or stories about boys and their fathers. Figure 6.2 illustrates boys enjoying time in the library.

SCENARIO Josh and Andrew as library users

Josh, aged 5, and Andrew, aged 3, now visit their local library regularly. Their parents had explained to the boys that the library was a place to be quiet and they behaved very well. On the first visit they stayed three hours; the boys were engrossed.

Simon, their dad, brought them on their third visit and was amazed how calm and absorbed they were.

Figure 6.2 *Boys enjoying time in the library*

Josh loves information books, particularly transport – cars, ships, rockets – and anything about dinosaurs and animals. At home his mum is reading him Roald Dahl books, serializing the *BFG*, *The Enormous Crocodile* and *Fantastic Mr Fox* (Dahl, 1982, 1978, 1970). During one library visit Josh found the CDs and brought them to show his mum; she had not realized they could be borrowed and the boys are now listening to stories in the car.

SCENARIO Young Tom the Pirate

Four-year-old Tom loves pirates – he has been known to dress up as a pirate, complete with eye-patch, hat and even temporary tattoos. He has a pirate playscape and pirate finger puppets. His favourite book is *1001 Pirate Things to Spot*, published by Usborne (Jones 2001).

Selecting books for children with special educational needs

Research on the Bookstart project has clearly shown that giving babies a love of books from the earliest age makes an enormous difference to language development and listening skills. Stories, songs and rhymes are also important in supporting bonding and developing a sense of well-being. This is no different for young children who are blind or partially sighted or deaf. This section looks at some of the resources developed to support babies and young children who have special educational needs.

Booktouch

Booktouch is a freely available Bookstart pack for blind and partially sighted babies and children, aged from birth to four years. Around 800 babies born each year are eligible for a Booktouch pack containing touch-and-feel books, some of which are in Braille. The pack and accompanying guidance leaflet were designed by Booktrust with advice from the Royal National Institute of Blind People (RNIB) and ClearVision (a national postal lending library). All babies need help in learning how a book works, which way to hold it, how to turn the pages and, eventually how to associate the marks on the page with language. The same is true for blind and partially sighted children, and many of the latter will eventually be able to read large print. Booktouch helps children become familiar with the concept of gathering information via their fingers. This is important for every child, but particularly for those who will go on to learn to read Braille, and read maps and diagrams by touch.

The pack also includes a leaflet with helpful tips about sharing books. Some of these tips will be the same as for any child – for example, all young children will enjoy it if you make sound effects to go with a story. But there are a few more considerations involved in reading with blind and partially sighted children, and advice is given on what kinds of pictures are best, what kind of text is easiest to read and what to consider when choosing books. Local authority visual-impairment teachers provided advice on the most appropriate books to include in the pack.

ClearVision

ClearVision is a national postal lending library of over 12,000 children's books with the text added in Braille or Moon (a simpler alternative to Braille). ClearVision books are designed for children with little or no sight to share with sighted children and adults. The collection includes tactile board books, simple stories for young children and stimulating books for newly fluent readers. ClearVision books are borrowed by over 800 families, schools, services for the visually impaired and libraries all over the UK. Anyone in the UK who needs children's books with a Braille text is welcome to join the ClearVision library. The books are ordinary children's picture books with added Braille (or Moon). They do not have enlarged print and are therefore not especially suitable for partially sighted children learning to read print. The books are designed to be shared and are suitable for any child who is learning Braille or who may do so in the future. Some of their 'readers' are babies and toddlers whose parents are keen to get them used to feeling Braille long before they learn to read it - in the same way as fully sighted babies see print everywhere before they can make sense of it.

ClearVision currently lends books to public libraries in the UK for an annual membership fee. Libraries can then lend on a local basis, enabling Braille readers to use the local library along with their family or school. A library's first loan will consist of 20 picture books or 10 books for newly fluent readers or a mixed loan of 10 picture books in grade 1 and 2 Braille and 6 books for newly fluent readers. ClearVision also lends books to families with visually impaired children throughout the UK. Membership is free for families, who are also welcome to contact ClearVision at any time to comment on the books or to request books on specific topics. It has 3500 titles and does not issue a booklist, so families need to provide information about the child (age, reading age, interests, classroom topics, etc.) and ClearVision will send appropriate books.

The way Braille is written in the UK is changing and Standard English Braille (SEB) is being replaced with Unified English Braille (UEB). This is already used in much of the English-speaking world, including Australia, Canada, New Zealand, South Africa, Nigeria and the USA. Ultimately it should mean more Braille materials (books, magazines, etc.) for everyone, because countries will be able to share resources (ClearVision, 2014).

Bookshine

Bookstart has added 'Bookshine' packs to its existing range of materials. Bookshine will help parents of deaf babies and children discover books together. The books and accompanying guidance materials for parents and carers have been chosen in partnership with the National Deaf Children's Society (NDCS) and parents of deaf children. The pack includes a touch-and-feel book and a book featuring simple British Sign Language (BSL) signs and an image of a child with a hearing aid, as it is important that deaf children see themselves in books.

Selecting books for the parenting collection

Library services will be very focused on promoting exciting materials for young library users – but don't forget the needs of their parents and carers. Most parents are not trained or educated about how to raise children. First-time parents, in particular, may be looking for information on how to bring up the new member of their family. In some cultures, parenting practice may be based on family tradition or experience. Where such traditional advice may not be available, information may be gained from professional practitioners. Families are also exposed to information and ideas through popular media: there are now many parenting magazines on the newsagents' shelves and 'nanny-says' types of programme on the television about coping with babies and toddlers. Parents who are well informed and feel confident and supported are better able to understand their role and provide good childcare. In communities where there is a lack of support and isolation in the parenting role, the adults are at risk of stress and depression. Libraries can support the information needs of parents and carers by providing a collection of parenting books and other resources, and by offering referral services when working in partnership with other organizations and agencies.

Leeds Libraries and Information Services has a 'family matters' collection in each of the libraries in Leeds. This includes books on family, feelings, health, new experiences, being safe and family learning. The 'healthy living' collections include books and DVDs designed to help families get healthy and stay healthy.

Parents need to know that the link between their involvement and the literacy environment of the home leads to a child's success at school. Familiarize yourself with reference materials and electronic resources aimed at parents and other professionals who support the family – this will be helpful in developing your role in the interdisciplinary teamwork. One way to provide education and support for parents and carers is to provide a collection of materials specifically aimed to meet their needs. These collections can include books, pamphlets, DVDs and audio books. Some parents may be first encouraged to use a computer in the library setting, and one idea is to bookmark websites on child development and parenting issues so as to promote computer literacy and encourage families to use the facilities. Experience has shown that it can be important to locate the parenting collection where it is easily accessible from the children's area.

Selection and management of the parenting collection

From a collection management perspective, the selection, acquisition, marketing and eventual weeding or withdrawal of the stock needs to be built into the ongoing work of the early years library. Agreement should be reached on the range of topics to be covered and the scope of the parenting collection. Who decides what goes into this collection? Are there selection criteria? Suggestions for topics to include would be general parenting, childcare, breastfeeding, toilet training, literacy and reading. There are some other considerations. The parenting collection should reflect the cultural diversity of the community it serves, but this may raise policy issues about the types of material you decide to provide. The parenting collection may be expanded to include material of interest to parents of school-age or teenaged children, as they may be the older siblings of your babies and young children. Some libraries target teen parents, who will have very specific support needs. Another policy decision is whether to provide duplicate copies of parenting resources in the main library collection and in branch and mobile collections.

Other resources in the early years library

In addition to the all-important books, the library can provide a range of exciting resources to encourage the development of language and literacy across the community. In this section we will discuss the provision of storysacks, treasure baskets and toy libraries.

Storysacks and storybags

Originally devised by Neil Griffith, a storysack is a large cloth bag containing a children's book and supporting materials to stimulate reading activities and make shared reading a memorable and enjoyable experience. The sack can contain soft toys of the book's main characters, and props and scenery that parents and other adults can use with children to bring a book to life even if the adult's reading skills are limited. The sack may include a non-fiction book on the same theme, an audio-tape of the story, a language-based game and a short guide containing questions to ask, words to consider and other ways to extend the reading activity.

Storysacks are a popular, non-threatening way of encouraging parents and carers to start sharing stories with their children, especially those parents with little positive experience of books. By encouraging children and adults to enjoy reading together, a storysack gives a child the chance to enjoy books at a variety of levels. Children can:

- develop their listening skills as the stories are read to them
- improve their vocabulary by talking about the contents of the sack
- develop their social skills and improve confidence
- explore different cultures and inclusion issues.

Storysack Ltd offers a wide range of commercially produced storysacks for sale, as well as tips on how to use the sacks. Further details are available from www.storysack.com. The company also produces a storysack rack - on castors, with storage space for holding big books. Although storysacks can be bought, another idea behind them is that you can get the community involved in a project to make storysacks or storybags. If you have parents who can sew, then decide on which book you want to make a storybag for and what you want in the bag and ask the parents to design it. By doing this you can get the whole community involved, and also raise their interest in their children's reading. Research evidence suggests that many adults, after they have been involved in a storysacks project, are motivated to take up opportunities for further study and so improve their own skills. Many libraries manage various storysack projects, aiming to reach people in deprived areas and groups at risk of social exclusion because of their language, culture or abilities. The themes of the sacks may address issues faced by these groups. The libraries work in partnership with community groups and their supporting agencies.

Based on the same principle as storysacks, Hampshire County Council has developed a number of story baskets as part of The Living Album project. These give children an opportunity to learn about Hampshire's Gypsy heritage and the Gypsy and Traveller lifestyles. Two of the baskets are housed in a 'Reading Wagon' storybox, adapted to look like a traditional Gypsy wagon. The story baskets each contain a storybook, a tape recording of the story with small cassette player, as well as 'smell cubes' and objects which relate to the story. Each of the selected titles not only relates to Gypsies and Travellers but also explores ideas and issues around acceptance, tolerance and inclusion. The story baskets enable childcare providers to discuss cultural and racial issues in a fun and sensitive way.

Babies love treasure baskets

The early years library can expand the range of resources to provide multisensory resources. The treasure basket is the perfect educational 'toy' for babies who are not yet able to crawl and is a great exploratory resource as soon as they are able to sit, propped up with cushions. The treasure basket itself is a basket made from a natural material such as wicker. It is filled with natural and inexpensive everyday objects from the real world and found around the home (as illustrated in Figure 6.3). They provide babies with sensory stimulation and help to develop hand-eye co-ordination, making of choices and preferences. The concept was developed over 30 years ago by Elinor Goldshmied, a child psychologist, from observing children and the way they gained knowledge of the world around them. She developed a method of play that helps babies and toddlers to learn naturally.

Figure 6.3 *Creating a treasure basket*

'Heuristic play' is the term used to describe play for babies and infants that actively encourages exploration of natural objects by using and developing their senses (Goldschmied and Jackson, 2004). A treasure basket is full of interesting objects that babies want to investigate and that they can play with, with little or no adult help. Often they will get very excited and will smile and clap, making 'happy' noises. By sucking, mouthing and handling objects, babies are finding out about size, shapes, smell, sound and texture. Goldschmied suggests that none of the objects in a treasure basket should be a 'bought toy' or made of plastic. In the highly manufactured 'global north' babies are already surrounded by plastic objects which are smooth, have no smell and no taste. By offering a range of objects which are not plastic you can increase the opportunities for a baby to learn and explore. In this age of consumerism, you can also help parents to understand that there are alternatives to brightly coloured and often expensive plastic toys. The contents should be selected with safety in mind, they require regular care and maintenance and should be washable, wipeable or disposable. They should be small enough to be held by tiny hands but large enough not to be swallowed. Table 6.1 gives examples of items you can include in a treasure basket. You can also try using a themed approach by devising a 'touch wood' basket, the 'bathroom basket' or the 'brush basket'. Another idea is to create a 'sounds' treasure basket filled with different musical instruments and sound makers.

Toy libraries

The constructive use of toys can help a child's development. Community toy libraries were first formed in England in the late 1960s, initially for children with additional needs. A report from the National Association of Toy and Leisure Libraries (2007) looks at the contribution that toy libraries make to securing better outcomes for children and the support they offer to parents and the wider community. The study drew on five case studies in areas of economic and social disadvantage in different parts of England. The report urges that consideration be given to including

Table 6.1 *Examples of items that can be included in a treasure basket*

Natural objects	Objects in leather, textile, rubber, fur
Fir cones	Puppy 'bone'
Large pebbles	Leather purse
Shells	Coloured-marble 'eggs'
Large chestnuts	Velvet powder puff
Big feathers	Fur ball
Pumice stone	Length of rubber tubing
Large corks	Tennis ball
Small natural sponge	Golf ball
A lemon	Small teddy bear
An apple	Beanbag
	Small cloth bags containing lavender, rosemary, thyme, cloves

Wooden objects	Metal objects
Small boxes, velvet lined	Spoons – various sizes
Rattles	Small egg whisk
Bamboo whistle	Bunch of keys
Castanets	Lemon squeezer
Clothes pegs	Garlic squeezer
Cylinders – bobbin, cotton reel	Bottle brush
Napkin ring	Triangle
Spoon	Metal egg cup
Egg cup	Tea strainer

Objects of natural materials	Paper, cardboard, etc.
Woollen ball	Little notebook with spiral rings
Little baskets	Greaseproof paper
Small raffia mat	Tinfoil
Wooden nailbrush	Small cardboard boxes
Toothbrush	Insides of kitchen-paper rolls
Shaving brush	
House-painting brush	

(Based on Goldschmied and Jackson, 2004, 108–10)

a toy library in every children's centre and within extended schools provision. Toy libraries can engage parents who otherwise might not use early years play services. When choosing new stock you will need to strike a balance between toys that are widely available and the more specialist items. Toy library toys have to be really sturdy, very safe and cleanable. They also need to demonstrate appeal to both boys and girls and represent all sections of the community. Greene (1991, 49) has suggested the following criteria for choosing toys:

* safety
* durability
* child appeal or play value

- aesthetic value - should be well designed
- teaching and learning potential.

As outlined above, safety is a major consideration when choosing toys for the library, so it is important to ensure that the products are well made, with no sharp or protruding parts that could injure the children. They need to be free from toxic substances such as lead, not easily broken, yet easy to keep clean. A further consideration is the need to match the toys to the stages of development and emerging abilities of young children. This is not only to enhance their ability to learn but also to increase their enjoyment of playing with the toy.

Toys for babies and young infants

Babies like nothing better than to reach out for objects and place them in their mouths. There are many books for babies that can be chewed and wiped clean, like board books, bath books and flannel books and these are ideal for babies and infants. It is therefore good to have on hand toys that babies can handle and suck, such as large rings, teething toys and squeeze toys. They like things that they can shake and that make a noise, so rattles of all designs are good, as well as objects with interesting textures, such as textured balls, vinyl and board books. All these toys can be good for developing listening skills, concentration, hand-eye co-ordination and gross and fine motor skills. As babies grow a little older, they love to move around and explore the environment. Toys that encourage movement, such as plastic and wooden vehicles with wheels that they can either ride or push along by themselves are good for the development of gross motor skills and concentration.

Toys for toddlers and young children

Toddlers are rapidly learning language. Good toys are things to play 'pretend' with, such as child-size furniture - kitchen sets with kitchen appliances, chairs and play food - or baby dolls and their accessories, like doll beds, prams and pushchairs. Dressing-up accessories and toy phones are also ideal for encouraging language acquisition, as are puppets, stuffed toys, plastic animals, sand and water toys. Young children love running around, jumping, climbing, rolling and rough-and-tumble play. It is therefore good to provide toys which encourage the use of their large and small muscles, such as balls for kicking and throwing, ride-on equipment, low climbers with soft material underneath, as well as toys for pounding on and hammering. They also enjoy problem-solving toys - so be sure to provide wooden puzzles, construction kits, blocks that snap together, objects to sort, as well as things with hooks, buttons, buckles and snaps or toys with parts that do things, such as dials, switches, knobs, lids and zips.

Children learn through play, and toys are their tools. The following suggestion from Family Place Libraries is a sample of age-appropriate toys available for very young children:

- infant non-shatter mirror
- small bead toy
- nesting cups
- shape sorter
- foam, cardboard or vinyl blocks
- cause-and-effect toy (with lids that are easily opened by manipulating various switches)
- knobbed puzzles
- Lego
- puppets
- small kitchen set (plates, cups, etc.)
- foldable train mat with magnetic train cars
- animal figures (farm, jungle).

Although toy library collections can require a significant investment in space, they offer a wonderful resource for many families.

Selecting DVDs

Age-appropriate DVDs can provide an excellent source of entertainment and be a valuable educational resource for young children. They provide visual and verbal stimuli and can be good for developing communication and extending vocabulary.

Selecting CDs

CDs of stories are good reading partners, as they allow the child to listen to a favourite story over and over again. They are also great for journeys in the car. In the Rankin family many long car journeys to holiday destinations were made bearable by listening to Roald Dahl stories. Dad particularly enjoyed *Danny the Champion of the World* (Dahl, 1975) and we all were word perfect on *The Enormous Crocodile* (Dahl, 1978). Listening to a story also allows children to match spoken sounds to words on the page.

Music resources: opportunities for listening and participation

The Early Years Foundation Stage (DfE, 2012) states that you need to promote opportunities for children to:

- share and enjoy a wide range of rhymes, music, songs
- link language with physical movement in action songs and rhymes
- develop phonological awareness through small-group and individual teaching.

Research on the impact of musical activities on the development of preschool children shows that regular contact with musicians has a positive impact on the development of communication skills and social, physical and cultural development (Music Manifesto, 2006). Consider the resources needed for music making and where to obtain them. Suggested items are rhythm instruments and keyboards, xylophones, maracas and tambourines.

Digital resources for young children

Very young children now access a range of technology on laptop computers, tablets and smartphones.

Granddad, James and Oscar (Figure 6.4) were playing on the iPad, but they wouldn't let Granddad JJ have a go. These two four-year-olds have become proficient at playing games on the iPad, on laptops and smartphones from when they were quite young. They could use touch screens, a mouse, space bar and arrows, etc. to manoeuvre objects around a screen to achieve the purpose of whatever game they were playing, whether it was building with Lego, interactive stories, Clifford's Thinking Adventures, Topsy and Tim or Tree Foo Tom.

Figure 6.4
No Granddad, we will tell you when it's your turn

Websites

- Popular websites for preschool activities include the BBC CBeebies and schools programmes. Find fun stories for babies, toddlers and young children, including fairy tales. Children can select activities to do with books and TV programmes - story time; make and colour; shows; games;

songs; radio. Watch! www.bbc.co.uk/cbeebies/
- Ladybird Books publisher's website has activities for young children and is organized into age and stages; things to do; favourite friends; blogs; digital and apps; and bookshop. www.ladybird.co.uk
- The BBC schools and learning centre online includes The Little Animals Activity Centre, which is a fun way for four-year-olds and older children to learn and play at home. www.bbc.co.uk/schools/laac
- TurtleDiary.com claims to be 'the learning playground for all the children who want to tickle their brain with our fun educational activities' (TurtleDiary, 2014). Games and activities are created by well-qualified teachers and educators who believe that learning should be easy and fun. The concepts are reinforced with the help of fun and educational activities. www.turtlediary.com

Sources of information for early years stock selection

There are many sources of information that you can use to support the process of selecting stock. Specialist journals and reader-development magazines are a good starting point.

Books for Keeps. This is a bi-monthly children's books review magazine. It often has a themed focus for each issue. The reviews are organized into teaching ranges. There are feature articles about different aspects of children's books, including production and promotion. The print version is available on subscription; the online version provides free access to reviews of thousands of children's books. The online version can be found at www.booksforkeeps.co.uk.

Carousel - **the guide to children's books.** This is the magazine of the Federation of Children's Book Clubs. Available via subscription and published three times a year, it is a well-illustrated publication with articles on children's literature and publishing and author interviews. It also includes book reviews - fiction and non-fiction - and reviews of audio books. Carousel, The Saturn Centre, 54-76 Bissell Street, Birmingham B5 7HX. www.carouselguide.co.uk

Achuka. This is an online magazine showcasing the world of children's books. URL: www.achuka.co.uk. There are also a number of non-specialist sources which are worth checking. Special features and book reviews appear in, for example, *The Bookseller, The Guardian, The Sunday Times, Times Educational Supplement* and *The Observer.*

Booktrust *Best Book Guide.* Booktrust publishes a free guide to its selected best books for ages 5 years and under. The *Best Book Guide* reviews can be downloaded from the website or requested in print format. Centre for Literacy in Primary Education.

Simply the best books for children: books for 0-7 years. Centre for Literacy in Primary Education (CLPE), ISBN 1872267327. www.clpe.co.uk

Riveting Reads: 3-6 by Derek Jowett (2005) School Library Association, ISBN 1903446317. This list of more than 250 books is arranged under a variety of headings, such as Starting Out and Families. They have been chosen with parents, library staff and teachers in mind and can be used at home as well as by teachers working in nursery schools, preschool groups and at Key Stage 1. www.sla.org.uk/riveting-reads.php

The Ultimate Book Guide (2008) This is a National Year of Reading guide aimed at new library members. It includes *The Ultimate First Book Guide* sections on recommended titles for early years, covering 0-2 years and 2-5 years. www.ultimatebookguide.com

The Ultimate First Book Guide: over 500 great books for 0-7 year olds by Leonie Flynn and Daniel Hahn, A&C Black (2008). The guide covers board books and novelty books, through to classic and contemporary picture books, chapter books and more challenging reads.

Publishers and booksellers. The websites of publishers and booksellers are a useful source of information on new titles. Bookshops specializing in children's books. www.booktrusted.co.uk/information/bookshops.php4

Picture book lists

The Good Reads website has an interesting range of booklists - e.g. the Caldecott Medal winners; Halloween; Really under-rated children's books; Best books for a new child's library, etc. etc.
https://www.goodreads.com/list/tag/picture-books

Scholastic asked more than 200 teachers, children's authors and children's literature experts to name the best picture books ever.
www.scholastic.com/teachers/article/teachers-picks-top-25-picture-books

Children's picture books that teach mathematics concepts (Christchurch City Libraries, NZ). Recommended for children aged 4-6.
http://librarybooklists.org/fiction/children/jpicture.htm

Booktrust has compiled its 100 Best Books for Children: 0-5 and requests that you take a look at its pick of the best books for 0- to 5-year-olds from the last 100 years. www.booktrust.org.uk/books/children/booklists/241

Lovereading4kids has compiled its 'Must Reads' of children's books.
www.lovereading4kids.co.uk/genre/ess/Bookshelf-Essentials.html

Booktrust

This is an independent national charity 'that encourages people of all ages and cultures to discover and enjoy reading'. The website provides free resources and recommendations for librarians, teachers and parents about books for all ages. Users can search the website for recommended books using keywords, genre and age range. Information is also provided on specialist children's bookshops, specialist children's literature magazines, publishers and organizations working with children's books and the children's literacy sector.
www.booktrusted.co.uk/books

Children's Stories net – free children's stories by leading authors. Anyone can register to receive free access to children's stories. This website frequently changes the free children's story selections from its library.
www.childrens-stories.net/reading-age/

IFLA World Through Picture Books. The aim of the World Through Picture Books project is to create an annotated list of picture books from around the world, recommended by librarians. The programme is led by IFLA section Libraries for Children and Young Adults, with support from partners IFLA section Literacy and Reading and IBBY (International Board on Books for Young People).
www.ifla.org/files/assets/hq/publications/professional-report/135.pdf

International Children's Digital Library - a library for the world's children. The International Children's Digital Library (ICDL), created in 2002, provides free access to children's books, in their original languages, over the internet. The ICDL Foundation's goal is to build a collection of books that represents outstanding historical and contemporary books from throughout the world. With children as design partners, an interdisciplinary team works with international experts in children's literature to make available an expanding collection of full-text historic and contemporary children's books. The mission of the Library is to encourage a love of reading, foster a readiness to learn and offer a response to the challenges of world illiteracy. At the time of writing the ICDL collection includes 4619 books in 59 languages. This is an interesting resource and you can search for books by continent and by title, author or keyword in dozens of languages. All the books in the ICDL can be sorted by title, author, illustrator, language and publication date. www.icdlbooks.org

Letterbox Library. This London-based, non-profit co-operative founded in 1983 provides multicultural and non-sexist books for children. It is a good source of American imports and the catalogue is particularly strong on picture books. www.letterboxlibrary.com/acatalog/index.html

www.lovereading4kids.co.uk. This website features books for the 0-5 age range and has useful 'like-for-like' author recommendations. The creators of the website say that Lovereading4kids has been created to be the ultimate children's online independent bookstore. Users need to register to use the site and an e-mail service keeps members up to date on the latest and best in their chosen age ranges. The message is that if young children have a favourite book or author, let them read it again and again, but also introduce a new author or book similar in style. The website's creators also suggest that parents can enjoy online time with their children, as much as watching TV with them.

Reading Is Fundamental (USA) - *Leading to reading.* This free, interactive resource is designed to help parents and childcare providers develop the language skills of their infants, toddlers and preschool children. Available in English and Spanish, it includes stories, lullabies, finger games and nursery rhymes. www.rif.org/leadingtoreading/en/babies-toddlers/

The Federation of Children's Book Groups. The Federation of Children's Book Groups (FCBG) produces a brand new booklist yearly, each year focusing on a new theme. The leaflets are written by people who are experts in their fields. Funded by both the FCBG and a variety of sponsors, these booklists are available for free and can be posted free of charge to anyone in the UK. In order to request a set, please e-mail info@fcbg.org.uk. www.fcbg.org.uk

The Red House Children's Book Award is the perfect opportunity to inspire pupils of all ages to get reading and discussing books. Its short list has three categories, including books for Younger Children, books for Younger Readers and books for Older Readers. Simply choose the category that suits your pupils, share and discuss the books, then vote for your favourites. www.redhousechildrensbookaward.co.uk/resources/index

Stories from the Web. This is a Reader Development Programme managed by Birmingham Libraries. The Early Years website is a pilot project funded by the Early Years Development Partnership Birmingham and aimed at 0- to 7-year-olds. The website also has activities aimed at older age groups. It is designed to develop language skills, confidence and an increased understanding of the world and aims to promote a love of reading from an early age. Using Stories from the Web will require guidance from an adult, as young children may need help in using the mouse and keyboard, explanation of what is happening on each page or help with reading and writing. The five activity areas are: stories, writing, games, drawing and the gallery. It is a members-only website offered on a subscription basis to library authorities around the UK. www.storiesfromtheweb.org

The Word Pool. This website aims to increase the profile of UK children's books on the internet. It is a well-established source of information for anyone interested in choosing or writing children's books. The Parents' Corner features books and links to help in parenting your children. This aims to be as comprehensive as possible and so includes the toughest part of parenting - caring for children who are unhappy, sick, disabled or emotionally scarred. In addition to books aimed at parents, the section includes reviews of some good children's fiction which may give parents an insight into their children's feelings. Users can sign up for a free monthly newsletter. The UK Children's Books Directory section provides links to the websites of a wide range of children's authors, illustrators, publishers and organizations. www.wordpool.co.uk

Equipment

Buyers' Guide Online is a useful source of information on library suppliers' products and services in the UK. Companies are listed alphabetically, by category and by the brand name of their products. The online service is supported by *The Annual Buyers' Guide Directory*, published in December of each year. www.buyersguideonline.co.uk.

Resources for bilingual books

Action Aid produces a range of multicultural books, teaching materials and resources to help teachers to bring a wide variety of cultures and traditions into the classroom. A catalogue is available on request. www.actionaid.org.uk

Fabula software. This software is designed to support bilingual literacy and allows teachers and children to create bilingual storybooks by inserting texts and scanned drawings or photographs into simple templates and adding special features of their own. The Fabula software, plus further information on the project and reading lists, is available free of charge on the website at http://fabula.mozdev.org.

The Global Dimension. This booklist from Leicestershire County Council Library Services for Education covers recent recommended multicultural fiction for ages 3+ to 16+. For details e-mail: lse@leics.gov.uk. This website also has a really good section on picture books - see the 2013 information page, www.pinterest.com/leicslse/2013s-best-picture-books.

Little Linguist specializes in multicultural resources for children that are suitable for use in early years settings and primary schools.

www.little-linguist.co.uk/multicultural-resources-for-
children.html?gclid=CIrA8p3lsr8CFWKWtAodMW8AvQ

The Early Years Foundation Stage (EYFS)

Everyone who works with children from birth to five in the UK will need to
know about the requirements of the Early Years Foundation Stage (EYFS),
revised in 2012 by the DfE. The EYFS is a statutory framework for high-quality
development, learning and care for all children from birth to the end of the
academic year in which a child has her fifth birthday. All early childhood care
and education providers are expected to plan for children's learning using the
EYFS framework, including all private, voluntary, independent and maintained
nurseries and reception classes and registered childminders (DfE, 2012). This
curriculum for young children from birth to five emphasized three 'prime' areas
of personal, social and emotional development; physical development; and
communication and language. Tickell (2011, 5) states that these are 'particularly
important for igniting children's curiosity and enthusiasm for learning, and for
building their capacity to learn and to thrive'. Young children learn best through
play, and the EYFS acknowledges the central importance of play, direct
experiences and active learning to support young children's learning effectively.
The EYFS should promote 'a secure foundation through learning and
development opportunities which are planned around the needs and interests
of each individual child' (DfE, 2012).

The role of practitioners – whether in early years settings, libraries or schools
– is obviously crucial to promoting young children's communication, language
and literacy – and the EYFS (DfE, 2012) is a really valuable resource that is freely
available. It will provide early years librarians with clearly accessible information
about the phases of young children's development not only in language and
literacy development but also across both the three prime areas and the four
specific areas of learning and development:

- literacy: reading; writing
- mathematics: number; shape, space and measure
- understanding the world: people and communities; the world; technology
- expressive arts and design: exploring and using media and materials;
  being imaginative.

The EYFS development matters document provides information about the
'Characteristics of Effective Learning', which emphasizes the importance of:

- playing and exploring: engagement: finding out and exploring; playing with what they know; being willing to 'have a go'
- active learning - motivation: being involved and concentrating; keeping trying; enjoying achieving what they set out to do
- creating and thinking critically.

'I think these are brilliant and really should be what we attend to throughout primary school. We report on these to parents. We have them clearly signposted on a wall display outside the classroom so that parents can see what we are doing.'
(Brock and Thornton, 2015, 182).

Tina Thornton is a reception class teacher who is passionate about providing high-quality early education experiences for young children. She endorses the EYFS as being a rich and valuable resource, not only for teachers, but for parents too. If early years librarians have some familiarity with the EYFS, then they can also direct parents to this freely available resource. Figure 6.5 is a sample page from the EYFS.

Conclusion

This chapter has aimed to provide you with a wealth of information about resources for early years libraries - books, toys and other delights to meet community needs, in particular the target audience of young children and their families. It has illustrated why early years librarians need to have knowledge of diverse resources such as treasure baskets, toy libraries, storysacks, Bookstart packs and the EYFS. You may not be able to access all the resources mentioned in this chapter, and you will know and discover many more, but we do hope that we have pointed you in interesting and valuable directions to make the most of your resource provision.

Issues and questions

- How can you develop and maintain a collection development plan for your early years library?
- Consider how to develop and share knowledge about diverse resources such as treasure baskets, toy libraries, storysacks and Bookstart packs.
- How can you provide a parenting collection to meet the needs of local families?

Communication and Language: Speaking

	A Unique Child: observing what a child is learning	Positive Relationships: what adults could do	Enabling Environments: what adults could provide
Birth - 11 months	• Communicates needs and feelings in a variety of ways including crying, gurgling, babbling and squealing. • Makes own sounds in response when talked to by familiar adults. • Lifts arms in anticipation of being picked up. • Practises and gradually develops speech sounds (babbling) to communicate with adults; says sounds like 'baba, nono, gogo'.	• Find out from parents how they like to communicate with their baby, noting especially the chosen language. • Ensure parents understand the importance of talking with babies in their home language. • Encourage babies' sounds and babbling by copying their sounds in a turn-taking 'conversation'. • Communicate with parents to exchange and update information about babies' personal words.	• Learn and use key words in the home languages of babies in the setting. • Provide tapes and tape recorders so that parents can record familiar, comforting sounds, such as lullabies in home languages. Use these to help babies settle if they are tired or distressed.
8-20 months	• Uses sounds in play, e.g. 'brrm' for toy car. • Uses single words. • Frequently imitates words and sounds. • Enjoys babbling and increasingly experiments with using sounds and words to communicate for a range of purposes (e.g. teddy, more, no, bye-bye.) • Uses pointing with eye gaze to make requests, and to share an interest. • Creates personal words as they begin to develop language.	• Try to 'tune in' to the different messages young babies are attempting to convey. • Share the fun of discovery and value babies' attempts at words, e.g., by picking up a doll in response to "baba". • When babies try to say a word, repeat it back so they can hear the name of the object clearly. • Find out from parents greetings used in English and in languages other than English, and use them in the setting. • Recognise and equally value all languages spoken and written by parents, staff and children.	• Find out from parents the words that children use for things which are important to them, such as 'bankie' for their comfort blanket, remembering to extend this question to home languages. • Explain that strong foundations in a home language support the development of English.
16-26 months	• Copies familiar expressions, e.g. 'Oh dear', 'All gone'. • Beginning to put two words together (e.g. 'want ball', 'more juice'). • Uses different types of everyday words (nouns, verbs and adjectives, e.g. banana, go, sleep, hot). • Beginning to ask simple questions. • Beginning to talk about people and things that are not present.	• Build vocabulary by giving choices, e.g. 'apple or satsuma?' • Model building sentences by repeating what the child says and adding another word, e.g. child says 'car', say 'mummy's car' or 'blue car'. • Show children how to pronounce or use words by responding and repeating what they say in the correct way, rather than saying they are wrong. • Accept and praise words and phrases in home languages, saying English alternatives and encouraging their use. • Encourage parents whose children are learning English as an additional language to continue to encourage use of the first language at home. • Support children in using a variety of communication strategies, including signing, where appropriate.	• Allow time to follow young children's lead and have fun together while developing vocabulary, e.g. saying 'We're *jumping up*', '*going down*'. • Plan to talk through and comment on some activities to highlight specific vocabulary or language structures, e.g. *"You've caught the ball. I've caught the ball. Nasima's caught the ball.* • Provide stories with repetitive phrases and structures to read aloud to children to support specific vocabulary or language structures.

Figure 6.5 *Communication and language: speaking (DfE, 2012)*

Key points to remember

- The selection of books and other resources to support the early years is a key role for the librarian.
- You need to know the needs of your market before you can begin to provide the resources.
- In an early years collection, provide materials in a variety of formats to encourage play, creativity and development - the emphasis is on having fun.
- Library collections for the early years are not just about books, as there are many ways to support literacy and the enjoyment of stories.

References

Branching Out (n.d.) www.opening thebook,com/archive/branching-out/page2.asp?idno=396.

Brock, A. and Thornton, T. (2015) Capable, Confident Children: a reception class teacher's pedagogical reflections. In Brock, A. (ed.), *The Early Years Reflective Practice Handbook*, Routledge.

Campbell, R. (2010) *Dear Zoo,* Macmillan Children's Books.

ClearVision (2014) www.clearvisionproject.org/news.asp.

Conteh, J. and Brock, A. (2006) Introduction. Principles and Practices for Teaching Bilingual Learners. In Conteh, J. (ed.) *Promoting Learning for Bilingual Pupils 3-11: opening doors to success*, PCP/Sage Publications.

Cooling, W. (2007) Books for Babies (Rosemary Clarke, Head of Bookstart, and Wendy Cooling, Founder and Senior Consultant, talks to Madelyn Travis about the scheme's origins and development), www.booktrust.co.uk/articles/documents.php4?articleid=48

Dahl, R. (1970) *Fantastic Mr Fox*, Allen & Unwin.

Dahl, R. (1975) *Danny the Champion of the World,* Jonathan Cape Ltd.

Dahl, R. (1978) *The Enormous Crocodile,* Jonathan Cape Ltd.

Dahl, R. (1982) *BFG,* Jonathan Cape Ltd.

Department for Education (DfE) (2012) *Statutory Framework for the Early Years Foundation Stage*, Department for Education, www.foundationyears.org.uk/files/2012/03/Development-Matters-FINAL-PRINT-AMENDED.pdf.

Edmonds, D. (2012) Outsourcing in Public Libraries: placing collection management in the hands of a stranger? In Fieldhouse, M. and Marshall, A. (eds), *Collection Development in the Digital Age*, Facet Publishing.

Feather, J. and Sturgess, P. (1997) *International Encyclopaedia of Information and Library Science*, Routledge.

Goldschmied, E. and Jackson, S. (2004) *People Under Three - Young Children in Day Care,*

2nd edn, Routledge.

Greene, E. (1991) *Books, Babies and Libraries: serving infants, toddlers, their parents and caregivers,* American Library Association.

Hill, E. (1980) *Where's Spot?,* Penguin Young Readers Group.

IFLA (2003) *Guidelines for Children's Library Services,* IFLA Children and Young Adults Section.

Jones, R. L. (2001) *1001 Pirate Things to Spot,* Usborne Children's Books.

Leeds Library and Information Services (2013) *Collections Development Policy April 2013,* www.leeds.gov.uk/docs/Collections%20Development%20Policy%202013.pdf.

McKee, D. (1998) *Elmer's Weather,*

Music Manifesto (2006) *Making Every Child's Music Matter.* Music Manifesto report no 2. A consultation for action, Music Manifesto.

National Association of Toy and Leisure Libraries (2007) *Toy Libraries - Their Benefits for Children and Communities,* NATLL and Capacity, www.natll.org.uk/pdfs/CapacityReportJune07.pdf.

Power, M. and Brock, A. (2006) Promoting Positive Links between Home and School. In Conteh, J. (ed.), *Promoting Learning for Bilingual Pupils 3-11: opening doors to success,* PCP/Sage Publications.

Rankin, C. and Brock, A. (2008) *Delivering the Best Start: a guide to early years libraries,* Facet Publishing.

Rosen, M. (2007) Children's Laureate. Acceptance, www.michaelrosen.co.uk/laureate.html.

Sullivan, M. (2013) *Fundamentals of Children's Services,* 2nd edn, ALA Editions.

Tickell, C. (2011) *The Early Years: foundations for life, health and learning,* An Independent Report on the Early Years Foundation Stage to Her Majesty's Government.

TurtleDiary (2014) www.turtlediary.com.

Van Orden, P. J. and Bishop, K. (2001) *The Collection Program in Schools: concepts, practices and information sources,* 3rd edn, Libraries Unlimited.

Whitehead, M. (2007) *Developing Language and Literacy for Young Children,* 3rd edn, Paul Chapman.

CHAPTER 7

Using digital media in early years library services

Francesca de Freitas and Tess Prendergast

Introduction

This chapter will focus specifically on the role of early years library work in the digital age. Digital media is now ubiquitous in the developed world. While the 'digital divide' remains glaringly apparent between society's most affluent and most underprivileged (Neuman and Celano, 2012), the wide availability of digital technology means that more and more children across a range of socio-economic and cultural groups now have access to digital tools in their daily lives with their families. How and why does this concern early years library staff? Simply put, just as libraries provide guidance about and free access to books and older-format audiovisual materials, so too should libraries provide guidance about and access to a range of digital resources from which families and the caregivers of young children can select what best suits their needs.

Digital media (sometimes called new media) exists and is being used by children in our communities in a variety of ways. In order to ensure that children are able to access the best that digital media has to offer, it is critical that communities can rely on the expertise of the children's librarian. In particular, tablet computers such as iPads, and the applications (apps) that are designed to run on them, represent an area of particular promise for early years libraries. Many of these apps are 'book-based', and this represents a natural place for early years library collections to jump into the digital realm. This chapter will focus on approaches to learning about tablets and apps and how they might be incorporated into your existing early years work in libraries.

Surveying the landscape of digital media in early childhood

While it would perhaps be reassuring to be able to use well-researched and proven best practices to make collection, programme and services decisions about digital media in early years library work, its rapid development over the past few years has not allowed research in this area of early childhood to play catch-up. However, due to its ubiquity and the fact that the marketplace for apps is both confusing and chaotic, the role that the library can play in helping families navigate this new digital media landscape has never been more important. A great deal of time and money can be wasted on low-quality apps, and parents and caregivers who want to provide children with digital learning opportunities face an overwhelming number of choices. Two things are very clear. First, we cannot wait several more years for published research to tell us how to do this 'properly'. By the time any research comes along, the formats and resources will have changed yet again. Second, families who have always relied on libraries to help them select the best materials for their children will be left to contend with the digital marketplace on their own if librarians do not step into the digital resources field and do what they do best: curate, evaluate, recommend, demonstrate and model the best of what is available in the new app format. This chapter provides a starting point for early years librarians to check on how they are proceeding with the development of responsive early-childhood digital media services, programmes and collections.

Brief literature scan about technology in early childhood

Early years librarians who are tasked with decision making about digital media for early childhood use should familiarize themselves with some of the existing and often ambiguous research about children and media. A well-known study by Zimmerman and Christakis (2005) suggested that exposure to media in the early years is associated with cognitive deficits and recommended no screen exposure for children under the age of two. Building on this work, another study suggested that children's language development is negatively impacted by television viewing (Tanimura, Okuma and Kyoshima, 2007). Interestingly, in an opinion piece that appeared in *JAMA Pediatrics*, Christakis (2014) has recently amended his personal views on the appropriateness of screen-media exposure in early childhood, particularly for children under two. Stating that 'judicious use of interactive media is acceptable for children younger than the age of 2 years', Christakis justifies his previous position by carefully analysing the specific affordances of the iPad: reactivity; interactivity; tailorability; progressiveness; promotion of joint attention; portability; and 3-dimensionality. Indeed, the literature about digital media in early childhood, although scanty, provides some evidence that some of the unique and very new features of current digital media (mostly in the form of tablets and developmentally appropriate apps) can and do support early learning in young children (Aronin and Floyd, 2013; Nemeth, Simon and McManis, 2013; Northrop and Killeen, 2013.) While no evidence has emerged whereby the tablet/app is proven to be 'better' at teaching things than older formats such as books, pens and paper, the suggestion is that many digital resources do just as good a job as other tools for children with typical development (Lynch and Redpath, 2012). There is also emerging research that points to digital media's positive impact on the communication and literacy development of children with disabilities (Fan, 2012; Windman, 2012). Also, some new research suggests that these digital tools are able to provide learning experiences whereby very young children (with and without disabilities) can be participants in their own meaning making in ways that are entirely new (Gillis et al., 2012; Shifflet, Toledo and Mattoon, 2012). Teachers report that digital media provides experiences that are quite unlike anything that previous generations of children had. While legitimate concerns about the amount of time children might spend in front of a variety of screens persist (Brown and Council on Communications and Media, 2011), the affordances of digital learning tools in early childhood, particularly as they apply to literacy development, should be thoroughly explored and understood by early years librarians. A recent UK study for the National Literacy Trust by Formby (2014) explored how changes in the use of screen-based activities affect some of the ways that both parents and practitioners can support children's development. One of the study's most interesting and relevant findings was that children from lower socio-economic levels showed more gains in literacy development when they had access to both print and digital books, as compared to print alone, suggesting that having access to digital media in their homes helps support their literacy growth. This study helps to solidify an early years library's rationale for providing access to digital early literacy learning resources for the benefit of underprivileged children. Finally, Guernsey (2012) provides a highly readable resource for both parents and professionals to explore research about media in early childhood. Her three-pronged approach (wherein consideration is given to the content, the context and the child) helps both librarians and parents to navigate the new digital terrain with confidence.

Developing a rationale for digital media in early years library services

Why are we bothering to talk about apps and library services? When digital media becomes available to young children and their families, we need to examine how it fits into our early years library services - and particularly into our two key service areas: providing advice to readers and modelling early literacy activities. By including apps in our readers' advisory and by modelling how to use those apps, we provide caregivers with new tools and show them how to use those tools to share early literacy experiences with their children.

Why provide readers' advisory for digital media?

Our library collections have already stretched to include digital media, as we offer e-books and downloadable audio books, subscriptions to online databases and annotated lists of recommended homework-help websites. It is not a large step to next address apps that are designed for and marketed to young children and their families. Many of the apps aimed at young children are based on or related to existing picture books, which makes us a natural resource for parents seeking help in choosing apps for their children. The skills and critical faculties we use to select and recommend books also work to help us select and recommend apps for a child. As mentioned earlier in this chapter, the haphazardness of the apps market means that parents and caregivers face huge challenges when it comes to choosing apps, and children's librarians are already trusted advisors in the area of early literacy.

Why model early literacy activities with digital media?

The reason why we have programmes in the library is not to lure children and their families in so that we can throw books at them! The audience in an early years story time is not the children, but rather their caregivers - we show them examples of how to talk, sing, read and play with their children. The picture books we read, the rhymes, songs and tickles we sing and the poems and stories we tell are all tools that we give to caregivers so that they can nurture their children's language and literacy growth. Apps are another literacy tool and, just like the others, it is the quality of the interaction between the adult and the child that provides the early literacy benefits - not the tool itself. So, just as we use story time to show caregivers different ways to share books with their child, we can use story time to show them how to share apps. The majority of media images of children interacting with portable electronic devices show a single, lonely child poking at a screen. This sets up two different problems - it contributes to the negative portrayal of 'screens' in early childhood and it gives the impression that an app is something a child uses by themselves. A parent is unlikely to hand their toddler a book and expect them to be able to use it by themselves, but the prevalent media imagery has given us different expectations for apps. By modelling apps in story time, we can show adults how apps can be a positive joint media experience - not just a child interacting with a screen, but an adult and a child interacting by using apps together. As with reading a picture book, it is the quality of that joint experience that will provide its early literacy benefit (Takeuchi, 2011; Fred Rogers Center for Early Learning and Children's Media at Saint Vincent College, 2012).

Providing app advisory for families and caregivers

There are different ways to help parents choose apps for their children, requiring varying degrees of effort, planning, expense and staff support. A selection of these are described below. If you intend to help parents in selecting apps for their children, it is important to support your information staff in learning about digital media, for example by having devices available for staff to play with, giving demos of apps at staff meetings or giving staff funding to purchase and try out new apps.

Create a list of go-to tools for finding quality apps

On your website, or in a handout, provide links to lists of recommended apps and app-review sources. This requires the least amount of effort and does not need to be updated frequently. The Vancouver Public Library (2014) has an online subject guide designed for early childhood educators that includes a range of both print and electronic resources designed to lead early years teachers directly to helpful resources for their work. A tab called Digital Resources has recently been added to the guide in an effort to connect teachers of young children with reliable sources of information about digital media, including readers' advisory for app selection. (http://guides.vpl.ca/content.php?pid=284726&sid=4726325)

Creating applists

Provide a list of recommended apps and sources of app reviews on your website and as a printed handout. Staff who are not familiar enough with apps to feel comfortable recommending one to a parent can hand them the list. It also gives you an opportunity to provide early literacy messages – annotate the list to describe an early literacy benefit for each app, and include a note about enjoying apps together with your children. This requires the least effort and will not need to be updated frequently. If you do choose to update the list regularly, the staff involved will become more confident and better able to advise parents. The following links provide many ideas about building applists and other resources for parents:

- http://westvanlibrary.ca/youth/early-years/ebooks-e-readers-tablets/sharing-apps-your-preschooler
- http://wvmlyouth.tumblr.com/
- http://littleelit.com/2014/03/26/power-to-the-kiddie-apps-by-kelsey-cole/
- http://edapps4sale.digital-storytime.com/index.php?Talking.

Providing access to apps

Provide devices in your library for families to play with. Let adults and children try out different apps that you recommend, without having to download or pay for them. This also provides access for families who do not have devices at home. Acquiring tablets (iPads or other devices) to use in your library setting may seem simple in theory, but going by what has been reported in blogs like Little eLit (littleelit.com) and ALSC (www.alsc.ala.org/blog/) on this topic, the process can be complex and time consuming. The intricacies of each institution's processes for new technology acquisition will of course vary, but, despite its complexity, initiating a digital media-device plan for the children's library will likely be worth the effort in terms of user satisfaction, ability to meet readers' advisory demands and parent–child engagement with your library's early learning spaces.

CASE STUDY

The Vancouver Public Library acquired five iPads to use for their children's section. The iPads are outfitted in sturdy kid-friendly cases and are safely tethered to tables in the children's library. The iPads are loaded with developmentally appropriate, engaging and interactive apps and are thought to enhance what is already a valued and responsive service at the Central Library Children's Library. Well in advance of the iPads' arrival, the librarian in charge of the project asked one of her employees whom she knew to be 'up on apps' to devise a list of recommended apps to be purchased and installed on the iPads before they launched. This librarian devised a multi-step strategy to evaluate and recommend a range of apps for the new iPads. First she devised sub-categories, then sought app-reviews from well-known app review sites. She also consulted the tumblr app list of a neighbouring library system which had already started buying apps for their iPads for children. She constructed a simple spreadsheet with sub-categories, app names, prices and links to the App Store. When the iPads arrived, technology systems staff assigned them with Apple IDs and passwords, and filled each with these age-appropriate, highly recommended apps covering a range of skills and activities, i.e. letter knowledge; animals; colours; simple games; book apps. The apps are divided into categories that align with early literacy practices: talking, singing, reading, writing and playing. The iPads have been available to families for over a month, and children's services staff are excited to see children enjoying the various apps, and families gathering together at the iPads to share the experience.

Holding parent-information programmes

Talk with your community's parents about how to use apps to promote early literacy. Hold programmes for adults, introducing them to children's apps and talking about criteria for choosing apps for children.

CASE STUDY

At Vancouver Public Library we ran an eBooks and Apps for Preschoolers programme for parents and caregivers who spend time with children aged 2–6. The goal was to demonstrate how you can use e-books and apps as tools for encouraging literacy. The programme was delivered over two 90-minute sessions, with informal homework/suggestions for practice in between.

The main messages were:

- The key activities to build literacy are talking, singing, reading, writing and playing.
- Stories are tools to help you do these things with your child.
- There are different ways to enjoy stories, including e-books, apps, songs, and toys.

The programme had the following structure.

First session
- Welcome, programme overview, definitions of e-books, apps and early literacy.
- Told the story 'Little Pea' by Amy Krouse Rosenthal, pictures by Jen Corace, using the picture book, then a flannel board and then the TumbleBooks e-book.
- Talked about some of the benefits and issues with reading e-books with children.
- Projected six apps on a large screen, describing different ways to use them to talk, read, sing, write and play with a child.
- Set homework – examples of ways to enjoy an e-book or app with a child.

Second session
- Welcome, quick review.
- Discussion of the experiences parents had playing with an e-book or app.
- Told the story Go Away, Big Green Monster! by Ed Emberley using the picture book, a flannel board story and then the app by Night and Day Studios, Inc.
- Projected six apps, describing different ways to use them to talk, read, sing and play with a child.

The parents took home a list of recommended apps and app-review sources, the list of suggested ways to play with stories using e-books and apps and an informal list of apps recommended by other parents during the programme. Feedback from the parents and early childcare workers was positive, and families especially appreciated learning about apps they could use in multiple languages.

Teaching healthy media habits with other adults who work with children

Early years library practitioners who are well versed in the issues surrounding digital media and childhood are in key leadership positions in their communities to develop and model how adults can help support the development and maintenance of healthy media habits, beginning in early childhood.

CASE STUDY

A local childcare resource centre invited a librarian from Vancouver Public Library to come and teach a two-hour workshop for a group of early childhood educators. The librarian developed a picture book-focused workshop that described and presented three different formats of picture books and how they could be used to support early literacy development. During the workshop she demonstrated some of each of the following formats: print, flannel board and app. After both the book and flannel board demonstrations and before demonstrating the iPad apps she had brought, she asked the group why they thought it might be important for early childhood workers to know about digital media. A middle-aged participant answered that since kids were using digital technology at home anyway, she thought she should know 'what it was all about'. Building on this statement from her peer, another participant said that knowing about digital media gives her the opportunity to carry on conversations with children about their digital media experiences (favourite games and characters, etc.). Both of these excellent points were probed a bit more as it became clear that this group of teachers valued their roles as primary caregivers of young children. Talking with children about what they like to do at home is an important part of language and communication support within the childcare/preschool setting and also helps to build connections between home and school (Sharon, 2005). The educators at this workshop viewed the children's interest in digital media as another way to connect with them. Then the discussion led to the role of early childhood professionals in helping parents to find and use the best of what is available on the market. The librarian emphasized that the recent emergence of hand-held tablet devices and the haphazard marketing of apps that run on them means that librarians and other educators have to play catch-up. She pointed out that, thankfully, several trustworthy app-review websites now offer substantial help to librarians and other early childhood educators as they select apps to use and demonstrate in their early-literacy resource provision (programmes and other services). The librarian at this workshop emphasized that everyone working in the field of early childhood should learn about digital media so that they are well positioned to help parents make the best decisions with regard to their children's digital learning.

Using apps in early years programming

Children's librarians who have been experimenting with the use of iPads and other tablet technology in their story time programmes talk about the successes and challenges in blog posts, webinars and other professional resources. This reporting on iPad/tablet use in story time has allowed creative collaboration to take place across diverse time zones and communities. The following section describes some of the programmes and apps that have been presented at the Vancouver Public Library.

Guessing and dancing at family story time

CASE STUDY

Vancouver Public Library holds a family story time on Sunday afternoons, advertised as 'Stories, songs, fingerplays, and rhymes for the whole family. Program will include stories for older children to share with their younger siblings.' The attendance varies from 10 to 40 and the group is culturally diverse. Children are accompanied by parents, grandparents, older siblings, relatives and caregivers. Some families attend regularly, but there are always newcomers.

We follow a similar structure each week.

- Welcome songs
- Two fingerplays
- A book
- Two action songs
- Middle item
- Two poems/songs/rhymes
- A shorter book
- Two calming-down songs
- Goodbye song.

By the middle of the programme, any latecomers have settled in and the kids have bounced off some energy and are ready to settle and are not yet restless or tired of paying attention. At this point in the programme we cycle through oral story-telling, flannel board stories, egg-shaker songs and stories with puppets. Last year we added apps to this list.

The room we meet in is small and it is not possible to use a wall or television screen during story time, so for this programme we use apps that work well without being projected on a large screen. This also means that there is no technical set-up required when we use our iPad during the story time.

We use the Animal Sounds app by Alligator Apps to play a guessing game. We hold the iPad facing away from the group and touch an animal. The app plays the sound that the animal makes and we ask the group to guess what the animal is. When they've shouted out some guesses, we turn the iPad around and show them the screen with the picture and name of the animal (as illustrated in Figure 7.1.) We play the sound again and spell the animal's name. We start with easy-to-guess animals, like farm animals, and then try harder, wild animals. We try to include animals that have been mentioned in the songs, rhymes or stories we're sharing in the programme that day.

Figure 7.1
Animal Sounds app by Alligator Apps

We use the Bunny Fun app by Auryn Inc. to help the group sing 'Head and Shoulders, Knees and Toes' in different languages. For this, we place the iPad on a chair with the screen facing the room so everyone can see it. We stand next to it and sing the song in English, demonstrating the actions. Once we've done this twice and people are familiar with the tune and the actions, we ask if they'd like to hear it in another language. We turn on the iPad, start the app and select one of the languages – we usually do Japanese first, as this is one of the common languages for this group. When the bunny hops into the screen, we ask them to guess what language that bunny speaks. Once we've guessed the language, we press the play

Figure 7.2
Bunny Fun app by Auryn Inc

icon and start the app moving and singing, as illustrated in Figure 7.2. We sing along softly and do the actions next to the screen. We play each language twice, usually singing the Japanese and French versions, and sometimes the Spanish or English if people are really enjoying it.

In our community there are parents who feel strongly about restricting their children's exposure to screens, so we take care to inform families at the start of the programme that we will be using a tablet to share a short, age- and subject-appropriate app. Thus far, the feedback has been positive, with families often asking to have the names of the apps to use later at home.

Mashing monsters

One Vancouver Public Library librarian describes her programme as follows.

At Halloween, I did a story time called Monster Mash. We had a monster-themed story time, ranging from classic monster stories like *Where the Wild Things Are*, by Maurice Sendak, to a puppet retelling of *Rhinos for Lunch and Elephants for Supper* by Tololwa M. Mollel, pictures by Barbara Spurll. We sang a monster version of 'Head and Shoulders, Knees and Toes' and finished off with the wonderful iPad app

version of 'Go Away Big Green Monster!' (as illustrated in Figure 7.3). This app has a 'read myself' mode, where children or adults can read the text themselves, a read-along with Ed mode, where the author narrates the story, and a sing-along mode, where you listen to a song version of the story. I chose the sing-along version, which I highly recommend as it is very catchy and fun. Everyone loved it! After the story time portion, the kids made their own monsters and played with colourful shapes and big googly eyes on the flannel board to create their own flannel monsters. I also prepared a handout that included the words to the monster songs we sang, the titles of the books we read, some monster-themed recipe and craft suggestions and finally a link to the free Make Me Monster app by

Figure 7.3
Go Away, Big Green Monster! app by Night & Day Studios, Inc.

CamMaxApp.com. I think this programme provided a good balance between traditional print and digital ways to have fun with monsters.

Telling stories on a large screen

At Vancouver Public Library we have done one-off story times in a larger room and taken advantage of the projector to put a story app on a big screen. This works well for large groups where they would not be able to easily see a picture book.

We've used the *Llama Llama Red Pajama* by Anna Dewdney app by Penguin Group as an extra-large picture book. We turn off the tablet's sound and read the words on the screen, just as we would a paper book. The slight animation and the large format work very well with a dramatic reading, especially the scene where the mother comes running up the stairs.

We've used the *Moo, Baa, La La La!* (by Sandra Boynton) app by Loud Crow Interactive Inc., projected on a screen to read to a large group. For this app we leave the sound turned on, but turn off the background music and the narration. We read the first part of each sentence, for example, 'A cow says ...', and ask the families to make the appropriate sound. When they're done, we touch the animal and have the app make the sound, as illustrated in Figure 7.4.

Figure 7.4
Moo, Baa, La La La! app by Loud Crow Interactive Inc.

Taking turns to play

A librarian at Vancouver Public Library talked about her successful Super Hero Party:

> I led a programme called Super Hero Party as part of the summer reading club special events. I had five stations for kids to circulate through: book nook; Captain Underpants Name Game (based on the books by Dav Pilkey); make a super hero/heroine craft table; super hero-themed puzzles and word games, and finally, the Super Hero photo booth iPad app. As the programme ran for two hours, kids circulated through the stations for as long as they wanted. They actually spent a huge amount of time in the book nook, which was crammed with what seemed like almost every super hero-themed book we have in the collection. They then took their ideas to the art table and created beautiful, sparkly super heroes and heroines of their own design. They had a great time at the Captain Underpants game and then took turns with the Super Hero photo booth app by Tasnim. The app works like this: you take a picture with the iPad camera and upload it to the app, where the kids then add their super-hero embellishments – masks, costumes, regalia, weaponry, etc. – to their picture. They could even add sound-effect words like 'BAM!' and 'POW!' The kids loved their transformations into super heroes and super heroines. We printed the pictures out for each child and then followed up by e-mailing the digital pictures to the parents for them to share amongst their friends. It was a real hit! I think this technology represents an easy way to roll digital experiences into our traditional hands-on art activities. The app activity was not a solo one: it was interactive and included facilitation and supportive help from a librarian, occasionally with input given by a parent or an older sibling.

Going further

We are looking at other ways of integrating digital media into our early years programming, and we take inspiration from the many early years librarians who share their ideas and experiences on Little eLit (Campbell and Koester, 2013). We are considering programmes specifically about using apps, for example, holding a parent-child tablet story time, where each parent and child sit together with a tablet in their lap and follows stories, songs, rhymes and apps, interacting with their own screen when appropriate. We are also looking at using apps to create our own digital media for use during story time, for example, displaying song lyrics, picture and word pairs or making digital flannel board stories. And we are keen to nurture inspiration by using apps along with our craft activities, helping parents and children to create their own digital media, for example, making pictures, videos or sock-puppet animations on a tablet.

Conclusion

Books, articles, conference programmes, webinars, workshops and toolkits about digital media in early childhood are emerging across the children's library services field of practice (see resources), indicating that this topic is of high importance in the field of early years librarianship. Many discussions have taken place about the rationale for providing access to digital media and apps in story time programmes. While some librarians prefer to leave the screens out of story time programmes, others argue that since parents are accustomed to taking librarians' recommendations for good material to heart, this is a perfect opportunity to make sure that parents who wish to use digital media with their children have expert help in selecting the best of what is available in the confusing app marketplace. Demonstrating a developmentally appropriate app during story time gives families a chance to see if they like it. They can ask questions about how and why or why not to use different apps and different ways to support their child's literacy learning across modes. Also, supportive conversations can take place between children's librarians and parents about the importance of selecting only carefully recommended apps, as well as the importance of setting sensible and developmentally appropriate time limits for children playing and learning with tablets. The goal of these conversations with parents and caregivers is to help to ensure that all children are able to participate in wide range of healthy, developmentally beneficial activities. It is thought that, without supportive input from an expert, many families may navigate the marketplace alone, randomly buying anything that is labelled 'educational', only to find that it is a poorly designed set of digital flashcards. We hope therefore that our readers will find opportunities to explore this topic in relation to their work with young children in libraries and that the examples herein will provide both inspiration and guidance to those who are just starting to incorporate digital media and apps into their libraries' services, programmes and collections.

References

Aronin, S. and Floyd, K. K. (2013) Using an iPad in Inclusive Preschool Classrooms to Introduce STEM concepts, *Teaching Exceptional Children*, **45** (4), 34–9.

Brown, A. and Council on Communications and Media (2011) Media Use by Children Younger than 2 Years, *Pediatrics*, **128** (5), 1040.

Campbell, C. and Koester, A. (2013) Little e-Lit: early literacy in the digital age, www.littleelit.com.

Christakis, D. A. (2014) Interactive Media Use at Younger than the Age of 2 years: time to rethink the American Academy of Pediatrics guideline? *JAMA Pediatrics*. doi: 10.1001/jamapediatrics.2013.5081.

Fan, T. (2012) *Enhancing Learning with the Use of Assistive Technology for Children on the Autism Spectrum*, online submission ERIC Number: ED531866, Master of Science in Education Thesis, Dominican University of California, http://eric.ed.gov/?id=ED531866.

Formby, S. (2014) *Practitioner Perspectives:children's use of technology in the Early Years*, National Literacy Trust.

Fred Rogers Center for Early Learning and Children's Media at Saint Vincent College (2012) *A Framework for Quality in Digital Media for Children: considerations for parents, educators, and media creators*, www.fredrogerscenter.org/media/resources/ Framework_Statement_2-April_2012-Full_Doc+Exec_Summary.pdf.

Gillis, A., Luthin, K., Parette, H. P. and Blum, C. (2012) Using Voice Thread to Create Meaningful Receptive and Expressive Learning Activities for Young Children, *Early Childhood Education Journal*, **40** (4), 203–11, doi: 10.1007/s10643-012-0521-1.

Guernsey, L. (2012) *Screen Time: how electronic media from baby videos to educational software affects your young child*, Basic Books.

Lynch, J. and Redpath, T. (2012) 'Smart' Technologies in Early Years Literacy Education: a meta-narrative of paradigmatic tensions in iPad use in an Australian preparatory classroom, *Journal of Early Childhood Literacy*, doi: 10.1177/1468798412453150.

Nemeth, K., Simon, F. and McManis, D. (2013) Technology in ECE Classrooms: results of a new survey and implications for the field, *Classroom Technology: Exchange*, September/October, 68–75.

Neuman, S. B. and Celano, D. C. (2012) Don't Level the Playing Field: tip it toward the underdogs, *American Educator*, **36** (3), 20–1.

Northrop, L. and Killeen, E. (2013) A Framework for Using iPads to Build Early Literacy Skills, *The Reading Teacher*, **66** (7), 531.

Sharon, R. C. (2005) 'Behind Closed Doors': discovering the literacies in our children's everyday lives, *Language Arts,* **82** (6), 420.

Shifflet, R., Toledo, C. and Mattoon, C. (2012) Touch Tablet Surprises: a preschool teacher's story, *Young Children,* **67** (3), 36–41.

Takeuchi, L. M. (2011) *Families matter: designing media for a digital age,* New York: The Joan Ganz Cooney Center at Sesame Workshop.

Tanimura, M., Okuma, K. and Kyoshima, K. (2007) Television Viewing, Reduced Parental Utterance, and Delayed Speech Development in Infants and Young Children, *Archives of Pediatrics & Adolescent Medicine,* **161** (6), 618–19. doi: 10.1001/archpedi.161.6.618-b.

Vancouver Public Library (2014) Early Childhood Education: digital resources in ECE, http://guides.vpl.ca/content.php?pid=284726&sid=4726325.

Windman, V. (2012) iPad Apps for Students with Autism, *Assistive Technology Roundup,* **32** (Generic), 28.

Zimmerman, F. J. and Christakis, D. A. (2005) Children's Television Viewing and Cognitive Outcomes: a longitudinal analysis of national data, *Archives of Pediatrics & Adolescent Medicine,* **159** (7), 619–25, doi: 10.1001/archpedi.159.7.619.

CHAPTER 8

Using play to enhance early years literacy in babies and toddlers: 'Read, Play and Grow' at Brooklyn Public Library

Rachel Payne

Introduction

A librarian covers a table with contact paper, sticky-side up. Little hands reach out and are surprised by the sticky sensation. He asks the children how the table feels and talks to them about the word 'sticky'. Every autumn, another librarian puts out a bowl of squash and small gourds, and even a medium-sized pumpkin, after her programme. She watches as the babies grab, pat and even roll the vegetables. As they do so, she says, 'You're patting the pumpkin! Let's all pat the big pumpkin!' The babies begin to learn that there are words ('pat') to describe their actions. In the summer, another librarian gives children cups of water and paint brushes and encourages the children to 'paint' the sidewalk in front of the library. She talks to them about what they have created and describes some of the shapes she notices in their work, such as squiggles and spirals, and the children may learn some new vocabulary to describe their world. All of these library activities are prime examples of play driving language development and early literacy. While some of these young children may not yet be talking, they are learning new words and new concepts in a meaningful, contextual way. And all of this happens through play.

Early childhood research has always highlighted the many benefits of play. The expanded and updated toolkit *Every Child Ready to Read* (American Library Association, 2011) features play as one of the five key early literacy practices (along with reading, talking, singing and writing) that parents should engage in with their children to promote reading readiness. A University of Iowa study reported that 18-month-olds who played with diversely shaped objects learned new words twice as fast as those who played with more similarly shaped objects (Perry et al., 2010). Another study of one- to two-year-olds found that those who played with blocks with their parents for just 20 minutes a day scored 15%

higher on language development tests and were 80% less likely to watch television (Christakis, Zimmerman and Garrison, 2007). These studies support what early childhood professionals have observed for decades.

At Brooklyn Public Library, we have been exploring how to construct play activities that get parents talking with their little ones. Through a couple of generous grants, we were able to develop Read, Play, Grow!, an early literacy curriculum of simple play activities using everyday household objects and materials. At their existing baby and toddler story-time programmes, library staff set up 'play stations' with interactive play activities for little ones and their parents to explore. At each station, 'play tips' are displayed, with suggestions for parents on things they can say to promote language development.

In this chapter I will give an outline of the curriculum, include some suggested play activities and detail practical tips for setting up 'play stations' in traditional story-time programmes or in full-scale play events, like Brooklyn Public Library's annual Big Brooklyn Playdate. Before we delve into the nitty-gritty of play, it is important to put play for babies and toddlers into context, so first I will discuss the ages and stages of play for little ones. I will also review what very young children learn from play, as well as adult interactions during play that best support early literacy, and I will address what impedes parents and caregivers being present and responsive during their children's play.

What does play look like for babies and toddlers?

Many people have a good understanding of what play looks like for children over three years and they may have vivid memories of playing super heroes with their friends or pretending a chair is a rocket ship. But play for infants and toddlers looks and feels a little different. Often it can be difficult for a parent, an inexperienced caregiver or a librarian new to working with children to know what kinds of play experiences are best for very young children. To begin, let's run through what play looks like for babies and toddlers.

Babies are always exploring. Many of the things they explore – their own feet, toys and even books – go directly into their mouths. We have more nerves in our mouths than in our hands, so if you want to get lots of sensory information about something (including taste!), there's no better place than your mouth. And from a very young age, babies are primed to put things in their mouths. Play continues to be about *sensory exploration* once they can start using their hands by reaching, grabbing, pulling and gripping a variety of objects, including their own bodies. Play is also about *social interaction*. How can I get the desired response from my parents and other caregivers? Gopnik, Meltzoff and Kuhl (2000) write extensively that babies are indeed physical and social scientists as they test theories about the world. What will happen when I shake this rattle? What will daddy do when I drop my spoon on the floor? Will mummy smile at me if I smile at her? Their mode of enquiry? Play!

While toddlers are also exploring the limits of their physical and social worlds, play begins to grow in new directions. During the first year and beyond, children begin to engage in *parallel play*, where they play side by side and often take notice of what their peers are doing without much interaction. *Symbolic play* begins to emerge at this time as well, which is when a child pretends one object is another. Puzzle pieces may be cookies or a pair of rolled-up socks may be a mobile phone. This kind of play is an important step in a child's literacy development. If a child can imagine that a shoe is a racing car, she is one step closer to understanding other symbols as well, such as letters and numbers.

What do babies and toddlers learn from play?

When I ask librarians to list the skills children learn through play, they often name concepts (colours, numbers, counting, letters, etc.) and social skills (sharing). They often mention how play allows children to develop their creativity. But play is also a way of researching the world. Through exploring cause and effect and experimenting with things around them, children are building their own understanding.

Play allows for self-direction. Children learn about what they *need* to learn about. A child learning to walk may enjoy cruising on the chairs in the library programme room. A child dealing with some separation anxiety may enjoy games of peek-a-boo; are my parents still there even if I can't see them? A child learning social skills may pretend to prepare food for grown-ups and enjoy the replies of 'please' and 'thank you' once it is served.

Play also promotes self-esteem in children. Since there is no product to be created or no explicit goal, children can feel confident about their play. While some children do get frustrated when their desires outstrip their motor skills and abilities, they often find a way to play with the materials in a way that is in sync with their development. For example, take a collection of toy kitchen items; all children can play with the toy plates and kitchen utensils at their own level. A baby may enjoy putting the plate in his mouth. A toddler may enjoy banging two plastic plates together to make some interesting noises. A preschooler may enjoy serving a pretend dinner to mum and dad. There are very few ways a child can fail at play, especially when surrounded by responsive caregivers.

With all the talk about STEM education (science, technology, engineering and mathematics), we often forget that play is similar to the scientific process. Young children are scientists and their playful explorations are mini-experiments. What is the best way to build my block tower? What will happen when I splash water in the bathtub? What does that rock feel like? In all of these experiences, children may not have the language to talk about what they are doing, but they are testing their hypotheses.

And finally, play is a powerful force in developing literacy and language skills. When babies coo, babble and smile at their parents or caregivers, they need a response. Researchers call this 'serve and return interaction' and believe it is the key in establishing strong brain architecture (Center on the Developing Child, video). If a baby makes a playful squeal (the *serve*), the parent notices, smiles and talks to the baby (the *return*). As children get older, they attempt to say certain sounds or even words. A toddler may say 'Bah' for ball and her grown-up will respond by saying 'Yes! That's a ball!' Through play, children learn language in a natural and organic way. They learn in the moment, in context and connected to real objects.

How can parents, librarians and others support literacy development during play?

Recent research in early literacy has noted that parents who are supportive and responsive to their children's chatter and other first attempts at language rear children who perform better on early language assessments. Parents who stroke, praise, and respond to a baby's babble, have children who make more attempts at language. While some parents have heard the message that talking to children is important, not all talk is created equal. Children whose parents take note of what their child is looking at and talk about it to them do better than children whose parents talk to them about things that the children aren't interested in (Bronson and Merryman, 2011).

Talking with a baby or toddler during playtime can sometimes feel awkward, particularly when a child is not talking back. That is precisely why parents should see these interactions modelled. Here is a composite transcript of one exchange that occurred in our library programmes during which an 18-month-old boy is stacking blocks made out of cereal boxes:

> **Librarian**: I like how you're stacking the blocks.
> **Child** looks at librarian for a few seconds and puts another block on top.
> **Librarian:** You put another block on top of the blocks. You've got a tall tower! Are you going to knock it down?
> **Child** looks at the librarian and then back at the tower and knocks it down with a smile.
> **Librarian:** Boom, boom, boom! You did it! You knocked down the tower!

While the child said nothing, he obviously understood everything the librarian said. The librarian put his experience into words and modelled to the parent things to say during play at home. She may have given the boy some new vocabulary or reinforced some words he already knew: 'stacking' and 'tower'. She helped him to learn or to extend his knowledge about new concepts, such as 'on top of' and cause-and-effect situations. All this from a simple, one-minute interaction!

Many librarians put out toys for kids to play with after programmes and leave the parents and kids to their own devices. Sometimes that needs to be done due to staff shortages, but I think we need to see playtime as a core component of our programmes, not an afterthought. It is important to model early literacy interactions with children. When parents and caregivers see library staff or other adults get on the floor to play and talk with children, they see at first hand how to engage them.

It is also important to understand what impedes parents from engaging their children. Many parents are mystified as to how to play with a very young child, particularly one who is still gaining language. What do you say to a baby who can only babble? What do you do with an active toddler on a cold and rainy day when going to the playground is impossible? In the *PlayReport* (Family Kids and Youth, 2010), a global survey of children and their parents initiated by IKEA, 45% of parents said that they didn't have enough time to play with their children. Even when parents did find the time to play, 26% said that they were 'too stressed to enjoy it'. We also surveyed parents and caregivers at Brooklyn Public Library about their challenges in playing with their children, and many mentioned struggling with how to engage a baby or toddler with a short attention span.

Even more troubling, research has also shown that low-income parents engage less in literacy-rich experiences than do their wealthier peers. The landmark Risley and Hart (1995) study noted that, by the time children are three, children from educated and high-income homes have heard 33 million words and their low-income counterparts have heard only 10 million. More recent research has noted that these gaps in vocabulary and language processing are leaving a mark on children as young as 18 months (Fernald, Marchman and Weisleder, 2012). The disparity in the amount of talk between babies and parents of different income levels and educational backgrounds is enormous, adding up to massive advantages or disadvantages for children in language experience long before they start preschool. The Risley and Hart study found that the more parents talked to children, using a richer vocabulary with more positive affirmations, the more their children's language use increased. When parents sit down to play and talk with their children they draw out babble and burgeoning language from babies and toddlers. All parents want what is best for their children, but many parents have not heard that play is itself a rich and unparalleled learning activity, particularly in the areas of language and literacy development. That's where we come in.

Play at the library!

When I first started doing programmes for babies, I thought of play as something fun for the parents and children to do after the programme. I didn't think of what I could do as a librarian to make play a core component of the programme and what I could do to facilitate it. Read, Play, Grow! was instrumental in helping me rethink all of this and move play to the front and centre.

When we began to develop the curriculum for Read, Play, Grow!, we knew we needed to find ways to encourage play at home. The activities we have created and model in our programmes are based on one idea: can they be easily replicated at home? We created simple play activities that parents and caregivers can try with everyday household materials. Cardboard boxes are blocks and plastic containers are stacking and nesting toys. We also bought some developmentally appropriate toys for babies and toddlers and found ways to replicate them with household items. Oven mitts could be puppets and clear plastic bottles filled with feathers or small rubber balls became 'discovery tubes'.

To encourage play and interaction, we set up 'play stations' for children to explore before or after the story time programme and displayed a simple activity or a home-made toy at each station. Each station has a sign (either in a sign holder or on a laminated sheet of paper) with various 'play tips'. These tips offer directions to parents, give parents some ideas for the kinds of things they can say to their child to promote literacy development and offer a few words about safety (if warranted). Some activities require more direction than others, so if additional staff or volunteers are available, we can enlist them to help guide the activity. The following are some of the 'play tips' that we have used in various programmes for babies and toddlers.

Baby tubes
What you do

Use an empty paper-towel roll to blow gently on your baby. You can also use the tube to play tug-of-war, to roll across the floor as your baby sits up, or to hide a sock or scarf for a peek-a-boo surprise. Older babies can pull out the sock or a scarf with a little help from you. Toddlers will enjoy stuffing the sock into the tube by themselves!

What you can say
- Describe actions as they are taking place, so your baby will begin to associate language with action: 'Mummy pulled the sock out of the tube!'
- When you blow through the tube, ask your baby questions. Even though your baby can't answer yet, you are helping her to learn new words. You can ask: 'Can you feel the air? Does it tickle? Does it feel like the wind?'
- You don't have to talk down to your baby, but babies do respond to animated and playful speech and the playful drama of it all, especially in games of peek-a-boo. It is OK to be silly!

Safety tip: Don't let your baby chew the tube.

Board book blocks
What you do

Get various board books of different sizes and line them up on their sides like dominoes and show your baby how to knock them over. You can also build low towers of books. Often babies and toddlers will knock them over after they have watched you do it first! Make a tunnel out of books. Get creative! Don't forget to read the books when you have finished building!

What you can say
- Make lots of sound effects as you knock the books over - it will keep your baby or toddler engaged.
- Ask your baby or toddler, 'What do you think will happen when we knock the blocks over? Will they fall down? They fell down!'
- You can even play peek-a-boo with books. Hold them in front of your face and say 'Where did mummy go?'

Peek-a-boo puppets
What you do

Take an oven mitt and glue or sew a simple face made out of felt on the front of the mitt. Use bold colours like white, black, red, yellow and blue. Fold the fingers of the mitt over to hide the face and then lift it up to reveal the face. Perfect for a game of peek-a-boo!

What you can say

- 'Where did the face go? Peek-a-boo! Here it is!'
- 'What colours do you see on the face? I see red and blue.'
- 'Where are the eyes? Where is the nose?'

Safety tip: Your child should be supervised while playing with this puppet.

Cereal-box blocks
What you do

Empty cardboard cereal boxes or other boxes can make great blocks. Stuff the boxes with newspaper to make them sturdier and tape the flaps closed. You can line up a few of them on the floor like dominoes and show your child how he can push one into the others and they will all fall down. Build a tower with the blocks. You can also talk about the pictures, colours or letters on the boxes.

What you can say

- When you line up the boxes like dominoes, talk with your child about cause and effect: 'What do you think will happen when we push the first box? Let's push it! Look! They all fall down!'
- As you build towers, compare them. Ask: 'Which is taller? Which is lower?'
- Point out letters on the boxes: 'Look, there's a T. Your name starts with T: Tom!'

Safety tip: If any of the boxes have sharp edges, cover them with tape.

Stack, nest, play!
What you do

If you don't have any stacking or nesting blocks at home, you can improvise! Stack up empty plastic food-storage containers (with the lids snapped on) for your child and see how tall you can build the tower before she knocks it down! Take off the lids and you have toys that 'nest.' Do you have a set of metal or plastic nesting bowls or measuring cups? Give them to your child to play with. She will enjoy taking them apart again after you have put them back together.

What you can say

- Talk about the shapes and colours of the objects your toddler touches,

'You have a big bowl. It's blue.'

- Say to your child, 'How tall can we make this tower?' Count as you place the containers on top of each other.
- As you put the nesting bowls/cups inside each other describe what you're doing. 'I'm putting the bowls inside of each other. Can you take them apart again?'

Safety tips: If you are giving your baby household objects to play with, make sure they have no small pieces that can come off or sharp edges. Always monitor your child when he or she is playing with these items.

No-mess finger painting
What you do

Take a large zip-closure freezer bag. Insert two colours of paint in primary colours (red, yellow or blue) or a primary colour and black or white. You don't need a huge amount. Squeeze the excess air from the bag and zip it closed. Tape the bag flat to a table with packing tape on all four sides. Now your child can move the paint around to mix the colours together. No mess!

What you can say

- 'What colours do you see inside the bag? Do you see anything else in the room that is the same colour(s)?'
- 'How does the paint feel? Does it feel soft? Does it feel squishy?'
- 'What happens to the colours when we mix them together?'

Safety tips: Keep the bag taped to the table. If the bag comes open, you can mend it with tape.

The Big Brooklyn Playdate

For the past three years, our Central Library has hosted the annual Big Brooklyn Playdate. Each time, over 100 babies and toddlers (and their parents or caregivers) have come out to play. Brooklyn Public Library staffers transform the Dweck Center - usually the site of gallery exhibits - into a baby-and-toddler play space with various 'play stations' around the room that parents, caregivers and young children can explore together. Again, we place signs near activities to give parents tips for things to say and ways to interact. Since 2013, we have borrowed an idea from the *Parent-Child Workshop* (Feinberg and Deerr, 1995) and invited 'roving experts' (child-development experts and others) to our event to be on hand to answer questions from parents.

We set up three 'zones' at the playdate, as a way to direct the children to appropriate areas, based on their development. There's the Baby Play Zone for pre-walkers, the Active Play Zone for walkers and the Block Play Zone, which is an area designed for more focused, less-boisterous play. Below is a description of what we do in these three large areas.

Baby Play Zone

In this area we securely tape variously textured or visually interesting materials to the floor to create an area for babies to explore on all fours. We have used rubber or fabric bath mats, bubble wrap, high-contrast patterned hand towels, metallic paper, small quilts, craft foam, placemats and zip-closure bags with visually interesting objects inside (feathers, sponges, leaves, seeds). We also place a large foam mat on the floor with several home-made and purchased toys for babies to explore who are not yet crawling. We put small rubber balls, ping-pong balls, jingle bells and feathers in tall, clear plastic bottles (securely sealed with tape) to provide an interesting visual tracking experience as parents tip the bottles upside down. We make 'mystery bottles' from clear plastic water bottles filled

Figure 8.1 *Baby Play Zone at the Big Brooklyn Playdate*

half with oil (vegetable oil works best) and half with water and food colouring. We leave scarves and 'Peek-a-Boo Puppets' out to encourage the classic game, as well as scarves stuffed into 'boutique'-style tissue boxes and paper-towel tubes. Along with a few classic baby toys, such as shakers, rattles and more, the babies play, babble and explore and some even practise cruising on the benches that surround the play area (see Figure 8.1).

Active Play Zone

This area is more appropriate for walkers and older children. We request a few large cardboard boxes from the library's mailroom and cut a variety of shaped holes and doors in them. For our first Playdate, we gave kids crayons or pavement chalk to decorate them with, but the children were so engrossed in crawling into and peeking out of the boxes that this proved unnecessary. Lots of language happens in and out of the boxes, with parents peeking at their children through 'doors' and 'windows'. We also bring out our parachute periodically for some even more boisterous play and remind parents that they can replicate this activity at home using a large bed sheet (personally, this was my family's lifesaver when we were stuck inside during Hurricane Sandy). To top it all off, we give away a few party-sized bottles of bubbles for the grown-ups to use with their youngsters.

Block Play Zone

In this area, we put out commercially manufactured foam blocks, stacking blocks, extra-large construction bricks and other building materials, along with our own home-made cardboard blocks. Early childhood educators often discuss the open-ended nature of blocks which allows for several different kinds of experiences and types of play (Wellhousen and Kieff, 2001). To this end, we also commandeer some of the large shopping baskets that patrons use at the library when browsing for books. This allows toddlers to fill up the basket with blocks and dump them out. Twos and threes enjoy engaging in dramatic play and often play 'store' with the cereal-box blocks (which are usually a variety of other food boxes as well). We've also added some play fruits and vegetables to the mix. It is wonderful to see babies to preschoolers engaged in the play that suits their developmental needs.

Play stations

Around these three large zones, we also have 'play stations' set up at child-size tables and staffed by staff or volunteers. We make shakers out of plastic bottles or paper cups, we play with home-made play dough, we create colour or texture collages and we create 'dot' art with file-folder colour-coding dots. The surprise hit of the Playdate has been an activity we call 'The Un-Sand Box' (see Figure 8.2). It is two large tubs filled with shredded paper from our office shredder. Who knew recycled documents could be so much fun? Larger paper shreddings work best. The activity generates lots of descriptive language and children and parents describe what the activity feels like. Kids love throwing, tossing and scrunching the 'snow' as many of them like to call it. Of course, the paper does go everywhere, but it can be cleaned up easily enough with a broom.

Figure 8.2 *The Un-Sand Box play station*

The annual Big Brooklyn Playdate is the biggest event we do for babies, toddlers and their caregivers at the library. The feedback is that everyone wants us to do it again every week. We publicize it on several local parent blogs and family websites, bringing in families with young children who have never been to the library before. Outreach efforts to local early childhood organizations have also brought us a group of teen mums from a local high school.

Two years into Read, Play, Grow! programmes, and after the first Big Brooklyn Playdate, we surveyed parents and caregivers about the programmes' effectiveness. A full 74% of respondents reported gaining new ideas to use with their children and 44% said they use Read, Play, Grow! activities at home. We are delighted that these simple activities are helping parents to discover what children already know: play is fun and powerful stuff.

Come out to play!

It is often said that parents are their children's first teachers, but they are also their first playmates. Parents are often bombarded with information about how to give their children the best start. We have multiple parenting books on our shelves with this information, sometimes offering conflicting advice. When my son was young, I sometimes got caught up in making sure I did the right thing. It was when I was relaxed and followed his lead that we had the most fun, laughing and playing together. Since libraries are often the first cultural and educational institutions where the very young can fully participate, we are uniquely positioned to support parents in these first interactions.

Whether we have set up appropriate activities or not, our youngest users are already playing at the library and it's usually in ways that drive the shelvers, security guards and custodians crazy. The youngsters are pulling books off the shelves, twirling on spinning racks and climbing through shelves. This is what young children do and need to do. Let's redirect this energy to more appropriate play. While it may be difficult for most libraries to replicate the large-scale, interactive exhibits and spaces of children's museums, we can create small-scale, temporary play experiences in our multipurpose programme rooms and even on the children's library floor out of very simple, everyday materials.

And while play belongs in our libraries, play needs to be front and centre in our programmes. Creating playful experiences in libraries helps parents to understand that play is central to a child's literacy and language development. When we get down on the floor and model positive, responsive interactions, parents see at first hand how to engage a young child with emerging language skills. We can help parents to connect the dots between language, literacy and play. We can let parents know that the best thing they can do to help their child grow and development is to connect with their child as they squeeze dough, stack blocks and peek through boxes.

Acknowledgements

A number of people helped to create, develop and test-drive the Read, Play, Grow! curriculum at Brooklyn Public Library. Special thanks go to Steven Lamonea, Christopher Lassen, Jeanne and Catherine Skrzypek for jumpstarting Read, Play, Grow! and to Jeanne McDermott and Katya Schapiro, who helped refine and evaluate it. Many thanks to the wonderful children's specialists and librarians, interns and volunteers at Brooklyn Public Library who field-tested it at branch programmes and at the Big Brooklyn Playdate. Thank you to the New York State Library and the Altman Foundation for their generous support of our Read, Play, Grow! initiative.

References

American Library Association (2011) *Every Child Ready to Read*, 2nd edn.

Bronson, P. and Merryman, A. (2011) *NurtureShock: new thinking about children*, Grand Central Publishing.

Center on the Developing Child (video) *Serve and Return Interaction Shapes Brain*

Circuitry, YouTube Video, https://www.youtube.com/watch?v=m_5u8-QSh6A, Harvard University.

Christakis, D., Zimmerman, F. and Garrison, M. (2007) Effect of Block Play on Language Acquisition and Attention in Toddlers: a pilot randomized controlled trial, *Archives of Pediatrics & Adolescent Medicine*, October, 967–71.

Family Kids and Youth (2010) *PlayReport*, IKEA.

Feinberg, S. and Deerr, K. (1995) *Running a Parent/Child Workshop*, Neal-Schuman Publishers.

Fernald, A., Marchman, V. and Weisleder, A. (2012) SES Differences in Language Processing Skill and Vocabulary are Evident at 18 months, *Developmental Science*, March, 234–48.

Gopnik, A., Meltzoff, A. and Kuhl, P. (2000) *The Scientist in the Crib: what early learning tells us about the mind*, HarperCollins.

Perry, L., Samuelson, L., Malloy, L. and Schiffer, R. (2010) Learn Locally, Think Globally: exemplar variability supports higher-order generalization and word learning, *Psychological Science*, December, 1894–902.

Risley, T. and Hart, B. (1995) *Meaningful Differences in the Everyday Experience of Young American Children*, P. H. Brookes.

Wellhousen, K. and Kieff, J. (2001) *A Constructivist Approach to Block Play in Early Childhood*, Delmar/Thomson Learning.

CHAPTER 9

Inclusive early literacy

Tess Prendergast

Introduction

In this chapter I hope to lay a firm foundation for early years librarians to consider their role in the provision of inclusive early literacy resources for children with disabilities (Kliewer et al., 2004). Over the past two decades, the work of early years children's librarians has evolved to include a significant role in the provision of early literacy resources for young children (Ward, 2007; American Library Association, 2011; Peterson, 2012). Much of this early literacy expertise is framed around the developmental trajectories of children who have typical development (Ghoting and Martin-Diaz, 2013). In order to best meet the needs of *all* children, including those with developmental disabilities, the public library's early literacy resource provision should include a range of inclusive approaches that are intentionally designed to be more likely to meet the needs of their community's developmentally diverse children (Prendergast, 2013). This chapter will lay out the rationale for building and increasing inclusive early literacy resources and supports in the public library setting.

Defining inclusive early literacy

In this chapter, when I use the term 'inclusive early literacy' I refer to early iteracy policies, discourses, programmes, practices and opportunities that consider the needs of diverse children and their families in order for children to participate together in the same setting. Inclusive early literacy ensures that young children with disabilities are able to experience early literacy alongside and in the same or similar ways as their age peers (Kliewer, 2008; Flewitt, Nind, and Payler, 2009; Mock and Hildenbrand, 2013).

Disabilities and exclusion

Before inclusive education, children with disabilities were routinely educated in separate environments alongside other children with disabilities. Prior to that, children with disabilities were often placed in institutions, with few or no educational opportunities offered to them at all. This harmful history contributed to the negative social perceptions of people with disabilities which persist today. For example, people with disabilities have often been presumed to be incompetent to acquire literacy (Kliewer, Biklen and Kasa-Hendrickson, 2006). Such presumptions, based on historically negative social reactions to disabilities, are not reflective of actual abilities or learning potential, particularly in the area of literacy acquisition. Recent research about inclusion in early childhood learning reveals persistent barriers to participation for children labelled with disabilities (Kliewer and Biklen, 2001; Flewitt, Nind and Payler, 2009; Purdue et al., 2011). Exclusion means that children with disabilities may be offered inadequate support for their literacy learning, and when they fail to learn to read, the underlying presumption of incompetence becomes a self-fulfilling prophecy (Zascavage and Keefe, 2004). To help counteract this persistent legacy of exclusion, library practitioners and all providers of early literacy resources need to recognize the need for, and participate in the provision of, more responsive social and educational support and acceptance for people with disabilities, *beginning in the early years*. Enacting mandates that aim to meet the needs of all community members means that public libraries have an important role to play in providing early literacy support to families whose children have disabilities. One of the chief ways this can be done is by carefully planning for and providing inclusive early literacy resources.

Expanding our notions of early literacy

Before practitioners are able to assess and address the inclusiveness of their early literacy settings and programmes, it is important to examine what their existing notions of early literacy actually look like. A commonly stated view of early literacy in the library profession, and one that draws on the American Library Association's resource *Every Child Ready to Read* (American Library Association, 2011), goes something like this:

> **Early literacy** encompasses everything that young children know about and do with traditional reading and writing before they can actually read and write traditional print.

Everything we do to provide children with experiences of reading and writing (as well as singing, talking and playing) supports this definition of early literacy.

Also, this definition can be further described in terms of a specific skill set that practitioners, parents and caregivers can target in early childhood. These are: vocabulary, narrative skills, phonological awareness, letter knowledge, print awareness and print motivation (Ghoting and Martin-Díaz, 2006; Diamant-Cohen and Ghoting, 2010; American Library Association, 2011). Research suggests that targeting and building these six skills will better prepare young children for success in reading once they arrive at school (Shanahan and Lonigan, 2010; Paciga, Hoffman, and Teale, 2011). This all makes a great deal of sense, and resources like *Every Child Ready to Read* have seen broad take-up across North America (McKend, 2010; Peterson, 2012), with newer research emerging which suggests that targeted caregiver training about early literacy skills leads to better outcomes for children in reading readiness (Campana and Dresang, 2011; Dresang et al., 2011).

Another view of early literacy draws on sociocultural literacy research (Hamer, 2005; Wolfe and Flewitt, 2010; Lawson et al., 2012) and allows for an expanded view of literacy in early childhood:

> **Early literacy** encompasses the broad range of experiences that young children have within their cultural contexts (i.e. family, school, community) with language (i.e. verbal and gestural/sign), all forms of social communication (including those that use digital technology tools) and symbol systems and artefacts to make meaning, often collectively referred to as multimodal literacies.

The first definition applies well to children whose development falls within expected norms. It works well for children whose spoken language, cognition and physical skills allow them to leverage what they know about traditional print reading and writing to acquire more and more knowledge about traditional print reading and writing. Research in this area suggests that by providing the recommended experiences that target these skills, children with normal development will likely become better prepared to succeed in reading. However, research about how children with disabilities learn early literacy suggests that skills-based early literacy learning, particularly those skills that draw on pre-existing phonological skills, may exclude a number of children whose spoken-language development cannot be leveraged for literacy skill development (Kliewer, 2008; Mock and Hildenbrand, 2013). Therefore, the expanded definition considers what a child with atypical development may be doing, as well as what he or she may need to be supported to do in order to express and develop his or her literate self. For example, children with a variety of disability labels may point, gesture, use bona fide or adapted sign language or use an assistive communication device to communicate. They may turn their heads or eye gaze or shift their body position to indicate engagement and communicate something quite specific (Flewitt, Nind and Payler, 2009). Therefore, this expanded definition of early literacy, one that encompasses all that a child may do with language, social communication, symbol systems and artefacts, including digital tools, allows early years library practitioners to recognize these experiences as legitimate early literacy expressions and experiences, and ones that must be both incorporated into and encouraged by the early literacy resources of the early years library. The overall aim of inclusive early literacy is to ensure that young children with disabilities are given the same or similar opportunities to have early literacy experiences as their age peers without disabilities and that they are provided with accommodations and support appropriate to their needs (Katims, 1994; DEC/NAEYC, 2009).

Inclusive early literacy research summary

The available academic research about early literacy and children's libraries is scanty (Stooke and McKenzie, 2011). However, the fields of early childhood education and early literacy have several studies from which early years library practitioners can begin to learn about, rationalize and plan for the mindful inclusion of children with disabilities into early years library programmes and services. Flewitt, Nind and Payler (2009) presented a case study that explored the early-literacy experiences of a child with disabilities in which they put forth a view of literacy as 'the development of shared meanings through diverse symbol systems in social contexts' (p. 213). They extended this understanding to a view of literacy as meaning making through the multiple 'modes' of communication that include gesture, gaze, movement, vocalizations and alternative and augmentative communication systems (p. 214). The authors captured details of the multimodal literacy events that occurred in various settings in the life of the case-study child participant, a 4-year-old girl named Mandy who attended two preschools: one inclusive community preschool and one specialized preschool for children with disabilities. They noted that the literacy opportunities present in Mandy's inclusive preschool setting far exceeded the literacy opportunities found in her specialized preschool setting. Mandy was provided with almost no literacy activities or experiences in her specialized setting, whereas in her inclusive setting she participated in the frequent and daily literacy activities of the classroom, alongside her age peers without disabilities. The authors persuasively argued that 'separating children from literacy experiences due to perceptions of their cognitive ability effectively devalues how they construct meanings in the social worlds they experience and, ipso facto, can breach the principles of inclusive education' (p. 213). Mandy's case illustrates the need for understanding inclusive early literacy 'as social practice rather than as a narrow set of technical sub-skills required for reading and writing' (p. 231). Early years librarians should therefore understand that the skills-based paradigm of early literacy as defined by *Every Child Ready to Read* and similar initiatives can sometimes cast children with disabilities as less than capable learners, and disregards other significant demonstrations of meaning making.

Rogow (1997) provided teachers with strategies for including children with a variety of significant disabilities in their classrooms. First of all, she noted that the fundamental principles of literacy 'apply to all children whether they have special needs or not' (p. 10). While acknowledging that many teachers are not specifically prepared to teach literacy to children with disabilities, Rogow encouraged the inclusion model as being of benefit to everyone as 'children learn to respect and feel comfortable with their differences; teachers develop their creativity and find new ways of stimulating, enriching, and enhancing literacy instruction ...' (p. 13). Rogow also emphasized the important role the teacher can play in a child's life by asking readers to 'imagine the influence of a teacher who believes in the capacity of a child with a disability to become an active and eager learner. Children flourish in the warming glow of a teacher's belief in their abilities' (p. 105). Librarians who hold similarly high expectations of all children will be better able to provide them with a range of tools from which to learn literacy.

Kliewer (2008) asserted that deeply entrenched attitudes and assumptions about non-verbal (or less verbal) children with disabilities contribute to the reality that many are simply not given the opportunities to learn and experience literacy in ways that build on the capacities they already have (such as using picture symbols and adaptive/digital technology) for making meaning. Also, children with disabilities are frequently involved in time-consuming therapies that seek to build other 'functional' skills. These and other factors tend to cast children who are labelled with developmental disabilities on less-successful literacy trajectories than those of their typical peers. Kliewer urged the consideration of different routes to literacy in children who are often deemed to be incapable of learning to read or otherwise engage with literacy, due to their labels and impairments. Much of Kliewer's research emphasizes the importance of creative adaptations to literacy lessons that allow non-verbal children, or children for whom spoken language is significantly impaired, to participate and contribute. The classrooms in his studies often provided adaptations that can be universally applied to all the children. For example, a non-verbal child required the addition of a box with illustrated song titles on cards so that she could take her turn to choose the songs to be sung at circle time (Kliewer, 2008). However, all the children enjoyed this method of choosing songs, so they all used it. The focal child's need to make her selection non-verbally was accommodated in the flow of this classroom and all children benefited from the opportunity to use print and picture symbols to demonstrate their choice of song. Many of the strategies found in the literature about children with disabilities can be applied to libraries' early literacy story time programmes with the same universally beneficial effect on all children. For example, a variation on the song-card activity is the song cube: a cardboard cube's six sides are decorated with song titles and pictures (Figure 9.1). At story time, children can take turns 'rolling the dice' to select a song (children with physical disabilities can be helped by another child or a caregiver to take a turn throwing the song box).

Figure 9.1 *Song cube*

A framework for inclusive story time

The most important thing about inclusion in the early years library is the consideration that is given to meeting the needs of diverse children *before* the development of the service, programme or resource. After carefully considering diverse needs and after learning about what accommodations and adaptations might be appropriate for including a range of children, it is likely that practitioners will discover that much of what they do each day is already inclusive. For example, providing hands-on learning materials (i.e. puzzles and blocks) for children to explore is inclusive. A diverse collection of picture books and non-fiction material aimed at young children that includes large print, audio, video, digital formats as well as Braille resources, if at all possible, is inclusive. Story times that frequently include movement, repetition and sensory learning with scarves, beanbags and bubbles is inclusive. Children with disabilities are more like other young children who do not have disabilities than they are different from them. Much (but not all) of what we know about and do for young children is inclusive. However, it is critical to consider that some of our commonplace early literacy and story time activities that are accessible to typical children may represent serious barriers to participation for children with disabilities. The following sub-sections describe some critical features of inclusive story times and offer some recommendations for adapting programmes to meet the needs of diverse young children, including those with developmental disabilities.

Pace

Conventional wisdom about story time presentation sometimes offers the advice to 'speed it up and mix it up to get their attention' (Rogers-Whitehead and Fay, 2010, 9). There is an enormous qualitative difference between being energetic and engaging and presenting a story time that feels like it is in fast-forward mode. A typical or precocious child might not mind being moved from one story, song, dance or rhyme to the next with dizzying rapidity, but a child with a language delay or a sensory disability will definitely mind. Children who, for whatever reason, cannot access language and literacy learning at such a fast rate will just disengage (Prendergast and Lazar, 2010). Their caregivers may also note their child's apparent lack of success in this setting and be hesitant to return. This is especially likely if the child has been particularly noisy in his or her protestations. None of this is the child or caregiver's fault. It is not even the presenter's fault, as he or she is doing what a great deal of conventional wisdom has told us about pacing in story time. Inclusive early literacy will necessitate the chucking of that particular piece of conventional wisdom, as it is neither true nor inclusive. Simply slowing down your rate of speaking, singing, transitioning and delivering each story time segment will greatly enhance the inclusiveness of your programme.

Engagement

Engagement on the part of the presenter is critical for inclusion. This is not the same as speed, or how fast you move from thing to thing so that they 'don't get bored'. Your energetic engagement needs to be genuine. You are having an engaged social interaction with a diverse group of children about language and literacy. This is authentic learning, and everyone's participation is meaningful and valued here. Eye contact, smiles and welcoming gestures send messages of encouragement just as well as your words do. Taking the time to look at and respond to each child in turn will help them to understand some of the social connections that are taking place in the programme. As the facilitator, you are modelling how communication and learning take place in this setting and everyone else will naturally take their cues from you. From a sociocultural standpoint, language and literacy learning is both a social and a cultural act (Heath, 1983, 2010; Kliewer, 2003; Street, 2003). From this viewpoint, we understand that language and literacy learning only happens when there is interpersonal connection. Socially engaging with participants in the story time setting also means that parents and caregivers are better able to develop sufficient trust in children's librarians to share with them additional insight and strategies for including their child.

Repetition

Repetition of story time elements is critical for inclusion. Repetition is never boring to young children (Diamant-Cohen, Estrovitz and Prendergast, 2013). Repetition should be offered in various ways and modes so that children have different ways to access new knowledge (vocabulary, concepts, etc.) over time. So, read a story, then tell it again with puppets or on the flannel board. Then sing a song about something in the story. Then act out a short segment of the story. Later, offer a craft that involves one of the characters or objects in the story. Show how to interact with an iPad app that relates to something in the story. Demonstrate one of many great story-creation apps in which children can create and tell their own stories, using words, pictures and narration and using the original story as a starting point. This range of activities does not have to take place within the same programme. In fact, this strategy can be spread over several weeks, with great success (Diamant-Cohen, Hetrick and Yitzhak, 2013). The idea is to offer multimodal/multisensory representations of key ideas. For example, repeating elements from Paul Galdone's classic picture book *The Three Bears* (Galdone, 1972) do not have to include porridge bowls, chairs and beds. A reimagining of this fairy tale could include black bean soup, beanbag chairs and beach towels, and bunnies instead of bears. Props could be very simple, inexpensive things like an empty food tin, a beanbag and a few soft-toy rabbits. The repetitive elements are what drive comprehension of narrative, and the creative reapplication of ideas drives cognition for all children (Salmon, 2014). This is literacy learning, and your modelling of this process for caregivers is of great importance, especially for caregivers who may be unsure of how to support a child with disabilities.

Routine

Routines in story time mean that things unfold in a fairly predictable sequence of events and come to be something that children as well as their caregivers can rely on. Various research studies suggest that the establishment and maintenance of routines in both home and school settings is important throughout early childhood (Wildenger et al., 2008). While predictable routines may be optional for many children, they are critical for children who struggle with information and/or sensory processing and have other disabilities, including autism (Stoner et al., 2007; Rodger and Umaibalan, 2011). If the child can trust the routine, he can participate better. One way to provide a predictable story time routine is to add a simple visual schedule to your programme and refer to it as you move through the segments of the programme one by one.

Group size

Early childhood research supports the idea that children at this age thrive in relatively small groups of their age peers with the presence of supportive adult facilitators (Frede, 1995). Think about the size of preschool classes and their adult to child ratio. There is simply not enough early literacy learning support to go around in large, crowded settings. Even with very effective crowd-control strategies, large story time groups are an enormous barrier to children with a variety of disabilities. Crowded rooms with lots of people sitting close together on the floor obviously make navigating with wheelchairs and walkers extremely difficult. Children who have sensory-processing issues and disabilities such as autism may be unduly distressed by the noises and movements of large groups of people. Crowded story time programmes are a complex barrier to address, as forcing people to register in advance causes its own set of access issues. One solution may be found by offering the same programme twice in a row, with a short break in between for two groups of attendees to change places. Another solution may be to offer a few 'small group' story times that are advertised as being able to admit only the first 15 families who arrive. As long as you continue to offer drop-in time slots (which may exceed 15 to reach your room capacity) you may be able to offer the best of both worlds to everyone who wants to participate. Over-crowding at story time needs to be viewed as a barrier to inclusive and developmentally appropriate early literacy resource provision. Solutions to over-crowding at story time should be patron driven and will necessarily vary from site to site.

What about 'special programmes'?

The professional literature has many examples of library staff's creative solutions to several kinds of participation barriers (Akin, 2004; Banks, 2004; D. Barker, 2011; Feinberg et al., 2014). Sometimes programmes are developed specifically for families of children who have disabilities to participate in together (Twarogowski, 2009; G. Barker, 2011; Leon, 2011; Prendergast, 2011). The idea is that the parents can relax a bit, knowing they are among their peers who understand their situation, and the programme content can be carefully geared towards the needs of the group and its characteristics. The examples that are most frequently found in professional literature discuss story time programme approaches for children with autism (Akin, 2004; Winson and Adams, 2010). Partnerships with organizations that support children with autism and their families mean that librarians can learn about the needs of children and families in their communities and work towards making their library's offerings more inclusive. However, from an inclusion standpoint, creating special programmes for special children should be conceptualized only as the first of many steps towards inclusion. Such special, separate, 'exclusive' programmes as are described in the professional literature are definitely a good way to gain the trust of families who have been reluctant to come to regular programmes. They are a good way to help familiarize their children with the routines of the library. They are a wonderful opportunity for parents to make connections with their peers who understand their lives (Prendergast, 2011). These may be necessary steps towards inclusion, with a few caveats. Try to avoid creating and then labelling programmes with only one specific disability in mind. Children are unique, and even children who share medical diagnoses may be much more different than alike. Also, the way that different disabilities are dispersed among the general population may make it difficult to fill an entire programme with one specific group of similarly diagnosed children. Another concern is that many very young children who have developmental delays are not yet diagnosed and therefore may not respond to invitations to participate in a programme aimed at a specific diagnosis they have not yet received. Finally, inclusive early-literacy programmes should never require the facilitator to know private medical information about any participant. Instead, parents can be encouraged to help you get to know their child and his or her characteristics and needs without feeling like they must share his or her label. A particular child's specific diagnosis may be something you have never heard of anyway, so there is no need to ask what it is. It is more important to build an atmosphere in which you can converse with her parent/caregiver so that you can find out what she needs to help her get the most out of your programme. You might find that she thrives on predictable routines, needs to touch things to help her learn and responds well to music. So, this child and her caregiver can be encouraged to sit in the same place close to the facilitator each week. She can be invited to look at the routine-of-the-day picture symbols before the programme begins so that she knows the order in which the action will unfold. The facilitator can make a simple prop for her (as well as all the other children) to hold while a story is told aloud. Pieces of felt or laminated pictures cut into the shape of a featured animal (Figure 9.2) could be passed around the room. The facilitator could ask what her current favourite song happens to be or let her

Figure 9.2 *Felt animal in child's hand*

have a turn rolling the aforementioned song cube and then lead the whole group in singing the song. It is doubtful that any of the typically developing children in the programme or their parents would even realize that the simple addition of these elements was in pursuit of this particular child's successful inclusion. Because they had been seamlessly woven into the already predictable and multimodal routines of story time, everyone would benefit from these adaptations. Inclusive early literacy means the creation of programmes that are designed to welcome and appeal to everyone, including the significant percentage of children with disabilities that live in your communities. As trusting relationships with caregivers are developed, practitioners can then learn to adapt even more strategies to maximize inclusion and participation by particular children.

Conclusion

Inclusion in early literacy and in all children's library services begins with the assumption that children with disabilities who are living in your communities can and should be able to benefit from the early literacy services of your library alongside their age peers. Inclusive early literacy involves *anticipating, planning and preparing for the participation of children with diverse development* and ensuring that they are provided with opportunities to experience and learn alongside their age peers.

Selected print resources

Feinberg, S., Jordan, B. A., Deerr, K., Langa, M. A. and Banks, C. S. (2014) *Including Families of Children with Special Needs: a how-to-do-it manual for librarians*, rev. edn, Neal-Schuman.

Klipper, B. (2014) *Programming for Children and Teens with Autism Spectrum Disorder*, American Library Association.

Prendergast, T. and Lazar, R. (2010) Language Fun Storytime: serving children with speech and language delays. In Diamant-Cohen, B. (ed.), *Children's Services: partnerships for success*, American Library Association.

Selected web resources

ALSC Blog: The official blog of the Association for Library Service to Children, www.alsc.ala.org/blog/category/special-needs-awareness

Autism and Libraries: We're Connected, www.librariesandautism.org

Inclusive Early Literacy: Exploring Early Literacy in the Lives of Children with Disabilities, www.inclusiveearlyliteracy.wordpress.com

SNAILS: Special Needs and Inclusive Library Services, http://snailsgroup.blogspot.ca

References

Akin, L. (2004) Autism, Literacy, and Libraries: the 3 Rs = routine, repetition, and redundancy, *Children & Libraries,* **2** (2), 35–42.

American Library Association (2011) *Every Child Ready to Read: teaching parents and caregivers how to support early literacy development,* http://everychildreadytoread.org.

Banks, C. (2004) All Kinds of Flowers Grow Here: the child's place for children with special needs at Brooklyn Public Library, *Children & Libraries,* **2** (1), 5–10.

Barker, D. (2011) On the Outside Looking In: public libraries serving young people with disabilities, *Australasian Public Libraries and Information Services,* **24** (1), 9–16.

Barker, G. (2011) Kids with Autism Get Their Own Story Time, *Salt Lake Tribune,* www.slrib.com.

Campana, K. and Dresang, E. T. (2011) Bridging the Early Literacy Gulf, *Proceedings of the American Society for Information Science and Technology,* **48** (1), 1–10, doi: 10.1002/meet.2011.14504801134.

DEC/NAEYC (2009) *Early Childhood Inclusion: a joint position statement of the Division for Early Childhood (DEC) and the National Association for the Education of Young Children (NAEYC),* Chapel Hill, www.naeyc.org/files/naeyc/file/positions/DEC_NAEYC_EC_updatedKS.pdf.

Diamant-Cohen, B. and Ghoting, S. N. (2010) *The Early Literacy Kit: a handbook and tip cards,* American Library Association.

Diamant-Cohen, B., Estrovitz, C. and Prendergast, T. (2013) Repeat After Me! Repetition and early literacy development, *Children & Libraries,* **11** (2), 20–4.

Diamant-Cohen, B., Hetrick, M. A. and Yitzhak, C. (2013) *Transforming Preschool Storytime: a modern vision and a year of programs,* Neal-Schuman.

Dresang, E. T., Burnett, K., Capps, J. and Feldman, E. (2011) *The Early Literacy Landscape for Public Libraries and Their Partners,* University of Washington, 1–34.

Feinberg, S., Jordan, B. A., Deerr, K., Langa, M. A. and Banks, C. S. (2014) *Including Families of Children with Special Needs: a how-to-do-it manual for librarians,* rev. edn, Neal-Schuman.

Flewitt, R., Nind, M. and Payler, J. (2009) 'If She's Left with Books She'll Just Eat Them': considering inclusive multimodal literacy practices, *Journal of Early Childhood Literacy,* **9** (2), 211–33, doi: 10.1177/1468798409105587.

Frede, E. C. (1995) The Role of Program Quality in Producing Early Childhood Program Benefits, *The Future of Children,* **5** (3), 115–32, doi: 10.2307/1602370.

Galdone, P. (1972) *The Three Bears,* Clarion Books.

Ghoting, S. N. and Martin-Díaz, P. (2006) *Early Literacy Storytimes @ Your Library: partnering with caregivers for success,* American Library Association.

Ghoting, S. N. and Martin-Diaz, P. (2013) *Storytimes for Everyone: developing young children's language and literacy*, ALA Editions.

Hamer, J. (2005) Exploring Literacy with Infants from a Sociocultural Perspective, *New Zealand Journal of Teachers' Work*, **2** (2), 70-5.

Heath, S. B. (1983) *Ways with Words: language, life, and work in communities and classrooms*, Cambridge University Press.

Heath, S. B. (2010) Family Literacy or Community Learning? Some critical questions on perspective. In Dunsmore, K. and Fisher, D. (eds), *Bringing Literacy Home*, International Reading Association.

Katims, D. S. (1994) Emergence of Literacy in Preschool Children with Disabilities, *Learning Disability Quarterly*, **17** (1), 58-69.

Kliewer, C. (2003) Literacy as Cultural Practice: some concluding stories, *Reading & Writing Quarterly*, **19** (3), 309-16, doi: 10.1080/10573560308214.

Kliewer, C. (2008) Joining the Literacy Flow: fostering symbol and written language learning in young children with significant developmental disabilities through the four currents of literacy, *Research and Practice for Persons with Severe Disabilities (RPSD)*, **33** (3), 103-21.

Kliewer, C. and Biklen, D. (2001) 'School's not Really a Place for Reading': a research synthesis of the literate lives of students with severe disabilities, *Journal of the Association for Persons with Severe Handicaps*, **26** (1), 1-12.

Kliewer, C., Biklen, D. and Kasa-Hendrickson, C. (2006) Who May Be Literate? Disability and resistance to the cultural denial of competence, *American Educational Research Journal*, **43** (2), 163-92, doi: 10.3102/00028312043002163.

Kliewer, C., Fitzgerald, L. M., Meyer-Mork, J., Hartman, P., English-Sand, P. and Raschke, D. (2004) Citizenship for all in the Literate Community: an ethnography of young children with significant disabilities in inclusive early childhood settings, *Harvard Educational Review*, **74** (4), 373-403.

Lawson, H., Layton, L., Goldbart, J., Lacey, P. and Miller, C. (2012) Conceptualisations of Literacy and Literacy Practices for Children with Severe Learning Difficulties, *Literacy*, **46** (2), 101-8, doi: 10.1111/j.1741-4369.2011.00603.x.

Leon, A. (2011) Beyond Barriers: creating storytimes for families of children with ASD, *Children & Libraries*, **9** (3), 12-14.

McKend, H. (2010) Early Literacy Storytimes for Preschoolers in Public Libraries, www.bclibraries.ca/ptplc/files/early_lit_storytimes_final_english_with_cip_electronic_nov10.pdf.

Mock, M. and Hildenbrand, S. (2013) Disability and Early Childhood: the importance of creating literacy opportunities and identities. In Larson, J. and Marsh, J. (eds), *The Sage Handbook of Early Childhood Literacy*, Sage Publications Inc.

Paciga, K. A., Hoffman, J. L. and Teale, W. H. (2011) The National Early Literacy Panel and Preschool Literacy Instruction: green lights, caution lights, and red lights,

Young Children, **66** (6), 50–7.

Peterson, S. S. (2012) Preschool Early Literacy Programs in Ontario Public Libraries, *Partnership: the Canadian Journal of Library and Information Practice and Research,* **7** (2), 1–21.

Prendergast, T. (2011) Beyond Storytime: children's librarians collaborating in communities, *Children & Libraries, the Journal of the Association for Library Service to Children,* **9** (1), 20.

Prendergast, T. (2013) Growing Readers: a critical analysis of early literacy content for parents on Canadian public library websites, *Journal of Library Administration,* **53** (4), 234–54, doi: DOI: 10.1080/01930826.2013.865389.

Prendergast, T. and Lazar, R. (2010) Language Fun Storytime: serving children with speech and language delays. In Diamant-Cohen, B. (ed.), *Children's Services: partnerships for success,* American Library Association.

Purdue, K., Gordon-Burns, D., Rarere-Briggs, B., Stark, R. and Turnock, K. (2011) The Exclusion of Children with Disabilities in Early Childhood Education in New Zealand: issues and implications for inclusion, *Australasian Journal of Early Childhood,* **36** (2), 95–103.

Rodger, S. and Umaibalan, V. (2011) The Routines and Rituals of Families of Typically Developing Children Compared with Families of Children with Autism Spectrum Disorder: an exploratory study, *The British Journal of Occupational Therapy,* **74** (1), 20–6, doi: 10.4276/030802211X12947686093567.

Rogers-Whitehead, C. and Fay, J. (2010) Managing Children's Behavior in Storytimes, *Children & Libraries,* **8** (1), 8.

Rogow, S. M. (1997) *Language, Literacy and Children with Special Needs,* Pippin Publishing.

Salmon, L. G. (2014) Factors that Affect Emergent Literacy Development when Engaging with Electronic Books, *Early Childhood Education Journal,* **42** (2), 85–92, doi: 10.1007/s10643013-0589-2.

Shanahan, T. and Lonigan, C. J. (2010) The National Early Literacy Panel: a summary of the process and the report, *Educational Researcher,* **39** (4), 279–85, doi:10.3102/0013189X10369172.

Stoner, J. B., Angell, M. E., House, J. J. and Bock, S. J. (2007) Transitions: perspectives from parents of young children with autism spectrum disorder (ASD), *Journal of Developmental and Physical Disabilities,* **19** (1), 23–39, doi: 10.1007/s10882-007-9034-z.

Stooke, R. K. and McKenzie, P. J. (2011) Under Our Own Umbrella: mobilizing research evidence for early literacy programs in public libraries, *Progressive Librarian* (**36/37**), 15.

Street, B. (2003) What's 'New' in New Literacy Studies? Critical approaches to literacy in theory and practice, *Current Issues in Comparative Education,* **5** (2), 77–91.

Twarogowski, T. B. (2009) Programming for Children with Special Needs: part one, www.alsc.ala.org/blog/2009/06/programming-for-children-with-special-needs-part-one.

Ward, C. (2007) Libraries as 21st-Century Learning Places, *Language Arts,* **84** (3), 269.

Wildenger, L. K., McIntyre, L. L., Fiese, B. H. and Eckert, T. L. (2008) Children's Daily Routines during Kindergarten Transition, *Early Childhood Education Journal,* **36** (1), 69–74, doi: 10.1007/s10643-008-0255-2.

Winson, G. and Adams, C. (2010) Collaboration at Its Best: library and autism programs combine to serve special audience, *Children & Libraries,* **8** (2), 15–17.

Wolfe, S. and Flewitt, R. (2010) New Technologies, New Multimodal Literacy Practices and Young Children's Metacognitive Development, *Cambridge Journal of Education,* **40** (4), 387–99, doi: 10.1080/0305764X.2010.526589.

Zascavage, V. T. and Keefe, C. H. (2004) Students with Severe Speech and Physical Impairments: opportunity barriers to literacy, *Focus on Autism and Other Developmental Disabilities,* **19** (4), 223–34.

CHAPTER 10

Music and rhyme time sessions for the under-fives

Shelley Bullas and Ben Lawrence

Introduction

Through the work we do as children's librarians, encouraging literacy and language development comes high on our agenda. Whether we are delivering story time sessions, class visits, training or rhyme times we are constantly linking them back to this overarching aim.

We are employed by Calderdale Metropolitan Borough Council and work in a team called Discover, which encompasses the Public Children's Librarians, Schools' Library Service and Museums Education Officers. Calderdale is located in West Yorkshire, England and is a semirural authority nestled between Bradford, Leeds and Kirklees. In Calderdale we have three Public Children's Librarians covering the 0–19 age range, with specialists in Early Years and Teenage library provision, overseen by a Coordinator. The delivery of all children's activities is undertaken by the professional staff. In the past, library assistants have occasionally delivered story time sessions, but rhyme times have always been delivered by the children's team, as this is seen as a professional role.

Singing and rhyme time sessions are perfectly placed in the local library. Not only does singing help to develop speech, language and communication skills as well as fine and gross motor skills, it also enriches the family unit, as it boosts emotional and social well-being.

Most library services now offer music-based activities for the under-fives. How group leaders go about planning and preparing for such activities is an interesting question. There are a wide range of resources about music making with the under-fives in early years settings, many of which include using simple percussion instruments. However, there are limited resources available which focus on singing in a library environment when both the children and parents are present.

As musicians we are well aware of the importance of choosing the right material.

Different group leaders will choose to sing different songs. However, some songs, particularly some well-loved nursery rhymes, are difficult for children to sing. Our chapter will help to guide you as group leaders on choosing materials and planning a well-balanced session. Group leaders are integral to the success of their group and it is important that they choose material which they enjoy.

This chapter will focus on running singing sessions in public libraries for young children and their parents and carers. We hope that the material in this chapter will be useful to anyone currently delivering rhyme times, but we also hope to inspire complete beginners. Librarians, library assistants, managers, early years professionals and students alike will benefit from reading the following chapter.

Singing with the under-fives and their families

For many of us, songs and nursery rhymes are our first encounter with the rich world of language and literature. Sounds surround babies as they develop in the womb, and when they are born they are already aware of their parents' voices. Singing is the most direct way of enhancing this family bond:

> Singing is a moment of intimacy, a concentrated bonding time when interaction between baby and adult is very focused. So singing can help mothers to build a strong, nurturing relationship with their babies.
>
> (Young, 2003, 27)

Nursery rhymes and songs have huge benefits to children as they develop. From the moment they are born, babies are able to use and explore their voices. Many of the nursery rhymes and songs that are popular today have been passed down from countless generations; therefore, they contain words which children may not encounter in a normal play situation. Ouvry (2004, 12) has highlighted the important role of music in 'passing on cultural heritage without the need for reading and writing'. Children who regularly experience nursery rhymes are more likely to have a richer vocabulary by the time they start school. Moog (1976, 113) found that 'between the ages of three and four ... girls and boys who are taught songs and games by their parents, brothers and sisters, or in nursery schools, have a clear cognitive advantage over other children'.

Unaccompanied singing and speaking are the most accessible and interactive ways of sharing songs and rhymes. When in a group setting, it is crucial for children to be able to hear their parents clearly as they join in. If there is a loud accompaniment, or noisy percussion instruments are being used, it limits this clear interaction. It is a misconception that singing has to have an accompaniment, whether live or a recorded backing track. The human voice is a wonderful instrument in itself and children need to be able to pick out the sounds and shapes of the language clearly. Children and grown-ups alike respond to good songs and rhymes with fun games and activities:

> Children enjoy group singing and will join in with small sections of familiar songs. Action rhymes, where the physical action reinforces the language, are particularly valuable at this age.
>
> (Pound and Harrison, 2003, 48)

Singing is the best way of internalizing musical skills, as the child has to create the sound from within, and the sound is personal and unique to them. To bang a drum, a child has to have developed some fine and gross motor skills, whereas babies are using their voices from birth:

> Children learn to sing - it is not something some can do and some can't, or just something that you pick up; it is 'learnable' and so teachable too.
>
> (Young, 2009, 75)

The way we plan and deliver our own rhyme sessions is directly informed by the writings and philosophical approach to music education of the Hungarian composer Zoltán Kodály. It is a methodical and sequential approach to music education, and in the early years has a huge emphasis on musical play. Katalin Forrai was hugely influenced by the teachings of Kodály and she further developed his approach by applying it to preschool music.

Songs and nursery rhymes have been handed down from generation to generation and are steeped in our cultural heritage. Kodály said 'Folksong is the school of good taste ... those who develop a taste for what is good at an early age will become resistant later to what is bad' (Rowsell, 2003, 4). A big part of the methodical approach of Kodály is about starting with simple ideas and gradually getting more complex, thus starting with shorter rhymes and songs with fewer notes and adding more notes as children become more experienced. It is worth bearing in mind that children's vocal chords are much smaller than ours and are therefore able to sing only a small range of notes. Susan Young highlights the importance of considering this when choosing appropriate material: 'It is important to provide children with some songs which are vocally achievable for them to sing ... Many nursery favourites lie outside pre-school children's current capabilities: the melodies are too wide-ranging and have tricky twists and turns' (Young, 2003, 51).

Singing works well as a library-based activity. People naturally congregate in libraries and, because it is a community space, it offers a safe, calm environment for music making to take place. Even though libraries have traditionally been 'quiet' spaces, most library services regularly offer some type of musical activity or performance. It is worth mentioning that some parents who are not current library users may be reluctant to attend a session which takes place in a library; similarly, adults with low levels of literacy or who have English as a second language may find the library building a barrier. However, many rhyme times take place in library spaces designed for children, and these by their very nature should be colourful, welcoming and friendly. Rhyme times are a fantastic introduction to libraries. As they grow, children will learn to associate their local library with the positive experience of rhyme time. They will become members of their library and choose books as part of their visit. Library staff will see a bustling, lively atmosphere with increased issue figures.

Planning and preparing your session

As Benjamin Franklin famously said, 'By failing to prepare, you are preparing to fail'. We, as practitioners, deliver our best sessions when we are at our most prepared. If you have a bank of songs, rhymes and activities, and a plan for every eventuality, or as many as you can think of, you will deliver a versatile and responsive session. Just as we wouldn't read a poor-quality story at a story time (or one we have not read before), the same applies to the songs and rhymes we choose for our sessions. Nursery rhymes are the bedrock of our rhyme time sessions in libraries. However, for those new to delivering, or those returning to it, it is important to refresh your knowledge. Refer to our resources section at the end of the chapter for some suggested places to start building your repertoire.

It is important to find songs and rhymes that you enjoy. Many books now come with CDs as well as printed music. These CDs are perfect for learning songs and rhymes, but we would always strongly advocate using the human voice, unaccompanied, when leading rhyme time sessions. Be aware of regulations in your country regarding the performance of recorded music. You will not be able to play recorded music in your building if you do not have the required licence; for example, in the UK this can be obtained from the PRS (Performing Rights Society). Susan Young speaks of the dangers of using some of the recorded music marketed for children in her book *Music 3-5*. She highlights the need to be wary of recordings that 'zip along at too fast a pace, at too high a pitch and with complicated words' (Young, 2009, 65).

It may seem rather time consuming to practise the songs initially, but once learnt thoroughly, they will stay with you for a lifetime. Find inventive ways to learn the songs, perhaps playing a CD whilst driving, or listen to them on your iPod as you exercise. Often practising in front of a mirror, which can seem embarrassing at first, will let you see the expressions you use.

How do I plan a well-balanced session?
How long should the session be?

This will vary from library to library. We recommend 30 to a maximum of 40 minutes.

How should the room be set up?

Try to limit distractions in the space where you deliver your session. Have a clear space to allow movement, preferably with little or no furniture or other hazards. Toys can be very distracting for you and the rest of the group. Parents can feel particularly stressed if their child is playing with toys rather than engaging in the session. Toys are tempting to all children, so if you want them to engage with the session, move all small toys to another room and cover larger toys with blankets, etc.

How should the families sit?

We find sitting in a circle on the floor the best way of delivering rhyme times. It brings everyone down to children's level, and everyone can see each other. Make sure you put some chairs out for adults who may struggle to sit on the floor.

What songs should I include?

Choose material that you like and enjoy singing. This enjoyment will shine through and will make everyone want to join in with you. Types of songs and rhymes you can include are

- welcome and warm up
- calming/lullabies
- energetic/physical action
- finger/simple-actions songs
- knee bobbing.

How many songs and rhymes should I include?

Our rule of thumb is 'less is more', and 'repetition is key'. Take your time with material and work hard to get the best from it. You may want to introduce a new song every so often.

What if I have a mixture of babies and toddlers?

This is when you will be grateful that you prepared so well. You should be able to tailor your session to suit the age range in front of you. Children of all ages love rhymes, but make sure you have a higher proportion of rhymes, tickling and knee-bobbing games if you have a session full of babies. If you have a higher proportion of toddlers, action rhymes and active songs may be more appropriate.

What if it goes horribly wrong?

Knowing your songs and their associated activities inside out will minimize mistakes, but you are only human. If something in your session does not go to plan, please try not to worry. Make light of any mistakes – you want to create a safe environment where everyone has a go. You wouldn't mind if families got the words wrong, so don't be hard on yourself. If an activity isn't working, move on to something else. Perhaps if everyone is looking sleepy or vacant you can try an active song like 'The Grand Old Duke of York', or if the group is noisy and unsettled, try a quiet, calming lullaby like 'Twinkle, Twinkle' to draw everyone in. If families aren't joining in, try using whispering voices and work up to singing voices. With a little bit of reflection you will soon be able to identify what went wrong, and with the hints and tips in Figure 10.1, will be able to make suitable changes to your plan.

- Every rhyme time session needs to be well planned and thought through.
- Like any good story, it needs a beginning, middle and end.
- In your repertoire you will need a wide range of songs and rhymes. Active, calming, interactive, finger rhymes, lullabies, parachute songs, etc.
- Try to start your session with the same song each week. A bright, simple, engaging 'Hello' song would work well. Children will become familiar with it and know that it is time to sit down with their parent.
- Plan sufficiently so you can adapt to the group's mood, and plan for different eventualities.
- Try linking songs. Are there any common themes? Perhaps singing all your songs about animals together, or your Space songs, etc., would work well.
- Make sure your equipment and resources are space appropriate. A big parachute in a small room can be fun, but may not be appropriate for safety reasons.
- If you are confident about delivering sessions, are you getting the best from your material? Is it time you learnt some new songs?

Figure 10.1 Hints and tips

Running and facilitating a group

Running a group comes with its own set of responsibilities and expectations. As a profession we must strive to raise parents' expectations of what libraries offer.

Free of charge does not mean a compromise on quality. Whether you decide to charge for attendance or make it a free event, most parents will expect the session to be well organized and led by a member of staff. Allowing for parental input in your session is all well and good, but parents will expect the session to be well structured and delivered with confidence.

Importance of family learning

The trouble is that, while children of this age love to sing and show a readiness and willingness to do so, fewer parents are teaching games and songs to their children – and it has been that way for a long time.

(Ouvry, 2004, 59)

As children's librarians we need to ensure that family learning is at the heart of every activity we deliver. According to NIACE (the National Institute of Adult Continuing Education), family learning is an activity which encourages children and adult family members to learn together. Rhyme time sessions are an ideal activity for family learning to take place. Sharing songs and rhymes are part of our heritage, and our aim is for parents and carers to take songs back into the family unit, so they become ingrained into daily life. You may need to emphasize the importance of singing the songs at home and explain to parents about the benefits of singing (bonding, language development, fine and gross motor skills). Repetition is vital to these benefits, and the songs and rhymes will have little effect if sung only once a week at your rhyme time session.

Henry always gets excited about coming [to rhyme time] and participates a lot. We always sing the songs at home and Henry has been singing some of the songs without me prompting him, which is great. Good ideas for me to use at home – I found my old hand-puppet spider and so we have been singing [the Spider Song] lots! Criss-Cross is our favourite.

Mum who frequently attends our rhyme time sessions

Parental involvement in the session

Parental involvement in library rhyme time sessions is crucial. Not only do parents play a huge role in what their child gets out of the experience, but they also contribute to the success of the event. It is therefore really important to have parents on side and to engage them from the start. Pound and Harrison (2003, 8) felt that 'It was not the musical abilities of the parents that made a difference but the high level of support that they gave their children'. Once parents are engaged in the activity and believe it is of value, their children will be able to get the most out of the experience. Engaging parents isn't always easy, but don't forget, they have made the effort to attend your session. Most of us will have met parents who love singing, but what about the parents who find the prospect of singing in public daunting? Many adults truly believe that they can't sing:

> Those who work with young children are aware that thoughtless negative comments can seep deeply into feelings and identity. However, putting down one's own singing ability or other people's singing is part of English culture.
>
> (Young, 2009, 78)

Encouraging participation

It is imperative that you create a secure, nurturing environment that immediately puts parents at ease. The moments before your session starts are a great opportunity for this. You can chat to parents, answer any questions they may have and get to know them and their children. Tell parents that they *can* sing and that it is really important that they join in. Even if they sing quietly, it is vital that their child can hear their parent's voice. Once the parents are at ease you will probably find that their children will relax too. It is also important to reassure them that it is perfectly normal for children to wander about or become restless and upset. Parents must never feel like they have to leave a session and should be free to manage these episodes, safe in the knowledge that the session will continue regardless.

Group dynamics

It is important to mention here that not all parents lack confidence. Some parents will need no encouragement at all and may be bursting with new ideas and songs to sing. This may work to your advantage by taking the focus away from unconfident parents. However, you need to be aware that overpowering parents can be off-putting to other participants and can also be very draining for you delivering the session. You will need to encourage them to maintain their interest, but also to curb their enthusiasm if they become too overbearing. You may also have parents who chat loudly throughout your entire session whilst their child runs riot. Whilst a bit of chatter is normal it is really important that parents participate with their child. Rhyme times are a learning opportunity and parents need to get involved so that their child can benefit from the experience. Just remember, *you* are leading the session. You need to be confident, and there will be occasions when you will need to be bossy. It is all right to be firm from time to time. If you feel that a parent is talking too much, patiently wait for them to stop. They will eventually realize that they are being disruptive and start to join in. It might help to set out some ground rules at the beginning of your session. If you decide to do this, make sure you make it light and friendly, as you want to maintain the relaxed atmosphere.

Asking parents for song suggestions can be a good way of encouraging them to participate. It can throw up songs that are inappropriate, either on a technical level or due to their content, but it is a great way of involving parents. Avoid falling into the trap of giving all responsibility over to the parents and carers. Too much free choice will create a chaotic session. If a keen parent suggests a song which is unfamiliar to you, ask them if they would be willing to share it with the group. They will either revel in the opportunity or shy away.

Top tip
We find that using a sack with either mini nursery rhyme puppets or laminated pictures on a large, squishy dice are great ways of creating an element of controlled free choice. Children love choosing the next song, and even very small children are able to grab a puppet or roll a dice.

Song sheets

It is not uncommon for nervous parents or carers to approach us to ask for song sheets, as the songs and rhymes may be new to them. We always do our best to reassure parents that they will not need song sheets, as songs and rhymes are repeated multiple times, across multiple weeks. If song sheets are used, parents will focus on the piece of paper rather than their child. The session is about sharing songs together and loving the language and actions in the songs and rhymes. If parents regularly attend your sessions they will automatically learn the song and rhymes by heart.

Things to consider

If at all possible, be around for ten minutes or so before the start of your session. This time is a great opportunity to get to know the families better. You may need to be on hand to point out where the toilets and baby-changing room are. It is also an invaluable opportunity to talk about library provision for under-fives. Taking the time to promote library membership, Bookstart or other reading initiatives to the entire family will make a lasting, friendly welcome to the library. You may also identify some families who need some extra support or guidance.

Throughout the session be mindful of your body language. Bright eyes and a friendly smile will of themselves create the welcoming atmosphere which is crucial to a successful rhyme time. It is your job to make sure that you know why you are delivering a rhyme time, and to explain to parents how they can get the best from the session. Welcome the group, and put it at ease with key information and messages.

Key points to remember
- Your job is to inspire a lifelong love of language and literacy through songs and rhymes.
- Planning and preparation are vital for a successful session. This will allow you to be responsive to the needs of your group.
- Enthusiasm is infectious. Make sure you are bright eyed, smiling and enjoying yourself.
- Repetition of rhymes and songs is key; they will become embedded in your participants' memories, making handouts obsolete.

Conclusion

Nearly all library services provide singing activities for the under-fives and their families. These activities form the foundations of language development for young children and therefore it is really important that group leaders are confident and the session is of a high quality. Even though there are limited texts which focus specifically on running singing sessions in the library environment, there are some fantastic resources which are available for practitioners to utilize. We have highlighted some of the logistical problems to watch out for when delivering sessions, and offered some strategies that work well for us.

There is no strict formula for a successful rhyme time session, and group leaders should choose material and a format which suits their style. As practitioners we feel that thorough preparation and practice will give group leaders confidence and aid their success. We have been heavily influenced by Zoltán Kodály, and we always strive to use the highest-quality material in a methodical, sequential approach. Choosing appropriate material is essential, and a list of recommended resources can be found at the end of the chapter. This list is by no means exhaustive and should serve as a foundation as you build up your own resource list.

Thorough planning and practice of session material is vital and this will boost the group leader's confidence. However, sessions can always be improved and sometimes things can go wrong. Try not to be disheartened, there is always something to be learnt. Ensuring that you have a relaxing, welcoming environment and organized, well-structured session will help to put you and the parents at ease.

Parents play a vital role in the success of the session and help their children to get the most out of the songs and rhymes. The real benefits take place when families share the songs and rhymes at home. Being enthusiastic in our delivery and confident in the reasons why we are running singing sessions will empower families to share songs and rhymes in their daily routine.

Suggested resources

Here is a list of the resources that we simply could not do without. We hope they will be of some use to you too.

Parachute

We have three parachutes, in different sizes - an extremely large one for big groups and venues, a medium-sized one, perfect for most situations, and a baby parachute for small groups. They are brightly coloured and are a source of great excitement amongst our families. Let your imagination run wild with the songs you use a parachute with. We purchased ours from YPO, which supplies public sector organizations with products.

Lycra

Available from most fabric shops/markets, Lycra is perfect for enhancing songs. This could be used for rowing, bouncing objects or hiding underneath. We have a selection of colours and sizes. Green works well for grass, and blue for the sea. We also have a piece of translucent Lycra with stars on, perfect for 'Twinkle, Twinkle'.

Puppets and soft toys

Puppets mean the world to children, and can really make songs and rhymes come alive. We have many finger and hand puppets, and have been accumulating them for some time. The British Kodály Academy is a great place to search for puppets. Soft toys can be found in most charity shops, too.

Scrunchy

A scrunchy is a tube of material with elastic inside. It looks like a giant hair scrunchy, hence the name. This is perfect for songs that require being in a circle and keeping shape. There is huge range of actions and directions to be explored with a scrunchy, for example, up-down, high-low, in-out and rowing.

Recommended songs and rhyme books

We are constantly collecting new material, and parents and other professionals are a great resource for learning new songs. We also use the books listed below. All have suggested games and activities for each song and rhyme.

A&C Black

To see A&C Black's full catalogue go to their website,
www.bloomsbury.com/uk/education/acblack-music, or e-mail
publicity@acblack.com.

Nicholls, S. (1992) *Bobby Shaftoe, Clap Your Hands*, ISBN 0713635568.

Roberts, S. and Fuller, R. (2004) *Livelytime Playsongs*, ISBN 0713669403.

The British Kodály Academy

For the BKA's catalogue go to www.britishkodalyacademy.org/resources.htm, or phone 02476411269.

Dietrich, H. M. (1995) *Rhymes, Mother Goose*, ISBN 9638457066.

Dietrich, H. M. (1999) *Fishy, Fishy in the Brook*, ISBN 9630385317.

Dietrich, H. M. *Children Songs*, no ISBN.

Forrai, K. (1998) *Music in the Preschool*, ISBN 9780958629706.

Waterhouse, C. (ed.) (2007) *How Can I Keep From Singing!* ISBN 0951259245.

GIA Publications, Inc.

For a list of all GIA publications please go to:
www.giamusic.com/music_education/index.cfm.

Feierabend, J. M. (2000) *The Book of Wiggles and Tickles*, ISBN 1579990533.

Feierabend, J. M. (2000) *The Book of Lullabies*, ISBN 1579990568.

Feierabend, J. M. (2000) *Bounces,* ISBN 157999055X.

Feierabend, J. M. (2000) *Simple Songs and Circles*, ISBN 9781579990572.

Feierabend, J. M. (2000) *Tapping and Clapping*, ISBN 1579990541.

National Youth Choir of Scotland (NYCOS)

A list of NYCOS publications can be seen at: www.nycos.co.uk/Publications.

Geoghegan, L. (1999) *Singing Games and Rhymes for Early Years*, ISBN 9780953826100.

Geoghegan, L. (2002) *Singing Games and Rhymes for Tiny Tots*, ISBN 9780953826117.

Geoghegan, L. (2005) *Singing Games and Rhymes for Middle Years*, ISBN0953826198.

Oxford University Press

Opie, I. and Opie, P. (1955) *The Oxford Nursery Rhyme Book*, ISBN 0198691122.

Online retailers

The British Kodály Academy, www.britishkodalyacademy.org
Dance in a Bag, www.danceinabag.co.uk/Catalogue.htm
Dickory Dock Designs, www.dickorydockdesigns.co.uk/home
Early Excellence, www.earlyexcellence.com/resource_centre.html
Puppets By Post, www.puppetsbypost.com
YPO, www.ypo.co.uk

Useful organizations

Bookstart, www.bookstart.org.uk
The British Kodály Academy, www.britishkodalyacademy.org
The Chartered Institute of Library and Information Professionals (CILIP),
    www.cilip.org.uk
Music and the Deaf, www.matd.org.uk
The National Institute of Adult Continuing Education (NAICE), www.niace.org.uk
The National Literacy Trust, www.literacytrust.org.uk
National Youth Choir of Scotland, www.nycos.co.uk

References

Moog, H. (1976) *The Musical Experience of the Pre-school Child*, Schott & Co.
Ouvry, M. (2004) *Sounds like Playing*, The British Association for Early Childhood
    Education.
Pound, L. and Harrison, C. (2003) *Supporting Musical Development in the Early Years*,
    Open University Press.
Rowsell, C. (2003) The Kodály Experience, *Libretto*, (2), 4-5.
Whitehead, M. (1997) *The Development of Language and Literacy*, Hodder & Stoughton.
Young, S. (2003) *Music with the Under-fours*, RoutledgeFalmer.
Young, S. (2009) *Music 3-5*, Routledge.

CHAPTER 11

Reaching your audience:
the librarian's role

Carolynn Rankin and Avril Brock

Introduction

This chapter is presented in two parts and we look first at how the librarian can provide opportunities for young children and their families to enjoy literacy and language development activities together. In the UK the library service can be regarded as a key partner acting as a bridge to the community by providing a welcoming atmosphere. We further discuss introducing a love of books to babies and young children and the role of stories and story-telling in helping to develop the imagination. Many early years librarians tell stories at sessions, providing entertainment and enlightenment for their local community. Acknowledging the skills required to effectively connect and engage with a family audience, we offer practical guidance for the librarian as performer. Continuing the theme of partnerships, we discuss three examples of outreach work by looking at Traveller families, teenage fathers and culturally diverse communities. Partnerships are a key aspect of campaigns and promotional schemes and we look at some UK-based initiatives. Part 2 of the chapter provides a superb range of case studies that presents early years library provision delivered by partnerships in Australia, Croatia, Denmark, Italy, Northern Ireland, Russia and Sweden.

PART 1 REACHING YOUR AUDIENCE
Providing a welcoming atmosphere

Librarians want to reach the family audience so as to encourage literacy skills and help build sustainable communities. The well-planned early years library will provide a range of wonderful books, toys, treasure baskets and other creative resources for young users and their families. The environment in which these resources are offered also merits consideration, as audiences can be encouraged by sending positive messages. The librarian has an important role in helping children, and the adults with them, to feel comfortable and welcome in the library or early years setting. In planning a welcoming environment, children's craft and art work displayed on the walls can encourage links with the local community. In Chapters 5 and 13 we discuss how the physical aspects of the library can be planned to create a positive environment. In addition to the physical environment, the social atmosphere and ethos created by the library staff is an important factor in making families feel welcome. Encourage your colleagues to consider their behaviour and the non-verbal messages they send, particularly when feeling concerned about something. It can be difficult to show relaxed, positive body language all the time. It would be useful to promote discussions with other colleagues about how to manage certain challenging situations. Remember that babies may not always show model behaviour when they visit - they can be irritable and cranky when teething and will probably dribble! The more independent toddlers and preschool children will look to adults for reassurance and guidance. The 'see me' stage of development can be irritating when your attention is demanded by boisterous youngsters - this isn't necessarily rude behaviour on the part of the child, but it is how they check that the adults are paying attention. Guidance and training can help all staff to be aware of their own positive behaviour. Libraries have a long history of providing services for their communities, and we have mentioned the interest in supporting the reading child. With increased interest in providing the best start for very young children and their families, librarians are reaching out to the wider community. As Miranda McKearney of The Reading Agency writes, 'the market opportunity is there for libraries to position themselves as the community hub for reading - social, lively, relevant' (McKearney, 2007, 40). We believe that libraries can reach their audiences by:

- modelling and encouraging parents to read with babies and young children from an early age
- providing a welcoming social space for families
- showing that parents are valued and that they are important as their child's first educator
- providing a variety of materials that can be borrowed, including multi-sensory, tactile books, story and information books, DVDs and storysacks
- creating exciting book displays to encourage parents and children to select a range of different books
- providing activities such as colouring and drawing, story activities, singing, puppets, crafts
- having story sessions at times to suit parents and carers, including dads
- offering dual language story telling sessions and providing dual language books.

(Brock and Rankin, 2008, 29)

Planning library sessions

In planning library sessions for the early years audience there are some practical things to consider. Publicity and advertising are important to ensure that your target market knows what is on offer and where. In planning the structure of your session, consider how long it will last and what format it will take. The venue also needs to be factored into the plan, as this will affect the activities you can undertake and the resources readily available – are you holding the sessions in the children's library or in a separate room in a library building, or are you going out into the community? It is a good idea to have a theme for a story session, such as numbers, weather, animals, colours, holidays, magic and enchantment, pets or nursery rhymes. Some library authorities have produced themed resource packs containing books, rhymes and song sheets, musical instruments, puppets, games, CDs and cassettes. These can be shared by a number of early years librarians.

It is also a good idea to plan the beginnings and endings of your sessions. Infants and young children respond well to what is familiar, and so it is a good idea to begin and end each session with the same simple songs. Some venues have a welcome song such as

'Hello Everybody'
Hello everybody, how do you do?
How do you do? How do you do?
Hello everybody, how do you do?
How do you do today?

The Reading Agency has provided an extensive checklist of 'Hints for Reading to Under 5s', including practical guidance such as coming to the story time with more books than you need – all of them stories which you like and have practised reading out loud. It is also suggested that you choose books with pictures that are big enough to be seen from the back of the group and choose stories that have lots of joining in – farmyard animal noises, counting or actions.

Running sessions: health and safety issues

Health and safety procedures should already be in place as part of the management operation in any library building, and practitioners should be aware of the requirements. A library space that is regularly used for early years sessions should already have a risk assessment checklist in place. Before holding any kind of session for under-fives it is good practice to do a 'baby and toddler audit', and a practical way to undertake this risk assessment is to get down to the child's level and look at the space you will be using for your library sessions. Check for potential hazards, such as plug sockets that may be particularly appealing to little fingers, shelving that may be used for climbing on and heating sources such as radiators. Ensure that you have child-size chairs and a clean mat or carpeting for story time. It is important to provide a safe environment for young children and their families, and health and safety requirements should be reviewed and documented regularly.

Planning layout and seating for parent and toddler sessions

Mums, dads and carers should be encouraged to stay with their young children for the story time and activity sessions, so it is important to plan the seating arrangements for the adults before the session starts (as illustrated in Figure 11.1). Considering this practical aspect of planning can make a difference to the success of the session. Remember that not all grown-ups may be able to sit on the floor with their young children or grandchildren on their laps, so do provide some adult-size chairs if they are available. Seating for adults is best kept to the sides of your story-telling area or arranged in a semi-circle to facilitate interaction. A closed circle will help to contain those babies who are starting to crawl! Experience has shown that seating adults at the back of the room sends the message that they are observers rather than participants, and will encourage

Figure 11.1 *Story-telling strategies – planning seating arrangements*

them to talk among themselves rather than joining in your session.

The young children can be settled on a story-telling mat or special area of carpet. As they are at floor level it helps if you are seated above them – this means it is easier for you to see them and they will be able to see the storybook and any other props you are using. Some venues have a designated story-telling chair. Ensure that you have given yourself enough room to work in and to enable you to easily reach the resources you will use during the session. It is worth checking other practical aspects of the activity venue; for example, it is better for any sunlight to be shining on you and not into the children's eyes, so think about the layout of the space.

Experienced practitioners also recommend trying to avoid the inevitable distractions of shared library spaces by seating children with their backs to windows and busy counter areas. It is also a good idea to give parents and carers permission to take their child out of the activity if the child is unhappy, so consider preparing another area with books and toys for young children who aren't ready to sit and listen with the group.

Timing: how long do your sessions last?

Young children have short attention spans and you may be running sessions for groups with a range of ages; the four-month-old baby may be joining her three-year-old brother for rhyme time. Practitioners discussing this question at an Early Years Library Network training day suggested that most sessions should last between 30 minutes and 1 hour. It is a good idea to vary the content of your events, as this helps to maintain the children's attention. Don't just fill hour-long sessions with stories, but include songs, rhymes and craft activities.

Involving parents and carers in your sessions

Some library practitioners suggest that you set out ground rules at the start of each session. Families attending for the first time may appreciate some idea of what to expect and what is acceptable behaviour. One practical tip is to check that all mobile phones have been turned off, as a courtesy, at the start of the activity time. Let the adults and carers know that you can build in time for them to talk together at the beginning or end of the session; this social interaction is very important for building relationships between the families and with the early years librarians. There is evidence to show the value of such contacts in supporting families where referral services are involved; we discussed partnerships with parents in Chapter 5.

During the library visit parents can be actively encouraged to let their babies and young children enjoy the experience of touching and handling the books. Carol Wootton's advice is:

> Do not turn young babies away, the younger you get them the better – it's lovely to see them develop over the weeks taking more notice and getting the parents to let them handle the books.
>
> Carol Wootton, Early Years Librarian

From a practical viewpoint, it is a good idea to suggest that parents sit with their children while you are doing stories and rhymes; this will encourage a sharing environment and should, hopefully, help to deal with any potentially disruptive behaviour.

Activities with glitter and glue

In addition to story time and rhyme time sessions, craft activities are a fun way to encourage families into your library setting. The early years librarians in Wakefield provide the following advice based on their 'Sticky Fingers' book-related craft sessions. Craft activities are best undertaken with adult supervision, and so this is a great opportunity to involve parents and carers.

Safety is important, so give glue and scissors to the adults. Attention spans will be limited, but simple book-related craft activities can help children learn to follow easy instructions and develop hand–eye co-ordination and motor skills. Using crayons and pencils gives small children the opportunity to practise holding writing tools. This type of session also helps to develop colour-recognition and counting skills. It is a good idea to choose a craft activity that the children can do themselves. Have a picture or a finished example to show them what they can do. Young children will lose interest if an adult has to do most of the work, so encourage parents not to take over.

Making books

A great way of helping children to understand how books work is to make them during an activity session. Many educators incorporate the making of books into their teaching of reading programmes with children of all ages. Whitehead (2007) explains that many young children discover for themselves how to make a book by folding one or two sheets in half and writing and drawing on the pages. During an activity session you can provide different kinds of coloured paper and let the children choose their pictures and the layout of pages. They can discover the power of becoming authors! Another idea is to make photograph books, as young children like to look at pictures of themselves. Until they grasp the idea of turning pages without tearing the paper, young children will need board or other indestructible books. Goldschmied and Jackson (2004) suggest an easy way of making indestructible picture books by using plastic envelopes. Use family photographs or pictures cut from magazines or catalogues and stuck onto card. Two sheets, back to back, go in each plastic envelope and the pictures can be changed or grouped in categories for older children. This is a good fun activity in a family craft session.

Making a reading tree in your library

When meeting young children and their families on a regular basis, making a reading tree in your library can be a good activity to encourage interaction and involvement. This is easy to start, as all you need to do is to draw a tree trunk and branches on a piece of paper or card and tape it to the wall. You can then involve the children in cutting out different leaf shapes from green card. Keep these leaves in an easy-to-reach place. Each time you read a story book in a session, write the book title and author's name on a paper leaf and add it to the tree. For every book they read together, encourage families to also add their story leaves to the reading tree. Begin by adding the leaves near the bottom and work towards the top. It will be great fun to see the reading tree growing week by week and it is a very visual reminder of the power of stories. This activity can also be done at home, as families can grow their own reading trees.

Dealing with other library users

One issue involved in developing library services for the under-fives may be complaints. Other library users may be concerned that the library has become a crèche and may object to the messy play and craft activities which are an integral part of your early years sessions. It is important that you respond promptly to any such criticism, following your local authority's guidelines for dealing with complaints. One solution might be to provide a trolley of books and materials available for other users when you are holding your sessions. It is a good idea to let other library users know when your sessions are held, so put up notices and provide leaflets; they can then make an informed choice not to use the library at those times. You can give examples of other library sessions that are more suited to older people, such as book clubs and coffee mornings.

Introducing a love of books to babies, young children, parents and families

Reading to babies and young children and getting them involved with books is one of the most effective ways of enhancing language development. Babies can learn to handle books and acquire vocabulary, while parents and carers provide the words that match the pictures, using a range of sounds and beginning voice gymnastics with enthusiasm (Brock and Rankin, 2008, 27). Many books are quite tactile, with different materials to touch and feel, flaps to lift up or buttons to press, and these early book-handling experiences can be a very interactive and interesting process. Babies are our youngest scientists and they will explore books with their eyes, hands, mouths and feet.

Early literacy can be encouraged by sharing books, so let parents know that it is valuable to get into a routine with their baby. Each night before bed, it is good to choose a book together, whether a storybook or a simple text with pictures and just a few words on a page. For many parents it is helpful to know that reading before bed can settle the baby and ensure that there are fewer interruptions during the night. This time together is important, it will help to strengthen relationships and help the baby to feel relaxed and safe. Talk to Your Baby is a campaign run by the National Literacy Trust to encourage parents and carers to communicate more with their children from birth. We discuss this in more detail in Chapter 5, in the section on partnership with parents.

Early literacy has been discussed in previous chapters, but here are some further reminders about how parents can be supported by providing them with information on this aspect of the early years. Encouraging early literacy by sharing books is important for the following reasons:

- It helps parent and child get to know each other better by supporting the bonding process.
- It encourages the joys of reading from a very early age and generates a love of words, stories and how to gain information.
- Reading to a restless baby or young child can have a very calming effect
- a baby will begin imitating sounds and words when read to over a period of time.
- Learning how to handle books, and how to read from them, can help to develop a good educational foundation.
- It helps to stimulate the imagination and an enquiring mind.

You can't start communicating with babies too soon, and early experiences are very valuable. Language-rich environments are important, and reading to babies is one of the most effective ways of encouraging language (Brock and Rankin,

2008). Sharing books with babies and young children is a great way of helping them to learn to talk. Reading aloud combines the benefits of talking, listening and story-telling and helps to build the foundation for language skills. Reading stories to children is thought to be *the* most important activity for their reading capabilities on entry to school.

You might also suggest some of the following read-aloud tips to parents and carers, provided by Reading is Fundamental USA. This guidance may also be useful information for staff in the early years library setting, as they will be interacting with families and can offer advice and encouragement.

- Hold the baby in your lap; make sure he or she can see the pictures.
- Play with words, sing and make up rhymes; include the baby's name.
- Expect babies to touch, grasp and taste, as that is how they learn.
- Offer the baby a toy to hold and chew while listening to you read.
- Read one or two pages at a time; gradually increase the number of pages.
- Let the baby turn the pages if he or she is more interested in the book than in listening to you read. He or she will still be learning about books and enjoying your company.
- Point to, name and talk about things in pictures; describe what's happening.
- Ask the baby: 'Where's the ...?' 'What's that ...?' Wait for a response.
- Encourage babies to join in – moo like a cow or finish a repetitive phrase.
- Stay on a page as long as the baby is interested.
- Put the book away and do something else when the baby loses interest.

Using treasure baskets with babies

The concept of the treasure basket for babies was developed by the child psychologist Elinor Goldschmied as a method of play that helps babies and toddlers to learn naturally. We discuss the contents of treasure baskets and the development of these resources in libraries in Chapter 6. In contrast to the shared activity of reading books together, playing with a treasure basket is very much a baby-only activity. The parent's or carer's role is to provide security by having an attentive but not active presence. Encourage parents to sit and watch their babies enjoying the treasure basket without interfering. Parents should resist the temptation to choose objects that they think their baby would like; that is not what heuristic play – the active exploration of natural objects in a multisensory way – is about.

Goldschmied and Jackson (2004) explain that one of the things an adult may find difficult to do at first is not to intervene but to stay quiet and attentive. Sometimes a baby may quietly gaze at a treasure basket for some time before deciding to reach out and investigate an object. When two or three babies are seated round the treasure basket they will need close adult supervision, and also protection from older mobile children. Babies are socializing when sharing a treasure basket. Though intent on handling their own chosen objects, babies are aware of each other, and for much of the time will be engaged in interactive exchanges. When planning the use of space in your early years library setting, consider including a quiet, safe space that can be used for babies to be seated with the treasure baskets.

Using picture books

For our youngest children, pictures are their introduction to the world of books. In a picture book the illustrations are as important as the text. Picture books help young children to understand that words convey meaning, well before they are aware of the text. Picture books help to build vocabulary, an important building block for reading. Books can help young children to identify letters, shapes, numbers and colours; names of people, animals, places and everyday things. Picture books and illustrations encourage children's vocabulary development, as the adult supplies the word or words for pictures (as illustrated in Figure 11.2). Picture books help infants and toddlers to begin to understand symbols and babies begin to understand the representative meaning of pictures as they touch, look at and share feelings about the picture with an adult (Bus and de Jong, 2006, 125).

Picture books can also be a good starting point for adults with poor literacy

Figure 11.2 *What can you see? Building vocabulary using picture books*

skills or those trying to gain competence in a new language. Angela Robinson (n.d.) explained how the Picture This project in Blackburn with Darwen was designed to encourage adults with basic literacy skills to share books with their children. It can be embarrassing for people to admit to poor reading skill, but this can be avoided by using picture books and encouraging parents and carers to share them with their children. Proficiency in reading isn't necessary when using picture books, as the illustrations usually tell the stories. A key achievement in the Picture This project was actually encouraging local families to attend, and it was important that the partner organizations working within the local children's centre helped with the promotion and publicity for the 6-week scheme.

Musical sessions: communicating through making music

Making music in the early years library is an activity in which parents can easily be involved. This should be a fun activity, and by exploring music and movement young children soon join in singing games and songs. You can create a treasure basket filled with different musical instruments and sound makers, such as spoons and pots. Music is a vehicle for expression and communication, just like language. You can try the following activities with babies as well as young children:

- Create sound effects with your voice - whistling, humming.
- Use bodies to create sound - use hands, feet, chest, knees, head for clapping, stamping, clicking and banging.
- Beat out the rhythm and syllables of each child's name.
- Repeat sounds and get children to appreciate the rhythm of syllables within words.
- Make musical instruments - shakers containing rice, beans, seeds, marbles, buttons.

To encourage sound and song you can try the following:

- Create a bag of animals for Old MacDonald's farm.
- Put models of a spider, crocodile, cat and mouse in a bag and invite the children to select an object from the bag to prompt the song.
- Make songs personal for children by including their names in a song.

For a detailed discussion on delivering rhyme time sessions, please see Chapter 10, by Shelley Bullas and Ben Lawrence.

A 'Communicate through Music' activity pack has been jointly developed by Music one2one and Talk to Your Baby to encourage musical interaction with babies and young children. It is designed for practitioners and professionals to help them to communicate the benefits of musical activities with parents and carers. The pack is designed to be a flexible resource and the materials can be freely copied and distributed. It includes the 'Babies Love Music' information sheet, which promotes the benefits of music and musical activities for use in your setting. Some libraries print this out to give to parents and carers.

Stories and story-telling

What's so important about story-telling? Well, stories are a means of learning about life. History, culture and family experiences are handed down through the generations by traditions of story-telling. New ideas, real-life issues and all sorts of characters can be explored and experienced through story. Listening to stories is an enjoyable experience and most adults and children are drawn into the listening process, whether it is one to one with an adult at home or in a group in your library. This is a great way to connect with your audience. Experience of stories helps everyone to understand the world in which we live, enabling us to make connections between what we are learning and what we already know. Swiniarski (2006), working in Salem in the USA, uses the concept of a 'global bookshelf' to promote a global educational theme of unity and diversity. Through using story-telling she aims for children to connect with others and to appreciate other cultures in an activity-based curriculum. The Early Years Foundation Stage (DfE, 2012) states that early years settings must offer opportunities for access to poetry, stories and non-fiction books, and this advice holds true for libraries.

Remember that children like to hear favourite stories over and over again, as they enjoy the unchanging themes and find reassurance in familiar endings. They will often ask for the same bedtime story night after night and won't let you omit any of the pages! Parents can be assured that this is quite normal. For a good example of this, see Brock and Rankin (2008, 72), where the mum of three boys aged 2, 3 and 10 years talks about their bedtime routine and the importance of stories, particularly *We're Going on a Bear Hunt*, which they love to hear again and again. Children pay attention to rhythm and repetition, characters and events, words and meanings. There is so much to discover in a good story. Children will develop their abilities as readers, writers, story-tellers and meaning makers from the stories they have heard. Listening to and reading stories from different genres is important, so consider the potential in your library setting for traditional fairy and folk tales, myths and legends, fantasy and adventure, fiction and non-fiction, family and animal stories.

It is important that staff working in a front-line role enjoy telling or reading stories. You will have read about story reading and story-telling in Chapter 3, but do enjoy this further advice from Carol Wootton, an experienced early years librarian from Wakefield, who offers some practical advice on story-telling and using books:

> Children are not going to judge you on your story-telling skills, they are just quite happy to be read to or told a story. Moreover, if you do it every day you soon become an expert! Hence the importance of early literacy. It also doesn't matter if a parent cannot read; we need to encourage them just to talk about the pictures with their child, and maybe make up a story with their child about the pictures. It is important to talk to children about the books as well as reading to them; this helps them to develop a love of books.

Carol Wootton's advice for making a quality story time is:

> Think about the ages of the children you will be reading to and have stories appropriate to all ages. Be aware how long each story will take to read. A half-hour session is long enough for young children and can be divided up into about 20 minutes of story-telling and 10 minutes for the activity, as a rough guide. But go with the flow, no two sessions are the same in early years work – if you have a lively group that have just found their feet, it's not easy to keep their concentration, however good you are!

The emphasis should be on having fun, but by providing prompts and support and asking key questions, adults and older children can assist in developing children's vocabulary and concepts. By posing problems and challenges you can encourage children to use their imaginations and develop their own story-telling skills. It is valuable to develop children's thinking through having conversations where there is equal interaction between adults and children and between children and children. Practitioners can help to create opportunities for 'sustained shared thinking' as described in the Effective Provision of Pre-School Education (EPPE) (Sylva et al., 2004) and Researching Effective Pedagogy in the Early Years (REPEY) (DfES, 2002) research, which involves the adult being aware of the child's interests and the adult and young child both working together to develop an idea or skill. From the librarian's perspective this means showing genuine interest by giving your whole attention, maintaining eye contact, affirming, smiling, nodding and offering encouragement. It also involves respecting children's opinions and choices and inviting them to elaborate by asking open questions. This supports and extends the children's thinking and helps to make connections in learning. In the most effective settings, practitioners support and challenge children's thinking by getting involved in the thinking process with them. Sustained shared thinking can only happen when there are responsive, trusting relationships between adults and children (Potter, 2008, 59). It is useful to explain the importance of these interactive conversations to parents, and how story can be a very valuable way into developing 'story-telling' relationships and being imaginative with their children.

Supporting separated families to share stories

There is also much value in family stories that can be passed down the generations, and family story-telling sessions are also a great way of involving grandparents. Invite families to contribute to your sessions by coming in to tell their stories, sharing them in writing, tape-recording them or creating a booklet of stories.

The importance of families sharing story-telling is exemplified in the work of Storybook Dads, an award-winning independent charity which aims to maintain family ties and facilitate learning for prisoners. Storybook Dads helps to maintain the vital emotional bond between parent and child by enabling parents to make bedtime story CDs, DVDs and other educational gifts for their children. Based at Dartmouth Prison, the scheme was started in 2002 by Sharon Berry and it has been successfully rolled out to over 100 UK prisons (including women's prisons, where it's called Storybook Mums). Any prisoner can record a story, regardless of their reading ability. The stories are digitally edited and sound effects and music are added. The children love these stories because they can hear their parent's voice whenever they want and this helps to maintain family ties. Over 20,000 beneficiaries were helped in 2012 and for many isolated and socially excluded families, Storybook Dads is a lifeline. The Storybook Dads scheme has been replicated in prisons across Europe, the USA and Australia.

This idea has been taken up by the armed forces and the Storybook Alliance now includes Storybook Soldiers, Storybook Waves and Storybook Wings. This helps to provide a link between parents who are away on operations and their children.

Stories in other languages: supporting the bilingual learner

The way a practitioner can structure stories through supporting bilingual children's language development in story-telling sessions can be very valuable. The adult can provide or model the language through story-telling while using props and 'this will enable children to gain confidence by repeating the vocabulary and language structures offered' (Brock and Power, 2006, 33). The children listen and feed the language back and these story-telling group activities can be very interactive and dramatic. There are valuable examples of how to do this using familiar stories such as 'Elmer the Elephant', 'Farmer Duck', 'The Owl Babies', 'The Gruffalo' and 'The Rainbow Fish' in Brock and Power (2006, 33 and 34). How to tell and read the 'Three Billy Goats Gruff' in English and Hindi/Urdu is demonstrated in Brock and Rankin, 2008 (pages 39, 40 and 48). An extract from the story of 'Send for Sohail' written in English and Urdu and how to use it with young children can be seen in Brock and Power (2006, 38-40).

Stories work with all children, but in particular with bilingual learners. It is very important to model the story, for the adults working with the children to actually become the Billy Goat, the Giant, Baby Bear. If we don't demonstrate, how can we expect the children to learn? An important tool is to 'shadow tell' the story: with the children playing roles, provide them with the words to repeat and they will expand upon them as they gain in confidence. Reading stories is fine, telling is fine, but neither of these is enough for children to become confident in using the words and phrases.

Using storysacks is a good way to support bilingual children (we discussed storysacks in detail in Chapter 6). Try to ensure that a range of stories from different cultures and backgrounds are available. Brock and Power (2006) suggest that one needs 'to be aware of the need to both affirm and extend the children - provide stories that they can see themselves in and stories that take them into environments other than their own' (p. 3). Many schools and libraries are now using storysacks that they have either made with parents or bought from commercial suppliers. Many of these stories have repetitive language that enables the children to tell the story easily while handling the characters and props. The following stories are very suitable for use with a storysack:

- Red Riding Hood and other traditional tales
- The Very Hungry Caterpillar
- Handa's Surprise
- Stone Soup
- Topiwalo the Hatmaker
- Mrs Wishy Washy
- Where the Wild Things Are
- Mr Gumpy's Outing
- Sandeep and the Parrots
- Send for Sohail.

(Brock and Power, 2006, 37)

Strategies for sharing stories with children: the librarian as performer
Ideas for making up stories in your library

There are so many wonderful story books available that you may have a difficult time choosing which ones to read aloud! Alternatively, you may feel confident to make up stories involving your own library setting. Carol Wootton, who worked as an early years librarian in Wakefield, offers some practical advice:

> If you feel confident about making up your own stories and see a scenario that you think could be used in story-telling with children, then jot it down in case you forget it. Many situations can be turned into stories for children. For example, if you are telling a story in a library, you can pretend that you have a resident animal that hides there, perhaps a mouse, rabbit or even a teddy. Tell the children what this little resident gets up to once the library has closed. Leave his little footprints around for the children to find - that makes it even more realistic for them! One week you can get the children to draw pictures for him and in the following week let them find a thank-you note from him. It can be great fun thinking up little adventures, and they don't have to last long, especially with younger children. You can plan to have a particular ending to your stories or leave them open ended and ask the children for their version of the ending. It is a fun thing to do.

As the teller, you must enjoy the story and want to share it with your young audience. There are a number of things to bear in mind when taking the story-teller' role:

1   Use props, costume and story resources to help set the scene.
2   Make use of your voice and of rhythm and tenor to create pace, surprise, suspense and anticipation.
3   Use gestures and movement to create effects of size, space, weather, action.
4   Pay special attention to how you portray your characters. Good characters bring a story to life, so put life into them with facial expressions, voice, gestures and body posture. You can characterize using intonation, emphasis, accent and dialect. Try to make each character different enough that they're easily told apart. When portraying two characters talking together try a 'cross-focus' technique where you make each one face a different 45-degree angle.
5   Tell and retell favourite parts of the story or repeat some sections for effect or comprehension.
6   Involve the children in telling and acting out the story.
7   Include children's names so that they feel they are part of the story (this

can also be a good way to hold their attention and involvement).

8   Incorporate personal and shared information about the local community to further develop a story.

It is a good idea to assess the children's listening abilities and engagement in the story. Young children do not have very long attention spans, so use ways of gaining and holding their attention. Try to maintain eye contact with your audience – this also gives you a chance to see what they are doing and how engaged they are! Some traditional story-tellers will sit in a special seat – there is a story-teller's chair and a story-telling cloak in the Writers Attic at Seven Stories, the Centre for Children's Books in Newcastle-upon-Tyne. Sue Wiggins, early years librarian at the Airedale Library and Family Centre in Castleford, wears a story-telling hat for her early years story time sessions. You could also use artefacts such as a magic carpet, an enchanted lamp, story wand or crystal ball.

Voice projection and performance skills

Some of us will have no problem at all in telling or reading stories aloud to an audience. Others will feel very nervous about the idea of a public performance – even if it is to a group of babies and their parents. Certain approaches and techniques will help you to prepare and have confidence in telling and reading stories and using your voice. Practise breathing deeply and correctly to project and sustain your voice. To check this, place your hand on your stomach. As you inhale and your lungs expand, you should feel your stomach push out. Many people do the opposite, holding in their stomachs and breathing only with their upper chests. Try to keep your back straight, so your lungs can expand fully. Don't push your voice too hard or use it unnaturally except when speaking as characters in the story. Practise using different, exaggerated character voices. During the story-telling performance try to relax your body, especially your throat and jaw muscles.

There are other practical things you can do to enhance the story-telling performance. This is about creating the right atmosphere and ensuring your young audience are engaged. Wearing a story-teller's hat or a story cloak can help to you assume the 'role' and play the part with confidence.

Reading aloud is an effective way to connect with your young audience, and Mem Fox's Ten Commandments provide valuable reading-aloud techniques. Mem Fox is an Australian writer who has championed early literacy for many years. Her *Read Aloud Commandments* have been included here as they are practical, humorous and also effectively summarize the message we want to share about reading stories out loud. The guidance is aimed at anyone involved with children, but you can reflect on how you feel about reading aloud in your library setting.

1   Spend at least ten wildly happy minutes every single day reading aloud.
2   Read at least three stories a day: it may be the same story three times. Children need to hear a thousand stories before they can begin to learn to read.
3   Read aloud with animation. Listen to your own voice and don't be dull, or flat, or boring. Hang loose and be loud, have fun and laugh a lot.
4   Read with joy and enjoyment: real enjoyment for yourself and great joy for the listeners.
5   Read the stories that the kids love, over and over and over again, and always read in the same 'tune' for each book: i.e. with the same intonations on each page, each time.
6   Let children hear lots of language by talking to them constantly about the pictures, or anything else connected to the book; or sing any old song that you can remember; or say nursery rhymes in a bouncy way; or be noisy together doing clapping games.
7   Look for rhyme, rhythm or repetition in books for young children, and make sure the books are really short.
8   Play games with the things that you and the child can see on the page, such as letting kids finish rhymes, and finding the letters that start the child's name and yours, remembering that it's never work, it's always a fabulous game.
9   Never ever teach reading, or get tense around books.
10 Please read aloud every day, mums and dads, because you just love being with your child, not because it's the right thing to do.

(www.memfox.net/ten-read-aloud-commandments.html)

Puppets

Another way of connecting with your young audience and their families is to use puppets. When telling stories it can be great fun to have story aids such as puppets, as they give your young audience something visual to focus on. Puppets can be used by adults to tell stories to children and by children to tell stories themselves. They are a great way to engage an audience, as they can encourage older children to chat, discuss the story-lines and offer advice on the outcomes and consequences. Children can emotionally engage with the puppets. If you are story-telling without a book, a puppet is a good prop to use. They don't have to be expensive and Carol Wootton suggests that home-made puppets work as well as any others:

Don't be afraid to use props such as puppets or a soft toy. I have a storybear that the children look after while I'm reading stories. Some people like to use puppets to give them confidence, because the children tend to look at the puppet rather than you. If you are good at doing voices you can make the puppet speak to the children, or you can have a silent puppet that whispers in your ear. It's not something you have to do; it's how comfortable you feel.

Staff at the Shadsworth Children's Centre in Blackburn with Darwen used a puppet theatre to stage a performance of 'Sleeping Beauty' as part of a monthly reading group project to encourage adults with basic literacy to share books with their children.

Reaching 'hard to reach' audiences

The phrase 'hard to reach' is used by 'government and other agencies to describe some groups, their families and children that are less likely than others to be using early years services' (Lane, 2008, 83). Care must be taken when using this term, as it can have negative connotations, and Lane (2008, 84) suggests that if services can consider 'whether they themselves are easy to reach', some of the potential barriers might be more easily broken down'.

It is recognized that librarians are good at reaching 'hard to reach' groups, particularly when offering services that promote social inclusion (Stevens, 2003). Where practitioners are tackling social exclusion, you may need to justify outreach time away from the library setting. It is a question of balance between making the library service as accessible and as appropriate as possible to the wider community and maintaining a quality service for those who actually visit the library.

CASE STUDY A librarian's reflection on the community her library serves

It's hard to get families into the library. We have plenty of school-age children, but we'd really like to get the younger children to come in too. I'm making that a priority. I've now started to visit and read stories in the Children's Centre next door. I found that most of the children are being brought to the Children's Centre by carers, but few parents seem to go there. It's very hard to make the connections. One grandma did not know her children's surnames and was not sure which father they had. It can be very difficult to get some parents to join libraries. We've found some would not enrol. They didn't want to fill in forms and we couldn't get them to bring their ID in. They had difficulties in filling in forms, as some had real problems with levels of literacy and couldn't fill in their address and postcode. Parents did not want the responsibility of having books in their homes. They wouldn't let the children borrow the books, as they thought they would have to pay fines. We try to be as welcoming as we can to draw these children and their families in through the doors.

Claire, community librarian

The next sections look at how libraries are promoting outreach work, using three examples: Traveller families, teenage fathers and culturally diverse communities. It is interesting to note that this challenging outreach work is often most effectively accomplished by using the power of partnerships with other key organizations.

Traveller, Roma and Gypsy families

Outreach is a fundamental aspect of working with Traveller, Roma and Gypsy families. Traveller Education Support Services (TESS) operate in most local authorities to improve access to education and other services for the children and families in these communities. Outreach can mean bringing families into existing local services or delivering a service directly to a family who have no means of access. These families may remain excluded from many mainstream services and opportunities, particularly health and education, as a service is effectively closed to someone who does not know about it and who has no relationship with it. Children may miss out on the Bookstart gifts, especially if their families are highly mobile. Libraries have been proactive in helping to reach these groups. Riches (2007) reports on story-telling services for the under-fives being made available on mobile libraries, and Sure Start librarians have arranged for book boxes to be given to Traveller communities. In some areas where there is no mobile library, the local library has arranged open days specifically for families from the Gypsy and Traveller communities. These open days allow the families to come together and be assisted to register as library users and find out what is available. In another example of outreach services, the Oswestry Sure Start Children's Centre has a mobile play bus with an on-board toy library service that visits sites, and the Sure Start librarian has organized story time sessions on site and a library box for 0- to 5-year-olds. The library service in Essex and the Essex Travellers' Education Service are bringing books to families living on Traveller sites in the county. Mobile libraries make weekly stops at a number of sites and also at primary schools with a high proportion of Traveller pupils. Preparation for this project included cultural-awareness training for librarians and careful selection of stock covering subjects known to be of interest to the Traveller community, such as non-fiction books on animal husbandry.

A number of key organizations, including the Society of Chief Librarians, have collaborated to make it easier for Travellers to return library materials, thus removing one of the barriers to the use of libraries by people who are on the move. Children and young people who are Travellers, looked after, refugees or asylum seekers (and their parents or carers) can return library materials to any library in the UK without any overdue charges being made. The receiving library will make arrangements to return the items to the originating library free of charge.

Teenage fathers

It is important that fathers are involved in interacting with their babies and form close relationships through playing with, chatting to, singing songs and telling stories with them. Sherriff (2007) has written about supporting fathers in developing positive relationships with their children. Significant barriers can make engagement difficult, e.g. cultural issues, negative perceptions of young fatherhood and poor referral systems. The need for projects, agencies and services supporting young fathers to adopt a planned approach to their work is stressed, as is the importance of networking and developing partnerships with other agencies and organizations in order to increase the chances of successful outcomes for young fathers, their children and their families (www.youngfathers.net).

In an example of good practice, a successful partnership in Leeds is encouraging teenage fathers to engage positively with their children. Leeds Library and Information Services support the Leeds Teenage Pregnancy and Parenthood Strategy and is working with FACT (Fathers and Children Together) to provide sessions that are both engaging and of benefit to the young fathers and their children. These evening sessions are held in Leeds Central Library and the FACT team accompany the teenage fathers and their children to the library. The Bookstart and Rhyme Time session encourages the fathers to read to their children and the group make musical instruments as part of the musical activity. This session also provides an opportunity for the young fathers to collect the free Bookstart packs for their babies. The follow-up session 'Library Tour and Digital Photography Time' encourages the group to interact with their children by taking photographs and learning to use Photoshop to edit the pictures. Feedback from the young fathers and FACT group has been very positive.

Culturally diverse communities

In today's society, particularly in, but not only in, inner-city areas, refugees, asylum seekers and economic migrants all need support services. Outreach workers from a variety of agencies are involved in providing these services. Such services need thoughtful marketing approaches, as it is important to encourage the communities and their families to access what is available to them. There are barriers to using local resources, including lack of knowledge about availability of and access to resources in the UK, misconceptions that using services may have financial implications and language difficulties. It may therefore be necessary to take these services, including library provision, out to the communities themselves, and experienced outreach workers can make a real difference.

CASE STUDY Bilingual Library Outreach in Bradford

The following statements made by parents to the bilingual outreach workers are about library outreach work in Bradford. They show how a lending library of toys and books for young children of playgroup age is highly valued by the community. The adults state how they love the storybook lending scheme and feel that they have become more confident in reading books to their children.

> I feel my daughter is learning very quickly and she always wants to play with her dad and me. I read books with her all the time, especially at bedtime.

> I always read books now with my child, whereas before I was afraid to take him to the library because he would tear the books. Since attending these sessions he can now handle the books properly and is more eager to share the books with other children and adults.

> I always borrow books and enjoy reading with my child. It has made me feel more confident to play with my child and given me more ideas about different ways of playing with children.

> I look at books with him. We go to the library, he enjoys going to the library. He chooses his own books and reads. He always wants me to sit down and read to him He tries really hard and uses the pictures to create his own stories, completely different from the actual story.

> At first I was very shy to read to my son in public. I had to be on my own when I read to him, where no one was listening and looking. I am more confident now and don't mind reading to him in front of other people.

> Although I can't speak English I do help her look at books and tell the story in my own language and also we talk about the things that are going on in the book and tell the story that way.

> It is very useful and we take a lot of books and toys home. It is useful because we don't have a lot of different things for her at home.

We think these statements by parents and carers are most interesting and valuable – they provide real insight into how much can be gained by encouraging families to access library services.

Promotions and campaigns in early years libraries

Campaigns and promotions are used by businesses to market products and services to particular audiences or target groups. Incentives are often offered to encourage the target group to take up the idea suggested by the marketing. In this sense, libraries can also be regarded as businesses, and national campaigns can be used to raise awareness of particular services and opportunities on offer. This section discusses some of the promotional campaigns libraries can use to reach out to the early years audience in the local community. Some of these are annual events that are part of a much wider community; others are an integral part of the ongoing business of the early years library setting. A connecting theme is the importance of working in partnerships.

Bookstart

Bookstart is the national early intervention and cultural access programme for every child run by the national charity Booktrust. Many early years librarians in the UK will be involved with this programme. Bookstart was the first national baby book-gifting programme in the world and encourages all parents and carers to enjoy books with their children from as early an age as possible (Wade and Moore, 2003). Bookstart began in the UK in 1992 with 300 babies; by 2001 there were over one million Bookstart babies. The scheme was initiated in 1992 by Booktrust, (working in co-operation with Birmingham Library Services, South Birmingham Health Authority and Birmingham University School of Education (Wade and Moore, 1998). Bookstart operates through locally based organizations by giving a free pack of books to babies, with guidance material for parents and carers. The aim is that every child in the UK should enjoy and benefit from books from as early an age as possible. Bookstart for babies aged 0–12 months aims to provide a canvas bag to every new baby born in the UK, containing baby books, a booklet for parents setting out information and advice on sharing stories with young children, a Children's Centres leaflet and a booklist and invitation to join the local library. These packs are distributed through health visitors, libraries and early years settings. The books are selected by a team which includes a health visitor and an independent expert on children's books. Choosing them is not as easy as it might sound: the varied cultural and social backgrounds of the children must be taken into account. In the majority of cases the Bookstart bag is given to parents by their health visitor at the eight months health check.

Bookstart Book Crawl

Libraries want to appear welcoming to the very youngest members of their communities. The Bookstart Book Crawl is a library-joining incentive for children aged 0-4 years. It encourages children under five to join the library and to borrow books by rewarding them with stickers and certificates. Birmingham Libraries encourages its youngest members to book crawl by using the enticing message 'There are great selections of gorgeous picture books to borrow including plenty of hardwearing board books to withstand sticky hands and sharp teeth!'

SCENARIO A reading milestone for Baby Ella

One bright spring morning Ella, aged 9 months, brought her mother, grandmother and aunt to the new Bookworms Library at Pinmoor Children's Centre in Wakefield. The baby was excited and looked around with wide eyes as she sat with her mum on the soft carpet. Ella bobbed her head in happiness and blew bubbles back at mum. Grandmother and aunt sat on adult-sized chairs and looked on with pleasure, glancing around the brightly coloured library, taking in all the toys, books and other playthings on display. This was an important day for the family, as they had come to celebrate with Ella. As one of the youngest members of the new Bookworms Library, the baby had reached the first of many milestones as a reader: she had achieved her first Book Crawl certificate. Carol, the early years librarian, sat on the carpet and presented Ella with her award. Mum smiled, grandmother and aunty laughed and clapped, Ella showed her delight by immediately sucking the edge of her certificate. We took a photograph. A snapshot moment – hopefully a lifetime of literacy ahead.

Chatterbooks groups

Older children, aged 4-12 years, are supported through the Chatterbooks national network of reading groups in libraries. Co-ordinated by The Reading Agency, the Chatterbooks scheme reaches families who may not have had a connection with libraries before, and the reading groups promote access to all kinds of learning in the community both for the young people who join and for their parents and carers. Every child joining a Chatterbooks group gets a pack with a reading diary, Post-It review pads, games and stickers. Library authorities who have signed up to deliver the scheme can access the Chatterbooks resources section on Their Reading Futures website.

World Book Day

World Book Day has been designated by UNESCO as a worldwide celebration of books and reading and is marked in over 100 countries around the globe. It is a partnership of publishers, booksellers and interested parties who work together to promote books and reading for the personal enrichment and enjoyment of all. World Book Day (WBD) entered its second decade in the UK and Ireland in 2008 and the initiative is well established in schools and libraries. WBD happens in school term time to help make the most of the opportunity to celebrate books and reading. In the UK and Ireland the core activities involve schools and preschool settings, with children receiving WBD book tokens. A main aim is to encourage children to explore the pleasures of books and reading by providing them with the opportunity to have a book of their own. The WBD event also offers a great opportunity for a wide range of reading and story-telling activities. Many schools and early years library settings celebrate WBD by having a dressing-up day, with both children and adults dressing as characters in their favourite book or story. Some settings provide reading tents with books and storysacks, others organize book sales, book donations and group sharing of favourite books. The WBD website provides a range of preschool resources, including downloadable colouring and activity sheets.

Issues and questions

- Do a critical review of the resources and activities provided in your library setting.
- Do the books in your setting reflect diversity in terms of genre, heritage and format?
- How can you use campaigns and promotions to market your services and connect with 'hard to reach' audiences?

Key points to remember

- Early story experiences can make a huge difference to language development, and stories and books are the routes into literacy.
- Cater for all age groups through providing a range of resources and activities.
- Entice everyone into your library setting - babies, toddlers, young children, parents and carers (including dads) - home and away; communities and businesses.

Useful organizations

Better Beginnings (Australia), www.better-beginnings.com.au
Family Place Libraries (USA), www.familyplacelibraries.org/whatMakes.html
National Reading Campaign, www.nationalliteracytrust.org.uk/campaign/index.html
Seven Stories, the Centre for the Children's Book, www.sevenstories.org.uk
World Book Day, www.worldbookday.com

References

Brock, A. and Power, M. (2006) Supporting Bilingual Learners in the Early Years. In
    Conteh, J. (ed.), *Promoting Learning for Bilingual Pupils 3–11: opening doors to success*,
    PCP/Sage Publications.

Brock, A. and Rankin, C. (2008) *Communication, Language and Literacy from Birth to Five*,
    Sage Publications.

Bus, A. and de Jong, M. (2006) Book Sharing: a developmentally appropriate way to
    foster pre-academic growth. In Rosenkoetter, S. E. and Knapp-Philo, J. (eds),
    Learning to Read the World: language and literacy in the first three years, Zero To Three
    Press.

DfE (Department for Education) (2012) Statutory Framework on the Early Years
    Foundation Stage (EYFS). Setting the Standards for Learning, Development and
    Care for Children from Birth,
    https://www.education.gov.uk/publications/standard/AllPublications/Page1/
    DFE-00023-2012.

DfES (Department for Education and Skills) (2002) Researching Effective Pedagogy in
    the Early Years (REPEY).

Goldschmied, E. and Jackson, S. (2004) *People Under Three: young children in day care*,
    2nd edn, Routledge.

Lane, J. (2008) *Young Children and Racial Justice. Taking action for racial equality in the
    early years – understanding the past, thinking about the present, planning for the future*,
    National Children's Bureau.

McKearney, M. (2007) The Reading Agency is Five, *Library and Information Update*,
    6 (12), 38–41.

Potter, C. (2008) Getting Young Children Talking in Early Years Settings. In Brock, C.
    and Rankin, A. (eds), *Communication, Language and Literacy from Birth to Five*, Sage
    Publications.

Riches, R. (2007) *Early Years Outreach Practice – Supporting Early Years Practice Working
    with Gypsy, Roma and Traveller Families. With transferable ideas for other outreach early
    years workers*, Save the Children Fund.

Robinson, A. (n.d.) *Picture This Project*, unpublished report, Blackburn with Darwen
    Borough.

Sherriff, N. (2007) *Supporting Young Fathers: examples of promising practice*, Trust for the Study of Adolescence.

Stevens, A. (2003) Libraries Put Vision into Action, *Literacy Today*, **37**, December, www.literacytrust.org.uk/Pubs/stevens.html.

Swiniarski, L. (2006) Helping Young Children Become Citizens of the World, *Scholastic Early Childhood Today*, November/December, 36-8.

Sylva, K., Melhuish, E., Sammonds, P., Siraj-Blatchford, I. and Taggart, B. (2004) *The Effective Provision of Pre-School Education (EPPE) Project: the final report*. A longitudinal study funded by the DfES 1997-2004, DfES Publications.

Wade, B. and Moore, M. (1998) *A Gift for Life: Bookstart, the first five years - a description and evaluation of an exploratory British project to encourage sharing books with babies*, Booktrust, 1998

Wade, B. and Moore, M. (2003) Bookstart: a qualitative evaluation, *Educational Review*, **55** (1), 3-13.

Whitehead, M. (2007) *Developing Language and Literacy with Young Children*, 3rd edn, Sage.

PART 2 INTERNATIONAL PERSPECTIVES: COUNTRY CASE STUDIES

Early years library provision is also delivered by partnerships in other parts of the world. There are a wealth of initiatives in operation, both in the UK and overseas, and we now present case studies of excellent practice from Australia, Croatia, Denmark, Italy, Northern Ireland, Russia and Sweden:

- Australia: 'Story time with Dad', by Carolyn Bourke
- Croatia: Early Reading Programmes at Zadar Public Library, by Dajana Brunac
- Denmark: Aalborg Bibliotekerne for all ages, including the youngest as V.I.P. library users, by Maria Sjøblom
- Italy: Nati per Leggere - book selection, by Giovanna Malgaroli
- Northern Ireland: Rhythm and Rhyme in Libraries NI, by Marie-Elaine Tierney, Jessica Bates and Andrew Carlin
- Russia: Moscow State Library for Children, by Tatiana Kalashnikova
- Sweden: Library activities for children 0-5 years old: some best practices from Sweden, by Ingrid Källström.

Australia

'Story time with Dad'

Carolyn Bourke

'Story time with Dad' is a multilingual story time programme run by Fairfield City Libraries (Sydney) in partnership with Uniting Care Burnside and The Smith Family. The programme is conducted in the libraries and is funded by the partnering bodies. The target audience is preschool-aged children and their fathers (or other male relatives) from communities speaking languages other than English. The sessions are run in a mixture of English, Arabic, Chinese and Vietnamese.

Background

The Fairfield Local Government area is one of Australia's most ethnically and socially diverse communities. Of a population of approximately 190,000, 70% speak a language other than English at home and 20% speak English either not well or not at all (2011 Census). 'Story time with Dad' is an imaginative response to a set of identified community needs which also addresses the issue of getting male figures in children's lives more involved in education, literacy and play.

'Story time with Dad' has been running since 2007, using trained male staff from the partnering organizations as story-tellers. The story-tellers employ a range of community languages in the stories, songs, games and craft. The programme models emergent literacy practices to men and encourages them to interact positively with their children. Each session is run in a mixture of languages, so, for example, a story may be read in Chinese and English. While reading a story about fish the story-teller will stop and ask all the children and dads to repeat the word for 'fish' in Chinese. The idea is that, regardless of language background, each attendee (both adult and child) will participate in stories and songs in several languages.

Partnerships

The project is the result of a partnership between Fairfield City Libraries and non-government agencies - The Smith Family, Learning Links and Uniting Care Burnside's Engaging Fathers programme - all under the umbrella of the Australian Government's Communities 4 Children programme. Speech pathologists and early childhood educators from Learning Links worked with male staff from the Libraries and Uniting Care Burnside to develop a story time programme where men read stories, sing songs and do craft activities with children in a range of community languages.

Challenges

One of the key challenges has been to attract men into an area which is traditionally and culturally seen as a female realm. The first sessions were run at our Fairfield branch library, which is considered a 'men's' library due to the large numbers of men who use the library each day to read the papers, play chess and socialize. It was hoped that these men, as a captive audience, would observe the sessions and take on board that other men using their community languages were reading and singing with children. Some of these men are community leaders, and so their influence is important.

We also wanted to get the children's fathers, uncles and grandfathers attending. Research done by one of our community partners indicated that men consider general information that comes home from school or other agencies to be directed at their wives. If you want a response from men, the communication needs to be personally directed to them. With this in mind, the children make invitation cards specifically for their dads. The response to a personal invitation from their child is much higher than any general promotional effort.

Another challenge is ensuring that male staff are visibly running the sessions and that their female counterparts take a very low profile. Our experience has been that our male staff enjoy running the programme, but that the female staff have to make a conscious effort to stay out of it!

Promotion

Although we do our key promotion directly to dads and granddads via their children, we also do general promotion to encourage men who aren't already connected with the libraries or our partner organizations to attend. This includes flyers in community languages, promotion through networks via e-lists or meetings, the local newspapers, the Council's events list, our website, electronic noticeboards in the libraries and the Council's intranet system to other staff.

Value to community

The importance of fathers modelling positive reading, language and social behaviours with their children cannot be overstated. For communities where many families speak a language other than English and literacy rates are low, this is even more crucial. Staff are role-modelling reading-engagement practices to fathers and other men in the community and empowering them to role-model this to their own children.

'Story time with Dad' encourages dads and granddads to read, tell stories and play with their children using their family language. It provides a fantastic opportunity for dads to spend time with their children while sharing books, learning and having fun. The programme helps dads bond with their children and aids language development and vocabulary learning. It also helps young children to develop skills needed for starting school, such as listening, working with others, telling stories and doing craft activities.

Evaluation and feedback

A short survey (translated into the three languages covered) is completed at the end of the programme to gather data on key achievements and includes questions such as:

- How do you rate the event?
- Will you be reading more to your child after today's session?
- What language do you speak?

The evaluation is overwhelmingly positive. Average attendance at each session is 16 dads/granddads, 17 mums and 30 children. Of the adults, 89.74% say that they will be reading more with their children after attending the 'Story time with Dad' session. Comments from dads include: 'It was excellent, keep going' and 'My son gave me the invite, it was fun'.

Future plans

Other important elements are the community partnerships that have developed and the opportunity the programme has provided for the male staff, who have grown in confidence and acquired new skills of great value to both the community and their own families. The programme has the full support of the participating agencies and will continue to model and develop male engagement, and therefore children's literacy skills, into the future.

References

2011 Census information, http://profile.id.com.au/fairfield/language.

CROATIA

Early Reading Programmes at Zadar Public Library

Dajana Brunac

Zadar Public Library started with early reading programmes in the early 1990s. Babies and toddlers are welcome to join the play time every day in the play area, which is available as long as the library is open. They can choose didactic toys from different categories (like reception, construction, imitation, etc.) and participate in play with other children, thus learning and socializing. They can sit in their parent's or the librarian's lap and listen to a story, or join the Nursery Rhymes programme (the sweetest programme of all). Parents can read books and magazines on parenting which are placed in the play area, or join the lectures and workshops provided by librarians or other experts. Most of all, they are keen to ask questions and learn about good-quality picture books. Librarians are happy to introduce the best writers and illustrators. Both parents and librarians are aware that, starting with toys, through picture books and children's literature, there is a good chance that a child will develop into a good and happy reader.

Training of librarians

Information science students can obtain Bachelor's, Master's and PhD degrees at some Croatian universities. In the fifth or sixth semester, students can choose an optional programme, Library Programmes and Services for Children and Young Adults, consisting of both theory and practice. The Croatian Center of Permanent Professional Education of Librarians provides the following courses on library services for children and young adults:

- The introduction and development of services for babies, toddlers and their parents in public libraries
- Tactile and other picture books in public and school libraries
- Promoting and encouraging reading among children and young adults
- Working with children and youth in public and school libraries.

The Croatian Children and Youth Services Section - a professional body of the Croatian Library Association - organizes an annual symposium for children's librarians. The Section has translated all of the IFLA Guidelines related to children and youth in libraries. It also provides the annual list of recommended books for children and parents.

Services for parents and caregivers
Parents' corner

Library services provide information and education. Primarily, this refers to toys and books available in the children's department. Librarians recommend and explain which skills can be developed by using specific toys, which picture books are suitable for a certain age, how to choose a good illustration, etc. There is a large collection of books and magazines on parenting. Parents Act is a programme in which parents talk on certain topics or share their talents.

Lectures and workshops

Programmes are provided by librarians or other experts. The Nursery Rhymes programme is conducted continuously, with a short introduction on the importance of rhymes. Other programmes are conducted periodically. Parents and caregivers are invited to attend these programmes, accompanying their babies and toddlers. During the lectures or workshops 'young librarians' - children and young adults recruited from other library activities - are charged with assisting parents. The lectures and workshops related to reading include:

- Nursery rhymes
- Meet the author
- Meet the illustrator
- Fairy tales today
- Why do paediatricians recommend early reading?
- Dyslexia and dysgraphia
- Christmas stories
- Santa reads to babies and toddlers.

Other parents' activities include:

- Responsible parenting
- Communication in the family
- Early speech development and speech therapy
- Breastfeeding
- Child health and vaccination
- Depression in children
- Carrying babies in a sling
- Complementary foods and introducing solid foods
- The most common injuries and poisoning of children - first aid
- Children and TV

- Children and new media
- How to make a puppet alive
- Children and Easter.

Story-telling

Story Time is a permanent programme which includes reading stories, rhymes, poems, riddles and other textual material to children, followed by an arts and crafts activity. The programme is conducted in the presence of both children and their parents, thus giving parents insight into their child's behaviour in the group and giving them ideas on how to be creative at home as well as in the library . The programme also gives them the opportunity to learn about good-quality picture books.

As a result of Story Time and arts and crafts activities put together, exhibits are organized in the children's department in order to present the children's work. Hand-made picture books (laporello type, etc.) are a part of the librarians' most precious collection.

Story-telling Afternoon is an everyday activity, conducted by young volunteers trained by librarians.

Bedtime Story, Stories in Pyjamas, Christmas Story-telling and Stories in Other Languages are programmes conducted occasionally, in co-operation with kindergartens.

The Zadar Reads programme

Modelled on several international programmes, the Zadar Reads programme was launched by Zadar Public Library in 2009. All kindergarten systems and preschool institutions in the city are included, participating in organized visits to the library, story-telling programmes, picture-book collecting for deprived children, visits by authors, exhibits, etc. Children's librarians provide kindergarten teachers with lists of recommended picture books and books on parenting, which are then distributed to parents.

Read to Me campaign

In 2013 (2013 being the European Reading Aloud year), the Croatian Children and Youth Services Section started the Read to Me! (Citaj mi!) campaign for promotion of reading aloud to young children. It is implemented on a national level in co-operation with the Croatian Paediatric Society, Croatian Reading Association, Croatian Association of Children's Literature Researchers and the

UNICEF office in Croatia, and it is sponsored by the Ministry of Social Policy and Youth. At Zadar Public Library the campaign is implemented through a number of key activities. Posters and flyers highlighting the importance of early reading to children are placed in all libraries in Zadar County, paediatric clinics, maternity hospitals and community health centres. The UNICEF office supported the distribution of a picture book at regular medical examinations in paediatric clinics, as well as reading programmes with parents, children and paediatricians. Some publishers supported the campaign by reducing prices of picture books for the youngest children, and Croatian Radio joined the campaign, adjusting its 'Bedtime Stories' programme to the youngest children.

Outreach activities

Children's librarians provide library services to kindergartens, paediatric and other institutions that might not have access to those services due to distance or other reasons. Outreach has an educational role and is conducted via mobile library visits or otherwise.

Challenges

Offering the early reading programmes usually presents some challenges, and sometimes even a risk as to how the new ideas will be accepted by other librarians, library users and the community. Programmes are introduced as a result of librarians' constant efforts to improve library services, which is done by following and respecting our patrons' needs. Although it is not possible, due to lack of staff, lack of space, etc., to meet all their needs and requests, all activities are expected to be good and valuable, accessible to all and, it is hoped, suitable for co-operation with parents or other institutions. Following the idea that librarians and parents are partners in a child's upbringing and education, we support the idea of a user-friendly library.

Values to the library and to the community

The library is often a first place for a child to meet other children outside the family environment. It should offer various programmes to children and parents and a choice of picture books dealing with different topics. Librarians introduce new social areas and knowledge, thus familiarizing children with them (family, community, diversities, ecology, holidays, etc.). This results in an increase in the number of library users, both children and parents, increased awareness of the importance of early reading, collegial sharing, promotion and realization of co-operation among institutions.

References

Guidelines for Children's Library Services, IFLA Libraries for Children and Young Adults Section, www.ifla.org/en/publications/guidelines-for-childrens-library-services.

Guidelines for Library Services to Babies and Toddlers, IFLA Libraries for Children and Young Adults Section, www.ifla.org./VII/d3/pub/Profrep100.pdf.

DENMARK

Aalborg Bibliotekerne for all ages: including the youngest as V.I.P. library users

Maria Sjøblom

Our beautiful main library in Aalborg is filled with people of all ages. The elderly learn how to use computers, students from the university meet in their study groups and children join our leisure clubs Manga Zone, Read Zone, Game Zone, or drop by to get a helping hand with their homework.

Being a library user is something you have to learn, and it is crucial that the habit should start at a young age; therefore we prioritize our efforts towards the youngest citizens in Aalborg. Our children's library is situated right by the main entrance. It's very visible to people entering the library and it's designed to look fun and inviting. The children's department is divided into three main parts. One room is for the oldest children, with books, movies and lots of computers. It's a room suitable for being noisy, hanging out and experimenting. The opposite side of the children's department, located close to the adult library, is 'Hulen' ('The Cave'), a red, cosy room with toys, books and tablets for the youngest, aged from 0 to 6. The room contains parking spaces for prams and room for adults, who must entertain themselves while the children are playing. Between these two rooms is 'Fantasi-rummet' ('The Imagination Room'), with small tables for eating lunch, sitting down to draw or just reading a nice book. The room has different levels to climb on, a small 'lake' to play in and toys to inspire the children to use their senses and bodies. But we don't just provide a room, of course. A library is so much more than that.

Baby Café for ages 0–1

Every month we have an open Baby Café for infants and their parents. The Baby Café is a nice, informal and educational meeting place that gives parents an opportunity to network and make new connections. As in other parts of the library, these connections cross social, economic and ethnic boundaries and are of great value for the participating parents.

Library staff host the café and use the opportunity to tell parents about books and other media they can find in the library. While they are doing this, the library staff also help to play with the infants and now and then lend a hand to warm a bottle. Every café is visited by a different expert, who gives a short lecture on topics like the sleeping habits of infants, healthy food, music for infants or physical or linguistic development. This spring we even featured one of our librarians, who sings hymns that are soothing for babies.

In Denmark we have specially trained healthcare nurses who visit new parents in their homes. They also visit our Baby Cafés to talk with the parents and provide advice on a wide range of topics. As a nice reciprocal result, our librarians are now being invited to participate in events for new parents in the health department.

When we first started these Baby Cafés we had about 20 participants, but after six months the number has increased to as many as 150 parents and babies - it's a bit chaotic, but a lot of fun. Warm relations are formed and some single parents are so grateful for the services provided that they are almost in tears when thanking the library staff. These babies are going to grow up to be regular library patrons - just like their parents, they will keep coming back.

'Linguistic fitness': getting ready for school

Children learn in different ways. Even the schools have adapted to the fact that some children are better off using their bodies to obtain new knowledge. But what about the libraries? Do we know enough about how children learn? And how do we use this knowledge in our libraries? Traditionally the library is for children who can sit quietly and either read a book by themselves or listen to a great story. In Aalborg we wanted to challenge this tradition and explore the tactile and kinaesthetic learning styles. We have invented the concept of 'Linguistic fitness' and initiated a project funded by the Danish Agency for Culture (an agency of the Danish Ministry of Culture). The target audience is children in kindergartens and preschools. To help create the project we enrolled teachers from the local school, Herningvejen, the kindergarten, Fyrtårnet, and a lot of students from University College Nordjylland (UCN).

The project team and the students from UCN experimented with different exercises and simple games to train the linguistic development of children while they were physically active. All of the games were tested inside the library with loads of happy, playful children and their teachers. These simple games really showed new ways to play with the alphabet, individual letters and language. All of the participating professionals learnt a lot of new ways to pass on the joy of letters, language and pre-reading skills to the children. These techniques can even be used before the children start in school.

Next step was to invite all the kindergartens and preschools in the municipality of Aalborg to join a big 'Linguistic Fitness' day held in May 2014. This event took place in a big park and more than 2700 children and 400 educators signed up. All of these preschools and kindergartens received an inspiration catalogue introducing the various games and rehearsed them. In this project the library has succeeded in connecting different institutions and different types of professionals to create a synergy in the community and create new ways of linguistic training so that the youngest children can become better readers in the future. The project will be followed by a national conference and it is hoped that we can adopt this knowledge about tactile and kinaesthetic learning styles in libraries all over Denmark.

The library reaches out to children everywhere

Our future library users are very important to us and we are careful never to miss a chance to reach out and tell people about the library. Our librarians can't teach a child how to read, but we can certainly teach them to love it!

ITALY

Nati per Leggere: NpL – selecting the bibliography of recommended books

Giovanna Malgaroli

Nati per Leggere (Born to Read) is an Italian programme which aims to promote the practice of reading to children from birth to 5 years. The programme was funded in 1999 by the association of librarians (Associazione Italiana Biblioteche – AIB), the association of paediatricians (Associazione Culturale Pediatri - ACP) and by a child-focused NGO, Centro per la Salute del Bambino (CSB). ACP has about 2000 Italian paediatricians and AIB links around 4500 librarians, libraries and information services. CSB is a non-profit organization committed to training and research on child health and development. These national associations work on a voluntary basis.

The programme is developed at local level by a grass-roots network of local stakeholders (librarians, healthcare professionals, school teachers and caregivers, non-profit organizations and individual volunteers) and it is financially supported mainly by the local public authorities. A central secretariat and a steering committee ensure co-ordination and external and internal communication, including editing the project website (www.natiperleggere.it), publishing informative and promotional material and handling the mailing list (npl-bib@aib.it), which links 4123 people interested in the programme all over the country. Further, they organize and supervise the training, develop training materials and provide technical support to the local projects, which now cover all 21 regions of Italy. At the local level, a commitment is made to carrying out the programme with the greatest of flexibility and with adaptations to the local situations.

The NpL strategy is based on establishing local co-operative structures, supported by public libraries, paediatricians and healthcare services, which can get involved in a continuous activity to raise awareness among families, education and health professionals that reading to children is a way to improve the cognitive emotional and social development of children and the parent -child relationship and to bring benefits to the whole community.

Selecting books to enhance reading within families with young children
Which books are worth sharing with children?

Since 2002, every two or three years, a specific NpL working group publishes a bibliography of recommended books for children from birth to five years of age. The annotated bibliography aims to guide professionals, volunteers and parents to make informed choices about books for young children and to enable all professionals to know about the best books and update their children's library collections. Each bibliography suggests 120 titles covering all the types of books available: board books and picture books containing nursery rhymes, traditional tales and fairy tales, brief stories about the child's daily life, books of words that help children to recognize and give names to things and emotions, books with introductory knowledge about a subject and books worthy of attention from children but also from parents and carers.

The titles are generally organized into 10 sections, the following being the ones used in the latest bibliography:

- Carezze in rima (Rhyme caresses: nursery rhymes, lullabies, poems and songs for children)
- Libri cuccioli (Baby books: first books with thick cover and pages with clear pictures and few words)
- Prima della buonanotte (Before goodnight: books with stories to help children to go to sleep)
- Che emozione! (What excitement!: books to help children to share good feelings and to face bad ones)

- Prime scoperte (First discoveries: first books to stimulate children's curiosity)
- Scopro il mondo della A alla Zebra (I discover the World from A to Zebra: books about animals, nature and reality)
- Una zuppa di fiabe (Fairy Tale Soup: traditional and new fairy tales)
- Storie per coccolare (Stories to cuddle)
- Storie per divertire (Stories to amuse)
- Grandi autori per i più piccoli (Great Authors for the Youngest: authors like Altan, Jeanne Ashbé, Eric Battut, Stephanie Blake, Eric Carle, Lucy Cousins, Donaldson-Scheffler, Leo Lionni, Iela Mari, Bruno Munari, Mario Ramos, Tony Ross, Maurice Sendak, Hervé Tullet, to name the internationally known ones).

Each section is introduced by a brief text or by key words to suggest to adults the reasons and ways to share books with young children.

Here is an example, the introduction to rhyme books:

A child prefers to listen to a book if the text contains Rhyme – Rhythm – Repetition [because] Rhyme makes memorization easy, produces a pleasant sound effect and comes almost with a smile, [because] Rhythm invites one to match the sound of the words with the movements of the body, [because] Repetition makes comprehension easy, favours choral reading, helps to predict the development of the story.

Books are cited with a reproduction of their cover, the names of authors and illustrators, the publisher and year of publication, the price and a brief description of the book. The bibliographies are published by AIB and distributed by AIB and CSB. They are normally purchased by local supporters of the programme for distribution to local libraries and for gifting to teachers, caregivers and parents.

The four editions to date of the bibliography *Nati per Leggere: una guida per genitori e futuri lettori* are available at the following web pages:

- www.aib.it/negozio-aib/npl/guida-npl-2012
- www.natiperleggere.it/index.php?id=22
- www.aib.it/aib/npl/libri03.htm3
- www.aib.it/aib/npl/libri01.htm3

Books to give to parents for reading to their children

Besides disseminating information about the best books that should be found in all libraries, day-care centres and kindergartens, NpL facilitates the giving of books to families without children's books in the home and where parents do not usually read. In fact, as is shown in statistical data (Morrone and Savioli 2008), the main factors influencing individual reading habits are the parents' attitude towards reading, including reading aloud to children, and the number of books available in the home. As is shown by experience in the USA- and UK-based programmes, the giving of books is one of the most effective ways to promote reading, particularly among families that for social and cultural reasons are not keen on this practice.

NpL recommends that books be given to parents during paediatric check-ups or in similar situations when at least one parent is present. In order to produce a wide choice of books to be gifted, since 2004 NpL has developed agreements with a growing number of Italian publishers. The books are selected on the basis of quality and should be interesting, attractive and suited to the handling, perceptive and cognitive abilities of children in their first five years, with special attention to shape, materials, size, content and communicative aspects. Books are sold exclusively to the NpL local programmes and supporters at a low price (€3.00-3.50).

Since 2004 we have published five editions of the special NpL books catalogue. The latest, published in 2014, includes 18 titles by 16 different publishers. The publishers that NpL is collaborating with represent a wide variety of the publishing houses devoted to children, from the very small and independent ones to the biggest ones. Included in the latest edition of the catalogue are: Babalibri, Bohem Press, Carthusia, Clavis, Editoriale Scienza, Edizioni EL/Emme, Gallucci, Giunti, Il Castoro, Interlinea Junior, La Coccinella, Lapis, L'Eubage, Mondadori, Panini, Sinnos.

A list and description of the NpL books is available at the web page: www.natiperleggere.it/index.php?id=20.

Reference

Morrone, A. and Savioli, M. (2008) *La lettura in Italia*, Bibliografica, pp. 36-47.

NORTHERN IRELAND

Rhythm and Rhyme in Libraries NI

Marie-Elaine Tierney, Jessica Bates and Andrew Carlin

Introduction

Libraries NI, which has been in operation since April 2009, is the largest library service in the UK and Ireland. It is a stand-alone library authority, and an arm's-length body of the Department for Culture, Arts and Leisure (DCAL) in Northern Ireland. Prior to 2009, Northern Ireland's public libraries were organized within five Education and Library Boards, so it was a radical shift to create a single library authority.

Public libraries are seen as politically neutral venues, which is particularly important in Northern Ireland. Libraries allow for all sections of society to engage, and provide an ideal setting for social inclusion and social interaction. Within Libraries NI there is a particular emphasis on providing services to areas of social need, which is in line with DCAL's Promoting Equality and Tackling Poverty and Social Exclusion agenda (www.dcalni.gov.uk). Rhythm and Rhyme sessions are held in public libraries across Northern Ireland and in various community settings such as play groups, especially in areas of social need. They introduce preschool children to favourite nursery rhymes, songs and stories in welcoming environments:

> Rhythm and Rhyme is a free programme of stories, rhymes and songs delivered on a regular or seasonal basis by Libraries NI staff (or held in partnership with Sure Start) for parents, carers and pre-school children (aged 0-4 years). The aim of the programme is to improve children's language and communication skills before they enter formal education.
>
> (Libraries NI, 2014a)[1]

The purpose of these sessions is to enhance children's development through the medium of rhythm and rhyme:

> singing rhymes with young children is an important step in building the foundations for reading and literacy. Listening to and joining in with rhymes and songs improves a child's vocabulary, communication and concentration skills and encourages an early love of books. It introduces the world in a fun way and improves the bond between the parent/carer and child.
>
> (Knox, 2011, 2)

It is hoped that the children who attend these fun, play-based activity sessions will develop the crucial foundations for later education (Wade and Moore, 1998; Ramos, 2012). Through the Rhythm and Rhyme programme, Libraries NI encourages parents and carers to spend time reading with children, to continue with the same rhymes and songs at home and to join in during the sessions themselves (and by doing so to be a role model for the children). Thus the impact of the Rhythm and Rhyme sessions extends far beyond the sessions themselves.

In 2012-13, 84 branches (88%) ran sessions for a total 88,524 participants - 48,577 children and 39,947 adults (Libraries NI, 2014b), and Libraries NI has been consistently exceeding its key performance targets in relation to the provision of Rhythm and Rhyme sessions. A key performance indicator for 2013-14 was that 75% of library branches delivered regular Rhythm and Rhyme sessions (the target for 2014-15 is 85%), with all libraries in areas of social need providing regular sessions (at least one session per month) to help develop early-learning skills (Libraries NI, 2013). Indeed, many of the larger library branches will have multiple weekly sessions to meet the demand. Looking to the future, Libraries NI intends to gain accreditation for its training in delivering Rhythm and Rhyme sessions and provide training to other organizations.

Evaluation

The Education and Training Inspectorate (2011) in Northern Ireland commended Libraries NI on its work to embed Quality Indicators in the Rhythm and Rhyme programme. Tierney (2013) undertook a study of Rhythm and Rhyme sessions in Libraries NI through a survey which was administered across three library branches (and covered four Rhythm and Rhyme sessions) and a focus group that involved eight participants at one Rhythm and Rhyme session (two grandmothers, four carers and two parents).

The survey found that 82% of adults attending one of the four Rhythm and Rhyme sessions and 69% of the children they were accompanying were members of the library. Of the children who were members, 64% had become members as a result of going to the Rhythm and Rhyme sessions. The sessions last approximately 30 minutes to 1 hour and 86% of the respondents were happy with the duration, with 14% indicating they felt it was too short. There was also a clear consensus that the adults regarded the sessions as being delivered at an appropriate level for the children they were accompanying.

The focus group revealed further perceived benefits of the Rhythm and Rhyme sessions - for both the children and the adults. For example, comments in relation to the benefits for the children included:

- My child is an only child and I know that coming here to these sessions has made a big difference to her. She was spending all her time with adults and was getting her own way all the time. But coming here she has had to learn to share with the other children and she knows that she has to take her turn. She mixes much better.
- It's been really good for her, it's helped her build up her confidence and interact with other children.
- He was shy before we came here ... Now he goes over to the other children and chats and shares the instruments. His confidence has grown and he interacts

better.

- I've noticed how engrossed they are when they're listening to the stories. They really concentrate.
- They listen more to what you're saying as well. I don't know if it's the stories or if it's following the commands or instructions in the rhymes but they definitely listen and seem to take in more.
- I think it prepares the children for school too. My older wee boy used to come here too and when he started school you could really see the difference in him compared with some of the other children. He mixed better, was more confident and his vocabulary was streets ahead, and I put that down to him coming to the sessions.

The strengths of the sessions for adults were also considered by some of the participants:

- I know it was mentioned earlier about it being good for the adults too but I would like to say that it's good for me because I never get the chance to mix with other mothers because I work full time and only now that I'm off on maternity leave it gives me a chance to chat to other mothers and exchange ideas.
- I have made so many friends and got advice and tips. I'd have been lost without it. So it's not only been good for the children but adults too.

Some adults also mentioned that the session they attended was very popular and that you needed to arrive early to be sure of getting into it. It is evident from the results that the general view from participants is an overall positive experience for those who attended the sessions. Some of the views presented by the parents and carers, such as coming to the sessions giving them 'a chance to chat to other mothers and exchange ideas', were an unanticipated consequence of the Rhythm and Rhyme sessions.

Recommendations and future research

1 Clearly, the programme of Rhythm and Rhyme sessions in Libraries NI is having a positive impact on the children and adults who attend. However, there is scope to continue the work of bringing Rhyme and Rhyme sessions into other community settings, particularly in more remote areas and in areas of social need. Further evaluation (beyond brief feedback forms) across the whole programme would also be valuable and provide an evidence base for future developments regarding Rhythm and Rhyme and the sharing of best practice.

2   Details of the Rhythm and Rhyme sessions (and evaluations of them) could be shared more widely and presented to relevant stakeholders across and beyond Northern Ireland, such as the Department for Culture, Arts and Leisure (DCAL), Department of Education, Parents Early Education Partnership's (PEEP's), Sure Start, Booktrust, practitioners and nursery school teachers - a consequence of which could be to bring together a holistic and effective early learning strategy for the under-fives.

3   The opportunity also exists for Libraries NI to contribute on a national scale to the dissemination of best practice for delivering early literacy programmes to preschoolers. Libraries as community partners actively support parents/carers in the development of early literacy skills and would be best placed to bring together good practice and harmonizing of policies.

4   Future research could examine the perceived benefits of Rhythm and Rhyme sessions for children with disabilities; their value for children for whom English is not their first language; the standardization of delivery across branches; and longitudinal evaluation involving the same group of children and adults.

Note

1   See the Libraries NI video 'The Benefits of Rhythm and Rhyme for Babies and Toddlers - Libraries NI' at: www.youtube.com/watch?v=hc5z-8kyao0.

References

Knox, I. (2011) *Monkey See Monkey Do*, Libraries NI Publications.

Libraries NI (2013) *Libraries NI Business Plan 2013-14*, www.librariesni.org.uk/AboutUs/OurOrg/Business%20Plans/Business%20Plan%202013-14%20(agreed%20by%20DCAL%20120813).pdf

Libraries NI (2014a) *Statistical Bulletin: participation in core library activities in Northern Ireland in 2012-2013*, www.librariesni.org.uk/AboutUs/OurOrg/Statistics/Participation_in_Core_Library_Activities_2012_13_Report.pdf

Libraries NI (2014b) *Annual Report and Accounts 2013-2014*, www.librariesni.org.uk/AboutUs/OurOrg/Annual%20Reports/Annual%20Report%20and%20Accounts%202012-13.pdf

Ramos, A. M. (2012) Learning to Read Before You Walk: Portuguese libraries for babies and toddlers, *IFLA Journal*, **38** (1), 78-85.

Tierney, M.-E. (2013) *Exploring the Impact of Rhythm and Rhyme Sessions in Public*

Libraries Across Northern Ireland on Pre-school Children, dissertation submitted for the MSc in Library and Information Management, School of Education, University of Ulster.

Wade, B. and Moore, M. (1998) An Early Start with Books: literacy and mathematical evidence from a longitudinal study, *Educational Review*, **50** (2), 135-45.

RUSSIA

Moscow State Library for Children: the A. P. Gaidar Central City Children's Library

Tatiana Kalashnikova

Preschoolers in Gaidarovka

The metropolitan area of Moscow has over 12 million inhabitants, of which more than 1.5 million are children aged up to 14 years. Moscow has a great variety of leisure institutions, including specialized children's libraries where young Muscovites are the main users. Our library serves children from 0 to 14 years. This is a defining period in terms of child development. Therefore the A. P. Gaidar library, or 'Gaidarovka', as it is known, provides library programmes for children not only of all ages but also with many different areas of interest. We will introduce you to some of them.

The programme Reading from Birth aims to involve expectant mums and dads in visiting the library. It prepares them for the fact that it will be necessary to attend to all aspects of a young child's development from the very first days of life. Often in our library you will meet mothers with prams, or with toddlers who are just starting to walk.

Our library provides toy books, books for the bathroom, soft tissue books and even musical books for the youngest visitors. In this way young children become accustomed to books and perceive them as something necessary in their lives. Young parents are offered books on psychology and pedagogy, popular literature on children's education and audio recordings. Parents receive help in choosing educational games for their children and information about different approaches to advancing their child's development.

Parents of children from the age of about one year are interested in speech development, choosing age-appropriate books to read to their children, toy books, etc. They can find guidance on these matters in reading lists for children from 0 to 3 years and the booklet 'Reading from Birth' produced by staff of the library service department. Children who join a library before their first birthday receive a set of books as a gift. Each year the number of participants in the programme increases. In every case we see positive results: parents whose babies have joined a library understand the importance of reading and books, read more to their toddler, and reading becomes their favourite habit. We hope that as the children grow older, their frequent visits to the library will continue.

The programme We Are Growing together with Books is aimed at children from 3 to 6 years of age and is the next stage of this important work. Preschoolers are defined as the most active library users. We work with them in several ways:

- working individually with preschoolers and their parents
- holding classes for groups of kindergarten pupils
- running hobby/special interest groups
- promoting developmental classes.

The 'Preschooler' hobby group brings together children who are not attending kindergarten. Its main task is to promote the children's development and to teach them to communicate and to socialize and build relationships with their peers. The chief activity in the preschool years is play, so the classes are based on the group play and joint creativity. The children listen to books, sculpt, draw, and watch and discuss cartoons together. Each lesson is devoted to a specific topic (for example, 'Seasons', 'The World of Fairy Tales', 'Transport'). Books, videos, games and creative activities are selected to fit the topic of these lessons. Classes take place twice a week. Every week thematic classes entitled 'Look inside the Fairy Tale' are put on for children from 2 to 5 years, as well as bilingual lessons titled 'Funny Animals' (for children from 4 years).

In group lessons, where children come from kindergarten with a teacher, the library organizes games, quizzes, reading hours and literary festivals to celebrate the anniversaries of favourite children's writers. Children can choose books, magazines, toy books, games, colouring books and creative materials for themselves, and can either take them home or take them to the library's cosy 'preschooler corner', where they can snuggle down with them. The library has a separate space for young children, as they need to be in a safe space, appropriate to their age, where they have a choice of interesting books and can feel that they are real members of the library - and be proud of it.

In the children's corner the books for the youngest children can be found not just on the shelves, but also 'travelling' in a small train and 'living' inside a fairy palace. Further, there are comfy beanbags on which to relax, soft, cube-shaped stools, a table with children's chairs - and armchairs for the parents. And if a child suddenly decides that she wants to be alone, there is a special chair with a curtain, where she can hide.

Some of the shelving in the children's area is allocated for books for the parents on subjects such as pedagogy, child psychology and children's health, as well as books for family reading. In this way parents can keep their children in view while searching for information for themselves.

Being able to access well-chosen, high-quality literature in the library makes the parents more competent and more confident. If they have a specific need they can obtain information about child development. They can also access information via the internet, including advice from a doctor or a teacher. Here we're talking situations when knowledge about the kinds of problems they can expect to face will help them to assess a situation quickly and effectively. This is one of the benefits that parents gain from visiting the children's library.

Library work with preschoolers and their parents is aimed at promoting understanding between them, creating a positive environment for the children's development and, last but not least, attracting children to read at an early age. We want to see babies with books in their hands first, before they move on to the electronic gadgets!

Preschoolers are now one of the biggest user groups in the library, and the fastest-growing one. This means that they will continue to come to our library throughout their early years, and on into adulthood.

SWEDEN

Library activities for children 0–5 years old: some best practices from Sweden

Ingrid Källström

In Sweden we have some nationwide library programmes for children, and they come with local adaptations in different parts of the country. One of them is Barnens första bok: Children's First Book. It started as a project around 1990 and was a success right from the beginning. In this programme libraries and the children's health centres work together. The parents of newborn babies go regularly to the children's health centres for advice and for check-ups for their babies. The local library co-operates in this activity. The parents receive a card from the paediatric nurse saying that they are welcome to visit the library and get a book gift in exchange for the card. This is very popular throughout Sweden. The libraries decide for themselves which book title they will give away, but most common are books of short stories and rhymes. When the parents first come to the library this is of course an excellent time to give more information about activities, reading, books and other things that the library has to offer.

Usually the libraries invite groups of parents to visit with their newborn babies and tell them specifically what the library can offer that is fun for baby and parent to do when they come together. Sometimes it can be the other way around, and the librarian visits the children's health centre. Libraries usually offer nursery rhymes, 'babybooktalks', sing-a-song sessions and other activities starting from the early years and through the school years.

Some libraries have been inspired by pedagogical theory, which they have tried to adapt to the library. The aim, of course, is to make the library more aligned to the needs of children. The thinking of the Italian physician, educator and philosopher Maria Montessori has been an inspiration, and also the ideas of Loriz Malaguzzi, the founder of the Reggio Emilia pedagogy.

'Sagostunden', a story-telling session, is a common activity for children aged 0–5 years in libraries all over Sweden. They can vary a lot. The children can be a group who already know each other and maybe come regularly to the library, or they may be a group with no connection to each other at all who are on a single visit. These different circumstances make the story-telling sessions different from one time to another and from place to place. Opportunities to collaborate with other actors who have an interest in children's culture, and also the possibility to create and develop the story-telling session on your own, are very much in the hands of the individual children's librarian. But activities like singing, painting and drama are usually appreciated.

Another activity is the Children's Bookjury. It started in 1997 and was inspired by an activity originating in the Netherlands. Anyone between the ages of 0 and 19 can be a part of the Children's Bookjury. Children can choose up to five favourite books and they can vote for any new book published during the past year. It does not matter whether the book is translated from another language or originally published in Swedish. No reprints are allowed. The children who vote can also win prizes, usually a book or maybe a visit by an author/illustrator to their school/preschool. The prize-giving ceremony is a big event. Several of the authors/illustrators who have won a prize in the Children's Bookjury say that this award is one of the most prestigious prizes an author/illustrator of children's books can get, because the award is made by the reading children themselves, and not by adult critics or other specialists in children's literature.

How to arrange and present the media for children in a library is always a matter of discussion. Many libraries use colours, symbols, objects and letters in different combinations to make it easy to navigate through the books and other media. Children's librarians are usually very concerned about the concepts children hold - the 'children's perspective'; that is, what you, as an adult, think is the best for the children - which might be quite different from the children's personal views. In work with even younger children, such as those of preschool age, it is really interesting to work with focus groups and workshops and really do your best to try to find out what in the library would attract the children the most. What *are* their needs and desires? These perspectives can be used in planning an area for children, with particular regard to furniture and the arrangement of the media.

Of course, it is always important to interact enthusiastically with the children - to greet them at eye level, in every respect - and smile!

Conclusion

As mentioned earlier, there is a wealth of initiatives in operation, both in the UK and overseas, and only some of them have been covered in this chapter. Do make time to visit the sources mentioned and glean further insight and ideas for professional practice. Also, make time to search on the web to discover more information, as in this way you can learn from what others are doing. Be proactive in contacting the agencies and organizations mentioned.

CHAPTER 12

Successful library activities for the early years and ways to promote books effectively

Anne Harding

Early years activities in libraries – and of course library books – can play a huge role in supporting babies' and young children's learning and development. This chapter will consider that role and identify effective library activities and book promotion for under-fives.

The benefits of library activities for early childhood learning and development

The acronym SPICE is a very useful reminder of early childhood developmental needs:

Social
Physical
Intellectual
Creative
Emotional.

Libraries are well placed to nurture all of these. Many readers will have witnessed young children learning how to take turns in rhyme times, just one example of the ways libraries help social development. Successful rhyme times incorporate plenty of movement – evidence of support for physical development. Anyone who has given or watched a library story time for young children and listened to their questions and comments will be well aware of its value for intellectual development. Craft activities foster children's creativity. Lots of picture books are wonderful for emotional development, helping children's understanding of their own and others' feelings.

Many countries define the areas of learning and development that should be supported in early years establishments. Libraries can and should bear these in mind when planning activities. This way they usefully complement what is happening in preschool settings and in the first years at school, so reinforcing children's learning. In addition, libraries can demonstrate their relevance to young children's education, making library visits more attractive to preschools and schools. In England the areas of the Early Years Foundation Stage (EYFS) (DfE, 2012) have much in common with those of other countries. The EYFS prime areas of learning are:

- communication and language
- personal, social and emotional development
- physical development.

There can be no question that libraries help communication and language. Rhyme and story times develop babies' and young children's listening and attention skills, help them to understand the spoken word and communicate with others and increase their vocabulary. Such activities also play a valuable role in terms of personal, social and emotional development. We have already seen some examples, to which could be added the fact that regular attendance at library sessions helps young children learn to manage their feelings and behaviour, and begin to share. Craft activities and rhyme times aid co-ordination and motor skills.

These are defined as the EYFS specific areas of learning:

- literacy
- mathematics
- understanding the world
- expressive arts and design.

Again, it is easy to think of ways in which libraries and books play a part. Surely nowhere is more important for early years literacy than the library. Crucially, libraries help children to enjoy books, making learning to read much easier, and rhyme times draw attention to word sounds in a highly enjoyable way. There is clear evidence of the benefits of rhyme in terms of literacy development (Booktrust, 2014). Libraries support maths too: number rhymes help with counting. Lots of picture books explore concepts like shape and size. Books are also wonderful for giving young children an understanding of the world. They learn about their own and other countries, about nature, about people. Any library activity in which children explore and use media and materials is all about expressive arts and design, as is any in which they have the opportunity to be creative and imaginative.

We should consider not just the direct impact of library resources and activities on babies and young children. Libraries also have the potential to develop the skills of parents and carers, enabling them to support their children better. Family learning is very powerful, and libraries are in an ideal position to support it. We know that parental involvement in a child's learning is more powerful than family background, size of family or level of parental education (Campaign for Learning, 2014), and that the earlier parents become involved in their children's literacy practices, the more profound the results and the longer lasting the effects (Mullis et al., 2004). Library practitioners can model and support good practice. They can help parents and carers to understand the importance of rhymes, books and book sharing and model good ways to aid children's learning. Many parents, if they read to their children at all, open the book, read the words, then shut the book. Through libraries, they discover how to engage children and make book sharing far more enjoyable and creative, and feel confident to use books, rhymes and creative activities at home.

Key ingredients of successful provision

If these are the benefits, what are the key ingredients of successful early years provision? First and foremost, everyone must feel welcome. Practitioners leading sessions need to welcome every participant, but welcome extends wider than this. How early years friendly does the library feel to the first-time visitor? Are all the staff on board? One glowering face as families come in can ruin a visit, and may mean that some never return. Is there a secure place to park buggies? How easy are nappy changing and breastfeeding? How safe does the library feel? Unless issues like these are addressed, again, families may come only once.

Fun must surely be the next priority. If the babies, young children and parents and carers attending library sessions don't enjoy them, they will not learn and they will not come back. No rhyme time, no story time, no early years venture of any sort will achieve its goals if it does not foreground pleasure. Is the children's area in itself an enjoyable place to spend time in?

Children love and need to be creative, as we have already seen, so make opportunities for this, remembering that joining in with a book and talking about it can itself be creative and that projects like making books are highly enjoyable. Sessions in which children create things to take home help to reinforce learning, especially if the activity in some way continues there. An example might be planting a seed after hearing *Jack and the Beanstalk* and taking it home to grow.

Play is crucial for young children's learning, so library activities need to include lots of it. A good rhyme time will of course just feel like play. Well-chosen books can too. Watch a child interacting with *The Very Hungry Caterpillar* (Carle, 2002), and what you see is play. Some Essex libraries offer creative play sessions in conjunction with local children's centres - a great idea. Good toys are very valuable, especially when used constructively - for instance, at the end of story or rhyme times. Use soft toys to tie in with rhymes and songs and to demonstrate actions.

As babies and young children learn through all their senses, it is always helpful to incorporate multisensory approaches. A book like *Handa's Surprise* (Browne, 2006) lends itself well if there are lots of fruits for the children to touch, smell and taste. Musical instruments in rhyme times are great: things for babies and toddlers to shake and to hear. Simple things like water, sand, feathers, leaves, balloons and bubbles and messy play are extremely popular and stimulate lots of discussion and learning. Soft toys, puppets and artefacts bring rhymes, stories and books to life and increase enjoyment, understanding and participation.

Participation

Participation is a vital part of successful early years sessions. No baby or toddler learns by just watching and listening. If they have taken an active part, parents and carers are much more likely to use at home those ideas that they have encountered in the library. (And of course we also need them to be engaged, as otherwise the children will be distracted.) What are good ways to make sure babies, young children, parents and carers are all involved? Small groups foster interaction and participation. Instruments, soft toys, puppets and artefacts encourage involvement by both children and adults. Encourage everyone to participate by using familiar rhymes that involve the adult and child doing things together: action, counting, tickling or cuddling rhymes. The best seating arrangement for rhyme times is a circle, as this encourages participation (and reduces the risk of small children escaping). Make sure small babies face their carer rather than facing outwards, as they can focus only on faces and objects that are nearby. Plan participative activities that link the artefacts, stories and books you aim to share, for example exploring light and dark with torches after reading *Peace at Last* (Murphy, 2007), or playing with cars on a floor mat after a car story. Acting books out is great. When choosing books to read aloud, choose ones that encourage children to join in, for instance books with lots of repetition.

Indeed repetition is very important for children's learning. In story times, young children often want to hear a book they have loved more than once. Reading it again will garner extra participation, enjoyment and learning. Research has shown that hearing the same book lots of times is better for children's vocabulary than hearing lots of different books (Bealing, 2011). Successful rhyme times use mostly the same rhymes and songs every week. Babies and toddlers look forward to them and develop the confidence to join in because they are familiar. It's great to have the same welcome song and the same goodbye one each time. Many Welsh library authorities support bilingualism by delivering some rhymes twice, once in Welsh, once in English. There is lots more detail about successful rhyme times in Chapter 10, about music and rhyme time sessions for the early years, by Shelley Bullas and Ben Lawrence.

At the start of this chapter we saw the early years areas of learning and development. Language and literacy are key aspects of learning that libraries can and should support. Speaking and listening are the cornerstones of language and literacy development and crucial for lots of learning, so encourage lots of talk during early years sessions. Clear, simple language is vital for babies' and children's (and parents' and carers') understanding and to develop babies' and children's language skills and learning. Sharing books and rhymes in libraries is beneficial in all sorts of ways, not least because they help young children to develop a love of language. Story-telling and story-tellers are fantastic. So too are local visitors - people like fire-fighters - talking about what they do and telling a relevant story or reading a book. It's worth remembering the other areas of learning when planning activities, to make sure they are relevant and helpful.

Planning and practicalities

Early years activities should feel informal. To achieve this, meticulous planning is vital, with clarity about the aims and expected outcomes. Risk assessments are crucial. Work out a safe maximum number of adults and children for under-fives events. As we have seen, careful thought must be given to practicalities like buggy parking, access to toilets and breastfeeding arrangements. It's well worth consulting local early years providers as well as users and non-users about under-fives provision. Session plans are a good idea, setting out what is to happen through the session, what resources and props will be used, what the practitioner will do and how children and carers will be involved. It's important to build flexibility into plans, since the number, age profile or needs of the visitors to a story time or rhyme time are often not as expected. Good planning ensures that you have a range of ideas and resources to suit any eventuality. Try never to be in a situation where you have to give an early years session without notice. Babies, young children and their carers deserve activities that have been thoughtfully prepared, and that takes time - something that unfortunately is in short supply in many libraries.

As much as possible, have the same practitioner each time. Consistency of staffing adds to children's and carers' sense of familiarity and comfort. Timing needs careful consideration: nap times need to be thought about, and school pick-up times. It's well worth consulting library users and non-users about this. Aim for a day of the week when there are not lots of other under-fives activities on offer locally. Whatever day and time you select, busy families need predictability and an easily remembered pattern. For example, 10.00 every Tuesday is memorable, while 10.00 on every fourth Tuesday is not. (The *last* Tuesday of every month is preferable, if staffing levels dictate monthly rather than weekly activities.)

For practical reasons, many library authorities offer one overall early years session per week. This is not ideal, as the needs of babies and toddlers and three- to four-year-olds are all very different. Children at the older end love fast-paced sessions and lots of action, but for babies these are bewildering. If at all possible, it is more effective to have separate sessions for different age groups. Enfield Libraries provide rhyme times for babies under one and not yet mobile, toddler times with stories and rhymes for one- to three-year-olds and story time and play for under-fives (Enfield Council, 2013). (It is of course flexible with families with more than one child.)

Try to have some activities at times when working parents can attend. Lots of library services now offer Saturday or Sunday under-fives events, sometimes targeted specifically at fathers and other male family members. Essex Libraries has Daddy Cool sessions with stories, songs and rhymes.

Most early years library provision takes the form of regular activities. However, one-off events can also be very valuable for attracting new and existing users, such as a very well-attended bedtime story session at Petts Wood Library in Bromley. A number of UK libraries run occasional family days with appeal across the age groups. For example, in March 2014 Glasgow Libraries mounted a Wee Write Family Day with rhyme times, book readings, art sessions and lots more as part of a Glasgow-wide book festival for children and young people.[1]

Ideally, not all early years provision will be for families. There is lots of value in providing visits to the library by toddler groups, preschools and nurseries. The emphasis should of course be on enjoyment, with plenty of rhymes, stories and interaction. Where they are possible, visits to early years settings are also very useful promotional tools. Some library services provide specifically for childminders. Others make sure they are invited to regular under-fives activities.

Put up signs throughout the library about early years sessions, to advertise them and to let other users know that noise levels will be higher than usual at those times. Many library users love seeing and hearing young children enjoying themselves in the library, but unfortunately, this is not the case for everyone. In this way the potential for dissatisfaction and complaints can be reduced. Do not worry if attendance is low to start with, as word will quickly spread, but do check that there are no problems with timing or access.

Monitoring and evaluation

The best early years provision evolves over time. Good monitoring and evaluation are very important. Keep a record of responses to the library and your activities. Some parents and carers find form-filling very off-putting. Oral testimony is equally valid. Listen to what the children say too, and watch how they interact with your sessions. And act on what you hear and on your observations about what works and what is less successful. Make sure good practice is shared throughout the library service. Monitoring can provide useful evidence about the value of your activities for senior managers and elected representatives. A few years ago Croydon Library Service conducted a survey about the effectiveness of its Saturday rhyme times. These were the very impressive results:

- 98% of respondents showed evidence of enjoyment
- 83% showed evidence of progression
- 93% showed evidence of acquiring new skills
- 72% showed evidence of a change in knowledge and understanding
- 52% showed evidence of a change in attitudes and values.

Catering effectively for early years entails catering for the whole family. A parent of a baby is quite likely to have a toddler as well, and perhaps older children too. That parent is not easily going to be able to attend an event for the baby or toddler without bringing his or her siblings. A flexible attitude means that the library welcomes the whole family to activities, even when the age range may not be quite appropriate for everyone. Themed family days can cater for lots of ages, for example Perth and Kinross ran a circus-themed day in March 2014, with a range of family-friendly activities, including a story time with puppets and a puppet-making workshop.

Inclusivity is a useful watchword. Thought should be given to how to involve young children with special needs, for instance making sure that anyone with a hearing impairment sits near the practitioner. Props to accompany rhymes and stories make them easier to understand for children with learning problems. They are also very beneficial for families with different mother tongues. It's great to share songs, rhymes, stories and books in a variety of languages. You may not know how to speak more than one language, but your visitors may be very happy to take the lead for a short while. Be sensitive to needs. For instance, teenage parents may require some separate provision, as activities where all the other parents and carers are very much older than them can be daunting. Do try to get men involved in library activities. Male role models are vital, but unfortunately often lacking in libraries. When a father accompanied a nursery group on a library visit and found and shared books about trains, the children, especially the boys, were enthralled.

It is well worth considering the value of partnerships with other providers – and not just children's centres, but organizations like local museums. Library and museum or library and archive co-operation in activities for under-fives can be very successful.

Marketing early years activities

What about marketing? The library service website is very important, and traditional flyers and posters have a role to play, particularly if they are displayed in places where non-users will see them: in health centres, religious institutions, shopping centres, etc. Make sure to emphasize that activities are free and anyone can come. Use Bookstart (www.bookstart.org.uk) as a marketing tool, with activities that tie in. It's important to remember that for huge numbers of children parents are not their main daytime caregivers. Grandparents need to be thought of in terms of marketing. Childminders have already been mentioned.

Outreach is crucial for reaching non-users. Visits to early years settings are very beneficial. A number of UK library services promote their offers at health centres. Some, for instance Hillingdon Libraries, have delivered one-off activities in shopping centres. Greenwich Library Service has done story times in local parks, and on one occasion joined forces with the National Maritime Museum to give an open-air rhyme time. It attracted hundreds of participants and increased take-up of regular library rhyme times.

Word of mouth is the best means of marketing that there is, and in these days of social media it is more powerful than ever. Think of the value of a positive write-up on Facebook or Twitter, like this tweet: 'Libraries offer a chance for my child to meet other children – rhyme time is an exciting part of our weekly routine!' Your users are your best ambassadors. This is from a father's blog post:

> Bounce and Rhyme was worth the wait. Sandy LOVES it. She's been doing it a while now ... so she's well versed in 'Zoom, zoom, zoom' and 'Five Little Monkeys.' She really enjoys all the movement and singing, and absolutely loves shaking her rattle in time with the other kids. There was a new lady leading it today and she was great. She did some new ones that ... I didn't recognise, so I learned something new as well.
>
> (Adventures of a Stay at Home Dad)

Promoting books and reading

There is no question about the importance of promoting books and reading. As Orville Prescott famously said many years ago: 'Few children learn to love books by themselves. Someone has to lure them into the wonderful world of the written word; someone has to show them the way' (Prescott, 1965). Library practitioners, with their knowledge of and access to huge numbers of inspirational books, are of course the ideal people to do it. Who knows better how to make books exciting and special? It is fabulous to hear a good book read aloud well. Young children who experience that joy are likely to find learning to read easier - they have seen how to do it - and to want to read. As mentioned earlier, children benefit directly from hearing stories and books in libraries, and they benefit indirectly as their parents and carers learn how to share books effectively.

What types of books work well for reading to groups of babies and young children? Given that we want to spread a love of books, the best aid to selection is to use books that you enjoy. Your enthusiasm will be contagious. If you find the book fun, so will the children. Use books with content that will stimulate lots of interest and discussion. Look for books with characters and plots that young children will relate to and understand. Choose books with good visual impact and good illustrations that can be seen from a distance. For babies, choose simple, colourful books with clear photographs or pictures of familiar things and everyday activities. Books that reflect home and preschool help children's understanding and make reading relevant. Pop-up books and books with flaps, textures and noises encourage enthusiasm and participation and are great for children with special educational needs and children who have little understanding of the language you are reading in, though they may not work well with large groups. Funny books are always popular. Books with rhyme, rhythm and repetition work well. They help young children's memory and understanding and develop their literacy skills, and are ideal for fostering participation.

Think about concentration spans. Babies and toddlers need short books with plenty to hold their attention, and not too many of them. They need more time than older ones to take in the words and the pictures. Older children, especially if they regularly attend your story times, will be able to concentrate for longer, but will still need books that provide lots of stimulation. Be sensitive to emotional needs. Lots of older children love *Where the Wild Things Are* (Sendak, 2000), but it can be terrifying for some younger ones. Young children are intensely curious and love learning. Intersperse story books with simple and attractive information books on topics that are likely to interest them.

Avoid books which reinforce stereotypes in text and/or pictures. Aim for inclusivity. Consider the implicit messages in the books you are sharing. There is a huge value to children experiencing a range of cultures and ways of living through books. Read dual-language books sometimes, even if you can read only one of the languages.

Good book promotion is not just about choosing effective titles; it's also about the method of delivery. What are good ways to make books come alive for young children? Children love hearing different voices for different characters. Use lots of facial and vocal expression and big body movements. Props really help them to understand and enjoy books. There are lovely *Gruffalo* (Donaldson and Scheffler, 1999) toys in lots of libraries, but home-made props or soft toys and puppets from charity shops can be equally effective. Participation makes all the difference. Even very little ones love joining in with the final words in rhyming lines. Three- and four-year-olds enjoy role play. A teacher introduced a reading of *The Tiger Who Came to Tea* (Kerr, 2006) by asking the four-year-olds in her class to imagine they had tiger ears and tiger stripes, a lovely way to make them receptive to the story. Dressing-up clothes are very popular. Simple art and craft activities related to books are fun, and help comprehension. For instance, children could make or paint tiger masks. Thematic approaches work well. You could accompany *Dear Zoo* (Campbell, 2010) with an appealing information book and an activity making pop-up pages with animal themes. For very young children the same book would be great accompanied with animal props and rhymes about animals.

Paul Kropp (1995) tells us that reading time should always be full of talk and play, even if that has little obvious connection with the story. It's through talk before, during and after book sharing that children make sense of what they are hearing and seeing, relate it to their own lives, and find wonder.

Conclusion

Wonder is an excellent word to finish this chapter. We have seen that library activities and library books are superb stimuli for babies' and young children's learning, and that they spread positive messages about libraries and reading. Well-planned sessions and well-chosen books deliver enormous benefits to children and families. The best are lots of fun. And yes, full of wonder.

Note

1   www.youtube.com/watch?v=Oa1NHGdbUTI&feature=youtu.be.

References

Adventures of a Stay at Home Dad,
      http://adventuresofastayathomedad.wordpress.com/tag/storytime.

Bealing, J. (2011) *'Again, Again!' Why repetition in reading helps children learn more*, University of Sussex, www.sussex.ac.uk/newsandevents/?id=7040.

Booktrust (2014) www.bookstart.org.uk/professionals/about-bookstart-and-the-packs/research/reviews-and-resources/the-benefit-of-rhymes.

Browne, E. (2006) *Handa's Surprise*, Walker.

Campaign for Learning (2014) www.campaign-for-learning.org.uk.

Campbell, R. (2010) *Dear Zoo*, Macmillan Children's Books.

Carle, E. (2002) *The Very Hungry Caterpillar*, Puffin.

Department for Education (DfE) (2012) *Statutory Framework for the Early Years Foundation Stage*, Department for Education.

Donaldson, J. and Schleffer, A. (1999) *The Gruffalo*, Macmillan Children's Books.

Enfield Council (2013) Toys and Stories, www.enfield.gov.uk/downloads/file/8122/under_five_leaflet_2013.

Kerr, J. (2006) *The Tiger Who Came to Tea*, Harper Collins Children's Books.

Kropp, P. (1995) *The Reading Solution: making your child a reader for life*, Penguin.

Mullis, R. L., Mullis, A. K., Cornille, T. A., Ritchson, A. D. and Sullender, N. L. (2004) *Early Literacy Outcomes and Parent Involvement*, Technical Report No. 1, Florida State University Family Institute, Outcome & Evaluation Unit.

Murphy, J. (2007) *Peace at Last*, Macmillan Children's Books.

Prescott, O. (1965) *A Father Reads to His Children: an anthology of prose and poetry*, E. P. Dutton & Co.

Sendak, M. (2000) *Where the Wild Things Are*, Red Fox.

CHAPTER 13

Designing family-friendly libraries for the early years

Carolynn Rankin and Rachel Van Riel

Introduction

This chapter considers the design approaches that libraries have used and reviews what makes for successfully designed library spaces for babies and young children and their families. Choosing, sharing and expressing views on books all start long before children can read, which makes the challenges and opportunities relating to library-space design for the birth-to-five age range important. The focus will be on provision for babies and young children in public libraries, but the discussion will also relate to library space in nursery schools and kindergartens.

In considering the environment and design of the early years space within the library, it is important to create a welcoming atmosphere and the ambience, layout, design, furniture and fittings will have a part to play. Guidance is provided on how you can negotiate with architects and designers to achieve this. We will encourage you to think about the use of colour, different types of furniture and equipment and how the books and resources are displayed.

While there is a reasonable amount of design guidance and information available on library spaces for older children and teens (Dewe, 1995; Lushington, 2008; Rankin, 2012), very little has been published on library design for the birth to five group. This means debates are still open and more evidence of impact needs to be gathered. We hope this chapter will raise questions and stimulate further discussion of how design can best meet the needs of this important audience.

The library as a community space: the case for the place

We will start by considering the role of the library building as a community space.

There is a strongly held view that libraries offer a welcoming, neutral space that provides opportunities for personal, cultural and community development in appropriate circumstances (Harris and Dudley, 2005, 18). Worpole (2013) cites the changing role of libraries and argues that designing libraries is about investing in people: 'If libraries have a reputation for being universally welcoming, the new renaissance in prestigious library development projects across the world should be welcomed as a sign that the library, both as a public facility and a learning space, has a future as a place to meet, read, share and explore ideas in what might be called a 'living room in the city'.'

In his book *The Great Good Place*, the urban sociologist Oldenburg writes about the importance of informal public gathering-places and why these are essential to community and public life. He identifies third places, or great good places, as the public domains on neutral ground where people can gather and interact. In contrast to first places (home) and second places (work), third places allow people to put aside their concerns and simply enjoy the company and conversation around them (Oldenburg, 1999). The library can, we suggest, be regarded as a 'third place' for children and their families, as it is a welcoming space for intergenerational encounters and where they can socialize and access resources. Carers of young children especially need third places, as being the only adult at home can become very isolating. When some third places are not welcoming to babies and toddlers, while others are simply not safe, it can be hard for parents and carers to find places to relax with others, which also cater for the needs of their children. The under-fives' area at the library becomes very significant in this context.

Schools, houses, offices, museums, libraries, streets and parks all combine to form the 'physical capital' of a particular place. The Commission for Architecture and the Built Environment (CABE) defines 'physical capital' as the potential value - financial, social and cultural - of the built environment. Every neighbourhood is made up of a collection of buildings and spaces which, when taken together with the cultures, commerce and behaviours of local people, determine the identity and quality of life in any given community (CABE, 2005, 33). Architecture and design communicate identity and values, and well-designed spaces are more efficient to manage and better cared for by the people who use them.

The presence of a public library (or early years library in a children's centre) can have a positive impact, enhancing the neighbourhood and providing a welcoming 'neutral' space for community engagement. Such free local spaces can be very important to young parents in helping to combat social isolation. We can now meet many of our needs from mobile devices at home - we shop from the sofa, chat online, download entertainment without ever having to open our front doors. Paradoxically, this can actually increase the feeling of social isolation.

Young mums have always been vulnerable to this, and one way of dealing with potential isolation is by going to spaces where you can meet others. Aabø and Audunson (2012) investigated public library use by the local community, focusing on social activities and how libraries function as meeting places. They found that public library use is very diverse, and state that the findings are important because of the need for meeting places across cultural, ethnic, generational and social boundaries in a complex, multicultural and digitized society. Going to the library makes a connection not just in the role as parent or carer of an under-five, it gives a feeling of connection with the wider community as well. Designing welcoming spaces for this key audience is an essential part of good library design.

Location, location, location ... the dilemma

One of the most visible ways of creating a child-centred library is to locate the children's area in the main library (Esson and Tyerman, 1991), as it can be argued that this raises the profile of the service by making it highly visible. A ground-floor location provides easy access for parents with small children and children with disabilities. However, controversy exists as to whether the children's library should be a separate room or an area in the main library, as there are advantages and disadvantages to both. Having a separate library allows children to make noise to a high level and makes it easier to put on activities such as film shows, musical events and messy crafts. Worpole (2013, 98) clearly states one of the issues around location: 'It is a matter of some debate as to whether the children's library should be seen as a place apart, self-contained and with its own safeguarding and child protection protocols, or more integrated with the adult library', and we can extend this discussion to include provision for the under-fives.

The problem is that the personal development needs of different age groups can cause conflicts. Noise and safety are very different for the 0–5s than for other age groups. Many libraries now have more open children's areas which blend into the larger space without hard barrier zoning, and problems can be resolved by what Rachel Van Riel calls 'managing through time not space', for example holding busy Rhyme Time sessions during school hours. However, there is still a view that a separate enclosed space is better, as everyone can relax, but this needs to be balanced against an alternative view that closing young children - especially toddlers and babies - off from everyone else does seem rather old-fashioned and patriarchal.

The design debate

Another debate to raise is the very nature of the design of library spaces for children.

In discussing the history of children's library design, Black and Rankin (2011) note a trend for themed, fantasy design and for funky furniture, such as reading towers and pods (see Figure 13.1), which encourage playful engagement in the library space. This approach provides a very strong visual demarcation between adult and child spaces and raises another area of contention identified by Worpole:

Figure 13.1 *The reading tower encourages playful engagement in the library space*

> It is also a matter of contention as to whether it should have its own design code – often colourful and imbued with fairytale imagery – or whether it should contain the same design palette as the rest of the library, avoiding charges of infantilisation.
>
> (Worpole, 2013, 98)

Worpole argues that not all library staff, let alone interior designers, are happy with the perceived 'infantilisation' of the children's library space. There is a danger that infantilization can result in a nostalgic design, where library staff wish to recreate memories of a golden past childhood, rather than a contemporary design with appeal to today's young parents. Worpole quotes a comment from CABE in describing a new library design: 'we think that a calmer aesthetic, less reliant on bright colour and organic forms could be more successful'. It can be argued that making children's libraries 'too young' will put off the 7-11s, who are harder to keep than the under-5s, who have no say in the matter. What is colourful and exciting to a 3-year-old may be a deterrent to an 8-year-old. It is easier to dress down a public library space age-wise with soft furnishings, rugs, cushions, toys than to give it temporary 'older' appeal.

Babies in the library: designing spaces for intergenerational encounters

Library space is a resource that needs to be well designed in order to meet the present and future needs of those who use it and to continue to attract users.

Major city public libraries are more likely to have the funding and investment to create the immediate 'oomph' or 'wow' factor, as suggested by McDonald (2007) in discussing the qualities of a good library space. You may not have the budget for high-impact features but planning how you use the basic elements of the space, the furniture and the bookstock will result in a better design which will create a pleasing impact and work better for your visitors. There is no space too small that it's not worth the application of design principles.

Mark Dudek, an architect specializing in design for young children, advises that

> Buildings should not merely satisfy basic needs, they should provide the right amount and kind of space for activities that will interest and stimulate their users. Most good architecture combines the practical with something less tangible; a sense of delight in the spaces which make up a building as a whole, which may even modify the moods of its users in a positive way. If designed skilfully, a building will help to make children's experience of their early years care a secure yet varied one.
>
> (Dudek, 2001, 8)

There is considerable evidence to show that the environment influences children's behaviour and plays a central role in learning (Roskos and Neuman, 2003), but this does not seem to have been readily translated into the design of library spaces for babies and children. The creation of welcoming but functional space is critical for encouraging and maintaining visits to the library, as families have other places they can choose to spend their leisure time.

In the USA the 'family-centered library' is a purposefully designed public space that welcomes very young children and families. Is it filled with developmentally appropriate activities and materials to encourage play, interactive learning and socialization (Feinberg et al., 2007; Kropp, 2004). Bohrer (2005) has reported on the growing number of USA public libraries that are transforming library spaces into dynamic learning centres focusing on developing literacy in young children.

The digitization of knowledge and the impact of new technologies have had an impact on reading and library practice. A key message is that innovative library managers have looked at other areas of cultural and leisure provision to glean design ideas. The design approach used in 'The Trove' at White Plains Public Library in New York has incorporated ideas from multimedia experiences in museums and theme parks (Miranda, 2012). If librarians want to continue to encourage use of the library there is a need to provide spaces that will attract and suit a range of young families and the 'digital natives' (Prensky, 2001), the born-digitals who have experienced sound and visual surroundings of ever-increasing complexity since birth.

To ensure that your library provides the best possible environment for the young children and their families who patronize it, it is important to take the time to consider the most appropriate and user-friendly layout, structure and design of the building. A well-designed building has a greater value to all involved.

An eye for detail: why should librarians be concerned about architecture and design?

The premise in this chapter is that librarians should be concerned about architecture and design and take an active interest in the place and space in which services are delivered to the user community. You may well be thinking 'I'm only involved as part of the team delivering services once the building is already constructed. The design issues are the concern of senior managers.' However, the current trend for multidisciplinary teamwork means that you could have the unique opportunity to provide input into a new project and be part of designing a building that suits the purpose you have in mind. Avoid being involved in the design and planning of the early years library space, and the result could be the creation of an area that you find unsatisfactory and unsuitable for your requirements. Architects and designers can have excellent ideas, but their priorities may differ from yours in terms of what is important in layout and use of space. You are the expert in terms of what is necessary, practical and desirable in the early years library. There are areas that it is possible and important to influence, such as access, entrances and exits.

Building design proceeds from the global (total square meterage for each area) to the detail of room data sheets, which specify requirements in terms of finish and electrics for each room. The building developers will want to finalize the various areas and finishes in order to plan costs at an early stage. There will then be pressure to complete the mechanical and electrical scheme - heating, ventilation, lighting, power and data -because, again, the building costs cannot be controlled without these being fixed. With a new building, all these will be tendered for well before any work begins on site, and often by the time library staff are consulted none of them can be changed. The earlier you can make contact with the building design team the better. Use the arguments in this chapter about the importance of good provision for the under-fives to justify your place at the table. If there is only one library representative allowed for the whole service, make sure you have regular meetings with them, so that you will be able to keep in touch and comment on what is going on from the under-fives' service perspective.

There are many aspects of the build where librarians must respect the expertise of other professions (architects, builders, designers) and amateur views will not be welcomed. However, there are key areas where your input is not only essential to getting the space right for your audience, but it can also help the whole design team to understand and deliver what is required. Below are some of the questions to raise:

Access and through-routes

Is the entrance in the right place? Easy to see and to use? What is the door system for buggies and wheelchairs? What are the sightlines from the entrance - is it easy to see where to go? Is there a clear route for buggies from the entrance to the under-fives' area? Tell the design team the likely numbers for under-fives' sessions - 20 toddlers involves how many carers, siblings, buggies at any one time?

Toilets

Where are the nearest toilets and are they accessible? Make sure baby-changing facilities are considered from the outset. For example, recent regulations in the UK have improved the standards for these, which mean that a pull-down baby change cannot be accommodated in a standard wheelchair-accessible toilet; you will need more space. Check also that the walls are strong enough for a pull-down baby change; pattresses can be added at an early stage but if you miss them (as one major project did recently) it will be expensive to add later.

Buggy parks

If the space is large enough, a buggy park is worth considering, but look at each case on its merits. In the UK many carers refuse to go very far from their buggies - it's not just the value these represent (which is considerable), it is that the whole eco-system for child/carer survival is located at the buggy, and people want things close at hand. Architects may give you a buggy park which won't get used. What does need looking at in every library space is how far buggies will spill out during under-fives' events.

Breastfeeding

Is there a comfortable space for breastfeeding? This does not have to be a separate room, as breastfeeding can be very discreet, but you need to think how you will support those who want to breastfeed.

Staff desk

In many new buildings the reception/enquiry desk is designed and built by the architect team. This is likely to mean that it becomes a feature piece, which may be beautiful but can also be space-hungry and off-putting. Modern library design aims to reduce the feature desk in favour of a more flexible relationship between staff and library visitors. Look at other options here and see whether the money saved can help you somewhere else in the building.

Connecting front and back office functions

How far away is the work area for staff? Book transit is a crucial part of the under-fives' service. The books are large in size and customers borrow large numbers at a time. Picture books and board books are the highest issuing area of the collection in most UK libraries. Every new library runs out of these books within a week of opening unless this is planned for. You don't need more shelves or kinder boxes – that will become overwhelming. You need space to store books to top up as shelves empty. Where will this be?

Refreshments

Carers will appreciate coffee facilities if you can add them safely. A free water cooler is always a boon to a parent with thirsty toddlers. The safest and best value water and vending systems are mains-connected rather than bottle-based, so they require positioning near to water pipes and electricity at an early stage.

As is recognized by CABE, you are the one who is left behind after the designers and planners have all moved on, and it is important that you should be happy with the end result.

CASE STUDY The shrinking library!

The library kept shrinking! This was happening during the design and planning stage of our first children's centre library and the room size was eventually cut down to the minimum. There was much negotiation and we had to take a cut on the potential staffing, but the library was included and we now have a very successful children's centre library. So my advice is: never miss a planning meeting – the librarian's voice needs to be heard!

Jean Gabbatt, Literacy Development and Resources Manager, Blackburn with Darwen

There's now a big difference between the super-library creating a destination point in a metropolitan area and the smaller branch library. Most new branches in the UK are and will be co-locations, as local government is rethinking provision to offer more services in one place. This saves costs, of course, but it can also be more customer centred. Librarians will be involved in these projects differently. It may be that you are a member of a multidisciplinary team planning a purpose-built setting in a children's centre, or you are involved in a refurbishment project in a public library setting. Perhaps you have been appointed to a new position and have inherited an existing children's library, or maybe you just want to take a fresh look at the current provision in your area. Whatever the scenario, it can be beneficial to have a regular review of the use of the spaces provided for babies and young children and their families.

There are many aspects to consider, and Table 13.1, based on McDonald (2007), can be used as a planning framework for considering the best qualities required in library space designed for the under-fives and their caregivers.

Table 13.1 *Library space for under-fives – a planning framework*

Functional	Space that works well, looks good and lasts well
Adaptable	Flexible space, the use of which can be easily changed
Varied	With a choice of learning, research and recreational spaces and for different media
Interactive	Well-organized space which promotes contact between users and services
Conducive	High-quality, humane space which motivates and inspires people
Environmentally suitable	With appropriate conditions for users, books and computers
Safe and secure	For people, collections, equipment, data and the building
Efficient	Economic in space, staffing and running costs
Suitable for information technology	With flexible provision for users and staff
Oomph or 'wow' factor	Inspirational space which captures the minds of users and the spirit of the institution

First impressions: the challenge

First impressions count! Consider this challenge. Try to imagine what your existing library setting seems like to first-time visitors. You may think it has a friendly, lively, busy and vibrant ambience, with everything clearly laid out using a carefully designed system. There may be lots of notices and posters, possibly in several different languages. Perhaps there are leaflet dispensers overflowing with free information about events, opportunities and activities on offer, or hundreds of colourful picture books displayed in kinder boxes. Nevertheless, to the anxious parent who has never used a library before and their 18-month-old child it may all seem quite overwhelming. The grandparent who remembers being told to keep quiet in a library as a youngster may not even consider visiting with their boisterous grandchildren.

The first impression children and parents gain from a library is its entrance and reception area. How well does yours measure up? Are visitors' first impressions likely to generate a positive experience? If you are involved in a brand-new build or a refurbishment project try to imagine what the ideal early years library should look like and how it should feel to the young children and families who use it. Libraries of various sizes and types are realizing the positive impact of creating comfortable and welcoming library environments for patrons of all ages. For years, school and public libraries have drawn in the very young and their parents with creative, enticing children's areas. According to Lushington (2002), a library should be easy to find, easy to enter and easy to use.

The importance of the environment and space

The physical appearance and location of buildings have an impact on the local community, but the environment inside is also important. As we look at the practical aspects of designing library space for very young children, let's start by considering some environmental factors. The childcare expert Friedrich Froebel (1782–1852) stressed the importance of environmental space. Froebel's view was that the first learning experiences of the very young are of crucial importance in influencing not only their later educational achievements but also the health and development of society as a whole. Froebel devised a set of principles and practices which would form part of an interactive educational process to take place in institutions which in 1840 he named 'kindergarten'. These principles also provide good advice when considering the design of early years library provision. Elements of a Froebelian Education for Children from Birth to Seven years include recognition of the uniqueness of each child's capacity and potential and recognition of the importance of play as a central integrating element in a child's development and learning. This pedagogy involves parents/carers and educators working in harmony and partnership. He proposed an environment which is physically safe but intellectually challenging, promoting curiosity, enquiry, sensory stimulation and aesthetic awareness and which allows free access to a rich range of materials that promote open-ended opportunities for play, representation and creativity (www.froebel.org.uk/elements.html).

The late Anita Rui Olds was a noted designer and psychologist with 30 years of experience in the design of children's environments. She felt that much emphasis is placed on the visual aspects of architecture, but it is really the feeling of buildings and our sense of well-being or dis-ease when we are in them that is at the root of the architectural experience (Olds, 2001, 22). She was the founder and director of The Child Care Institute, an annual training programme helping architects, designers and childcare providers to design spaces.

Environment as the third teacher: the Reggio Emilia approach

Environments can play a crucial part in the ethos of a setting and can be a key factor in ideologies behind education, care or services. Northern Italy is home to the Reggio Emilia programme of early childhood education, which has gained an international reputation since the first schools were started by parents in 1945, in the aftermath of the Second World War. It is now a city-run, sponsored system designed for all children from birth through six years of age. The Reggio Emilia approach recognizes the environment as the third teacher - parents and carers being the first two. Great attention is given to the look and feel of the early years setting. Space is organized for small- and large-group projects and small, intimate spaces for one, two or three children. Displays are at both adult and children's eye level and the furniture is designed to be multifunctional. Reggio settings make a marked use of natural and artificial light, with floor-to-ceiling windows and pale walls that offset the colourful artwork done by the children. The outside environment is also a source of colour and texture, and plants are widely used in the classrooms as well as in interior courtyards (Community Playthings, 2006).

The Reggio approach has an understanding of the young child which recognizes the whole child and acknowledges that the child's wider world of family and community are core to her experience of childhood.

Architecture and design – buildings – planning and designing spaces for the under-fives

It is important to try to visualize the environment through a child's eyes. Consider the following challenge:

> Get down on the floor and move around at child level. If you lie on your back and look up (a baby's perspective), you will realise that even ceilings are relevant!
>
> (Community Playthings, 2006)

Anita Olds (2001) has identified five factors which contribute to a truly great room layout, to a design that guides and encourages children to learn through play:

- Location: where is it in relation to other physical features and other activity areas?
- Boundaries: how well is the area defined?
- Variety: is there enough to keep the children interested?
- Storage: the materials children need in each activity area should be stored conveniently to hand, and displayed attractively for effective use.
- Mood: is the mood of the area appropriate to the function? Is it home-like?

Olds (2001) also reminds us that decisions involving functions, budgets and material performance are improved when people knowledgeable in these areas contribute their experience and expertise to the design. We should ask architects and contractors to provide cost estimates for alternative designs and materials. It would be good to see models and mock-ups of areas so that staff can evaluate the 3-dimensional aspects of a space. You can role-play the use you plan to make of each space to test out the requirements. A collaborative process encourages people to think about how we are currently doing things and how we would really like to be doing them in the future. In making suggestions about early years library provision don't be constrained by what you may already have, but consider innovation. This is very true of consultation too, as people find it hard to express what they want other than in terms of what they have already. Asking people to describe their ideal library, its ambience and what people can do in it, may help.

CABE was the UK government's advisor on architecture, urban design and public space between 1999 and 2011. Funded through central government, it aims to promote the role of quality design in new buildings and produces a range of publications on planning and design. CABE merged with the Design Council in 2011 and continues to offer expert advice on the built environment.

Well-designed spaces are cheaper to manage and better cared for by the people who use them, and they will be better used and more popular. Doing design well requires more than an understanding of aesthetics - looks are important, but the usefulness of the end product is what is really important.

The role of the librarian client; and consultation opportunities

A well-designed building is one that contributes to the business, is suitable for its intended use and is built to last. As the librarian with professional expertise in providing services for the early years, you may be asked to be part of a project team working alongside other specialists in the development of a new centre, or to make contributions to planning discussions. Either way, you will need to interact with the architects and designers commissioned to develop the plans. Architects generally seek staff input initially, but may not always check out the consequences of design solutions later on. The client's role is very important in the design-and-build partnership. To be a successful client you can look at other early years building projects to get ideas, and talk to people involved in similar projects about their experiences. Consultation with the library user community is also important.

When discussing the design of the early years library setting with the architect, it is important to be clear about what you want. Dudek (2001) comments that, 'Early years practitioners often ask architects to create a "homely" setting - a subjective and imprecise term that could mean all sorts of different things. It is vital that reflection about form and style go beyond this basic kind of definition.' The architect needs to know how the building will be used, who the clients will be, its purpose and how it will complement its surroundings. Once this broad picture has been defined, it would be helpful, where possible, to include parents and children in the discussions to allow the architect to fill in the details. This will enable a better understanding of the project and the path will be set to ensure that it sets off on the right footing. Dudek concludes, 'It is crucial that the architect or architectural practice selected to oversee the project is in tune with your needs, willing to be flexible and to take your views and those of the community seriously' (2001, 77).

It is really important to have an understanding of what you want to achieve before you meet an architect or design team. Things that are really important to you may not be included in the final design brief, so be well prepared and assertive in stating your requirements. As stated earlier, architects will undertake consultation with clients to establish needs, but requests are not always followed through.

Sources of advice

There is considerable practical advice and expertise available for those about to embark on a major building project for the first time. For example *Building for Sure Start: integrated provision for under-fives* (DfES, 2004) is potentially useful for anyone involved in new buildings for the under-fives and will have information for early years librarians involved in public library projects. Another best-practice online guide aimed at the client is *Creating Excellent Buildings: a guide for clients* (CABE, 2011). This is divided into the four main stages of a building project - preparation, design, construction and use of the building. The Designing Libraries website (see below) includes an Essential Design Guide on *Managing a Successful Library Design and Furnishing Project*. The State Library of New South Wales (2012, 97-9) provides a useful guide to children's areas which recognizes that there are 'different learning, developmental and socialization behaviours to address' in catering for children at different stages of development.

One of the best ways of approaching your library design project is to learn from others, and decision making can be supported by looking at what has been achieved elsewhere. Feinberg and Keller (2010) offer practical advice on the benefits of visiting other libraries during busy periods to gather information and be inspired with good ideas for creative use of space. Seeing what works and what doesn't can be enormously helpful in planning your own projects. You can get ideas for design and use of space by looking at what has already been built, and one valuable resource is the Designing Libraries website, a freely accessible resource for anyone interested in design and innovation in libraries. This was established in 2004, with funding from the Museums, Libraries and Archives Council (MLA) as part of its Framework for the Future programme. Designing Libraries is a gateway to the world of libraries and a source of information on all aspects of the design and use of library spaces, including virtual as well as physical, spaces, with examples of practice from around the world. It is also a guide to products and services, innovation and development in the industries that partner with libraries in the areas of design, technology, content and consultancy. It includes:

- a buildings database, providing a permanent record of library building, refurbishment, improvement and extension projects in the UK and Ireland
- a resource for interactively sharing expertise and experience on library planning and design, through discussion forums and e-mail lists
- a directory of web links and sources of information on libraries, library organizations, library buildings, library design, technology and innovation.

A number of examples from the database are in Sure Start partnerships such as Britwell Play and Learn Library in Slough and Lowestoft Library, which is a shared building. Also included are the Toy Library in Handsworth Library, Birmingham and Platt Bridge Community First School, a new extended school which includes a Sure Start children's centre and nursery provision (www.designinglibraries.org.uk).

Librarians with expertise in early years provision may not have the loudest voice when it comes to making decisions about the design of the building, but your professional knowledge and expertise can have a very positive impact on the planning discussions. Make sure your professional voice is heard. You should ensure that you are consulted about the needs assessment and to determine specific space requirements.

Practical stuff about designing
Space/room planning: some things to consider

Remember that a collaborative process encourages people to think about how we are currently doing things and how we would really like to be doing them in the future. You can plan the use of new space, but keep in mind that the fixed features of a building can constrain its interior design. Where possible, built-ins should be kept to a minimum to allow greater flexibility. Try to keep to two doors per room, as a room with too many doors will lose valuable corners and floor space for quiet activities. To free the corners for activity areas, any door should, ideally, be in the centre of a wall. Try to avoid built-in partitions and shelving, as this will result in less-flexible space. In the planning stage also consider electrical outlets, plumbing, floor surfaces, lighting and the all-important natural light from windows.

The shape of the room is also important. Bishop and Rimes (2006) argue that many architects underestimate the design challenge of early years spaces. These include the distinctive educational and organizational requirements of the Foundation Stage of the National Curriculum; the importance of the whole environment – indoors and outdoors – for experiential, interactive learning; the SEN and Disability Act 2001; and the need to integrate education, childcare, family support, adult training, health and other services in children's settings. There is an architectural trend away from rectangular rooms, but Bishop and Rimes feel that unless the new shape gives children more playing space, it can be detrimental. You need to make up your own mind on this. Furniture can be used to break rectangular space into more friendly, curved areas. The Airedale Library and Family Centre in Castleford incorporates a curved wall made of glass bricks as part of the children's centre. The staff feel that this is a positive feature and use it as a display space.

Design to create boundaries

Boundaries increase a child's security and focus, protecting their activities from traffic and other distractions, encouraging longer-lasting, sustained play. Think about different uses in the space available, then design quiet corners for reading and noisy, stimulating space for role play and group activities. Even in a small room, you can create well-defined activity areas and children will show a higher degree of exploratory behaviour and social interaction. Display and shelving can act as boundaries and a carpet can be a visual boundary when used to designate the reading corner. Children will instinctively recognize the most secure space in a room. Often the corner directly opposite the entrance is a good place for a quiet area where they can crawl into a cubby-hole or reading hideaway for a bit of privacy. You will also want space for events like puppet shows and story-telling.

Design to create interactive spaces

Children's facilities are often designed to attract children with playful concepts. The architects BCA designed the younger children's library in New Lenox Public Library in the USA around a 'reading tree' that provides a fun place for parents to share a book with their children. Making dens and dressing up are an integral part of children's play, and role-play areas allow children to try out well-known and new roles in a safe environment.

Flexibility is important, and there are advantages in being able to offer a variety of room layouts. This allows for seasonal changes and for catering for different groups with differing needs. New staff members will have fresh ideas, while space that may be shared by a number of partner organizations needs to be flexible to their different needs. You can use portable screens and dividers to create small, cosy, safe places for individual work, or expand the area for a story-telling group gathering. A psychological barrier may be enough; these don't always need to be tall or sound-proof.

CASE STUDY Generating ideas for exciting interactive space

'The Trove' in White Plains Public Library, New York, was opened in October 2005. It is a children's space re-modelled from the old space. The director, Sandra Miranda, wanted to recreate the library for a new generation that is used to being entertained, engaged and active. She looked at museums, playgrounds and bookstores for ideas.

On the outside, the building is a late modernist structure which opened in 1974. It wasn't designed, using off-the-shelf solutions, and planning the project took several years. The library staff decided what they wanted for the children and worked with a team of other professionals – architects, theatrical designers and fabricators and lighting specialists – to get the end results that they wanted. The Trove provides different environments and experiences for children from birth through to age eleven. The name was suggested by a branding firm, based on the idea that 'A trove is a collection of valuable items discovered or found'. White Plains library has created a multisensory, multimedia space. You actually enter The Trove through a jagged brick opening in the wall on the library's second floor – a motif for the traditional library blown apart! The Compass is the focal point of the Trove and serves a number of purposes – information, reference, assistance with circulation and printing.

Each of the environments is very different. The areas closest to the opening are for older children, while areas for younger children are deeper inside The Trove, where it is more contained and intimate (Miranda, 2012).

See further information at www.thetrove.org.

Where literacy is the most important objective, you need to think about how the books themselves can be made exciting. A dramatic themed concept can overwhelm the books and result in children enjoying the space but never feeling tempted to pick up a book and explore it. Successfully themed libraries will incorporate engagement with reading and not just with play. One approach is to use illustrations from children's books so the wall display connects to the activity of sitting and reading with a carer, and recognition is triggered across the space to the book and back again. If you are clever in placing these you can create a lot of visual fun. Children's authors may give permission to use their images for free, as Simon Bartram, creator of *Bob, Man on the Moon*, did at Gateshead Library, for example.

There is a particular challenge in balancing the need to encourage families to use the library facilities and promoting access to resources to support literacy development.

In many younger children's libraries, it is well recognized that a play area makes the space more attractive. The problem is that often the play feature – a train or a castle, for example – is presented as the most enjoyable activity. The message, therefore, becomes: 'here's where you climb, hide, role play and have fun'. Children immediately run to it on entering and regard it as the best bit of the experience. Meanwhile, the books sit firmly spine-out on the shelves, passive and inert. The message is: 'here's the boring bit that you only go to when you're made to'. Well-designed furniture for libraries brings the books and the play elements together, so that the magic of books is an integral part of the enjoyable experience.

(Van Riel, 2012)

Book display: different age groups

Choosing books together is an important activity for parents and young children and it is vital to make book selection an enjoyable experience. Whitehead (2007) provides observations on the setting, believing that careful thought and organization must go into the environment in which children hear stories and investigate books. Although Whitehead is primarily writing about the early years classroom setting, her ideas are applicable to library environments for babies and very young children. She suggests that the books should be displayed on tables and low shelves, with their attractive covers showing or opened at interesting illustrations. A large, unsorted collection of books can be overwhelming and very unappealing and it is suggested that an early years collection should be small, and changed frequently (Whitehead, 2007). Versatile, low shelving will allow books to be displayed at child's-eye level. Book displays for older children and adults will use spine-on display to maximize storage, but it is not easy for small children to get books from a tightly packed shelf. The storage and display of picture books in mobile kinder boxes also allows for easy browsing by children and their parents, but it is important that the kinder box shows enough of the covers. Many old-style kinder boxes only show the top section of the cover and a child can only see one book at a time. Children glance at the first book and if that doesn't appeal, they won't always invest the effort to see what is behind it. Flicking through the books is also difficult for small fingers when the books are heavy. Library staff sometimes justify the acquisition of furniture which doesn't meet the physical needs of under-fives by saying that most book choosing is actually done by parents and carers. This may be true, but choosing independently is an essential part of reading for pleasure and under-fives' library spaces need to do everything possible to encourage this. Children can make their own choices based on the visual of the cover long before they learn to read (see Figure 13.2).

The Opening the Book company produces a range of play furniture which can double as book display. Its Reading Tower has an upper level with paperback shelving for older children and a lower level with picture-book shelving for younger children. The sides have metal panels to encourage magnetic games.

Figure 13.2 *Typical old-style kinder box*

Easier to look and touch kinder box

Another book-display idea is the reading tunnel, which combines play with choosing.

Furniture and equipment: for little people and for big people

Do shop around to get ideas and look at what others are doing. Durability is important, but also consider style and colour combinations. You will have a choice within your budget range, but don't feel you have to settle for what is the cheapest. Furniture for the early years library setting should be child sized, and sturdy enough to withstand energetic use. It will receive much greater wear and tear than in the average home. From a safety point of view, make sure that edges are rounded to avoid injuries. When choosing furniture it is important not to simply stick to bright, primary colours to 'stimulate' children. As will be discussed in more detail later in this chapter, it can have the opposite effect of making some children hyperactive. Consider the type of materials available and the impact this will have on the feel of your library setting.

It is important to provide an inviting space, enhanced by carpeted floors and appropriate furniture. The exposure to language and literature begins with books and reading, so you need spaces where babies, young children and their caregivers can spend time with books. Comfort is an important consideration. Think carefully about the seating provided for adults, as not everyone wants to relax on floor cushions, however inviting they may appear! You also need some chairs that are low, yet scaled to fit adults, so parents and staff can interact at child level. When considering the purchase of furniture such as tables and chairs, ask your suppliers to let you try it out before you decide to buy and involve parents in helping to choose. A book loft, or raised area, can be an asset in a children's setting. This can be used to help develop children's imaginative play and is a great place to curl up with a book. If it is free of detail it can be used for open-ended play, with the children's imagination determining the scope of play, rather than prescribed adult ideas.

There are a range of companies who supply furniture for the children's library market. Bunnett and Kroll (2006) have described how one early years setting used a variety of different seating arrangements, using benches, stools and chairs of different heights. With these additional options, it provided interesting physical movement challenges for the children and the space felt more home-like. You can suggest that parents can improvise and create a book den. This is any inviting, fun place for children to read in. While a comfy chair will often do, a large cardboard box with cut-out windows and door makes a great reading den or cave. Just add a few cushions for comfort. A reading tent is also a great place for creative play and can be quickly made by draping a sheet or a blanket over a table or a clothes horse. A woodland or jungle effect can be created by using large house plants. What better place to read animal and nature stories together?

Carpets and soft furnishings

Carpet is one of the best ways of ensuring that there is softness in a room and to make it comfortable for small children to sit and crawl on the floor. Carpets can act as a room divider, showing where a story time or group activity area starts. You can use a rug or carpet to help create a reading corner. Some libraries have a brightly coloured alphabet rug to encourage number and letter recognition. This doesn't have to be permanently installed, but can be a large, loose piece with bound edges. This would give you more flexibility in using the available floor space. Floor cushions can be used individually or to settle children down together for a story time session. Ideally these should be washable!

Signage and guiding

The signs in your library are an important part of the communication system with users. Dewe (2006, 27) discusses how to improve the appeal and signage of library buildings by adopting the ethos of the bookstore, supermarket and other retail outlets. Consider the impact on your users and avoid having too many signs and signs with too many words or which are too big or too small. Dewe suggests that signs and guiding perform three main tasks:

- to inform: plans, opening-time notices, safety procedures
- to direct: arrows to destinations
- to identify: when a destination has been reached, such as toilets, information desk, baby-changing facilities.

Furthermore, as Olds (2001, 246) advises, the presence of signs clearly denotes an institution, so the fewer the signs, the more residential and intimate the setting will appear. Using familiar words rather than library jargon on signs will help here. Use of too many languages gets visually confusing and can appear tokenistic, while a well-placed sign in a relevant language can make all the difference to the welcome offered to a specific community. Start thinking about signage early, but final placing cannot happen until you can stand in the space and check the sightlines and possible locations.

Where possible and appropriate, make signs visible to children as well as adults. Child-level devices are desirable - objects to spin, buttons to push, a sequence of photographs of children or animals all help to welcome young ones.

Children can interpret signs which use logos or symbols, for example a crawling baby or the outline of a boy or girl. Signage giving children visual and text pointers to what is available should be a strong design feature. Makaton language programme signage can also be displayed and so provide children and families with special educational needs (SEN) full access to resources. Leeds Library and Information Services are providing access to Boardmaker software to enable staff and users to make simple signs. Be careful, however, of over-signing the books with lots of categories or labels - let the cover designs do the work of appealing to your young audience.

Storage

Storage needs to be considered in the early planning stages for the children's library. Storage should be safe, located close to the point of use and aesthetically pleasing. You can make some storage facilities accessible to children, as they can gain a sense of accomplishment from helping to pack up after a rhyme time or playtime session. Shelves or storage compartments need to be within reach and clearly labelled with simple pictures. This would be good for musical instruments or song sheets. Obviously, in a library setting some storage space will need to be out of the children's reach and may be better behind the scenes in a store cupboard.

Stimulation, mood and sound

Children's growth, development and learning are directly affected by the amount of stimulation in their lives. King (2007) writes about the effect of sound and colour on young children. With their still-developing senses of sight, hearing and touch, they are super-sensitive. We may be unwittingly over-stimulating them with bright primary colours, hard surfaces, loud music and bright lights. It is interesting to note that the aforementioned Reggio settings in northern Italy are not painted in bright primary colours (Community Playthings, 2006, 18). You may actually want to create quiet areas in the library setting by using calming, neutral colours. There are times when you want children to become enthusiastic and involved, but you don't want to over-stimulate.

Colour

We respond to colour with our whole body, and colour can often be a cause of over-stimulation. Nursery-age children are especially responsive to colour. They prefer bright, warm colours, but because they are so sensitive, surrounding them with lots of primary colour can be over-stimulating. King (2007) suggests that hyperactivity, stress, inability to concentrate and even aggressive behaviour can result. Changing the interior colour scheme is one of the easiest and least expensive ways to transform a children's setting. Olds (2001, 213) explains that colour can alter the apparent size and warmth of a room; influence our estimation of volume, weight, time, temperature, and noise; encourage introversion or extroversion; induce anger or peacefulness. As a form of energy, colour affects our physiology as well as our mind and emotions.

Noise

When designing a library, the impact of 'noise' is an important aspect for consideration and it is often overlooked. In a shared public library building there may be some tensions when adult and children's service are sharing space. The adults tend to find the noise from children's library settings intrusive and undesirable, especially when sound from children's activities spills over into 'adult' (quiet) areas of the library. In everyday life both adults and children are constantly pounded by noise. However, unlike adults, who have learnt to 'tune out' unwanted noise, children are particularly sensitive to auditory stimulation. Their response is often hyperactivity and irritability. It is important therefore to consider how you can dampen undesirable noise by using

- curtains, textured wall hangings, carpets
- furniture, lofts and platforms of varying heights
- sound-absorbent ceiling materials.

Because children and the furniture they use are close to ground level, noise can travel relatively unhindered in the space above their heads. To give a room a more intimate atmosphere, its reverberant qualities can be reduced by adding absorbent surfaces and by varying ceiling and furniture heights. The installation of sound proofing to improve acoustic quality may be considered at the design stage, though this will inevitably have cost implications.

CASE STUDY Early Literacy Play Space at Loudonville Public Library: designing for babies in the library

Debra Knoll and colleagues at Loudonville Public Library in Ohio decided to make a radical change in how they provide service to babies and their caregivers, by rethinking the layout of a section of the children's area. They wanted to be able to point to a specific place for parents to visit, for professionals working with families to refer and for babies to play and learn. This action resulted in the construction of a research-based, intentional play space. Based on observational research, they developed the idea of a simple place for babies. 'It should be respectful of infants, neutral in colour, soft and inviting, include pre- and early literacy elements, and provide a level of comfort for adults. We wanted the area to look intentional, permanent, and aesthetically pleasing.'

A corner of the children's department was turned into an enclosed, permanent play area and a padded, curved bench seat was installed to form an enclosed yet airy corner in which babies could play. The bench also contains carefully detailed, custom-designed alphabet blocks mounted on vertical spinners. The play area includes a large mirror and a pull-up rail to support balance and gross motor activity. A computer workstation is provided for the adult caregivers, and there is a nursing corner with glider rockers designed for the comfort of nursing mothers and safety of little children.

(Knoll, 2014)

Refreshing spaces: making a tired space into something better

Not all of us are lucky enough to be involved in designing a new space but there are many principles and tips in this chapter which can help to improve your existing space as well.

Start by identifying what is working well and what is working less well for under-fives and their carers. Ask staff and users for their views on this. Make a list and then prioritize the areas that need the most attention. Articulate the arguments that support what you need – is the priority a new carpet, a feature piece, moving the existing furniture to create new spaces?

Clearing out and de-cluttering costs nothing and can make a huge difference. You probably have a collection development policy that includes guidance on weeding material – how frequently do you manage to implement it? Consider what materials or areas in your library currently detract from the environment. If your library has overcrowded shelves, open rubbish bins, scruffy notice boards and tired-looking signage you can take steps to improve things. If you have too many clashing styles and colours, all acquired at different times, plan how you will gradually simplify this over time by working to a smaller colour palette.

It is also a good idea to plan for the future, as styles will change and things will get worn out. A positive approach will involve staff in creating a long-range plan for keeping furnishings and fittings fresh and up to date. This will involve regular cleanings and a replacement policy.

Conclusion

In conclusion, this chapter has considered the physical environment in which early years library services are provided. The library has a continuing role as a valued, trusted community place that can offer learning via experience for the digital natives. Choosing, sharing and expressing views on books all start long before children can read, and the challenges and opportunities relating to library-space design for the birth-to-five age range are up for debate. We hope this chapter will have provided practical guidance on the issues.

Useful organizations

CABE, http://webarchive.nationalarchives.gov.uk/20110118095356/http://www.cabe.
    org.uk/home
Community Playthings, www.communityplaythings.co.uk
Designing Libraries, www.designinglibraries.org.uk
Opening the Book, www.openingthebook.com

References

Aabø, S. and Audunson, R. (2012) Use of Library Space and the Library as Place, *Library and Information Science Research*, **34** (2), 138–49.

Bishop, M. and Rimes, M. (2006) *Better Building Design for Young Children*, Community Playthings.

Black, A. and Rankin, C. (2011) The History of Children's Library Design: continuities and discontinuities. In Bon, I., Cranfield, A. and Latimer, K. (eds), *Designing Library Spaces for Children*, De Gruyter Saur.

Bohrer, C. N. (2005) Libraries as Early Literacy Centers, *Public Libraries*, May/Jun, **44** (3), 127-32.

Bunnett, R. and Kroll, D. (2006) *Transforming Spaces: rethinking the possibilities*, Community Playthings.

CABE (Commission for Architecture and the Built Environment)(2005) *Physical Capital: how great places boost public value*, CABE.

CABE (2011) *Creating Excellent Buildings: a guide for clients*, CABE,
    http://webarchive.nationalarchives.gov.uk/20110118095356/http://www.cabe.org.
    uk/buildings.

Community Playthings (2006) *Spaces: room layout for early childhood education. Your guide to space planning and room layout*, Community Playthings.

Dewe, M. (1995) *Planning and Designing Libraries for Children and Young People*, Library Association Publishing.

Dewe, M. (2006) *Planning Public Library Buildings: concepts and issues for the librarian*, Ashgate.

DfES (Department for Education and Skills) (2004) *Building for Sure Start: integrated provision for under-fives,*

Dudek, M. (2000) *Kindergarten Architecture: space for the imagination,* 2nd edn, Spon Press.

Dudek, M. (2001) *Building for Young Children: a practical guide to planning, designing and building the perfect space,* National Early Years Network.

Esson, K. and Tyerman, K. (1991) *Library Provision for Children,* AAL Publishing.

Feinberg, S. and Keller, J. R. (2010) *Designing Space for Children and Teens,* American Libraries, http://americanlibrariesmagazine.org/features/03142010/designing-space-childrenand-teens.

Feinberg, S., Deerr, K., Jordan, B., Byrne, M. and Kropp, L. (2007) *The Family-centered Library Handbook,* Neal-Schuman Publishers.

Harris, K. and Dudley, M. (2005) *Public Libraries and Community Cohesion – developing indicators,* MLA.

King, J. (2007) *The Environment in your Nursery. The effect of sound and colour on young children,* Community Playthings, www.communityplaythings.co.uk/c/resources/articles/environments/mood.htm.

Knoll, D. (2014) Babies in the Library – Creating a Truly Baby-friendly Early Literacy Play Space, *Public Libraries,* **53** (1), 44–7.

Kropp, L. G. (2004) Family Place Libraries: building strong families, strong libraries, *Journal of the Library Administration and Management Section of the New York Library Association,* **1** (1), 39–47.

Lushington, N. (2002) *Libraries Designed for Users: a 21st century guide,* Neal-Schuman Publishers.

Lushington, N. (2008) *Libraries Designed for Kids,* Facet Publishing.

McDonald, A. (2007) The Top Ten Qualities of a Good Library Space. In Latimer, K. and Niegaard, H. (eds), *IFLA Library Building Guidelines: developments and reflections,* K. G. Saur.

Miranda, S. (2012) Case study: Imaging, explore, discover – welcome to The Trove at White Plains Public Library, New York. In Rankin, C. and Brock, A. (eds), *Library Services for Children and Young People, Challenges and Opportunities in the Digital Age,* Facet Publishing.

Oldenburg, R. (1999) *The Great Good Place: cafes, coffee shops, bookstores, bars, hair salons and other hangouts at the heart of a community,* 3rd edn, Marlowe & Co.

Olds, A. (2001) *Child Care Design Guide,* McGraw-Hill.

Prensky, M. (2001) *Digital Natives, Digital Immigrants,* www.marcprensky.com/writing/Prensky%20-%20Digital%20Natives,%20Digital%20Immigrants%20-%20Part1.pdf.

Rankin, C. (2012) Library Place and Space Transformation – Designing for the Digital Natives. In Rankin, C. and Brock, A. (eds), *Library Services for Children and Young People, Challenges and Opportunities in the Digital Age,* Facet Publishing.

Roskos, K. and Neuman, S. B. (2003) Environment and Its Influences for Early Literacy Teaching and Learning. In Neuman, S. B. and Dickinson, D. K. (eds), *Handbook of Early Literacy Research,* The Guilford Press.

State Library of New South Wales (2012) *People Places – a Guide for Public Library Buildings in NSW,* 3rd edn, State Library of New South Wales.

Van Riel, R. (2012) Making Space for Reading – Designing Library Spaces for Children in Public and School Libraries. In Rankin, C. and Brock, A. (eds), *Library Services for Children and Young People, Challenges and Opportunities in the Digital Age,* Facet Publishing.

Whitehead, M. (2007) *Developing Language and Literacy for Young Children,* 3rd edn, Paul Chapman.

Worpole, K. (2013) *Contemporary Library Architecture: a planning and design guide,* Routledge.

CHAPTER 14

Planning: organizing projects and money matters in the early years library

Carolynn Rankin

Introduction

The theme in this final chapter is planning. All organizations, and indeed individuals, need to plan for their future success and sustainability. Planning is a vital activity at all levels and we discuss some of the issues associated with planning in organizations and multidisciplinary teams. Financial planning is discussed as a very important means of allocating resources to enable development. We also look at some practical aspects of project planning, as many early years librarians have opportunities to set up schemes and initiatives, often in partnership work. Impact and evaluation are also discussed, as these are important stages in the planning cycle for any project or activity.

As a main theme in this book is early years literacy and the enjoyment of books, we have included a section on planning sessions for babies, young children and their families. The final sections look at planning at the individual level and we discuss aspects of continuous professional development (CPD) and developing skills for the reflective practitioner.

Organizational planning: strategic, tactical, operational

To be an effective early years library practitioner and to undertake a planning role in the workplace, it is helpful to understand the ways in which your parent organization and library and information services work. In most organizations the senior managers lead formal strategic planning processes to determine long-term plans, strategies and direction for the business. In the not-for-profit sector in the UK, organizations and agencies will consider how to meet the requirements of government agendas such as the Early Years Foundation Stage and partnership initiatives such as Bookstart and Talk to Your Baby.

The purposes of an organization are often expressed through its mission statement and corporate aims, which are then broken down into more specific objectives. Table 14.1 shows the characteristics associated with different levels of purpose in a typical hierarchical organization.

Table 14.1 *Levels of purpose in an organization*	
Level of purpose	**Common characteristics**
Mission	Visionary and far-reaching Central and overriding Sometimes implicit, i.e. unwritten
Corporate (strategic) aims	Identify goals for the whole organization Formulated by senior management Set stakeholder expectations Often expressed in terms of 'market share'
Unit (operating) objectives	Identify goals specific to units of organization Practical and operational Reflected in activities and tasks of the unit Expressed in terms of 'outcomes' or 'outputs'

Another way of expressing this activity is by means of basic questions. At the strategic management level the question is 'Why?' This most senior level carries overall accountability for the success of the organization. Staff working at this level will determine the mission and the corporate aims by undertaking long-term planning and strategic development. When the direction for the organization has been determined, the next basic question is 'How will the corporate aims be achieved?' The 'how' question is implemented by managers operating at a tactical level in the hierarchy. They will interpret aims at the level of the business unit and undertake medium-term planning to achieve the objectives of the organization. This level of management has a co-ordinating role and often controls systems and resources. Further down the hierarchy, operational managers are responsible for delivering what needs to be done on a day-to-day basis and who needs to do it. Operational targets are usually short term, and monitoring is done at local task level. The overall process should ensure that the organization achieves its objectives, with everyone in the organization involved. This is a very simplistic overview of an organizational structure, but has been included to help explain the potential challenges in partnership work.

SMART objectives and goals

If objectives are to be useful in helping an organization move towards achieving its goals they need to be clearly understood by everyone working towards that end. One way of doing this is to set SMART objectives. This stands for Specific,

Measurable, Achievable, Realistic and Timely. These criteria can be used to evaluate how useful an organization's objectives actually are.

- Specific: objectives should be clearly identifiable and focused, as the organization needs to know what exactly it is trying to achieve.
- Measurable: the organization needs to know whether the objective has been achieved or exceeded, or how far short it is falling.
- Achievable: the organization needs to ensure that the resources (skills, funds, time) necessary to achieve the objective are provided.
- Realistic: those who must work to achieve the objective must feel that the expectations of managers are realistic.
- Timely: a deadline should be set by which the objective must be achieved, or when progress towards it will be assessed.

Some sources add two additional qualities to the SMART goals, making them SMARTER. Here the E stands for evaluate and the R stands for re-evaluate. We rather like these additions, as they are a reminder that goals must constantly be evaluated and re-evaluated, as will be discussed later in the chapter.

When describing your work plans as a series of objectives it can be helpful to use this approach. Evans and Alire (2013, 97) say, 'Once you establish the goals and objectives, it becomes relatively easy to identify appropriate activities, policies and procedures as well as the resources required to achieve the desired results.'

The challenges of partnership work: planning shared objectives

We have already identified that partnership working is seen as an important strategy for tackling complex issues such as social inclusion and supporting the lifelong learning agenda (see Chapter 5). Many UK workplace settings now require services or projects to be delivered by a series of teams, each team a multidisciplinary one made up of professionals from different backgrounds (Atkinson, Doherty and Kinder, 2005; Rankin and Butler, 2011). Partnership working can present challenges and barriers, particularly in cross-sector partnerships, where participants are from different organizations and agencies. Some of the difficulties may involve having different strategic objectives and priorities, working to different time-frames, or differences in organizational culture. Practical difficulties, such as differences in systems and procedures, may be quite frustrating at an operational level.

On a positive note, Allan (2007) identifies many benefits from working in partnership, based on her discussions with directors of library and information services and project managers. These include enhanced access to people, resources and organizations and ownership of projects. The involvement of a wide range of people from different professional backgrounds can enhance the quality of the project outcomes. Being part of a successful partnership can boost morale. Individuals working on a collaborative project will have the opportunity to develop their knowledge and skills through teamwork and this will enhance CPD.

Planning and organizing projects

What is a project? In contrast to managing and delivering your core services, which are financed on a recurring basis, a project can be expected to have the following features:

- a clearly defined set of objectives or outputs
- specific start and end dates
- will involve the investment of resources for future benefit
- can be planned, financed and implemented as a unit
- has geographical or organizational boundaries.

A project is different from managing and delivering core services, which are managed on a recurrent, ongoing basis. A new service may have been initiated as a trial project to get it up and running. Early years library practitioners may be involved in capital projects involving new buildings, moving into a new early years setting or perhaps refurbishing an existing setting. Other practical examples might be developing a marketing campaign for the library, setting up a new parenting collection in a branch library or running a storysack workshop for the local community. Managing projects involves using various management skills and activities, such as:

- carrying out some research to identify gaps in provision
- setting objectives to decide what is to be achieved within a specified time-scale
- developing a plan to decide what needs to be done and in what order
- allocating resources and managing people in order to achieve the objectives of the project
- communicating with the stakeholders – disseminating information about the progress and the outputs
- evaluating the project against the set objectives.

Organizations need to consider the staffing resources that will be involved in running the project and the management systems and structures required to deliver the outputs. These will depend on the size and complexity of the project.

A small-scale project is sometimes run as a pilot or a trial to test out a new service idea and gain feedback before rolling it out on a full scale.

Allan (2004) has written about project management tools and techniques for information and library practitioners. Teamwork is vital. Projects to be delivered by multidisciplinary teams can fail because of a lack of clarity about the objectives. Where team members do not share a common goal, there is likely to be a conflict of interests. It is a good idea to involve all partners in planning from the start. Senior managers may need to be persuaded that projects need dedicated time from co-ordinating members to ensure successful outputs.

Action plans can be used in projects to show who is doing what and the time-scale involved. Gantt charts, laid out on a grid, are helpful for project management because they show the project schedule and associated tasks at a glance. A Gantt chart shows the time phases and activities of a project so that they can be understood by a wide audience. Specialized project management software is used when there is a high level of complexity, but you can use a spreadsheet or the table feature in your word processor to create a basic outline for planning needs. Gantt charts are easy to read and can be used to show recurrent tasks and milestones. In simple projects you can very effectively use a whiteboard or flip-chart paper and Post-It notes for the same purpose.

Figure 14.1 is an example of a simple Gantt chart showing the scheduling of tasks and the time-scales involved in planning a storysack workshop for a local community.

Task	January	February	March	April	May	June
Planning meeting with partner organizations to agree storysack theme and to allocate budget and staffing	■					
Book activity room for the workshop	■					
Order resources – books, sewing materials, etc.		■	■			
Produce publicity material and advertise event			■	■		
Brief staff and plan workshop session Prepare resource materials				■		
Order refreshments for the workshop					■	
Issue press release, invite local paper/radio station to provide coverage on the day					■	
Run the workshop Gather evaluation evidence					■	
Prepare evaluation report for partner organizations						■

Figure 14.1 *Gantt chart: scheduling a storysack project*

Planning budgets and money matters in the early years library

Budgeting involves the allocation of resources among the competing activities, programmes and services provided by an organization. Put simply, this can be seen as a series of goals with price tags. Operating budget or revenue budget are the terms used to describe year-by-year budgets, generally drawn up on an annual basis to fund current operations. A different budget source, the capital budget, will be used for high-cost improvements or major investments such as a new building. Another type of budget is the single-purpose grant from government agencies, commercial partners or charitable foundations. These special budgets are often allocated on a competitive basis, may be time limited and could include both capital and operating funds. Collaborative partnerships often attract this form of finance, and your parent organization may be involved in such schemes. Funding available for special projects usually has to be allocated and used within specific time-scales and may need to be treated separately for accounting and auditing purposes.

Budget headings for the everyday running of an early years library might typically include:

- staffing/payroll costs
- accommodation costs: rents, cleaning, heating and lighting
- books and other resources such as DVDs and CDs
- toys and play equipment, treasure baskets
- craft materials and other stationery
- magazines and newspapers for the parenting collection
- staff development and training
- publicity and marketing
- office supplies and consumables
- IT equipment
- library management system, including maintenance contracts
- projects and programmes
- travel and subsistence for outreach work.

Financial management in information and library services is very important and the future success of a library service may be dependent on the effective planning, organization and control of the financial resources. You cannot afford to neglect financial matters and, according to Roberts (1998), improving budgetary practice should be seen as a strategic goal for all information and library service managers. In the present economic climate it is not enough to ensure that expenditure is kept within budget, as managers are generally expected to provide the best level of performance for the available finance and may have cost targets and income targets as part of the process. Library managers are now required to justify expenditure on particular items or for the whole service, and Corrall reminds us:

> Most information service managers are faced with decreasing financial and human resources, but increasing customer demands and wider delivery options, requiring complex decision making, which in turn requires effective management information systems - particularly information on costs.

(Corrall, 2000)

Library practitioners need to take responsibility for developing their own knowledge and skills in financial management and for encouraging staff working with them to do the same. All practitioners should be aware of the financial context in which they work and have some knowledge of the financial performance indicators on which their services are judged (see chapters in Evans and Alire, 2013; Roberts and Rowley 2004). The ability to cost activities has become more important with diminishing resources and increasing accountability, but an inherent problem for libraries is that the work is very labour intensive. Roberts (1998) suggests that many performance measures are incomplete if a financial dimension cannot be included.

Budgets can have several purposes, both as plans for the distribution of resources and as tools for the prediction of costs. At one level the budget for your early years library service can be your action plan expressed in financial terms, and this can act as a control mechanism and an evaluation tool for your activities. Viewed another way, the budget has a role in the translation of your organization's strategic plans into practical, everyday service-delivery outcomes. Practical wisdom suggests that you should keep a close eye on your budgets and commit funds well before the end of the financial year. Experienced practitioners will keep a wish list, because when a tranche of money becomes available, you have to take the opportunity and allocate it quickly.

Planning and evaluation

Public libraries are complex institutions, and defining value in the context of their offering is open to considerable debate. A significant challenge for public libraries is determining what data should be collected (Halpin et al., 2013).

There is an increasing demand for evidence of effectiveness in provision, and other chapters of this book have commented on the importance of meeting the needs of the user community and evaluating what is being provided. This is done to assess how well you are meeting the objectives and targets set for your service. In library services provided for young children and their families, parent satisfaction is one of the key indicators that the library is meeting its objectives. A good example was provided by Barratt-Pugh and Allen in Chapter 4 and also in the case study on Rhythm and Rhyme in Libraries NI on page 252.

Sue Roe, a very experienced children's librarian, says that

> measuring impact is still very difficult. You need to record comments and feedback from children and parents effectively, and make use of evidence and reporting from partners such as Booktrust and The Reading Agency. When collecting the statistics for other organisations such as Booktrust about Bookstart or Booktime you can use the forms for your authority's benefit too - local figures/feedback/activity reporting for Bookstart/Book Crawl etc.

Powell (2006), in providing an overview of evaluation research, says that it should enhance knowledge and decision making and lead to practical application. Libraries have traditionally gathered and maintained statistical records, and the early years setting will be interested in having data on the number of registered borrowers, the number of books loaned, the number of visitors, events and family learning activities and the numbers attending. Monitoring can enable you to provide evidence about the level of activities - the number of things you are doing. In order to justify expenditure in the early years library you do need to provide quantitative evidence - measuring how many sessions were offered, how many participants from the target group used particular services, how much of the budget was allocated to stock acquisition for early years resources and so on. So at one level your organization will need information about how you have used the resources allocated. Data about your services and projects can be collated and analysed to provide information for annual reports and feedback to funding partners. However, Feinberg and Feldman provide something of a challenge when they say

> Librarians think of evaluation as coming at the end of the process so it is easy to put off and neglect. But the planning process is cyclical. Evaluation streamlines all activities of the library, completes the planning process for any one activity, and provides the tools for change and growth in public library services ... Without the identification of goals and objectives at the beginning of the process, there can be no meaningful evaluation at the end.
>
> (Feinberg and Feldman, 1996, 103)

Measuring impact and effectiveness

We feel that there is also a need to go beyond simply measuring the various library processes through performance indicators. There is much interest now in the social impact of library activities. One way of exploring the big question of how libraries contribute to the cohesion and development of their communities is to use the concept of social capital; this was discussed in some detail in Chapter 1. Measuring impact is much more difficult than collating statistics. How do you know that you are making a difference? How can you prove that you are making a difference? When planning monitoring and evaluation approaches, consider how you will demonstrate the impact of your work and how the qualitative evidence and quantitative data can be interpreted to tell the story of your library provision.

As Powell (2006, 106) notes, it is relatively straightforward to measure the inputs or resources of a library, more difficult to measure true performance and even more challenging to measure impact/outcomes or how the use of a library or information service actually affects users. Other researchers (Bawden et al. 2009; Crawford, 2006; Markless and Streatfield, 2012; Neuman, 2009) have identified this challenge in determining the unique offering and value of the public library service:

> In a target driven world there is a danger that library services will not be judged on the quality of material and services and the unique experience they offer, but simplistically on how many people come through the doors.
>
> (Usherwood, 2007, 127)

Evaluation as a form of research can be used to assess the value or effectiveness of social interventions or programmes (Seale, 2012, 567). We can look again at some of the evidence gathered by Wakefield Library and Information Services. The early years librarians there have made a significant impact on the lives of many young children and their parents in areas where literacy levels are particularly low. Here are some points from their impact assessment:

- Approximately 95% of families using our early years libraries in Wakefield have never used libraries before and their perceptions of books, reading and learning are being positively changed.
- Many families are without access to computers in the home. Parents (and children) have been able to develop IT skills in a non-threatening library environment, either to access information or to get help with preparing CVs and job applications.
- Professional help has enabled local parents to enrol on IT/Basic Skills training

courses, take a leading role in the community through fund raising, chairing meetings, volunteering within the Sure Start community and successfully gaining employment.

- Children with little or no confidence and poor communication skills have started to interact at story sessions and developed new social skills in the friendly environment.
- Families who feel isolated, including Asian families, asylum seekers and Travellers, have discovered a safe, non-threatening environment in which to access support with literacy and information.
- Where families have needed additional support from other agencies, librarians have been able to assist with the referral process.

Evaluation studies have to inform and be useful for decision making and practice – whether gradually, in an incremental policy-making process, or directly used to adjust less-complicated decision-making processes at the micro level (Abma and Widdershoven, 2013, 570).

We agree with Professor Susan Neuman when she states: 'Without research, however, we have no evidence – and without evidence, it's difficult to claim victory' (Neuman, 2009, 133).

We have endeavoured to sprinkle examples of impact evidence throughout the chapters of this book by providing comments and feedback from practitioners and parents and carers. We hope that, as effective practitioners, you will be proactive in using guidance on how to gather such evidence in support of your early years library services. The more refined your evidence collection, the clearer the picture you will have of the impact your service is making. Markless and Streatfield (2012) also write about evaluating the impact of your library, discussing success criteria, impact factors and what counts as impact evidence. They provide practical guidance on thinking about evidence and on deciding your approach to gathering it using techniques such as questioning, interviewing and observation.

Professional practice

It is also a good idea to evaluate your professional practice at the operational level. You may be working as part of a team or have responsibility for leading a team in delivering particular services. Systematic evaluation will improve services for children. Teamwork needs to be reviewed regularly so that you can learn from success and improve on weaknesses. You can seek feedback by carrying out regular evaluations of your sessions. The Early Years Library Network suggests that at the very least you should keep a log of the stories and rhymes used in sessions, note how many attended and record any local circumstances that may have affected the turnout. It's also a good idea to keep a log of the weather, as bright sunshine may encourage your regulars to head to the local park, whereas pouring rain may keep people at home. If you have a team of staff you can review the sessions that colleagues are delivering and give feedback on them. One suggestion is to record sessions so as to enable your team to analyse the content and reflect on the outcomes and impact. It is important to act on the results.

Some questions to ask in reviewing and evaluating teamwork in delivering the early years library sessions might be the following.

- What went well?
- What didn't go so well and could be improved?
- How could we do this differently next time?
- Who else needs to know about this activity? (Sharing the messages with your partner organizations and user community.)

Personal development planning: managing your own CPD

This final section is about planning your own personal development. CPD is about ensuring your own personal development and continued competence.

The CILIP Professional Knowledge and Skills Base (PKSB) maps the knowledge and skills in the library, information and knowledge professions. It can be used as a self-assessment tool for professional development and to demonstrate your unique skill set to employers. It is also a framework for skills analysis, staff training and development plans. The PKSB aims to reflect the breadth of the library, information and knowledge profession. It brings together the areas of professional and technical expertise required across the profession with the generic skills and capabilities that are required. Ethics and values are at the centre, as they underpin the work of practitioners in the sector. Professional expertise and generic skills are the key sets of knowledge and skills which make our profession unique. Professional expertise and generic skills have been set within the wider library, information and knowledge sector context and the wider organization and environmental context because it is important for practitioners to maintain current awareness and understanding of the wider profession and have a good knowledge of the world outside their own workplace.[1]

One aspect of your development as an early years library practitioner is to network. According to CILIP (the Chartered Institute of Library and Information Professionals), networking is a means of meeting other people to open up opportunities and to obtain or exchange ideas or information. A professional network can help you to build a strong support structure that will enhance your career in the years to come. The most successful information professionals will use networks to:

- get expert advice
- exchange ideas
- get a second opinion
- test new ideas
- gain moral support
- engage in collaborative problem solving.

It is not always possible for early years librarians to attend professional events, but conferences, seminars and training events are a good place to network and can help to broaden your contacts. Look closely at your development needs and those of your colleagues and find out who supplies the required training. In the UK this might be the CILIP Youth Libraries Group, ASCEL (the Association of Senior Children's and Education Librarians), the National Literacy Trust, The Reading Agency or other organizations promoting early years literacy. Running joint training sessions with colleagues from other professions can be a good way to network and get productive partnerships off the ground. Consider planning a series of short meetings to exchange ideas or to make a five-minute presentation on your work area.

The reflective practitioner

Reflection and reflective practice are core values of professionals and have a key role in professional training. Reflection is promoted in a range of disciplines, particularly in education, health and social care, and is an essential part of professional practice (Moon, 2004). In many professions reflection is approached consciously and deliberately and 'reflective practice', as it is termed, is regarded as an important dimension of professionalism and a key to learning.

Reflection is about analysis, about delving into an issue or problem to explore different perspectives from a range of aspects and standpoints. The more complex or tricky the problem or issue is, the deeper the analysis required, as you think around and into the heart of it, working out what feels right. Emotion and intuition also play important roles in the reflective process. The process of reflection through engaging in reading and research and developing professional, practical and personal experience generates knowledge and skills that enable understanding, empathy and professional practice that can make a difference to children and families. Reflecting on practice is to generate thinking to improve practice (Brock, 2015).

Reflection involves questioning, and thoughtful criticism and analysis. It enhances learning and is an essential part of CPD. Reflection can be described as a thinking and learning process, following an activity, that enables you to use your past to inform and develop your future. It is at the heart of learning from experience because it is the way that you draw out the maximum information from experience. The insight that we gain from this 'reflective questioning' can help us to make decisions, resolve problems or plan our work more effectively. Reflection can also help you to develop self-awareness and have greater clarity about what you want to achieve.

The challenge for the reflective practitioner is to interconnect understandings derived from tacit knowledge gained from experience and practice with explicit knowledge gained through education and training.

Margaret Watson, a former President of CILIP says that

> since information is at the core of the information society, information workers and other knowledge workers will be key players in this society. In order for information professionals to play their role effectively, they will have to be individually and collectively pro-active in addressing the competency issues that enable them to remain relevant in a dynamic environment.

Moyo (2002) says that reflective practice can help us to

- determine why we do things in professional practice
- make informed, reasoned decisions in practice when there are competing alternatives
- better understand and ultimately improve our practice.

By developing critical analysis skills the reflective practitioner can examine a situation, identify existing knowledge, challenge assumptions and envision and explore options. You can help to prompt reflection by keeping a learning diary, asking questions, seeking feedback and allowing yourself time to consider situations. Reflective journal writing can enhance reflection, critical thinking and self-awareness. Becoming a reflective practitioner should help you to become a more effective manager.

CPD is important in any profession, not only to keep abreast of the ongoing policy and latest initiatives addressed in Chapter 1, but also to take on board new practices and knowledge within a particular discipline.

Atkinson, Doherty and Kinder (2005) suggest the adoption of a self-critical and reflective approach to an individual's professional identity and work as a key factor for successful multi-agency working. But what is a reflective approach? Reflection can be related to learning situations where we are trying to make sense of new material or where we need to make sense of knowledge and understandings we have already learnt. Moon (2004) uses the term 'cognitive housekeeping' to capture some of the essence of this sorting out of ideas. Some of the outcomes of reflection are the building of theory, self-development, decision making or resolution of uncertainty, and empowerment or emancipation.

Through developing a critical, reflective approach to practice, practitioners can become more articulate, secure and able to justify practice in the face of challenge (Adams, 2010).

Reflective practice involves critical thinking, and enquiry is a highly complex process. Our own values as practitioners will affect how we approach reflective enquiry.

Conclusion

So, to summarize this chapter, you have to deliver the objectives of the organization, and to do that successfully you have to plan all the types of resources - policy, people and places - that we have discussed throughout the book. Of course, planning is vital and it is best accomplished through collaboration and communication with others. Policy needs to be implemented - and effective planning arms you with courage and confidence and helps you to be in control.

Issues and questions

- How will you evaluate the success of your service, particularly when working in partnership with other agencies?
- How will you keep effective and manageable records of what works well in your activity sessions?
- How can you gather evidence of the social impact of your services and the added value you are providing? This may be vital for your service's future sustainability.

Key points to remember

- Make sure that your objectives are SMART or SMARTER.
- Use the guidance available from other practitioners. Remember to access them through the organizational sources cited in this chapter and throughout the book - you don't have to reinvent the wheel!
- Take responsibility for your own professional development. Nothing stands still, and change is inevitable - so be proactive in deciding how you meet change, but sustain what you value.

- Don't avoid (or be frightened of) handling your own budget, or someone else will do it for you and you may not get what you want!

Final comments

Remember the importance of listening to your client groups. Listen to people – community members, parents and children. Even very young children, as you will have seen from some of the case studies and scenarios presented throughout the book, are very capable of indicating to you what they are interested in and whether or not you are meeting their needs.

We hope that this book has given you confidence to do the job of an early years librarian, make a difference and face the future. Early years practitioners – educators, carers and librarians – really do have very important roles to play.

The end!

Note

1   See more at: www.cilip.org.uk/cilip/jobs-and-careers/professional-knowledge-and-skills-base#sthash.ZnWvc1UE.dpuf.

References

Abma, T. A. and Widdershoven, G. A. M. (2013) Evaluation as a Relationally Responsible Practice, In Denzin, N. K. and Lincoln, Y. S. (eds), *Collecting and Interpreting Qualitative Materials*, 4th edn, Sage Publications.

Adams, S. (2010) Putting the Bananas to Bed! Becoming a reflective teacher. In Moyles, J. (ed.), *Beginning Teaching, Beginning Learning in Primary Education*, 3rd edn, Open University Press/McGraw-Hill Education.

Allan, B. (2004) *Project Management Tools and Techniques for Today's ILS Professional*, Facet Publishing.

Allan, B. (2007) *Supervising and Leading Teams in ILS*, Facet Publishing.

Atkinson, M., Doherty, P. and Kinder, K. (2005) Multi-agency Working Models, Challenges and Key Factors for Success, *Journal of Early Childhood Research*, **3** (1), 7–17.

Bawden, D., Calvert, A., Robinson, L., Urquhart, C., Bray, C. and Amosford, J. (2009) Understanding Our Value: assessing the nature of the impact of library services, *Library and Information Research*, **33** (105), 62–89.

Brock, A. (ed.) (2015) *The Early Years Reflective Practice Handbook*, Routledge.

Corrall, S. (2000) *Strategic Management of Information Services: a planning handbook*, ASLIB/IMI.

Crawford, J. (2006) *The Culture of Evaluation in Library and Information Services*, Chandos.

Evans, G. E. and Alire, C. A. (2013) *Management Basics for Information Professionals*, 3rd edn, Facet Publishing.

Feinberg, S. and Feldman, S. (1996) *Serving Families and Children through Partnerships: a how-to-do-it manual for librarians*, Neal-Schuman Publishers.

Halpin, E., Rankin, C., Chapman, E. L. and Walker, C. (2013) Measuring the Value of Public Libraries in the Digital Age: what the power people need to know, *Journal of Librarianship and Information Science*, published online ahead of print 3 September 2013, doi: 10.1177/0961000613497746.

Markless, S. and Streatfield, D. (2012) *Evaluating the Impact of Your Library*, 2nd edn, Facet Publishing.

Moon, J. (2004) *Handbook of Reflective and Experiential Learning: Theory and practice*, Routledge Falmer.

Moyo, L. (2002) CPE Anywhere, Anytime: online resources for the Information Society. In *Continuing Professional Education for the Information Society: 5th World Conference on CPE for the LIS Profession*, IFLA.

Neuman, S. B. (2009) *Changing the Odds for Children at Risk: seven essential principles of educational programs that break the cycle of poverty*, Praeger.

Powell, R. R. (2006) Evaluation Research: an overview, *Library Trends*, **55** (1), 102–20.

Rankin, C. and Butler, F. (2011) Issues and Challenges for the Interdisciplinary Team in Supporting the 21st Century Family. In Brock, A. and Rankin, C. (eds), *Professionalism in the Interdisciplinary Early Years Team: supporting young children and their families*. Continuum.

Roberts, S. A. (1998) *Financial Cost Management for Libraries and Information Services*, 2nd edn, Bowker-Saur.

Roberts, S. and Rowley, J. (2004) *Managing Information Services*, Facet Publishing.

Seale, C. (ed.) (2012) *Researching Society and Culture*, 3rd edn, Sage Publications.

Usherwood, B. (2007) *Equity and Excellence in the Public Library*, Ashgate.

Index